UNIQUELY CELTIC

THE SOUL AND THE SPIRIT

Frank Rafters

Grosvenor House
Publishing Limited

The right of Frank Rafters to be identified as the author of this
work has been asserted in accordance with Section 78
of the Copyright, Designs and Patents Act 1988

The book cover picture is copyright to Frank Rafters

This book is published by
Grosvenor House Publishing Ltd
28-30 High Street, Guildford, Surrey, GU1 3EL.
www.grosvenorhousepublishing.co.uk

A CIP record for this book
is available from the British Library

ISBN 978-1-78148-971-0

For my beloved family and friends

"Contents"

"Acknowledgements"

Over the years, an incredible array of information sources have been amassed regarding not simply the history of Celtic Football Club, but Scottish Football and the sport as a whole. These do not simply take the form of books, but of websites, fanzines, newspapers and much more besides. With every new project, there is that little bit more out there for both present and future generations to enjoy, but rest assured, the task of producing new pieces would be made exceptionally more difficult without the past efforts of authors, historians and fans in producing the previously mentioned information sources. As such, I must take this opportunity to thank those responsible for the following works and publications.

"An Alphabet of the Celts – A Complete Who's Who of Celtic F.C (Eugene McBride and Martin O'Connor with George Sheridan)"

"A Lifetime in Paradise (James Edward McGrory)"

"Celtic: A Biography in Nine Lives (Kevin McCarra)"

"Celtic F.C. Cult Heroes (David Potter)"

"Celtic 1888-1995, The Official Illustrated History (Graham McColl)"

"Glasgow Celtic 1945-1970 (Tom Campbell)"

"James 'Dun' Hay, The Story of a Footballer (Roy Hay)"

"Oh, Hampden in the Sun... (Peter Burns and Pat Woods)"

"Played in Glasgow – Charting the Heritage of a City at Play (Ged O'Brien)"

"Rhapsody in Green – Great Celtic Moments (Tom Campbell and Pat Woods)"

"Sean Fallon – Celtic's Iron Man (Stephen Sullivan)"

"The British Newspaper Archive (and all of the titles available therein)"

"The Celtic Graves Society"

"The Essential History of Newcastle United (Paul Joannou, Bill Swann and Steve Corke)"

"The Evening Times"

"The Glasgow Herald"

"The Glory and the Dream (Tom Campbell and Pat Woods)"

"The Roar of the Crowd – Following Scottish Football Down the Years (David Ross)"

"The Scottish Football Museum"

"The Shamrock: A Celtic Retrospective (Website and Fanzine) (Paul)"

"The Story of the Celtic, 1888-1938 (William Patrick Maley)"

"Tommy McInally – Celtic's Bad Bhoy? (David Potter)"

"Willie Maley: The Man Who Made Celtic (David Potter)"

"London Hearts - www.londonhearts.com"

"The Celtic Wiki - www.thecelticwiki.com"

Lastly, I must offer my sincere thanks to everyone who assisted me with the work which eventually culminated in the publication of this book. Without those people who agreed to be interviewed, the assistance of proofreaders, and indeed all of you who supported my previous endeavour, this would not have been possible.

"Uniquely Celtic"

Celtic Football Club is special. It may not be surprising for a Celtic supporter to say that, but it is the truth nonetheless, and it is my aim to show you why this is the case. Indeed, to make such a brief statement is easy, but to adequately explain why it is accurate is a substantial challenge and requires much more than a solitary sentence. In the past I have discussed the effects that we the fans can have on our Football Club – attending matches and backing the team to the hilt – but now, please allow me the opportunity to consider the ways in which our Football Club can affect us, both on an individual and collective basis.

In order to be successful in this objective, let us compare the ways in which the Celtic support view their Club against the thoughts of somebody with no interest in football whatsoever. After all, if we are to dissect a topic of discussion so far reaching and of such a scale as Celtic Football Club, we must understand the basics first and foremost.

For example, to a footballing novice, a match is just a sporting endeavour contested on a piece of grass by twenty-two players, overseen by a referee and their assistants. Yet, to a Celtic supporter, it is so much more. Combining elements of gladiatorial blood and guts style combat (figuratively speaking) and the pantomime duels between good and evil, each football match tells its own unique story in one way or another. No two fixtures are ever wholly identical, and in that unpredictability lies much of the wonder of the beautiful game. These tussles give people the opportunity to come together and share a common bond, laughing and cheering as their side vanquishes a foe or commiserating as one whenever they themselves are defeated.

Equally a goal, logically speaking, appears to be nothing more than a ball passing between a set of upright pillars connected by a crossbar before making contact with some netting. Yet, to a Celtic supporter, it is so much more. It can be the source of ecstasy or despair; acclaim or criticism; marvel or controversy. Goals can make heroes and villains almost instantaneously, and given the correct scenario, they can be life changing, sending people to distant countries or keeping them stuck at home. For example, had Henrik Larsson not scored in the second leg of the UEFA Cup semi-final against Boavista, our mass pilgrimage to Seville may never have occurred, and this is just one of an almost endless plethora of examples which could be cited. Although, having said that, neither matches nor goals alone can account for my opening assertion.

Continuing in this line of thought, one could observe that managers and players are simply human beings, just like the rest of us, and that they do not automatically deserve the adulation often directed their way. Indeed, on one level this assertion is correct. Yet, to a Celtic supporter, they are so much more. At the present moment, we have a fine team in possession of substantial potential, led forth by a talented and passionate manager. Certainly, there is an affinity between him, his playing squad and the supporters, and this is of critical importance if future successes are to be attained.

Finally, to the untrained eye, the Celtic shirt is just green and white fabric stitched together to form a garment of clothing. Yet, to a Celtic supporter, it is so much more. Indeed, it is the pre-eminent symbol of "a people and a cause" as the great Tommy Burns once said. Other clubs from all around the world – England (Yeovil Town), Germany (Greuther Fürth), Ireland (Shamrock Rovers), Kenya (Kibera Celtic), Mexico (Santos Laguna), Portugal (Sporting Clube de Portugal), South Africa (Bloemfontein Celtic), Spain (Eibar and Racing Santander), Switzerland (St. Gallen), Turkey (Bursaspor) and many others besides – have worn their interpretation of the green and white Hoops at some point or another, but if one were to ask a selection of football fans from across the globe whom a similarly Hooped shirt represents, I have no doubt in my mind that the majority would say it was the colours of Celtic Football Club. Instantly recognisable, portraying not only a football team but the common ethics and values of the people who wear it, the Celtic shirt is much more than a simple sports top. Yet, despite all of this neither the coaching staff, their playing squad nor the Celtic shirt alone can justify my opening statement.

Now, please do not think that I am casting aside all of the factors which I have previously mentioned, for I wholeheartedly believe that they constitute integral parts of Celtic Football Club, but unlike the two areas which I am set to discuss momentarily, they could be mimicked by anyone with enough determination and the correct means. All football clubs host matches and score goals; some clubs could buy our players or tempt our manager away should they wish; and a few have taken our iconic shirt as an inspiration for their own, but that is where the imitable factors end. Whilst our sport, manager, players and shirt are all important, they do not represent the be all and end all of Celtic Football Club – only the soul of our supporters and the spirit of our history do this – and neither of these traits can be manufactured or bought. Indeed if they could be, they would be tremendously valuable commodities in the modern game, which has become increasingly corporate and devoid of passion in some instances.

Ironically, these particular factors which make Celtic so special are generally the most difficult to sufficiently describe in words and yet, they are undoubtedly of the utmost importance. Our supporters are the lifeblood of our Club, representing it with incredible faith and infectious enthusiasm. Without them, Celtic Football Club would not be what it is today, and in each and every one of them, there is proof that the legendary Jock Stein was correct when he said: "Football without the fans in nothing." Equally, the history of Celtic Football Club sets it apart from the rest of the footballing world. Formed in a time of widespread social division and exclusion, "for the maintenance of dinner tables for the children and the unemployed", charity and equality have been central to Celtic's success from day one. Again, in this sense, the words of another managerial giant from the Club's past, Willie Maley, continue to ring true over a century and a quarter on from its foundation: "It's not his creed nor his nationality that counts, it's the man himself."

Make no mistake about it, Celtic Football Club and its supporters, are special. Though our financial clout may be restricted in the modern day and some media outlets malign or vilify us with apparent regularity, none of this – nor anything else – should diminish this point.

The fact that Celtic are supported by men and women of every age, every ethnicity, every religion and none from all over the world is something of which we should be tremendously proud and hold dear to our hearts, as it is the envy of many other clubs. The impact which Celtic can have in people's daily lives must never be underestimated, nor that which any individual can have on the Club, and it is my hope that in these pages, I will give you an expanded insight into how and why this is so.

Celtic Football Club is that feeling when time seems to slow down as you realise a goal bound effort is going to find its target; Celtic Football Club is that reaction as the net bulges and vast swathes of humanity explode with jubilation; Celtic Football Club is the emotion as we bid farewell to a departed idol, whose achievements have attained immortality; Celtic Football Club is the belief that a mighty foe such as Barcelona or Real Madrid can be toppled midweek, despite the fact that a disappointing domestic loss was suffered the preceding weekend; Celtic Football Club is the mantra which says charity must always be our objective, even as the generations pass; Celtic Football Club is the joy on a young child's face as they gaze in wonder at the modern day magnificence of Celtic Park for the first time; and yet above all else, Celtic Football Club is as much about the support's hope for our next match, regardless of what it may be, as it is about our unparalleled history which blends sporting and social aspects together like no other.

The people, stories and triumphs discussed within this book are "Uniquely Celtic".

"The Man with the Iron Chest"

Born in the tiny mining village of Woodside, Ayrshire, on the ninth of February of 1881, James Hay would not have had the easiest of starts in life. The youngest of nine siblings, James would never meet his older brother and namesake, born in 1869, who passed away a little after his first birthday. Also, it appears another one of Hay's elder siblings died very young.

According to the evidence submitted by representatives of the Ayrshire Miners' Union to the "Royal Commission on Housing (Scotland)" towards the end of 1913 – over three decades on from Hay's birth – Woodside was "a village of thirty-six houses", which were "very small" (with many the same size, if not smaller, than most modern day living rooms) and "of a poor type". The individuals who penned this evidence, James Brown and Thomas McKerrell, claimed the outside toilets referred to as "closets" were "unspeakably dirty", something "the womenfolk complained bitterly against." "Open sewers" are then mentioned, before a brief reference is made to the "keen interest" and pride the men of the village had in looking after their gardens. Finally, in summation, the report states "The people here are of a good type, and deserve better accommodation."

Now, to reiterate the point which I have made above, it is clear that the living conditions in Woodside – just as they were in many other such villages, and not simply those within the realms of Ayrshire – were very poor indeed. One wonders then, with some justification, just how bad matters must have been over thirty years previously, upon the birth of James Hay. Yet, as has been the case now and again across the course of history, such difficult upbringings can on occasion produce some of the finest, most industrious, and toughest sportsmen of a generation – all categories into which Hay fits comfortably when one casts an eye over his career with the benefit of hindsight. After all, the small village of Glenbuck in East Ayrshire also produced the Shankly brothers, the most famous of whom, Bill, was born in the same year that Brown and McKerrell handed over their report to the Royal Commission. Perhaps it is of no wonder then that James Hay was made of stern stuff, particularly when one considers that he, following in his father's footsteps, first ventured into the depths of a local coal pit at ten or eleven years old.

Described by one writer as "a mere boy in years but a man in stature" at the age of just fifteen, James opted to sign for Derbyshire side Glossop sometime around the turn of the century, but due to the intervention of family members, he was forbidden to go and as such reneged on his agreement. Spending his early footballing days with Woodside Annbank Juniors, Hay was given a trial at Celtic in the May of 1900, but as he returned to Annbank (the senior side) about a week later, one can surmise that the folk at Parkhead did not think he was up to their standards – not yet, at least – as it is well known that the Celts kept a keen eye on several young men whom they once had on trial, often signing them a matter of years later.

Thereafter, during a goalless Scottish Cup match against Dundee on the eleventh of January 1902, Ayr's regular inside-left William Aitken suffered a bad injury which would rule him out for the foreseeable future. As such, the men in control of the club were left with no choice but to attempt to secure a suitable replacement as quickly and efficiently as possible. With their knowledge of local players, Hay was quickly identified as their target, but they would first have to trudge through miles of snow in order to reach his home and present him with their offer. This did not put them off however and after agreeing terms, James Hay would sign for Ayr Football Club (one of the two clubs which would merge together to form Ayr United only eight years later) for the princely sum of two pounds.

Somewhat ironically, James would make his debut only days later versus the team against whom his predecessor had sustained the injury. The fixture was contested at Dens Park in front of the biggest crowd any Ayr side had ever played before at that point in time, with over eleven thousand spectators in attendance (some six or seven hundred are said to have been away fans). Ayr would lose the replay by two goals to nil, with one football journalist reflecting that Hay "was timid and uncertain in his movements". However, the same correspondent also latterly praised the debutant's work once he was forced to move from inside-left to left-half when one of his new teammates retired due to injury. Nobody would have known it at the time, but it is clear this would bode well for Hay habituating defensive roles on the field of play.

In the months which followed, James would enjoy some success in the crimson and gold colours of the old occupants of Somerset Park, as Ayr finished eighth in the second flight of Scottish Football at the end of the 1901-02 season, before surging forward to jointly hold the third position at the end of the following campaign, only two points off promotion to Division One.

Having signed for Celtic on the nineteenth of March 1903, there is some contention as to whether the Parkhead side paid fifty pounds or one hundred pounds to attain their new player's services. However, according to Hay himself in a series of newspaper articles which he would write many years later for the "Dundee, Perth, Forfar and Fife's People's Journal", it appears to have been the former of the two, although a caveat was attached as he jokingly recalled. "There was a...proviso when I went from Ayr to Celtic. My club got £50 down, and there was a suggestion that they would get an extra £25 if I should turn out to be a success in the team. It was only quite recently that I heard this story and was also informed that the extra £25 had not come to hand. I am still wondering if this means I was not a success, but I think it will be unwise for me to offer further comment."

Standing at five feet and seven and a half inches in height and weighing twelve stones, James would make his senior debut as the Celts kicked off their league campaign by welcoming Partick Thistle to Celtic Park. Amidst a heavy autumnal shower and before a crowd numbering only five thousand or so, the home side edged out their opponents by two goals to one. The media coverage surrounding this game, published both before and after the fixture itself, may prove to be of some interest to you. Beginning with the former, an article contained within the "Edinburgh Evening News" on the Friday immediately preceding the tie was not overly kind to Celtic, nor its recent intake of youth players, saying "Celtic Park will be opened by Partick Thistle. Last year in the corresponding game, Celtic won rather easily. Comparing the teams for tomorrow, there is less certainty about a repeat victory. There does not seem to be anything impressive in the following list: McPherson; Battles, Strang or McLeod; Moir, Young (late Bristol City), and Hay; Muir, Somers, Bennett (late Rutherglen Glencairn), McMenemy and Quinn."

Now, without going off on a tangent, I do hope the author of the previous piece lived long enough to have been proven wrong by many of the players listed in that squad, several of whom went on to form the backbone of the greatest Celtic side ever up until that point which, of course, proceeded to win an unprecedented six domestic league titles in a row as well as several Scottish Cups and other trophies before a decade had passed. James Hay would prove an integral part of this footballing force also, as I shall discuss in more detail shortly.

Returning to the media coverage of the opening day of the 1903-04 season, the gentleman writing for the "Dundee Evening Courier" earlier in the week was of a much more optimistic nature. "Too much attention need not be paid to the collapse of the Celtic in March and April last. Then the competitions as far as honours were concerned were closed to them, and apathy reigned. When they put forth a fresh team in the Charity ties a difference was seen, and on that showing alone we are justified in predicting bright things of the Celts this season. From goal to centre there is more youth about the eleven than usual, and there has been retained just a sufficiency of older blood to infuse discretion. McPherson has Junior Internationalist Adams to share the goal with him, and at the back figures Battles and Watson, the old firm, with two young ones in Strang and D. McLeod, of Dunfermline. At half Moir, Loney and Orr are reinforced by P. Watson from Dykehead; James Hay – a real good one this – from Ayr; and Young, from Bristol Rovers..."

Equally, as for the actual match itself, very little is said of Hay – who was ironically missed out of the Celtic line-up (which featured only ten players) in the match report published subsequently by the "Glasgow Herald". Regardless, James Hay, both as an individual and as a member of a team of the rise, would soon be making himself such a well-known and much-loved figure that nobody could forget about him.

Celtic began the 1903-04 league season brightly, winning six of their first eight games, but two unexpected losses against Third Lanark (both coming by virtue of a three-one scoreline), meant that as Celtic travelled to Ibrox midway through October, they trailed their opponents by a point whilst sharing second spot with the impressive Cathkin Park outfit. However, although the Celts had already amassed almost half the points which they did the previous year, a quick glance at the league table of the time indicated that they faced an uphill task if they wished to become the champions of Scotland again. Yes, Rangers only led the table by a solitary point, but the Ibrox club had already scored twenty-eight goals in their eight fixtures played thus far, whilst their closest competitors at this point – Celtic and Third Lanark – had scored only fifteen and fourteen respectively. As such, Rangers were considered to be the favourites for the first derby match of the season, but this would be to no avail as the tie finished goalless.

Subsequently, a run of six victories and one loss from the seven fixtures interceded before Rangers travelled to Celtic Park for the return tie on New Year's Day. This saw Celtic do their best to keep pace with the teams above them – particularly the Ibrox side – who had played a few games more than they had at this stage. Again, Celtic would hold their opponents to a draw – two-all on this occasion – but both sides would squander chances to assert any sort of stranglehold on the league the following week as they were each defeated in high-scoring visits to opposing grounds. Whilst Rangers fell by five goals to four at St. Mirren, Celtic dropped points thanks to a four-three loss against Airdrieonians. James Hay scored his second goal in only three matches from the penalty spot that day, but Celtic were fighting against a home side with a numerical advantage, for poor Hugh Watson, a young man on the verge of winning his first Scotland cap, suffered a horrendous leg break in the first half of proceedings. Regrettably, Hugh never did play for Scotland, with Celtic supporters reflecting he never looked the same upon his return from injury. In time, he would fall out of the reckoning at Parkhead and eventually move across the water to join Belfast Celtic.

Eventually, when the season came to a close, some of you may be surprised to discover it was neither Celtic nor Rangers who were crowned as the champions of Scotland, but rather – for the one and only time – it was Third Lanark. Having quietly gone about their business picking up remarkable victories and crucial points here and there, they topped the table at the end of proceedings by four points from Hearts in second, with Celtic and Rangers tied for third place a further point behind. Ironically, had Celtic's two league defeats against Third Lanark gone the other way, it would have been the Celts who would have earned the right to call themselves champions.

Regardless, whilst Third Lanark did overcome Celtic in both league ties, the Celts won a crucial Scottish Cup semi-final fixture against the Cathkin Park side to set up a mouth-watering final tie with Rangers – the day upon which Jimmy Quinn would immortalise his name by scoring a hat-trick after Celtic had gone two down to bring the trophy back to Parkhead. Therefore, it will come as no shock when I say the majority of the newspapers which covered the Final spent the majority of their column inches gushing with praise for the Bhoy from Croy – and rightly so. Other Celts were complimented though, with the "Dundee Courier" saying "McLeod and Orr at the back were quite invincible...Lonie [spelt incorrectly as was often the case early in his career] and Hay were also good." Coincidentally, for a matter of record, it is perhaps worthy of note that the "Edinburgh Evening News", the newspaper which had been relatively scathing in its criticism of the young Celtic side preseason, said the following: "Months ago for some reason...the Celtic were set down by some of their not over-friendly critics as a poor lot...well the Celtic have by their final triumph shown the fallacy of all that. They have proved themselves to be...a set of gritty players with a touch of football genius here and there."

As James Hay's first season at Celtic Park came to a close, one would presume he would have been rather happy with how things had gone thus far. One season previous, he had been playing in the second tier and yet now, at the age of just twenty-three, he had a Scottish Cup winners' medal to his name. Equally, he should have taken much pride in the fact that as a newcomer to the squad, he had featured in all but two of Celtic's twenty-six league matches and each of their six Scottish Cup ties, cementing a place in the side for himself for seasons to come in the process. Also, as I have made reference to, when one considers that this was a team on the up, with some very good players competing for starting places, it is a testament to Hay's ability and attitude that he held his spot with a firm grip during that first season. Also, it is notable that due to a change of kits near to the start of the 1903-04, James Hay was one of the first eleven Celtic players ever to wear the green and white Hoops, a great honour indeed.

The following league campaign, that of 1904-05, would start well for Celtic and James Hay, as he was one of the five men who scored on the opening day of the season as the Hoops eased past Partick Thistle by five goals to nil at Meadowside Park, Thistle's last home before their eventual move to Firhill in 1909. Only a few weeks later, Hay would double his goalscoring tally for the season by netting the winning goal in a hotly contested three-two victory away at St. Mirren. As the autumn turned to winter, he would find himself being asked to play out of position on several occasions by Celtic manager Willie Maley, as cover for veteran full-back Willie Orr, who had signed for the Parkhead Club when James Hay was sixteen. Operating at full-back on an erratic basis, James watched William Black, a new signing from Queen's Park, do his best to cover his usual position.

Here, Black would enjoy some success, before eventually moving on to Everton at the end of the campaign, but it must be said that although Black was a Celtic player for just one season, making only a handful of appearances, he was involved in controversy in that time. Having won the aforementioned away tie against Partick Thistle with some ease, Celtic welcomed their guests to the East End of Glasgow on the seventeenth of

December, 1904. On a day upon which the weather was recounted by the "Glasgow Herald" as "conditions of the worst possible description – a drizzling rain falling during the entire game", the tie went ahead on a pitch which was "greasy" and "muddy" according to the same newspaper.

Celtic took the lead thanks to a counterattacking move wonderfully finished off by the great Peter Somers, but allowed their opponents, who debatably had the better of the first half, to equalise prior to the break. In the moments following the interval, the visitors again asserted their unexpected dominance and, thanks to a mistake from Hay, described as follows, Partick Thistle took the lead: "On resuming, the Thistle at once attacked, and Hay stopping the ball instead of clearing, Kennedy rushed in and scored."

From here on in, the Celts took the initiative in the match and for the first time that day, laid consistent siege to the Partick Thistle goal. Eventually, this pressure told as a foul committed in the box gave the Hoops a penalty kick, which James Hay dispatched calmly to redeem his earlier error. However, it was then, in the final minutes of the match when both teams were giving their all in search of an elusive winning goal that controversy flared. William Black was the unfortunate subject of an overly aggressive tackle from James Sommen, and the injury which Black received forced him to be carried from the field on a stretcher. As such, Celtic carried on with ten men, but so incensed by the previous tackle was "Sunny" Jim Young that he flatted Sommen almost as soon as play had resumed, and was subsequently sent off, leaving the Celts will only nine men come the final whistle. However, it is noteworthy that Partick themselves finished the match – which ended in a two-all draw – a man down, for Sommen too had to retire from the tie and be carried to the pavilion after Young avenged his fellow half-back William Black, who would not reappear in the starting line-up for approximately six weeks thereafter. Somewhat bizarrely, a brief snippet contained within the "Nottingham Evening Post" in the days which followed this match, revealed the following: "A director of the Partick Thistle Club presented each member of the team with a gold watch for having drawn the match with the Celtic on Saturday."

As for James Hay, although he was forced to play out of position every so often that season, he did achieve the prestigious feat of appearing in every match which Celtic contested, both in league and cup competitions, throughout the entirety of the 1904-05 season. During that league campaign, Celtic lost fewer matches than they had done for three years and as such, come the final whistles on the last round of fixtures that year, jointly topped the league standings with Rangers. Of course, none of this would have been the case had it not been for a stunning Celtic victory at Ibrox in what was to be the Celts' penultimate league encounter of the season, as the visitors not only dominated the match but also the scoreline, running out four-one winners and giving rise to an rare possibility referred to by the "Edinburgh Evening News" on the Monday following Celtic's triumph at Ibrox Park.

"Our Glasgow correspondent writes: The possibility of a tie for the League Championship is now a probability. Rangers have three games to go, Celtic one, and success in these will work out at a total of forty-one points each."

Subsequently, before turning our collective attention to the play-off itself, allow me to highlight the following passage from the same newspaper which discusses the remarkable determination and desire which Celtic displayed whilst sealing their victory at Ibrox Park: "On Saturday, Celtic did play the only game that is possible to beat the Rangers present team; an untiring, worrying sort of a game. It is a long time since we had football under such stormy conditions as prevailed at Ibrox, and the clubs may wait long enough ere [before] they have a similar experience. More against the Rangers' nappy style was the footing, and when they attempted the open style they were not in it with Celtic, who seemed to be playing for even a bigger stake than the championship, so courageously and strenuously did they force matters."

Thus, thanks in part to Rangers winning all three of their remaining matches, and also to a six-two victory for Celtic over Motherwell at Fir Park, there would be a play-off for the Scottish League Championship title for the second and final time (the first involved Dumbarton and Rangers at the end of the inaugural 1890-91 Scottish League season, but after the play-off was drawn both sides were declared joint champions).

The build-up to this play-off tie, coming only a year after the gargantuan Scottish Cup Final between the two clubs, was rather intense. Yet, whilst there was the inevitable anticipation present within both sets of supporters, some consternation and controversy also surrounded the fixture from the fans of both Third Lanark and Queen's Park, as well as some within the Scottish press. Essentially, the two aforementioned clubs were set to play a Glasgow League tie at Cathkin Park on the sixth of May 1905, the day upon which it was agreed the Scottish League play-off would take place at Hampden Park just across the road. It is not surprising then to note that both clubs, particularly Third Lanark, were unhappy as they felt the presence of such an important fixture nearby would seriously hamper their attendance (and more importantly, their gate receipts). A journalist from the "Edinburgh Evening News" explains:

"Our Glasgow Correspondent writes: In selecting Hampden Park for the venue of the deciding game for the League Championship the clubs concerned acted wisely. That the game, however, should be played on Saturday in opposition of the Glasgow League match at Cathkin Park between Third Lanark and Queen's Park has created some [bad] feeling and straight talking. The former club especially, resent the counter attraction, an effort – to modify the effect which will result as the clashing of the games – made by their representative at the League meeting on Monday being futile. The influence of the present League Championship clubs is too great, and now those who have, in the past been gracious to and patient with them, cry out. It is needless at this time of day to ask why the League meetings are not open to the Press…Third Lanark have a decided grievance, more so than Queen's Park, who will share to a certain extent in the profits accruing from the Scottish League match on their own ground at Hampden."

Focusing on the play-off match itself, the same correspondent continues his article, making particular note not only of the importance of the tie, but of the fact nobody was sure at the time quite how many fans would attend.

"For the second time in the history of the Scottish League a deciding game for the championship is necessary, and the meeting of the Celtic and Rangers tomorrow will be akin to a national cup final. It remains to be seen whether, in spite of its attractive nature, the patronage will be in keeping with that which has graced former meetings on special occasions, of the clubs interested. I fancy it will, but may be mistaken. We have had a lot of Celtic-Rangers this season, but the appetite of the football patron seems insatiable."

The match proceeded as planned and Celtic edged what was considered not to be a particularly great footballing spectacle by two goals to one. The "Glasgow Herald", one of the few newspapers to cover the event in any significant detail (and even then it received far less attention than a Scottish Cup Final would have at the time), reported the match as follows: "Celtic's League Triumph – The tie for the League Championship, which was decided on New Hampden on Saturday, drew a crowd of about thirty thousand, which was much in excess of what could have been expected in view of the prolongation of the competition beyond the limits of public interest, and certainly the game provided was not at all in keeping with the attendance. Play in the first half showed the Rangers a cleverer combination than their opponents...However, the second half saw matters reversed, for they abandoned their fine open game for the less profitable one of close passing, and this proved their undoing, for the Celts halves were able to checkmate their every move, and kept them out of shooting range. Twice in a couple of minutes Celts broke through and scored, goals which with ordinary care could have been saved, and for the rest of the game Rangers were seldom dangerous, unless when Robertson got their only goal. Celtic thoroughly deserve the championship if for nothing else than their plucky, uphill fight in the far end of the season, a season which has been remarkable for the vacillating promises of Airdrieonians, Partick Thistle and Rangers for leading position."

Therefore, Celtic were the champions of Scotland for the first time in seven years, and with a young and improving team at his disposal, blending a potent mixture of flare and strength, Willie Maley and his side began a period of dominance which Celtic Park would not witness again until the glorious days of the Lisbon Lions.

The spring of 1905 would also see James Hay selected to play for his country for the first time, as the Scots welcomed Ireland to Celtic Park for their second fixture of the British Home Championship. Having lost their previous match by three goals to one against Wales in Wrexham – with one of the Welsh goals coming from the legendary Billy Meredith – Scotland would have known all too well that they would require a win if they were to have any hope of winning the Championship outright for the first time since 1902. Ireland had managed a one-all draw with England in Middlesbrough prior to their encounter with the Scots, so could not be considered pushovers by any means.

Briefly returning to Hay's newspaper series previously mentioned, we are given a brief insight into what his first call-up to the Scotland squad meant to the young man. "This brings me to the subject of internationals. How well I remember the first for which I was chosen. There is a thrill about the first game for which a man is chosen for his country which cannot be repeated. He may get the big game after having figured for a number of years in the less important events, and this certainly brings a big amount of satisfaction, but it is not to be compared with the rapture which comes with the first."

As was often the case at this point in time, the international selectors had a habit of picking more players from the club whose ground upon which the tie was going to be played than they perhaps would otherwise. As such, five Celts – James Hay, Donald McLeod (the great full-back destined to die on the battlefields of World War One), Jimmy McMenemy (a man who would go on to become an undisputable Celtic legend in his own right), Peter Somers (the clever inside-forward a couple of years James' senior) and Jimmy Quinn (the sensational striker who remains Celtic's fifth highest goalscorer) were chosen to make their international debuts in this tie. The rest of the side was made up of several representatives from Heart of Midlothian, with members of the Partick Thistle and Third Lanark clubs also included.

Scotland would ultimately go on to win the fixture by a scoreline which would suggest a relative amount of ease was involved – four goals to nil – but that is not to say it was a breeze for the home side, nor that all of the Scots on show were thought to have enjoyed good performances, as the following extract from the "Dundee Courier" in the days succeeding the match shows: "The Scots forwards took a long time to settle down, due principally to the weakness of Peter Somers and the masterly way Connor, the flaxen-haired Glentoran centre half, was stopping Quinn, while the slovenly way the home half-backs gave the ball to the forwards had not a little to do with the ineffective form shown. Hay and Gibson were great sinners in this respect, especially the latter, who found the Tottenham pair much too clever for him and was left little time to make up his mind what to do with the ball when it came his way…Hay never touched his club form, and preferred banging the ball to placing it."

Whilst a few of the Celtic players who featured that day would enjoy some level of praise from the sporting press, only Peter Somers would retain his place for the crunch tie with England in London, which would see the English secure the British Home Championship after a one-nil win. James Hay would have to wait until almost four years had passed until he would be chosen to pull on a Scotland jersey once more, but even after a relatively poor debut, he would win over his international detractors in time.

As 1905 turned to 1906 and the Celts cemented their position as league winners for the second time running, James Hay repeated his achievement of the previous year by featuring yet again in every single one of Celtic's league and cup matches, playing all but one in his familiar half-back role. Coincidentally, the only occasion upon which he reverted to full-back saw the Hoops suffer one of their few defeats that season, going down by a single goal to nil away against Aberdeen.

Thereafter, as the Celts prepared for the 1906-07 season and full-back William Orr turned thirty-three over the course of the summer, James Hay was selected by Willie Maley to take on the role of Club captain, undoubtedly as great an honour then as it is widely considered to be in the modern day. It marked another significant moment in the rise of Hay, who had still been playing second tier football a little over three years prior to taking up the captaincy at Celtic Park. When one takes a moment to think of the style of play personified by James Hay – a hard tackling, unforgiving man when it came to defence but a determined, quick moving and on occasion rather skilful figure when driving his side forward – it is rather apt that during his first six league games as Celtic captain, the Hoops kept six clean sheets whilst scoring a cumulative total of twenty goals themselves, with Hay netting one of these himself on the first day of the season away at Motherwell. It has also been said that James Hay was the first protestant captain of Celtic Football Club, although personally I have my doubts about this owing to the fact that his predecessor was married in a Methodist wedding ceremony. Regardless, this point may appear to be of little practical significance – as, of course, it was considered by the Celtic support of the time – but when one casts an eye back across history and the sectarian policies employed across the city for many years, the relative importance of this decision becomes clearer to behold.

It was then, with Celtic's 1906-07 league record thus far reading seven wins from seven matches, with twenty-two goals scored and only one conceded, that misfortune would befall both Celtic and, in particular, their captain. One week prior to Rangers' league visit to Parkhead, the Hoops travelled to Dens Park to take part in a fixture which would be significantly hindered within the first few moments of play. According to the "Glasgow Herald", who first recounted how this tie had drawn the largest ever crowd to the stadium, with no less than twenty-five thousand paying spectators in attendance: "The match had an unfortunate beginning, both teams playing ten men practically from the outset. Fraser, the Dundee outside-left, was the first victim, being so badly injured about the head in a collision with McLeod that he had to be conveyed unconscious off the field, while a few minutes later Hay, in a passage with Webb, had the misfortune to get his collarbone fractured. These mishaps robbed the game of a part of its interest."

Latterly, in a piece clearly tacked on to the bottom of the previous quoted article, the same newspaper provided an update of Hay's condition two days after the incident, as well as offering a rough estimate of how long the Parkhead faithful would have to wait to see him in the Hoops once more.

"James Hay, the captain of the Celtic, who was injured at Dundee on Saturday in the course of the football match…was temporarily attended to in the Infirmary there. He was afterwards taken to Glasgow by train and conveyed to the Royal Infirmary. In that Institution he was placed under the charge of Dr. Fitzwilliam – who, by the way – was some years ago a well-known rugby player. Dr. Fitzwilliam found Hay to be suffering from a fractured collarbone. However, he will be able to leave the Infirmary this afternoon, though it is expected it will be fully six weeks before he is able to again play for Celtic."

In fact, it would be eight weeks before James Hay would return to the Celtic line-up, as they beat Port Glasgow Athletic by four goals to nil at Celtic Park a few days shy of Christmas 1906. During his absence, the rest of the squad continued their fine form, firstly defeating Rangers by two goals to one, before victories against the likes of Hibernian and Falkirk followed. Only a three-all home draw with Clyde caused the champions to drop points without the presence of Hay, who held his place in the squad for all but two matches upon his return.

Throughout the remainder of the league season, Hay would make several appearances once more at full-back, covering at both left and right-back, as Celtic strode forward to secure another Scottish League title by seven points, even whilst drawing four of their final five matches. However, the fact that the destination of the league flag looked virtually certain in the closing months of the campaign did have its benefits for the Celts, who were able to focus their attentions on attempting to capture the Scottish Cup for the first time in three years. Despite the Hoops playing a total of eight matches in the competition that season en route to the final – four of which were replays and second replays, it must be said – Maley rarely tinkered with his chosen eleven for these affairs. The rear-guard six of Adams in goal, McLeod and Orr at full-back, and Young, McNair and Hay at half-back went entirely unchanged throughout this period, conceding only three goals in total.

Of course, whilst every player most certainly played their part in Celtic's Scottish Cup run of 1907, I must give special credit to the newly installed captain. Two consecutive draws with Morton, a hardworking if somewhat average top flight side, led to a second replay being held at Celtic Park in an effort to finally decide the tie one way or another. Played before thirty thousand spectators, this game came a fortnight after the first encounter between the teams, and as Jimmy McMenemy opened the scoring amidst a relatively dominant first half display from the home side, some present may have expected the Hoops to finally pull away from their opponents. However, this was not to be the case, as after the interval Morton appeared resurgent, eventually equalising through Lindsay. Yet, as another draw appeared ever more likely, it would be none other than James Hay who would score a vital header (only his second goal of the season) two minutes before the cessation of play to drag his team through to the next round of the Scottish Cup.

Having dispatched Clyde and Morton in the early rounds, the Celts would face Rangers – a side whom they had lost to a little over two months before at Ibrox on league duty – at the quarter final stage. Although Celtic would go on to win this cup tie by three goals to nil, a more comfortable scoreline than many would have predicted, the "Dundee Evening Telegraph" published on the following Monday tells there was far more to the fixture than the game itself.

"The competitions for the national Cups are nearing a close, and with excitement at fever heat in those districts still represented it is little wonder that the financial returns are big. Comment has been made that the drawings at English ties are always far in excess of those realised in Scotland. There was an exception to the rule on Saturday, when Rangers and Celtic played before a crowd which paid more to witness the game than has been paid in any tie in England this season. A new record for the sixpenny gate was established at Ibrox. The official total was £1,910 – gate, £1,370; stands, £540. The crowd was so dense that one of the exit gates was burst open, and, before order could be obtained, large numbers had gained free admission. In the rush several persons were crushed, and had it not been for the admirable service rendered by the mounted police the disorder might have had more serious consequences. It may be mentioned that the largest sum netted in any one English Cup tie this season was £1,831 at the replay between Bolton Wanderers and Everton."

Continuing along similar lines, the same newspaper then turns its attention to the contest itself:

"There were big crowds at the four English matches on Saturday. The biggest was at Sheffield, where 37,830 saw the Wednesday defeat Liverpool by 1-0. This was little more than half, however, than that which went into the enclosure at Ibrox to see Celtic soundly whack the Rangers – the extent of the victory, 3-0, was as surprising as the financial returns – many thousands could not be accommodated...The prevailing excitement did not in the slightest affect the Parkheaders, who early settled down to a telling game. The Rangers were weak in comparison, and only seven minutes had gone when Bennett, getting the better of May, centred nicely, and Somers, cleverly catching the ball up, hooked it into the net. This reverse fairly roused the Rangers, but somehow, even allowing that Adams got some nice ticklish shots to hold, they were not such a dangerous side as the Celts, whose halves were ahead of the Rangers' trio. The Celtic inside three played the game to perfection, despite the fact that the Celtic centre was badly winded by Hendry, and as time wore on the Rangers' prospects did not improve. They might, however, have survived the one goal, but another put on by Hay just on the interval proved the turning point, and when early in the second half Hamilton notched a third goal for Parkhead the result was settled."

A hard fought trio of semi-final clashes with Hibernian would follow, the first two of which would end in goalless draws, but eventually another three-nil success would see the Celts progress into the Scottish Cup Final. There, they were set to face Heart of Midlothian, the current holders of the tournament and the side who last eliminated the Celts from the competition.

Almost fourteen months on from that disappointment though, the Celts would make amends at Hampden Park, racking up another victory with a three-nil scoreline. Yet, although in the end it would turn out to be a rather simple win for Celtic, that was not the feeling held by many as the half-time whistle sounded. Having had the wind blowing in their favour, the Parkhead side had seemingly thrown all they could at the Hearts' defence without scoring. Therefore, as was the way in the early days of football, before the landscape and construction of stadia nullified the wind factor to a large degree, some expected a much stronger, more offensive looking Hearts performance in the second half. However, they would be disappointed (and those supporting the Celts elated), as the "Dundee Evening Telegraph" relays:

"The less said about the last half-hour so far as Hearts are concerned the better. In the most remarkable fashion they "snuffed out." It was a complete collapse. That a side should have striven so successfully against such strong forward and half-back ranks as possessed by the Celtic aided by the breeze in the first half, and then gone under to the extent of three goals when everything had turned in their favour seems incomprehensible. Yet so it was, Celtic in the end triumphed in easier fashion than even the most rabid Irishman had any cause to expect at the interval."

Unsurprisingly, there was much praise dished out in the direction of Celtic's forward line, but for the rest of the Celtic side and the Hearts' goalkeeper also, as the same newspaper article describes: "Beaten three times, yet the hero of the Hearts' side! Allan, the goalkeeper, was without doubt the best player afield. He was tested and not found wanting in the initial period – that, too, notwithstanding that the ball was wet and slippery, the footing none too secure, and Celtic's shooting of the low, swift, along-the-ground type...Had the Hearts' halves been in keeping with the backs, or in the same line with Celtic less work would have been thrown on Reid and Collins but save for McLaren at centre half, who was Quinn's watchdog, the Hearts' trio were a long way behind Young, McNair and Hay."

Therefore, as the Scottish Cup Final of 1907 made its way into the annals of history, so would Willie Maley, James Hay, and the rest of the Celtic side soon after, for it would be the first occasion upon which the Football Club won both the Scottish League Championship title and the Scottish Cup in the same season – the first of many modern day "doubles". Notably, although the Celts did not officially win the League title until the days following the Cup Final, this was all but a formality. Earlier victory in the Glasgow Cup meant that as the previous Dundee newspaper phrased it, a treble of trophies would soon "adorn the sideboard of the club President; and all that is required is the securing of the Glasgow Charity Cup to establish a record without equal in the history of any Scottish Club."

Emphasising this point, one correspondent writing for the "Scottish Referee" around that time said: "To be captain of a team which has won this season the Scottish Cup, the Glasgow Cup, the Scottish League Championship and played itself into the final of the Glasgow Charity Cup…is, I boldly submit to you, the greatest captaincy ever held in Scottish Association football; in fact, I might venture to make it British, if you please. The qualities of captaincy are, in my opinion, ability, tact, and geniality. All three James Hay has in judicious measure."

Sadly, a narrow one-nil defeat to Rangers in the final of the Glasgow Charity Cup (or the Glasgow Merchants' Charity Cup, to give the competition its full title) denied the Celts – and James Hay in his first season as captain – a clean sweep of silverware, but good things come to those who wait, and only a season later, Celtic would win every tournament they contested, a feat they would not replicate until the time of the Lisbon Lions.

Stability in terms of playing position did not accompany the start of the new season for James Hay, who again found himself being moved along the half-back line or retreating to full-back here and there in order to cover for other players who were unavailable for selection. Before continuing, it is perhaps worthy of note that such dexterity was of great assistance to the side as a whole, and it is clear Mr. Maley must have trusted his captain's ability to play away from his usual position of choice, such was the regularity with which he was deployed to different areas of the field. The early part of the season also saw Hay score two goals in one match (a rare event) – albeit both from the penalty spot – as the Celts beat Third Lanark by three goals to one at Cathkin Park. This was a crucial victory improving the morale of the side if nothing else, for having started the league season with five consecutive victories, two draws followed by an away loss against Aberdeen meant they had gone three matches without a win as they travelled to the South Side of the city. Eight wins from their next nine matches, kick-started by this triumph against Third Lanark, would see the champions heading in the right direction once again. In saying that, they were still four points behind surprise league leaders Falkirk at this point, but the Bairns had played two games more than the Celts and therefore two victories in their ties in hand would see the Parkhead side join them atop the standings.

Regardless, the last of these nine fixtures, coming only days before Christmas at home against Kilmarnock, saw the Hoops run out the victors by four goals to one. However, it would also signal the last time upon which James Hay, who missed a penalty that foggy afternoon, would appear in a starting line-up until a few days before St. Patrick's Day, approximately eleven weeks later. Initially, the reason for this – certainly with regards the first tie he would miss, a goalless draw against Airdrieonians – was seemingly unknown, as several newspapers published the day before quoted him in the starting elevens which they expected to be selected. It was only Hay's absence from the Celtic side for the New Year's Day Glasgow derby with Rangers which appears to have forced some clarification on the matter.

The "Dundee Courier", published on the day following Celtic's two-one victory over their rivals explains the situation, beginning with the headline "Serious Illness of Celtic's Captain": "I learn with regret that Hay, the popular captain of Celtic, is threatened with appendicitis, and yesterday his place was taken again by Mitchell. We all wish the Celt skipper a speedy recovery."

A little over a week later, another newspaper said Hay "is to enter a private nursing home to be treated. It is not likely that he will be available to help his club for some time". Yet, despite the inevitable blow which losing their captain for a prolonged period would have struck on the Celtic team, they continued to go about their duties in admirable fashion. The fact that, a few draws aside, the Celts won the rest of the matches they played during Hay's absence, progressing from the early rounds to the semi-finals of the Scottish Cup (knocking out Rangers at Ibrox in the process) is a testament not only to their individual skills, but to their collective character.

Upon the return of Hay in mid-March, Celtic continued their drive towards retaining the Scottish Cup and winning another Scottish League Championship to boot. Firstly, a comfortable five-one victory in the Scottish Cup Final against St. Mirren would take place on the eighteenth of April before a crowd of approximately sixty thousand spectators at Hampden Park. This would be the last occasion upon which the Celts would lift the famous old trophy at the national stadium for fifteen years thanks to the infamous riot which would occur at the 1909 Cup Final. Interestingly, before delving into any detail regarding the tie between Celtic and St. Mirren, the "Glasgow Herald" made particular note of the people who helped to make up the crowd that day.

"The day has arrived when the Final Tie of the Cup, no matter the contestants, will draw forth the eager thousands as no other match, barring the English International, will. That was proved on Saturday. The purely partisan element would not account for the enormous attendance, and it was evident that not only was the spectatorate drawn in the main from the great unattached, but that the majority of this class came to swell a St. Mirren triumph. They were disappointed, and took no pains to conceal their disappointment, but none denied the merit evident in the victorious eleven."

Clearly then, Celtic were not everyone's team of choice in 1908, although it must be said that some of this feeling may genuinely simply have been attributable to the fact that they seemed to be winning almost everything at that point. Anyway, as for the match itself, the same newspaper as quoted previously said: "Opening with a confidence that showed the practiced foot and head, Celtic, by delightful forward play and grand backing up from the halves, took a very decided grip of the game early on. To the rabid enthusiast there was possibly too much elaboration, too much clever play without real result, but judged critically and viewed from the usual standard of play of the Parkhead club the very fact of the grace and intricacy of movement being indulged in bespoke a win. Final or no final, the eleven played their usual game and won without being unduly stretched...Weir's dash and McNair's calm made a happy blend. Loney and Hay were untiring and resourceful to a degree at half, and it was a pleasure to watch how their assiduous feeding was appreciated by the forwards..."

Celtic would go on to win it all that season, making that of 1907-08 debatably the greatest in the Club's history until that of 1966-67. The following year, James Hay was back to his imperious best, playing in all but a couple of matches over the course of the entire league and cup campaign, leading his side to a fifth consecutive championship title and what may well have been a third successive Scottish Cup victory, had the trophy not been withheld by the Scottish Football Association following the trouble which ensued after Celtic and Rangers drew the replay of the 1909 Final. Undoubtedly, this event was great both in terms of scale on the day and significance thereafter, but having covered it in some detail in my previous work, I shall refrain from doing so herein so as not to tread the same ground again.

Of all the seasons during Celtic's "six in a row", ignoring the first of these titles which was decided by the much discussed play-off, it would be the season of 1908-09 when the Celts would be pushed closest by any other side, with Dundee ultimately finishing only one point behind them in second place. The importance attached to results early on in league calendars can often be much maligned, particularly in the modern day when three points are awarded for a victory, but as with James Hay's first season at Celtic Park, in which Third Lanark's early wins over the Parkhead side proved crucial come the end of proceedings, similar events were to occur in 1908. Only six matches into the domestic campaign, Celtic had lost by two goals to one at Dens Park before they won the reverse fixture around five weeks later by two goals to nil. At first glance, the two results essentially cancelled each other out, and with twenty-eight matches still to be played after the latter result, few would have thought them to be of vital importance at that stage, but in time they would be proven to have been so, as Dundee would have won the championship had they been victorious in the return tie.

The following season, that of 1909-10, would not only see James Hay pick up the last of his six Scottish League Championship winners' medals, but the Ayrshire man would also score his final goal for the Celts, which would come only five minutes into a three-one away win at Fir Park a week before Christmas, a Saturday upon which the Hoops were the only top flight side to win away from home. This would not quite be his last hurrah, but sadly that time was gradually beginning to draw near. On the international front, however, matters were looking decidedly more positive, as after having been called up to the Scotland squad for the first time in four years in 1909, Hay found himself captaining the side as Wales visited Rugby Park in 1910. The Scots won this fixture by a single goal to nil, but would fall to a reverse of this scoreline upon their visit to Belfast for their next international – Hay's second as captain. The last time upon which James Hay would lead his country out onto the field of play would come a year later in the spring of 1911, as Scotland faced England at Goodison Park, equalising with only moments left in the tie to secure a one-all draw. Of course, it is a great honour for any Scot to captain their country, but to do so in an international match against England, particularly during the period in question, must have made Hay proud indeed. Although he would not lead any Scotland side thereafter, James Hay did register another five outings for his country in the years which followed, culminating in a three-one victory over England at Hampden Park in 1914.

Focusing on domestic matters once more, as with all runs of consecutive titles, Celtic's historic succession of league flags in the early part of the twentieth century had to come to an end at some point. This would be the case in the 1910-11 campaign, where the Celts finished a disappointing fifth, eleven points behind champions Rangers, with Aberdeen, Falkirk and Partick Thistle occupying the intervening positions. Despite opening the season with a three-nil win over Airdrieonians at Celtic Park, the Hoops would lose their next three league matches, crippling their chances from the outset. In all, Celtic suffered eight league defeats that season, with six coming prior to New Year. To contextualise this somewhat, during Celtic's "six in a row" era, the Club only lost a total of twenty-three league matches in six seasons, indicating there had been a notable slump in form. This was unsurprising and in footballing terms, debatably somewhat inevitable, but there was still one piece of silverware to be celebrated, as the Celts brought home yet another Scottish Cup. Before briefly turning our focus to that and the end of Hay's time as a Celtic player, it is noteworthy that although it took a couple of years to reach the heady heights of League Championship glory once more, it was not long before Maley replaced some of the cogs which made up his side and got them firing on all cylinders again. Between 1913-14 and 1918-19, Celtic would win another five domestic titles, four of which came in successive seasons.

Returning to the matter at hand, James Hay would win the Scottish Cup for the third and final time as the captain of Celtic Football Club after he and his side overcame Hamilton Academicals in a two-nil replay win in the middle of April, 1911. A fortnight later, Hay would make his final senior appearance in the green and white Hoops as the Celts rounded off their season with a goalless draw against Aberdeen at Pittodrie. It is of credit to Hay and the rest of the defensive unit that despite their fifth place finish, Celtic conceded sixteen fewer goals than any other side in the Scottish top flight that season – but it was their lack of goals scored which predominantly came back to haunt them.

As for James Hay, having made a request to the Celtic board for a new contract with improved terms, it was made abundantly clear to him that this would not be forthcoming. Therefore, in rather sad and acrimonious circumstances, the captain, still with a few years of top class play in him yet, left Parkhead behind for

Newcastle United. James' counterparts in the famous half-back line of Jim Young, Willie Loney and James Hay continued to appear as a duo for a couple of seasons yet, and whilst nobody can say for sure how long Hay could have remained a fixture in the starting eleven at Parkhead, it is certain his departure would have been felt by his former teammates and also the Celtic support.

Of course, what was Celtic's loss was to be Newcastle's gain, as Hay quickly set about establishing himself as a first team regular in a side which had won three English First Division titles during the last six years and had also lifted their first F.A. Cup only a year earlier (in fact, they had appeared in five of the previous seven F.A. Cup Finals). In his first season at St. James' Park, Hay and his new teammates would rise up the league table once more to finish a very respectable third. As a point of note, the following piece of information may well highlight the competitiveness of the English league at that point in time. During the 1911-12 season, Newcastle United won eighteen of their thirty-eight matches and finished third from twenty teams. Preston North End, who ended the season nineteenth and were relegated, won thirteen of their thirty-eight fixtures. Only eleven points separated the sides, despite the latter finishing sixteen places lower in the league standings. No club won more than twenty league ties that season.

Over the next few years, the great Newcastle team of the previous decade began to fade away, as did their performances, finishing fourteenth at the end of the 1912-13 campaign. At this stage, James Hay – still a relative newcomer in the north-east – was given the prestigious honour of being named the new captain of Newcastle United Football Club. Indeed, Hay was held in such high regard by the black and white faithful that they soon dubbed him "The Man with the Iron Chest", in respect of the remarkable thrust and endeavour with which he approached the game. During the two seasons in which he would hold this position, his side finished eleventh and then fifteenth in the league table, latterly only avoiding relegation by four points.

However, it is worth remembering that this was a very different footballing England to the one which we know in the modern era. Chelsea and Tottenham Hotspur were the only two London clubs present in the top flight of the domestic game, and nobody could deny the real powerhouses of the sport in England were then the north and midlands with the majority of clubs clustered there. Everton were the league champions, with Oldham Athletic finishing only a point behind them in second. One cannot help but feel a tinge of regret when casting an eye back to history, for nowadays not even Everton, undeniably a big club with a large following, have any hope of ever winning such an honour again without either a notable change in the footballing landscape or an incredible injection of financial resources. As it happens, the bottom three in the table that year were Manchester United, Chelsea and Tottenham Hotspur.

With the outbreak of World War One, domestic football in England – unlike that north of the border – was halted after the end of the 1914-15 campaign, and would not resume against until the 1919-20 season. Undoubtedly, James Hay would have gone on to record many more appearances for Newcastle United had external factors not stood in his way, but regardless of this, he remains a well-loved figure in the proud history of that football club. Subsequently, Hay was allowed to leave English Football behind him and he returned to his roots, as one may have expected only a few months shy of his thirty-fifth birthday, joining Ayr United. This venture did not go well initially, with Hay's first two matches in December resulting in defeats away at Falkirk and at home to Celtic. Of the latter tie, the "Glasgow Herald" said the following: "Ayr Disunited – At full strength and under normal conditions Ayr United would have made the Celts' task much more difficult, though on the season's form victory would have been the champions just the same. But the absence of Getgood and Niven had an unsettling effect on the home team which Hay's presence did not allay."

However, in the New Year and beyond, Ayr's form would improve markedly, and to the surprise of many, they eventually concluded the season in fourth place – their highest ever league finish – having won more than half of their matches played. When one considers that they had only won five from fifteen prior to the aforementioned loss against Celtic, this fightback becomes all the more remarkable. Sadly though, a downward spiral for Ayr and Hay would follow, as they finished the next campaign in fifteenth before ultimately coming bottom the following year. Perhaps unsurprisingly, one newspaper reported that "Hay was barracked mercilessly by the Rangers support" on a trip to Ibrox with Ayr in the early part of 1917. Clearly his reputation as one of the finest Celts of his era had not been forgotten.

In the years thereafter, having been called up to fight in the ongoing war, Hay joined the Royal Field Artillery in France, serving as a gunner, whilst also returning to the coal pits during his time back in Scotland. In footballing terms, a loan spell with Hearts followed before James Hay moved to Clydebank, where he would eventually hang up his boots for good and progress into a managerial role. During this time, finding himself in dire need of personnel, Hay turned to his old friend and mentor Willie Maley in search of assistance. As one would expect, Maley happily obliged, and loaned Hay three players. I shall leave it to the words of one of those men, a certain James Edward McGrory, to recall his memories of this period. The following excerpt is from McGrory's own book, "A Lifetime in Paradise".

"Jimmy Hay, the immortal from the Celtic half-back line of Young, Loney and Hay, had around that time taken over as the manager of Clydebank and being short of players asked his old colleague Willie Maley for some help in young Celtic players on loan. He got me and two others. The biggest shock for me in joining Clydebank was a cut in wages. Celtic had been paying me £5 a week but the Bankies told me they could only afford to play me £4. Being an eternal sucker in the subject of wage negotiations, I accepted."

Of course, Jimmy McGrory would famously go on to score at Celtic Park as Clydebank beat the home side there for the first time ever, but despite the young Jimmy's best efforts, he couldn't help his temporary team to avoid relegation that year. In the summer of 1924, with Ayr United's present manager leaving them behind for the equivalent role at Cowdenbeath, a good side who would actually finish in fifth place only two points behind Celtic the following season, James Hay subsequently left Clydebank to manage his old side. It would be here that his football career, in all seriousness anyway, would come to a bitter end.

Sadly, he and Ayr United would struggle. With an interfering board who possessed a liking for picking the teams which the club would field, Hay was marginalised to some extent, doing his best to coach the players but never truly having the authority or control held by the likes of his old boss a few miles up the road in Glasgow. According to one member of his family, James was a nervous manager, and often retired to the recesses underneath the stand (or even out into the street beyond) during important matches, asking people to come and update him with relevant information at periodic intervals. This may come as a revelation of sorts to some of you – after all, Hay was as tough and fearless a man on the field of play as any other – but it does tell us two critical points about him as a manager. Firstly, he cared deeply about the performances and results achieved by his sides, and secondly, he was undoubtedly a man who felt as if he was under a lot of pressure.

The division between Hay and the Ayr United board would culminate in an incident which remains infamous to this day. With this in mind, I shall cut a long and complicated story short. Essentially, according to James Hay, prior to a vital match with fellow relegation candidates Third Lanark in March 1925, a director of Ayr United Football Club, Mr. Thomas Steen, attempted to bribe the man set to referee the upcoming fixture, Mr. Tom Dougray, in exchange for his assurance that the Ayrshire side would walk away from Cathkin Park with an important victory.

Undoubtedly, this was an incredibly serious allegation for any manager to make against the director of a Scottish football club, but particularly so against Mr. Steen, who had also been the Treasurer of the Scottish Football Association since 1907. However, by accusing Steen, James put himself on a collision course with the director which would culminate in the downfall of both men, but such prolonged conflicts often result in the destruction of the parties involved. Hay, refusing to withdraw his accusations and offer an apology, was suspended by the

Scottish Football Association in January 1926 and subsequently left his job as the manager of Ayr United. Steen, despite some legal wrangling, eventually lost his roles with both the Scottish Football Association and Ayr United before the end of 1927. Late in the November of that same year, Hay would finally see his suspension from any involvement in the Scottish game lifted. However, with the exception of a scouting tenure with Newcastle United, he would never enjoy any further work in football, instead finding employment as an insurance agent.

James Hay died on the fourth of April 1940, aged fifty-nine, at his home in Marchfield Road in Ayr. Undoubtedly a famous figure within the footballing world despite his largely forced withdrawal from the game, his funeral was well-attended by the famous and anonymous alike. As his old teammates, Willie Loney, Jimmy Quinn and full-back pairing Joe Dodds and Alec McNair looked on, Willie Maley – who had only retired from his role as the manager of Celtic Football Club a little more than two months previously – rose to deliver the sort of speech for which he had become renowned, praising his departed friend and adding a dash of sentimentalism here and there as he did so. Later that day, Celtic welcomed Rangers to Celtic Park and, before a crowd of approximately thirty thousand spectators, the flag flew at half-mast in the East End of Glasgow for Ayrshire's departed son. For the sake of recordkeeping, Rangers won the match by two goals to one, having been awarded the softest of penalties when they trailed the home side by a single goal. The spot kick was given by one Matthew Dale, a referee whose name I would ask you all to remember, for he shall be spoken about at some length in a later chapter.

I cannot finish a piece such as this with a veiled reference to a referee, particularly when the importance of the protagonist's endeavours in the green and white of Celtic Football Club was so great. In all, James Hay played three hundred and twenty-four times for Celtic, scoring twenty-three goals whilst picking up eleven full international caps for Scotland. He also made one shy of one hundred and fifty appearances for Newcastle United and eighty-five for Ayr United. Critically, he captained each of the club sides mentioned in this paragraph, as well as leading his nation on to the field of play on three occasions. Whilst controversy will forever surround the name of James Hay, I believe it is his true legacy of skill, vision and fortitude which must be remembered as the years continue to pass. His ability to read the game before him was legendary, and the manner in which he conducted himself is worthy of much admiration also. An integral part of what remains one of the greatest Celtic sides ever James Hay, the lad from a tiny mining village in Ayrshire, is one of the few men who can truly be described as a Celtic legend.

In closing, I will leave you with the words of Mr. Gethin from Galashiels, who penned the following poem honouring James Hay in the style of another Ayrshire man, Robert Burns, and submitted it to a newspaper as so many others did a little over a century ago. Written when Hay was injured and unavailable for selection for the Hoops, it captures the love and respect the Celtic supporters of the time held for their captain.

"Long life tae ye, my trusty frien'
Prood leader o' the White an' Green;
In mony a hard-fought fight you've been,
An truth to tell,
Fu' mony a trophy won ye've seen
An' won right well."

"An Ayrshire laddie bred and born,
In' still as fresh as dewy morn,
O' tricks that are o' meanness shorn,
Ye've aye approved,
The Celts your loss wad fairly mourn,
Were ye removed."

"A real hard-working honest player,
When the Celts are pressed ye're always there;
Ye'er energies ye never spare
Tae see them through.
There's mony a team wad prosper mair,
If led by you."

"Ye're upright conduct oft has earned
The highest praise frae a' concerned;
Ye're pluck and grit have often turned
A threatened fa'
Tae victory, an' that well-earned
In spite o' a'."

"Long may ye strive, then, Jamie Hay,
Tae lead the Celts to victory,
An when ye're time is up, we'll say
(An wha'll dispute),
'Ye were a champion in yer day,
Without a dou't'."

"The Chronicles of Willie Maley: "The First Instalment""

In this set of chapters, you will find excerpts from a series of articles written by Willie Maley during World War One for the "Weekly Mail and Record". These are first-hand accounts of many of the stories and events which took place during our Football Club's formative years, and as such, I hope you will find them both informative and enjoyable. Therefore, I shall leave you in the capable hands of Mr. Maley for short periods throughout this book.

"The Beginning of His Career in Sport"

"This week we give, as promised, the first instalment of the life story of Willie Maley, the Celtic F.C. manager. In the course of this series Mr. Maley will recall many thrilling incidents in the history of a club which has achieved wonderful success and created many records."

"By Willie Maley, Celtic F.C. Manager"

"To give you a sketch of my career, and incidentally the rise and life of the Celtic club to date, is a big order, and means a delving back into the past. In this process it is quite possible that my memory may at times lead me astray on dates and figures but, as far as I can, I gladly give it to the football world which has known me and borne with me for the past twenty-six years."

"I was born in the ranks of the 21st Royal Scots Fusiliers, of which my father was then an acting sergeant, in the barracks at Newry, Co. Down. My father was born in Ennis, Co. Clare, and my mother came of a Kerry family, so that I am "Irish". My family, consisting of four brothers, are in their birthplaces emblematical of the British Empire, as the eldest, Charley, was

36

born in Barbados, Tom in Portsmouth, myself in Ireland as I have stated, and Alick, the youngest, in Cathcart, Scotland."

"My earliest recollections of football concern Cathcart. In the early 1880s there was a team there called the 23rd R.R.V. connected with the volunteer regiment of which my father was instructor for many years – till his death in 1896. In my mind I can see the big strong fellows who made up this team, and played the game in the kick and rush style of their day. Strength and dash were absolute necessities [then]. The games which counted most outside the Scottish Cup were the inter-village games, which were played home and away each year. Cathcart had a good team, and had many desperate fights with Thornliebank, Nitshill, and Barrhead in these far-away days."

"Thornliebank's Advance"

"In 1880 our village had been stirred tremendously by the fact of Thornliebank, the local rivals, having attained the honour of being finalists for the Scottish Cup against the then invincible Queen's Park. Great hopes, I remember, were held out for a country victory, big expectations being built on the speed of one Anderson, the Thornliebank outside-right. He was a speedy man...It was not to be, however, and the Queen's won the Cup by three to one."

"I played some junior football at home with a team called Hazelbank, but we had neither funds nor conveniences to enable us to get into Cup-ties until about 1886, when we played in the Glasgow Junior Cup, going out in the semi-final to Govan Fairfield by three to one. In this game, we stripped at the side of the pitch, which was beside the railway in Kinning Park, near the old Rangers' ground. Incidentally, one of our team, who had come straight from his work, had his pockets rifled as the game was going on. We also played in the Renfrewshire Junior ties, but here again we failed to achieve fame."

"In these Junior ties I came across several men against whom I later on figured in Senior football, such as Billy Johnstone and the two Oswald's, of Third Lanark, "Spriggy" Rae of Rutherglen, for which team, by the way, I played two or three games in 1886. Another man I met as a Junior was "Fisty" Britten of Clyde. He played for a team called, I think, the Carrick, and in a Junior tie we played against this team. I remember we played my brother Tom, home from college (and at that time a Senior playing for the London Caledonians), under an assumed name. Tom won us the game all right, to the consternation of the Brigtonians, who had reckoned on making us easy prey. They tried hard to discover Tom's identity, but failed."

"Tom, at this time, returning from Hammersmith College, where he had been studying, played occasionally for 3rd L.R.V. [Third Lanark], and latterly for the Hibs. I was asked to play for Second Third [their reserves], and did so on several occasions, and also played twice for the first eleven – once against Rangers. The team did not attract me, and I had really made up my mind to stop football and take to the Harriers [athletics] at this time. In the office in which I was employed I had as companion Andrew Dick, one of the most energetic men the Clydesdale Harriers ever had, and he induced me to take up his pet game. I tried it on several occasions, but sustained a very bad fall in the closing dash of a race at Busby, which laid me up for some days and really closed my Harriers career."

"When Willie Maley Played For Third Lanark"

"After my short spell of track racing in 1887, I played some few games for Second Third Lanark [as I have said], in the first eleven of which my brother Tom had then taken a regular place, having finished his studies in London. But I never felt at home there. In their ranks, I had my first football "jaunt" as we termed it at home. It was to Dumfries, to play the Vale of Nith, and we won by three to one. I had to leave Cathcart about 6.45 a.m. to walk into town to catch the 8 a.m. train for Dumfries, and I was a proud boy setting off that morning in possession of my first football bag (a present from my mother). We had a fine time of it at Dumfries, driving to the Sweetheart Abbey, a place still fresh in my memory."

"In 1887 I travelled with my brother Tom to Alexandria to see the village team, Netherlee, play the Levendale, the nursery at that time for the famous Vale of Leven. The game was a draw, but the Vale won the following Saturday at Kilmarnock."

"What a big, hardy lot the two teams were! They gave and took their knocks quite cheerfully, and I can tell you they were demons to charge. It was fierce, and yet it did not look so bad as a similar exhibition would today, with all our restrictions and penalties, and I sometimes wish we could have a bit of the old days over again, if only for a variety to the tripping and ankle tapping of today."

"It was at this time I first met Michael Dunbar, a Busby man, and therefore a serious rival to Cathcart. He played for Cartvale, who were at the time a real good team, Dunbar and Calderwood making a great left wing. They were both taken up by Cowlairs, who were the "country gleaners" of that day. My clubmate (in time to come), through friendship with my brother Tom, and with Johnnie Colman (destined later also to play for Celtic), who played at that time for Netherlee, played a few games for the Netherlee team, composed of Cathcart men. We four little dreamt of the football history we were all to make. Mr. Dunbar and I were, after that, particular chums, and in all our Celtic wanderings we were bedfellows."

"Tom's Temptation"

"In December 1887, the Celtic Club was getting underway, and Tom was approached to join the new Irish club. Previous to this, a few attempts had been made to form such a club, and the title of the Glasgow Hibs was proposed. It fell through, as did a later one of more anon. Tom was playing well for Third Lanark, and they were not inclined to let him slip."

"My father, when in Dublin, just before his discharge from the army, had been friends with a Pat Welsh who [later] asked my father to come to Glasgow to settle down. This the family did, and strange to say their first home in Glasgow was in the parish of St Mary's, Calton, where the Celtic sprang from. Pat Welsh, being a keen footballer, when he heard the Celts wanted Tom and myself to join, visited us at Cathcart in December, 1887. Along with him were the lamented Brother Walfrid, and the never to be forgotten John Glass (R.I.P.). Needless to say, the soft tones of Pat Welsh, aided by the blarney of Bro. Walfrid, and the wonderful promises and possibilities so ably at all times put forward by John Glass, earned for the Celtic the consent of both Tom and myself to do our little best for them; but I may honestly say that when our good friends had gone home we both thought that the club we had joined would have a short life, and go the way of many others started with almost as much enthusiasm."

"Are You Okay Up There Wee Man?"

At times, writing can be a somewhat tedious pursuit, whilst at others, it has the potential to be exciting indeed. The long hours associated with the proofreading and editing processes are mediated by the characters whom you can be fortunate enough to meet along the way and the pride in a good job well done come release day. Gracefully, I have been incredibly lucky to spend time with some truly outstanding individuals (such as the late, great Bill Boland) in penning this book and its predecessor. Equally, I have become firm friends with many people – not only those featured in either work – but those I have met at functions and the like also. Now, allow me to begin this chapter by simply stating the following of its chief subject – he is a remarkable gentleman.

Born on the twenty-first of March 1962, Gerry Cleary was not your typical baby boy. Having suffered the harmful side effects of Distaval (Thalidomide), a so-called "wonder drug" which was targeted at – amongst others – pregnant women suffering from morning sickness, Gerry was born with severely deformed legs and a wasted left arm. In all, he had only one fully functional limb, his right arm. Having said that, it is indicative of the character of the man in question that he wholly considers himself to be one of the lucky ones. After all, many of the babies affected by the drug were stillborn or miscarried.

In the modern day, Gerry stands approximately three and a half feet tall, but whatever the man lacks in physical stature he most certainly compensates for with a wonderful, kind-hearted philosophy towards life. Born in Paisley, Gerry initially lived in Nitshill before a short time in Cathcart was followed by a move to East Kilbride, the town which he still calls home to this day.

As the eldest of four siblings (Diane, Louise and Michael), Gerry maintains that he was aware he was different to everybody else from a very early age. However, admirably, he quickly made the decision to accept this fact and move on as best he could, even as a child. Just as any small boy does, Gerry spent a significant portion of his early life out and about with his friends, using jumpers for goalposts and finding hours of entertainment where adults would only see, for example, a tree.

"As a kid I had two favourite pastimes above all others," Gerry told me, "Playing football – you know, proper football, not that stuff on games consoles which they play now – and climbing trees. Strange though it might sound nowadays, collecting bird's eggs was a rather popular hobby back then, so it was through that I discovered my talent. It turned out I was actually well suited to climbing. I had a lot of upper body strength, and because I was much lighter than all of my pals, I could climb up a lot of trees which they simply could not. It gave me a great sense of freedom then, I really enjoyed it."

In retrospect, all of Gerry's favoured childhood activities paled in comparison to his love of the sport of football and his unbridled adoration for one particular Football Club, Celtic. As I have previously mentioned, the young Cleary was not simply a spectator to the beautiful game, he was an active participant. In fact, for someone who might appear at first glance to have no legs at all, he gleefully recalled to me that not only was he a decent enough player, but also had certain attributes none of his friends could ever hope to replicate. At first, that could seem to be a rather bizarre statement, but when one considers it with an abstract mind, Gerry's point becomes clear. For example, he was able to head home much lower driven crosses than most men, a feat he thoroughly enjoyed and memories of which continue to bring a smile to his face many years later.

As a young child, Gerry's parents Mae and Jimmy fought fiercely so that he could be given the opportunity to attend a mainstream school as opposed to one for children with special needs. Such a tale may sound somewhat unlikely today, especially for a child who was not mentally handicapped in any way, but attitudes were very different in the sixties. After all, fifty years is a long time for progress to occur. Regardless, whilst some stereotypes and uninformed opinions suggested that those affected by a disability were not normal people, in reality nothing could be further from the truth.

Gerry's parents won their battle with the help of some teachers, and the young man spent many years being educated at St Leonard's Primary and St Bride's Secondary in East Kilbride. In these surroundings, he would form friendships which would last a lifetime and meet a girl by the name of Karen who would one day become his wife, but he would face adversity also.

At the age of seven, Gerry was taken to Glasgow's Victoria Infirmary where he was to be fitted with artificial legs. Of course, the prosthetic limbs of the time were of a much poorer quality than those which are available nowadays, and whilst Gerry respects the hospital staff for doing their best with him, it was apparent from early on in our discussions that the young boy did not like the end result one bit. "They were heavy, cumbersome wooden pieces", Gerry told me, "which didn't look remotely right or fit well. They were horrendous, but my parents made me wear them to school for a period regardless. I developed a habit of arriving home in at the end of a day and taking them off before I did anything else, so they eventually understood that I was far more comfortable just being me."

Similarly, the artificial limbs which I have described previously formed a pivotal role in Gerry's earliest trips to see Celtic. The sixth of March 1971 saw Raith Rovers travel to Celtic Park for a Scottish Cup quarter final tie and, for the first time, Gerry Cleary would be a spectator as the Hoops romped to a seven-one victory. As one would expect, such a performance was a spectacle to behold for a first timer in particular, and as Gerry openly admits, he was very fortunate to be able to watch the likes of Tommy Gemmell, Billy McNeill, Jimmy Johnstone and Bobby Lennox in the flesh. However, whilst everything seemed to go swimmingly well on the pitch that night, matters were not quite so positive off of it.

Gerry's late father, Jimmy, was a regular follower of Celtic when his son was just a boy. He attended many matches with his best friend Tommy, and saw them not only as sporting ties, but as an excuse for a good day out with drink aplenty. Therefore, by Gerry's own admission, he feels that his father believed his presence cramped his style. Stood unsteadily on his artificial legs that night against Raith Rovers, James had to pay extra for him and his son to access the main stand. After all, although he would make the odd trip to the terracing in future, such areas were not really fit for Gerry's needs, particularly not in the months following the Ibrox disaster of 1971. Therefore, although he thoroughly enjoyed his first match at Celtic Park, it is fair to say the young Gerry became somewhat disillusioned in the weeks and months which came thereafter.

Perhaps naively, as many other boys have done in the past and some will do in the future also, he assumed that now he had attended one home match – overcoming the relative inaccessibility he faced climbing flights of stairs amongst other obstacles – that he would find himself accompanying his father to fixtures with an increasing regularity. This wasn't to be the case, and in truth such occasions would be rarities in future, causing Gerry to feel strong levels of resentment towards his father at this point in his life. Nowadays, with Gerry himself a man in his fifties, such feelings have tempered somewhat, as he now says he can partly understand where his father was coming from.

However – and I doubt any of you will be surprised by this – Gerry soon found his own solution to this problem. Instead of going to many matches with his father, he would have none other than Celtic player Ronnie Glavin (who lived only a few streets away) and neighbour Tony McGuinness (a businessman who resided in the same street) to thank for arranging much of his transport to games in the years approaching the mid-1970s.

As Gerry reached his mid-teens, the Thalidomide Trust, an organisation set up to distribute compensation from the company which produced the drug, began to split up a total of over thirty million pounds in damages for those affected by the product's side effects in the form of annual payments. The size of the sum which each individual received was directly linked to the severity of their respective disability, and once Gerry was granted his initial share of money, he bought himself his first car, had the relevant hand controls fitted and started driving lessons. Having subsequently passed his test, the young man predictably saw this as an opportunity to follow Celtic all over the country. As Gerry said himself, it might not have been the most exciting vehicle in the world – a brown Ford Escort estate – but it was functional, giving him a new found sense of independence, and finally allowing him to offer lifts to his friends and family, rather than having to rely on their assistance as he had done in the past.

From the start of the 1980s, Gerry and his friends found themselves following the Celts religiously in the Ford which I have just mentioned. Of course, this did mean that Gerry often played the role of the designated driver whilst his pals enjoyed a good drink, but he was happy enough. After all, he was watching his favourite football team on a regular basis, and that in itself is a blessing each and every time any of us do so (hard though that may be to accept after a poor result or performance).

Anyway, in the months and years which followed, Gerry would come to an arrangement with Jim Kennedy (an ex-Celtic player responsible for the distribution of away tickets prior to the days of an established ticket office) in order to access match tickets for him and his friends. At this point in time, the demand to follow Celtic was high, and therefore Supporters' Clubs were often only granted a percentage of the tickets for which they had applied for any given fixture. As such, the "Sons of Warsaw Celtic Supporters' Club" (the invention of Cleary and his companions), generally picked up seven or eight tickets for each tie. Their membership totalled over thirty people and in most similar situations, this would generally cause some levels of friction. Not for the "Sons of Warsaw" however, as the majority of their members had no desire to watch Celtic at all. Now, allow me to explain – for Gerry and his friends to be allocated tickets they needed to either join an existing Celtic Supporters' Club or start their own and, as you can see, they chose the latter of the two options. New Supporters' Clubs were required to have a minimum of thirty listed members at the time, but as there were only seven or eight individuals hoping to receive seven or eight tickets, the decision was made to register other people as members simply to fill numbers. These included Rangers supporting colleagues and family members who had no interest in football whatsoever, and as such this formula "worked a treat".

Whilst interviewing Gerry, I had decided to hold off on what I considered to be an important question until I felt the time was right. My query, which concerned whether or not he had ever felt endangered whilst in a large football crowd – partly due to his size and relative lack of mobility – was not one I wanted to seem crass or provocative, but as the East Kilbride man sat in his armchair and began to recall his trip to the 1985 Scottish Cup Final, I felt an opportune moment had presented itself.

Gerry replied, "In all honesty Frank, it's rarely been a great issue for me. Thanks to the help of Jim at Parkhead, I sat in the stand at home and away matches on the vast majority of occasions, but there were a few fixtures I had to go out on to the terracing for. The 1985 Scottish Cup Final was a prominent example of that, but I didn't often feel scared at the football. My friends, as well as the rest of the Celtic support, were great with me. If we did find ourselves in the midst of a large crowd, they'd form a wee ring around me and become pretty vocal with those nearby if the situation warranted it, but most of the time there was no problem at all. Well, nothing other than the fact it's not hellish easy to see the game from the terracing when you're three and a half feet tall unless you happen to be down at the front."

Of course, the 1985 Scottish Cup Final, the hundredth such occasion upon which the famous old trophy would be contested, was the subject of much interest. As Celtic prepared to take on Dundee United, Gerry knew that without a ticket for the stand, his only option to watch the match live would be from the open terracing. Due to the movement of turnstiles at the Celtic end from their traditional locations on the street up to the peak of some stairwells, there were many reports in the days which followed the match of crushing being an issue outside particular areas of the ground. This was not an all ticket affair, and as such Gerry and his friends, who were fortunate to avoid the overcrowding issues externally, paid at the gate in order to gain entry to the game. However, in the middle of such a large mass of people, the chances of Gerry finding his way down to the front of the terracing were slim. Undeterred, Cleary simply put the skills which he had mastered as a youth in practice, quickly and nimbly climbing one of Hampden's famous floodlight pylons. As was the way of things at this point in time, the young Gerry was not the only one to have such an idea, although one would naturally assume that he may well have been the sole disabled fan to attempt to scale such a structure that day.

"The view was great", recalled Gerry, "None of my pals seemed to be too worried that I had climbed away up the pylon, but a few other fans who didn't know me offered shouts of concern. You know – "Are you okay up there wee man?" – that kind of thing, but they all meant well. Most people were shouting words of encouragement anyway, it was all good natured. When Celtic scored the equaliser through Davie Provan – my favourite player at that point – and then the winning goal thanks to Frank McGarvey, I naturally found myself celebrating and leaping about as best I could whilst up this pylon, but as I stopped and actually took in the sight of the Celtic fans below me, I couldn't help but notice the entire structure swinging and swaying from side to side. Clearly, the combination of a few fans on the pylon and tens of thousands jumping around below made it move. Anyway, to sit there and watch so many people celebrating deliriously on the terracing was something special. It was a bird's eye view of a great day for our Football Club, and I feel very lucky to have attended the game and been part of it all."

In 1987, Gerry would marry his long term girlfriend, Karen. Two years later, the birth of twin sons Declan and Sean meant that their lives would never be the same again. Born on the twenty-sixth of October, Declan suffered from jaundice for a short time, and as a result of this he and his brother were only released from hospital on the fourth of November. Celtic were scheduled to face Rangers at Ibrox that afternoon, a match with an added degree of tension attached to it, as Maurice Johnston was set to line up against his former club for the first time. A conflict of interest therefore arose, as Gerry had a ticket for the fixture.

Having asked the boys' doctor whether or not they would be allowed home as the days passed and the derby game approached, the proud new parents of two baby boys were finally allowed to take them home on the morning of the match. However, the true meaning of an apparently innocuous visit of Gerry's two friends – supposedly popping in to see the kids – only a matter of moments after their arrival home soon became clear to Karen. Between ten and fifteen minutes after Gerry and Karen had pulled up at their house, with Declan and Sean in tow, Gerry and his friends would depart for Ibrox. To this day, Gerry has mixed feelings about his decision, something which Karen described as "pathetic" at the time and is still a minor bone of contention.

"It probably wasn't my proudest moment", he lamented, "We'd only just made it up the road. There was no milk or bread or anything of that sort in the house, and although I thought I was there for twenty minutes or more, Karen maintains I was only home for ten minutes at the most. I hadn't really adjusted to the effects which parenthood would have upon my life at this point, and it was perhaps somewhat naïve of me to think I could go to the game without causing any problems. However, after missing our famous trip to Love Street in 1986 and the celebrations which followed, I was loath to not attend any Celtic game at that point in time. In truth, with the benefit of hindsight, I can see why Karen wasn't pleased. I was maybe a bit out of order insisting that I went to that match at Ibrox, but to be fair, I'm sure most Celtic supporters could read this story and understand how something like this might come to pass. My two friends came in, held a twin each briefly, said they were "lovely", and then a few seconds later I appeared at the bottom of the stairs. They then handed the kids to Karen, who had one twin in each arm, said "cheerio" and the three of us walked out. She still hasn't forgiven me for that, but I think karma had its way of getting back at me that day, because Maurice Johnston scored the only goal of the game in the last minute of normal time and we lost one-nil. It was just as sickening then as it is now."

Unsurprisingly, Gerry's rate of attendance at away matches would plummet in the years following the birth of the twins, as he was occupied by more important matters. Bizarrely, due largely to a twist of fate, his involvement in football as a whole would actually experience an upsurge as the boys grew. Whilst they were still only five or six years of age, Gerry would take Sean and

Declan to training sessions held by two older gentlemen with an affiliation to one of the local amateur sides, East Kilbride Burgh. At this point, there were training sessions but no actual team for the age group in question, and so the coaches looked to the parents of the boys for volunteers to take such a side.

Gerry, whose continuing absence from Celtic's away matches was still causing a proverbial itch which he couldn't seem to scratch, put his name forward and in time would find himself as the manager of the "Burgh Blacks", the nickname given to his side to distinguish it from the other Burgh teams. Wearing blue and black vertical stripes and a kit not dissimilar to that worn by Inter Milan (whom we shall discuss later), Gerry developed a decent enough side initially, without enjoying any sort of spectacular success. However, the departure of one coach who was an ardent supporter of the team's use of the four-four-two formation presented Gerry with an opportunity to change systems a few years later. This was something he had been considering for some time but had always met resistance when voiced.

"I'd been taking the boys for years at that stage and in the past few months I couldn't help but shake the feeling that four-four-two wasn't doing us justice", he told me. "I didn't believe we had the players to operate that system as it should be, but I did feel three-five-two, which at the time was a pretty unpopular formation, may have suited us better, so I decided to get the boys together and we agreed to give it a try. Of course, a couple of years after that Martin O'Neill would introduce the same system at Celtic also."

Indeed, it was a bold move for Burgh, as they were the only side in their league to implement such a tactic in the late 1990s, but soon its respective worth became apparent as they started to accrue a collection of league and cup wins. It may sound clichéd, but for a significant period of time, the opposition sides just didn't know how to deal with it. However, that was not to say it was all plain sailing, as whilst matters on the park improved Gerry came under pressure as a manager from his beloved wife of all people, as he would make the decision to leave the twins on the bench more often than not.

Gerry expanded on this point: "It would have been all too easy for me to make the boys the first two names on the team sheet every week, and a lot of other managers at that level of the game did that then and almost certainly do so now, but I couldn't justify it as it wouldn't have been fair on anyone involved. It was my job to put the best team on the park that I possibly could, and I'd like to think that nowadays, the twins can understand why I made the decisions that I did and respect me for them. In saying that though, it did cause a bit of friction at the time, particularly between me and Karen, but I had to stick by my choices."

Gerry, his fellow coaches (John McDonald, Derek Strickland, Mick Cleary and Ricky McCrorie) and their East Kilbride Burgh side would experience some great highs and gut-wrenching lows during their time together, emotions which often directly conflicted with those personal feelings Gerry experienced as a Celtic supporter. For example, one morning in late May 2005, Burgh travelled to league rivals Broomhouse and returned not only with three points thanks to a four-one victory, but as league champions also. Gerry then watched Celtic's final match of the league season on a big screen in East Kilbride, where two late goals from Motherwell striker Scott McDonald would turn his elation to despair as the Celts watched the title slip from their grasp. Yet, hugely disappointing though this was, Gerry recalled it was nothing compared to the few painful defeats endured by his Burgh side, with the most notable being a late equaliser and subsequent penalty shootout stealing a place in the Scottish Cup Final away from them: "I always felt awful when we lost a big match. Naturally, I considered myself responsible for the team, so it hurt me."

Despite this, when asked to ponder his managerial experience as a whole – which came to an end after fifteen years on the sidelines – Gerry would not allow such results to overshadow the accolades which he and his sides achieved. He said: "When I look back on it all now, I have to say that I absolutely adored that era. It filled a huge hole in my life having stopped going to Celtic's away games, but it was much more than that. I've always felt I've known my football, but having had such an involvement with youth players for so long I do believe it gave me an even better insight into the tactical realms of the game. However, as you might expect, the best thing about it was the boys – each and every one of them. Watching them all grow and develop together, making mistakes and learning from them, battling for each other, and more often than not playing some really impressive football gave me the greatest satisfaction of all. I suppose it's perhaps those feelings of happiness and contentment with regards what we all accomplished which means I have no desire to ever go back to management. It was a fantastic time in my life and I wouldn't change it for the world, but it's over now."

The late 1990s would also see the birth of Gerry and Karen's third son, Aidan. Having focused on Gerry's time managing a football team, allow us to return to his life as a Celtic supporter. Gerry would enjoy opportunities to again attend some of the most important away matches which Celtic had either enjoyed or endured (depending on whether or not you happen to be of a nervous disposition whilst watching the Celts), as we all followed the "Road To Seville" from living rooms, pubs and stadia across Europe. Early on in this run, Gerry travelled south to Blackburn to see the Hoops dispatch the Rovers by a two-nil scoreline which was actually a much more comprehensive victory than the result alone would suggest.

Of course, one must remember that both the Blackburn manager Graeme Souness and also their captain, Gary Flitcroft, had been disparaging towards our chances of progression – with the "men against boys" quote uttered by each of the two men undoubtedly being the most infamous example of this. In the days which followed the second leg, lines such as "men against Bhoys" became very popular within the Celtic support. Gerry proudly recalled that he did not wait as long as that to make his feelings about the incident known, instead having a tricolour made for the trip south by a Rangers supporting friend of all people. The message on the banner was both simple and devastating in its nature, reading "Gary Who?"

For the sake of clarity, I should say that Mr. Flitcroft did enjoy a fairly successful if somewhat unremarkable playing career, appearing for Manchester City (prior to their financial injection), Blackburn Rovers and Sheffield United, but never attaining a senior international cap. He is now, at the time of writing, a director of Chorley Football Club, who play their football in the National League North (formerly known as the Conference North), one of the sixth tiers of English football. With the benefit of hindsight at our disposal, I feel it is safe to say that whilst we all would wish Gary the best for the future, neither him, his Blackburn side or their manager could even lace the boots of the Celts who made it all the way to a European final in 2003.

Anyway, continuing onwards, Gerry would also travel to Anfield in the quarter finals of the UEFA Cup, and having seen Celtic survive one or two dicey moments that night, the pleasure associated with John Hartson's stunning goal which continues to resonate through time and the subsequent thoughts of a semi-final and maybe – just maybe – a final beyond it filled him with unbridled joy.

"The prospect of us actually reaching the final itself had never really crossed my mind before we knocked out Liverpool", he told me. "They were a good team, and although we obviously did the business at Anfield, people forget that they gave us a fright on occasion that night – it wasn't all a walk in the park – but I suppose that was the mark of a good Celtic team, the defence held firm and the midfield and strikers provided enough of a threat going forward that we were able to win the game. To top it all off, of course, we had Big John's goal – it was an absolute cracker!"

In the weeks which followed, Celtic would battle their way past Portuguese side Boavista to earn their place in their first European Final in thirty-three years, and as far as Gerry was concerned, there was no way he could not travel to the Andalusian capital of Seville to witness it for himself.

"We had no idea of how we were going to make our way there amidst the chaos of people booking planes, trains and boats all over Europe simultaneously. Eventually, we plumped for flights departing from Liverpool which involved stopovers in Munich on the outward leg and Frankfurt on the way back, with Malaga being the Spanish airport which we frequented. The only problem with these was that they were a week apart, but it gave us an excuse to turn the trip into a proper holiday of sorts", recalled Gerry.

The potential issue of tickets, which in truth was a story in itself, was solved by a friend of Gerry's, Alan Craig, a Rangers fan, who had access to corporate tickets. Unsurprisingly, this act of kindness still means a lot to Cleary.

Carrying on our focus into the city of Seville, this was to be a "watershed moment" of sorts of Gerry, as the man himself so aptly described it. This was not because of the football, but because of his gradually decreasing mobility. In the weeks leading up to their journey to Spain, Dom Smith, a close friend and colleague had asked him whether or not he'd considered using a wheelchair during the trip, something which Gerry had never done previously. Initially, Gerry was very resistant to the idea, but soon found that his body and his mind were telling him two totally different things. Until the spring of 2003, he was still playing the odd game of five-a-side football and using shortened clubs on the golf course, but as Gerry explained that would soon to come to an end.

"I could feel my legs were going. The mornings after I'd played either game I was knackered, I could barely walk, and at that point I began to realise my sporting days were done. When I finally came to that realisation and accepted it, I was a bit less reticent about the thought of the wheelchair and I decided to give it a go. In all honesty, it turned out to be one of the best decisions of my life, and I never thought I'd have said that when the idea was first mentioned."

Naively, those of you reading this will perhaps immediately make the same mistake I did about the greatest benefits of Gerry's wheelchair use. The feeling of increased mobility, particularly in the heaving crowds and relentless heat which encompassed Seville, was the subject of the line of questioning I pursued whilst interviewing Gerry, but he quickly informed me that this was not the best thing about it. He explained this as follows: "It might sound somewhat strange, especially to able bodied folks, but the relative anonymity which the wheelchair brought with it was absolutely magnificent. You need to keep in mind, I have a pretty unique appearance. There really aren't too many other people out there who look anything like me physically and as such, if I walk through a shopping arcade or down a busy street, people do tend to look at me. Partly, that's why so many folks recognise me even if they don't know me, because I've got a memorable appearance. However, I almost immediately realised that when I was in the wheelchair, most people didn't even give me a second glance. It was strange, but it was fantastic. You know, a wee man with wee legs wandering along transforms into just any other bloke in a wheelchair – it was surreal – but I wasn't complaining. I got used to the idea very quickly, and obviously, it must be said that the boys pushing me about did make navigating the city a lot easier, and I'm still thankful to them for putting in the effort which that must have required, especially in those temperatures."

In the months which followed, Gerry would return his rental wheelchair and purchase one of his own – and yes, it is green. After all, these things are important in life. Over a decade later, a different wheelchair, albeit the same colour as the one previously mentioned, would accompany Gerry to the Italian city of Milan, as his beloved Celtic prepared to face a side with whom they shall be forever linked, Internazionale. There, he would be joined by his three sons and one of their friends, but before continuing, I must make some reference to the intervening decade.

At this point, during one of my discussions with Gerry, he revealed to me the details of a health scare which is most certainly not restricted to those who suffered the harmful effects of Thalidomide, but is more prevalent within those affected by the drug. However, in an admirable style typical of the man and his character, the manner in which he recounted the events of the night of the nineteenth of May 2010 (two months after his retirement from managerial duties), and the resulting impact thereafter, were both frank and positive.

"It was the night of the Copa del Rey Final, and being someone who'll watch almost any football match quite happily, I settled myself down for what I hoped would be an entertaining game."

Sevilla, who had won the same tournament in 2007 (their second such triumph in two seasons), were set to take on Atletico Madrid, themselves the holders of what was now the Europa League, having beaten Fulham in the final a week earlier.

Gerry continued, "During the game, my left arm started to give me some grief, but the odd ache and pain now and again was common then, and as such I just ignored it. Sevilla won the match two-nil against an up and coming Atletico Madrid side, and I went to bed after having watched the trophy presentation. Around three in the morning, I woke up and the first thing I was aware of was the intense pain emanating from my left arm. Feeling horrendous, I clambered out of bed to the toilet, making it clear to Karen that something was wrong. I was sweaty and ashen faced, and before I knew what was happening, Sean had bundled me into his car and raced to the nearby accident and emergency department at Hairmyres Hospital. It turned out that I had suffered a heart attack, and so they fitted two stents and kept me in for four days. The initial shock of it all caused me to lose almost two stone in weight, and I know it gave my family a hell of a fright. Looking back on it though, I can't say it affects me too much nowadays. I've just got to get on with things, life is there to be lived and whilst I know I'm not going to be around forever, I'm determined to enjoy it as much as I can for as long as I can."

Gerry's youngest son, Aidan, has grown up to share the same love of Celtic Football Club embraced by his father and older brothers. He is a young man whom I have had the pleasure of speaking to for many hours alongside Gerry during some of our interview time, and although perhaps a little shy at first, he certainly proves himself to be knowledgeable and passionate when the subject of conversation inevitably turns to the green and white Hoops. However, due to the fact there is almost a decade in age difference between himself and his older siblings, Aidan's only European away trip prior to Milan – that of Benfica in 2012 – saw him travel as a boy amongst men. This is not to say that he would not have enjoyed himself, but as I can compare this to my experience of travelling to Seville at the same age with later trips to the continent, I can attest to the fact there is a notably different dynamic present dependent on the respective ages of the travelling party.

Therefore, in the days which followed the draw for the first knockout stage of the 2014-15 Europa League pitting two famous footballing sides against each other, Gerry decided to treat his sons to the trip of a lifetime. After all, prior to this Celtic had not faced Inter Milan in competitive football in over forty years. Critically though, having told the rest of the family – and myself – of his ruse, Gerry kept the trip a secret from his youngest son until the whole family visited on Christmas day, thereby allowing Aidan to open a present containing an Inter Milan shirt. Unsurprisingly, having been put on the spot to some degree, it took the young man a few seconds before the proverbial penny dropped, but once it did the whole family were met by an elated reaction.

Despite the improvement in Celtic's overall form under Norwegian manager Ronny Deila, few truly hoped of dispatching an Inter Milan side which, by their high standards, many with a knowledge of Italian football considered to be fairly mediocre. Equally, even fewer would have held such expectations when the Hoops found themselves two goals down after less than fifteen minutes of the home leg against "I Nerazzurri" (the black and blues), yet it was then that an ultimately fruitless but damn enjoyable comeback began. As such, when the final whistle blew that night at Celtic Park only a minute or two after John Guidetti had drawn an incredible match level at three-all – as celebrations continued to ensue all around the stadium – Gerry and his sons knew they would travel to Italy still in with a small chance of seeing their side progress to the next round of the competition.

"As you would expect Frank, we were all really looking forward to the experience", Gerry told me as he began to recall his memories of the trip which would follow, "Particularly after we managed to claw back the early deficit in the home leg. We were set to fly from Manchester, so in order to save the hassle of having to pick everyone up individually in the morning and adding to what was already set to be a long drive, all of the boys stayed at the family home the night before we departed. One of the twins' pals Gerry Kelly, an ex-Burgh player as it happens, was set to accompany us. There was a buzz about the place, but I must confess I did get a bit of a scare, because I woke up in the middle of the night with a really sore elbow on my good arm. It happens every so often, reminding me that I'm maybe not as young as I once was, but generally if I can sit and rest for a day or two it passes. However, I'm the only one in the family who can drive my car, as it has hand controls which are individually configured to me, so I knew I'd have to cover more than two hundred miles the next morning regardless. Anyway, once I'd calmed down enough to think clearly about it, I eventually ended up manoeuvring a pillow underneath my arm once into the driver's seat so my elbow would have something to rest against. It wasn't the most pleasant start to the journey I could have envisaged, but we got there and that was the main thing. Once we arrived at the airport I just forced myself to have a couple of beers to ease the pain a little, for purely medicinal purposes, of course."

As for the Italian city itself, Gerry's thoughts and perceptions were actually somewhat different to those which I have heard many other Celtic supporters discuss regarding Milan. Of course, it is perhaps worthy of note that in any large settlement, particularly one which is home to over one million people within the city limits and another four million beyond, our opinions are often formed by the areas which we see and the people whom we meet.

Anyway, Gerry continued: "I thought Milan was alright. The main square was lovely – which is hardly a surprise since it is famous for that attribute – and the area in which our small hotel was located was actually quite nice also. I've heard a lot of people criticise Milan, and they may well be correct in doing so, but we never really entered any areas of the city which gave us any cause to do so. It was clear some parts were industrial in their nature, so perhaps not the most picturesque places on Earth, but you expect that in any big city which you visit. Still, the most important thing from our point of view was that we had all made the journey safely and that there were thousands of Celtic fans coming from far and wide to join us, so we were very much looking forward to it as match day finally arrived."

"The day of the game was great. We headed out, had some pizza and a couple of beers for lunch in a small restaurant in which the "large beers" were a litre in size, before making our way into the city centre. We'd found out about the localised alcohol ban which had been imposed there so Sean and his pal Gerry headed back out to the hotel which had a wee supermarket next to it to see if they were far enough away to be unaffected by the restrictions, whilst the rest of us made ourselves comfortable in the square. The boys appeared a while later in a taxi after not being allowed back on to the subway with their carry out. The atmosphere was buoyant, particularly in the nice weather, but as a result of all the beer I soon encountered a potential problem – finding an accessible toilet. I know it's the sort of thing most people never have to think about, but sometimes they are not as easy to find on the continent as they can be here. Anyway, one of the boys wheeled me over to the McDonalds on the edge of the square, only to be met with two big bouncers on the front door. To be fair to the guys, they were great, and once I'd explained myself not only did they help me through the crowd inside, they told me they'd be happy for me to return as many times as I liked over the course of the day, so that took a big weight off my shoulders and allowed me to just enjoy my time in the square. Aidan had a chance to have a couple of beers too, although not as many as the rest of us, but I think he really enjoyed that as he felt he was part of the group as an adult."

Later that day, Gerry and the lads arrived outside one of the world's most famous football stadia, the Stadio Giuseppe Meazza, often referred to as the San Siro.

"The wheelchair facilities they had there – or certainly the ones which I was given access to – were fantastic. Gerry Kelly and I were in with the Inter supporters, right down by the pitch, whilst my boys were away up in the gods alongside the rest of the Celtic support. The people were lovely, and a few of them were kind enough to give me the odd memento, such as an Inter Milan badge. Symbols of friendship such as that mean a lot when travelling abroad in Europe, and I'm glad to see the mutual respect between the supporters of the two football clubs is still present today, almost fifty years on from their first and most famous meeting in Lisbon. Also, to top it all off, Gerry and I managed to get a few beers inside the stadium, despite the fact that Sean and Declan had told us not to drink any more."

"As for the game itself, the result was a bit frustrating. The sending off of Virgil van Dijk changed the entire match, and I have to say that up until that point in time, I thought we'd given a pretty good account of ourselves. I was impressed by Gary Mackay-Steven's willingness to run at their defence in particular. For any young man to do that is great to see, but particularly so when they've only just moved from Dundee United and all of a sudden find themselves playing at a stadium like the San Siro. It's a shame Ronny chose to sacrifice him following the red card, but as I say it was a ridiculous decision to dismiss Virgil in the first place. Inter Milan's late winning goal was magnificent, and I have to admit, even if it is somewhat begrudgingly, that a strike of that quality was worthy of settling the tie once and for all. On the whole though, it had been a great trip, and one which I personally am very happy I was able to be a part of."

In closing, I must reiterate the fact that one of the reasons I love writing and interviewing people is that, more often than not, I seem to form firm friendships with those whom I have been fortunate enough to speak to. In this sense, Gerry Cleary is no different, and I have no doubt that I will continue to spend time with him in the future, not as an interviewee but as a good mate. He is a truly remarkable man, although I know he does not have the sort of character to admit that, but I believe it to be the case regardless. Certainly, it would have been an easier choice for someone affected by Thalidomide to shy away from many aspects of life, but instead Gerry has decided from his earliest days on this Earth to face them head on with determination, vigour and an infectious personality.

As I said at the outset of this chapter, what Gerry Cleary may lack in physical presence he really does make up for in terms of character and personality by simply being himself. He has overcame many obstacles in his life, but he has endured, and is now not only a husband to his wife and a father to his three sons, but a grandfather also. I hope he has many fruitful years in front of him in this sense, with regards to both his family and his Football Club, and also that one day he – and all of the other individuals affected by the harmful results of Thalidomide – will see the justice they have strived for, as it is unquestionably deserved. Gerry Cleary, ladies and gentlemen, a man short in stature, but one of the biggest men I have ever met.

"Celtic by Numbers:
"We Owe So Much, to So Few""

Numbers are wonderful. From their early beginnings on stone tablets and cave walls, through to their modern uses in powerful computers and elaborate formulae, they allow us to quantify the world around us in a way which all of us can understand. Unlike the written word, numbers are a universal language of sorts, and when it comes to sport in particular, they allow all of those with an interest in any given game to indulge in the statistics behind it.

Like any other sport, football has many numbers which are intrinsically linked to it – eleven (players on each side), ninety (intended duration of a match in minutes) and even the lowly number one (number of balls in play), to name but a few. Equally, Celtic also has many numbers which shall forever be associated with the Football Club and its achievements, whether one considers a small number such as seven (the iconic jersey now linked to a band of Celtic greats) or a much larger figure like one thousand, nine hundred and sixty-seven (the year of the Club's greatest triumph). In this short chapter and three others which follow periodically in this work, I hope to give you all a greater insight into our Football Club's statistical past.

Of course, as football fans and presumably as Celtic supporters, all of you will be fully aware of the significance of the numbers I have referenced previously. They are figures which are so engrained into our psyches that we often take them as read, and some would say that they are naturally more adept at recalling memories which can be quantified numerically than anything else. Granted, the majority of football supporters aren't going to have any interest in theoretical mathematics or the history of numerology, but when it comes to remembering other facts and figures which they consider to be more important, such as dates and scorelines, some fans can be quite remarkable indeed.

Before we continue, I would like to encourage you to have a think about any person you know who exhibits the qualities I have mentioned above. After all, I feel it is fair to speculate that most of us will know someone who can pluck seemingly impossible pieces of information from their minds with apparent ease. I hope these statistical segments will not only take you on a numerical journey, but that it will also allow you to appreciate those football fans who do possess exceptional memories – specifically Celtic supporters in this case.

And so, where to begin? Well, I suppose the earliest days of the Football Club's existence would be a good place to start. On the twenty-eighth of May 1888, Celtic defeated "a side of Rangers" by five goals to two at the old Celtic Park. As you would expect, this was a day of many firsts for Celtic, as the first eleven took to the field; Neil McCallum became the first scorer; Tom Maley netted the first hat-trick; and, beginning a trend which would continue for over a century, Celtic had a goal disallowed for offside.

On the terracing stood a crowd of approximately two thousand people, one of whom was a young boy named Dan Drake, but he shall reappear later in this book so I shall save his tale until then. Men were charged six pence each for entry to the ground, with women and children admitted free of charge, so Celtic's total gate receipt for the first match the Football Club ever took part in came to a little under twenty-two pounds sterling, less than most individual match day tickets cost in the modern era.

In fact, at the end of the 1888-89 season, Celtic had taken in almost four thousand pounds through a variety of gate receipts, season ticket sales and loans, whilst donating over ten percent of this figure to charitable causes including the St Vincent de Paul Society (their largest beneficiaries), Poor Houses, Poor Children's Dinner tables and the Little Sisters of the Poor – certainly not an insignificant amount for charities and good causes in desperate need of support. Make no mistake about it, there were people in the late nineteenth century who owed their very survival to the formation of Celtic Football Club and, consequently, one must presume there are descendants of such individuals currently living in Glasgow and around Scotland who would not be here today if it weren't for the charitable donations put forward by the Football Club in its earliest days. That, in itself, should remain a source of immense pride for everyone associated with Celtic in the modern day.

Returning to the subject of numbers, we know that by the end of the Club's first season in existence, less than forty pounds had been gathered from season ticket revenue. Of course, season tickets were not popular then as they are now, but when one considers the fact that with the money they spend on some present day Champions League tickets, they could have paid two thousand people into the ground for Celtic's first match, or covered the cost of every season ticket for that inaugural campaign, it is quite a thought. In all, Celtic finished the 1888-89 season with approximately one hundred and sixty pounds in the bank, and less than a pound currently in the form of cash. To think this early endeavour would one day rise to the top of the sporting world is truly astonishing in many ways, and perhaps what makes this story so special is that it is not a work of fiction, but of fact.

The creation of the Scottish Football League in 1890 would only accelerate the Celtic story, as well as giving birth to a countless array of numbers and statistics. With forty-eight goals scored and only twenty-one conceded, Celtic began a run of concluding league campaigns with positive goal differences in 1890-91 which would continue until the start of the Second World War.

Fast-forwarding to the modern day and considering the Club's fortunes as a whole, one can say that at the end of the 2014-15 season, Celtic had scored eight thousand, eight hundred and twenty-five league goals, whilst conceding four thousand and eighty-seven, during the four thousand and sixteen league matches they had played thus far. Averaged out, Celtic score approximately twenty-two goals for every ten they concede. Well, there's a piece of useless information for you – or is it? Because when you start to delve deeper into the numbers, interesting little bits and bobs begin to appear.

For example, a quick bit of maths determines that four and a half percent of Celtic's league goals were scored by Jimmy

McGrory alone (one in every twenty-two). Adding Jimmy Quinn, Patsy Gallagher, Henrik Larsson and Bobby Lennox into the mix (our second, third, fourth and fifth highest league goalscorers respectively) brings this percentage up to over twelve and a half percent, meaning that between one in every eight Celtic goals ever scored in league competition was scored by one of five men, and if you take a few moments to consider the plethora of goalscoring talent ourselves and generations before us have seen wear the green and white, that is quite a thought. Indeed, these five men scored more league goals in the Hoops between them than the entire Celtic squads of the day did from the start of Rangers' nine in a row run (1988-89) up to and including the season in which we went to Seville (2002-03), with some room to spare.

Continuing on in this vein, another relatively quick calculation tells us that over thirty-eight percent of all of Celtic's league matches from the inception of the Scottish Football League until the present day, as I write this, have seen Alec McNair, Billy McNeill, or Paul McStay feature on the field of play.

Again, take a moment to consider that – for every three league matches Celtic have played throughout the entirety of our existence, from 1890 and the inception of the Scottish League system until the end of the 2014-15 season, over one third of them will have seen one of those three men take to the field for the Parkhead Club. Perhaps it is just me who feels this way, but I cannot help but be astonished by such a statistic, and if nothing else it adds to the gravitas and stories of these three great Celtic men.

Turning our attention to the Celtic support briefly, I have been able to calculate another statistic which I suspect will be of some interest to you. Over the years, Celtic's total home league attendances have now surpassed the fifty million mark. With the average attendance figures I used for every competitive Scottish league season thus far (2014-15 being the last), the exact number was a little over fifty-one and a half million, or the approximate population of South Korea in the modern day.

Of course, two things are important to note about this number. First of all, this does not mean that over fifty million individuals have watched Celtic play league games at both the old and new Celtic Parks, as the vast majority of them will have done so time and time again. Secondly, it is impossible to ever calculate this total exactly, as over the decades countless people will have attained access to matches for free and, on occasion, only approximate attendances are given in newspapers and the like (rounding up or down to the nearest hundred or thousand, for example).

However, it is astounding to think that since the Millennium, the turnstiles at Celtic Park have spun more than fifteen million times for home league games alone. Of course, if one were to consider domestic cup competitions and the European arena also, this figure would undoubtedly rise far higher. For example, Celtic Park had a similar total number of visitors for matches in some recent seasons as tourist attractions such as the Houses of Parliament, although the attendances at places such as these seem to fluctuate far more than those at Parkhead. Of course, Celtic Football Club, despite their occasional inconsistency, tend to deliver far more than the average politician!

"Our First Captain:
"No Kelly, No Keltic!""

Much has been written by many people about the earliest days of Celtic Football Club, with a couple of the most notable early figures, Willie Maley and Dan Doyle, having had entire books penned about their lives and exploits. As a man who runs a website called "Maley's Bhoys", you could be forgiven if you expected me to write a chapter solely devoted to Mr. Maley in this, or indeed my previous, work. One day in the future, I may well do so, but as with any author writing about Celtic Football Club or someone associated with it, I would not wish to do so until I felt the time was right and I could do the great man justice. After all, not only have people written extensively about Willie Maley, but he also penned a book himself – "The Story of the Celtic (1888-1938)".

Instead, I have decided to write about Celtic's first captain, James Kelly, focusing largely on the period during which he was a member of the playing squad at Celtic Park. In conjunction with this, I also wish to give you all a relatively detailed insight into those earliest seasons as a whole, charting the ups and downs of a Football Club destined for greatness, alongside Kelly's individual tale. In the modern day, names such as Lionel Messi and Cristiano Ronaldo are almost universally recognised by people regardless of their relative interest or disinterest in football. Likewise, on a domestic level, most folks will probably know who the heroes of the day are, whether it be Billy McNeill or Henrik Larsson. Therefore, with that in mind, you must understand that in the late 1880s, the brightest star of the time was none other than James Kelly. He was born on the fifteenth of October 1865 to an Irish Catholic family living in Renton, West Dunbartonshire. Whilst little is known of his formative years, it is apparent that he would have been surrounded by the new and emerging game of football as a child, with the likes of Dumbarton, Renton and Vale of Leven Football Clubs all being formed in 1872.

References to a Renton player by the name of "Kelly" featuring in team line-ups can be found in newspapers as early as the January of 1884, whilst the more specific "J. Kelly" first appears in 1885, so one must presume he joined the football club prior to or around this time if the first man mentioned in indeed James. Less than twenty-years on from his birth, Kelly would find himself as a member of Renton's first ever Scottish Cup winning team, as they defeated Vale of Leven by the virtue of a three-one scoreline in a replay of the final after the first match had finished goalless. Renton had only featured in one such Scottish Cup Final previously, away back in 1875, when they lost to Queen's Park. However, one year on from Renton's first success, Queen's Park would again spoil the Dunbartonshire side's day, overcoming them in the Scottish Cup Final of 1886. The following season, Renton actually took part in the English F.A. Cup, first knocking out Accrington and then Blackburn Rovers before eventually falling at the third round stage to Preston North End. They also secured Dunbartonshire Cup for the first time, battering Vale of Leven by five goals to nil in the final.

In February 1888, a couple of years on from their last Scottish Cup Final heartbreak, Renton, Kelly and their supporters would have much to smile about again as they secured their second (and subsequently last) Scottish Cup triumph, hammering Cambuslang by six goals to one and setting a record for the largest margin of victory in such a tie which has never been surpassed (at the time of writing). Notably, Celtic did equal this margin overcoming Hibs by the same score in 1972, but no matter.

In March that year, James Kelly would receive the honour of featuring as a Scottish international for the first time as they welcomed England to Hampden. However, whilst this would be a memorable day for the twenty-two year old, it would turn out to be so for all the wrong reasons, as the Scots endured what was then their worst defeat against the English, losing by five goals to nil. Whilst much of the terminology used by the Scottish press in the days following this fixture (which made references to the game being a "funeral" and the Scots supporters being in "mourning") may seem somewhat exaggerated, the magnitude of this result becomes more apparent when one considers the fact that England did not beat Scotland by five goals again until April 1955, only eventually surpassing this margin of victory in 1961. However, the loss of 1888 was not the fault of the debutant Kelly, particularly after the Scots had been considered fortunate to win the previous year's match against a continually improving English side.

Perhaps the most famous achievement of Renton Football Club would come only a matter of months after their previously discussed Scottish Cup triumph, as they took on West Bromwich Albion (winners of the English F.A. Cup) in a match dubbed the "Championship of the United Kingdom and the World". The Scots won the friendly tie by four goals to one, giving them reason to refer to themselves as the "Champions of the World". This view was only reinforced a few weeks later as Renton overcame Preston North End (runners-up to West Bromwich Albion in the 1888 F.A. Cup Final) in a testimonial match for the benefit of the Queen's Park legend, Walter Arnott. Nowadays, some people may look at such a claim regarding the status of "world champions" in the 1880s as a bit of a fallacy. In a sense, they would be correct, but when one considers the fact that the game of football was still in its infancy and only played to any serious level in and around Britain and Ireland, one can understand where Renton were coming from. After all, it would have been a fine marketing tool indeed for them to make such a claim.

Regardless, less than ten days after Renton's triumph over West Bromwich Albion, James Kelly would be persuaded to represent Glasgow's newest Football Club for the first time. In this respect, the influence which John Glass [the man who would become the Club's first President and an incredibly important individual from its very inception] had over James was instrumental, and his success in securing him as a Celtic player must be seen as one of the great man's finest achievements. Do not forget that Scottish football was an amateur pursuit – at least officially – at the time of Celtic's foundation. As such, any footballer could pick and choose who they wanted to play for without being held down by a formal contract. With this in mind, it was common to see players from one club turn out for other outfits in friendly matches and the like. Indeed, this was the case when Kelly first played for Celtic, who made his mark by scoring the second goal in the club's first match, a five-two victory over "The Swifts" (a conglomeration of Rangers' first and reserve teams) on the twenty-eighth of May 1888.

It must be said that John Glass showed a degree of cunning to persuade Kelly to feature in this first game, which was an admirable feat in itself, for it laid the groundwork for what was to come. Allegedly, Glass appealed to Kelly's good nature, highlighting that as the match in question was being held to raise money for charitable causes, it may benefit the overall financial total were he to feature, as his presence had the potential to attract a larger crowd to the tie than that which would have been there otherwise. However, at that point Kelly was reticent about committing himself to any single team, but he would become sure in time, particularly when a large financial incentive was offered to him. As for the match itself, the "Glasgow Herald" described both the first goal ever scored by Celtic Football Club – netted by one Neil McCallum, also of Renton – and James Kelly's debut goal which followed it.

"A mistake by Meikle gave Celtic a corner kick. Dunbar placed the ball in front of goal, and McCallum was enabled to head the first point of the game." [Celtic 1, The Swifts 0]

"A foul against the light blues further enhanced the prospects of the home team. The ball was kept in dangerous proximity to Nichol's charge and to avert what proved to be only a temporary and insufficient relief, the Rangers were forced to concede a corner kick. Like the former, and placed by the same player, Kelly, who was playing a judicious game, headed the second goal a few minutes before half time." [Celtic 2, The Swifts 1]

Neither James Kelly nor Neil McCallum would feature in the Celts' second match, another friendly, this time against Dundee Harp, and last minute replacements had to be called up. However, this did not seem to faze Celtic much, as they triumphed by a single goal to nil regardless. Both men would return for the

Football Club's third match against Mossend Swifts, which resulted in Celtic's first draw, with the scoreline being three goals apiece upon the sounding of the full-time whistle. This was thanks in part to two goals from James Kelly and one from the aforementioned McCallum, as the old Renton boys began to solidify themselves as Bhoys, earning the growing adoration of thousands in the process. Kelly's two goals that day, coupled with his header against "The Swifts" also meant that for a brief period he was, along with Tom Maley, the highest scoring Celtic player of all time – with three.

A couple of weeks later, having suffered their first defeat against Clyde, the Celts lined up for their first ever tournament match against Abercorn in the Glasgow Exhibition Cup. The contest resulted in a one-all draw, with Celtic taking the lead midway through the first half before Abercorn equalised just prior to the interval. No goalscorers are referenced sadly, although it is known that James Kelly did play on that summer's evening in Kelvinside. He would also feature in the Celts' next three friendly matches, which included a three-two win over Hibernians and a six-nil drubbing of Airdrieonians, but no mention was made of him specifically in the match reports of the time, which were often tremendously short in nature.

To exemplify this brevity, allow me to quote to you directly the entirety of the "Glasgow Herald" article which covered the Glasgow Exhibition Cup semi-final between Celtic and Partick Thistle in late August (Celtic defeated Dumbarton by three goals to one earlier in the month to reach this stage of the competition):

"Played last night on the University Recreation Grounds before a large turnout of spectators. About twenty minutes before the finish Ferguson, the Partick Thistle left wing forward, twisted his leg and had to retire. Near the close of the game, the "Celts" by a determined effort, scored. Nothing else was done. Result: – Celtic, 1 goal. Patrick Thistle, 0 goals."

Only a couple of days hence, James Kelly would captain Celtic as they made their first venture into what was undeniably Scotland's biggest and most prestigious tournament, the Scottish Cup. Having been drawn against Shettleston, the Celts emerged the winners by five goals to one at Celtic Park on a wet, windy day which made playing conditions difficult at points. Notably, the Celtic goalkeeper, William Dunning, is said to have used "his smartest tactics to avoid disaster" on "several occasions", so it is clear that the match was somewhat closer in nature than the scoreline may suggest.

Now, this match was not only critical for the Celts in terms of their Scottish Cup progression, but with regards to Kelly's time as a Celt also. Previous to this, having only played in friendlies and Glasgow Exhibition Cup matches for Celtic, James was not strictly their player until he had made an appearance in a major competitive tie (which, without any league in operation at that point, could only be a the Scottish Cup fixture).

The most important point is that James Kelly could have gone anywhere he liked, north or south of the border, with interest from several other clubs (most notably Hibs) well known to him. Yet, he ultimately chose to sign for Celtic, and this acquisition alone was essential for the Football Club, as numerous other men, all of whom wanted to play with a talent such as Kelly, followed suit, forming the bulk of the Celtic squads in those early years. John Glass' ambitious plan to land one of football's biggest names had been successful. Indeed, such was the importance of this procurement that the phrase "No Kelly, No Keltic!" became popular in some circles, hinting that many of the players the Club attracted on the back of Kelly's arrival would not have been signed otherwise, and that the Club may not have been sustainable as a result.

Less than a week later however, Celtic would be beaten in a knock-out tournament for the first time, as Cowlairs ran out two-nil winners in the final of the Glasgow Exhibition Cup, having scored on either side of the half-time break. Although it is generally accepted that Cowlairs were the better side on the day, much was made of the ill treatment dished out to the Celtic players by many of those in the crowd who were supporting the Springburn club. This led to the infamous after-dinner speech given by John Glass, the man who played an integral role in the establishment of Celtic Football Club, who said, "Celtic will yet win to their proper position, and those who scoff today will one day have to applaud."

Glass had made his position very clear, resolutely defending Celtic Football Club even in its earliest days. Ironically, a little over a fortnight later, Celtic would face Cowlairs once more, this time in the second round of the Scottish Cup. On this occasion, before approximately seven thousand spectators at Celtic Park, the Celts certainly taught their opposition a lesson, winning comfortably by eight goals to nil. James Kelly scored that day, but that may not surprise you when one considers that more than half of the outfield Celtic players found the net during the match. Kelly is credited with an assist in the tie also, delightfully flighting over a corner kick from which Michael Dunbar headed home Celtic's second. One newspaper said the following of Celtic's four second half goals, including James Kelly's strike: "In the latter half Cowlairs had to act pretty much on the defensive, McLeod doing some fine work. Out of a scrimmage Tom Maley placed a fifth goal, and in like manner Dunbar scored another. After relaxing their efforts temporarily Celtic put on a spurt, and Kelly, with a long shot, and McCallum, out of a tussle, each added a point, making the result – Celtic, 8 goals; Cowlairs, nil."

Of course, this was a very positive result for the young Celtic, but the most critical thing about it was not the progression to the third round of the Scottish Cup with which the Celts were rewarded (nice though it undoubtedly was), it was the fact that Club, and all of those involved with it, had shown categorically that they would stand up for themselves, using attractive football and strong support as opposed to insults or innuendo in order to do so. This was the Celtic way then and I would like to think it remains the Celtic way today.

As the season continued, Celtic progressed in both the Scottish Cup (beating Albion Rovers and St. Bernard's) and the Glasgow Cup (annihilating Shettleston and scoring eleven goals in the process). Having dispatched Shettleston, the Celts were set to face Rangers for the first time in their history. For many, including myself, Celtic's debut match towards the end of May 1888 was against Rangers in all but officialdom, but for those of you who may come across a supporter of the Ibrox club who claims the five-two victory was not the first true Glasgow Derby, I would suggest you simply tell them about this match instead. After all, I'm sure it would bring a smile to most of their faces.

Two things about this fixture remain undeniable – firstly, that it was our inaugural trip to Ibrox Park to face Rangers and secondly, that we absolutely outclassed our hosts, winning by six goals to one. Remarkably, Rangers actually opened the scoring on that blustery October day. However, the home side's lead would not last long, as goals from Willie Groves and Michael Dunbar put the Celts ahead prior to half-time. The following newspaper report tells of the events of the second half, hinting at the joy that such an emphatic result brought to the members of the Celtic support who made the short trip to the South Side of Glasgow.

"The second half began unfortunately for Rangers. They took the ball to the Celtic goal, but notwithstanding all their efforts, they failed to get it through. The Celts continued playing capitally, but they showed, if anything, a little less spirit than in the first period, and lost some opportunities. Tom Maley had a throw-in about midfield, and, following the ball up, he sent it in and Coleman sent through. No sooner was the ball set in motion than Tom Maley again distinguished himself by heading the fourth goal, amid the greatest enthusiasm of the supporters of the East End club. A few minutes later Dunbar scored a fifth goal – being three points in about five minutes for Celtic. As the end drew nearer the Rangers seemed to become disheartened. Kelly made a sixth goal. Time ended – Celtic, 6 goals; Rangers, 1 goal."

However, despite such a positive result at Ibrox, Celtic would fall in the semi-finals of the Glasgow Cup less than a month later when they faced Queen's Park for the first time before seven thousand fans. If the previous triumphs against Cowlairs and Rangers were proud days, this afternoon was not to be, for violence erupted both during the tie and after a poor result. However, before discussing these events, I feel I should describe the match itself to some degree, wherein Celtic went down by two goals to nil against the Spiders. "The Scotsman" said the following, making specific note of the terrible weather conditions and what was, in all likelihood, the earliest goal Celtic had ever then conceded.

"This match played on Celtic's ground of Parkhead was generally regarded as the most important yet played in connection with the Glasgow Cup [this was only the second season in which the Glasgow Cup tournament was contested]. Upon its decision largely depended the location of the cup itself."

"The Queen's lost the choice of ends and kicked off towards the south. In a minute a regular daisy-cutter from the toe of Berry [a Queen's Park inside-forward] just got through low down at the corner. Notwithstanding a perfect downpour, a greasy ball and a soft pitch the play now raged furiously from end to end. The Celts put in some excellent work, but they were met by a dogged half-back line..." [Celtic 0, Queen's Park 1]

"The Queen's Park forwards seemed to gain in confidence from the excellence of their defence, and troubled the Celtic rearguard frequently, and occasionally very dangerously. The dirty weather and heavy ground seemed to suit the Queen's, and they rattled away in determined style. The Celts' precision of passing and excellence of manipulation seemed to be greatly handicapped by the adverse conditions, but they could fairly claim to have had the best of the play, though not the most dangerous tries at goal in the first half. When the teams crossed over, the Queen's led by a goal to nil."

"The hard play of the first half did not appear to have had any appreciable effect on the players, who again went at it vigorously [after the interval]. The Celts were first over, and for the first few minutes had the best of it. Then the Spiders took up the running, and from a third corner in succession, Robertson headed a second goal for the visitors amidst great cheering. The reverse did not seem to improve the Celts' play. It lost its effectiveness, and became erratic and wild, while the Spiders were now playing better than ever, and tried severely the good home defence." [Celtic 0, Queen's Park 2]

It was at this point in the proceedings that things began to turn nasty. Whilst "The Scotsman" remained rather democratic in its reporting of the events, saying "A portion of the home crowd who had got inside the enclosure dragged one of the officials into the crowd, where he was badly handled…" the "Dundee Courier and Argus" was less willing to pull its punches (rather like some in the crowd it seems). It said, beginning its article with a headline which read "Queen's Park v Celtic –Disgraceful Rowdyism": "The presence of the priests at the Celtic Park on Saturday and the vigilance of the Celtic Committee prevented what would otherwise have resulted in a serious quarrel. When the Irishmen saw that their favourites were being hopelessly worsted, a large number of unruly young men, some of whom under the influence of liquor, took umbrage at the referee, Mr. Sliman, who, it should be stated, was performing his arduous duties in the most unbiased manner."

Returning to the coverage of the match itself from "The Scotsman" for a moment, we can see how the game was played out.

"Fortunately the prevailing excitement did not reach the players, who, although playing hard and vigorously, did not descend to foul play. For the greater part of the last half the Spiders completely outplayed their opponents, who, although coming very near to scoring, had in the end to retire with the most unexpected defeat of two goals to love against them."

The "Dundee and Argus Courier" then continued its discussion of the behaviour exhibited by some within the crowd: "At the close of the game the crowd bolted over the field in all directions in search of the referee, who in the meantime had happily made his way into the pavilion with the teams. If he had not, there is no saying what might have happened. Baulked of their prey, the unruly mob rushed to the pavilion, and in the most cowardly manner kicked Smellie and Gillespie [two Queen's Park players who had not yet made it inside], the latter of whom they said "won the game for the Queen's.""

Now, whilst I must categorically state that I do not condone such violent actions, it is interesting to note from a historical point of view that even in the first year of Celtic Football Club's existence, there was a general feeling within a section of the support that the team they followed were not being treated fairly by Scottish officials.

This is most certainly indicative that such beliefs in an unspoken bias are not merely modern phenomena. It is worth highlighting, once again, that Queen's Park were firmly seen as the so-called "establishment club" of the nineteenth century in Scotland, which again ties in with the previously mentioned feeling of favouritism from officials. Whether there is any truth to such suspicions is a matter for another day, and one which is undoubtedly wide ranging and very difficult to categorically prove or disprove one way or the other, but it is certainly not a new opinion. For the record, Queen's Park became heavy favourites to win the tournament once they had dispatched Celtic, and subsequently went on to do so, beating Partick Thistle by eight goals to nil in the Glasgow Cup Final.

Moving on, Celtic's poor form (although some would say it was notably tinged with bad luck) continued as a week later they were knocked out of the Scottish Cup by Clyde. Of course, many of you may know that Celtic reached the Scottish Cup Final in their first season in existence, and you would be correct in that regard, but it does not change the fact that in late November 1888, the Celts were knocked out of this competition before being reinstated. "The Scotsman" said:

"In the second period the Barrowfield [Clyde's home prior to their move to Shawfield in 1898] men acted strictly on the defensive, and won an exciting game by one goal to nothing. The Celts had as much of the play as their opponents, but Chalmers in goal played one of his best games, and saved marvellously. The Irish team, of whom so much was expected, are now out of the two principle competitions, the Scottish Cup and the Glasgow Cup. They will have the opportunity, however, of playing for two other trophies, and unless bad luck continues to dog their steps they may with some confidence look forward to gaining one cup at least."

Around ten days later, the same newspaper reported on the decision to brand the first match null and void: "Scottish Football Association – Last night the monthly meeting of the committee of the Scottish Football Association was held...The Celtic protested against the Clyde being awarded the cup tie played on 24th November, because the ground was unplayable, and that for the last fifteen minutes game was played in darkness. Mr. Harrison, the referee, explained that the teams started to play a cup tie with the consent of both captains, that for the last eight minutes he could not follow the game, and that the game was late in starting, part of the delay being caused by several Clyde players having to remove bars from their boots. Mr. Reid (Airdrieonians) moved that the protest should be sustained and this was seconded by Mr. J.B. Walker (Renfrewshire Association). Mr. Boag (Partick Thistle) proposed that the protest should be dismissed. Mr. Graham (Renton) seconded. On a division, the protest was sustained by seven votes to four and the tie was ordered to be replayed on the ground of Celtic on Saturday first."

Therefore, having been given a second chance – albeit with due cause – Celtic were not going to waste it and suffer another defeat, taking a two goal lead within the first ten minutes of proceedings at Parkhead. However, they then let two goals slip within a minute midway through the first half, and thus found themselves level with their opponents again after twenty-five minutes. Whether complacency played any part in this comeback is entirely speculative, but the subsequent response from the Celtic players, taking the lead again before half-time, hinted that this was not a problem for them. In fact, a quick glance at a newspaper report from the time suggests that Clyde were initially allowed back into the game due to nothing other than human error: "The Clyde men were prominent, and Cherrie put a ball into Dunning's hands, which the custodian let through. The Clyde attacked strongly, and within a minute thereafter Cherrie equalised with a splendidly judged shot."

Interestingly, another newspaper report said the following of the match, suggesting Clyde were fortunate to only be a goal behind come the interval, before telling of how the defeat could have been far heavier for the visitors on a different day, hinting at Celtic's overall superiority: "During the first half the Celts had matters nearly all their own way. They were never seen to more advantage, and played one of the most scientific games witnessed this season. Their passing was swift and accurate, while their half-back play was admirable. The Clyde played a hard game, and had it not been for the excellent defence of Chalmers in goal, they would have fared worse than they did."

By the close of proceedings, both Tom Maley and Willie Groves had hat-tricks to their names, and the Celts secured their place in the next round of the Scottish Cup, sending out a clear message to all of the other sides who remained in the competition as they did so, having won by nine goals to two. Notably, one newspaper correspondent saved the bulk of his praise not for either of the two previously mentioned goalscorers, but for the Celtic captain, who was credited with an assist for one of Tom Maley's goals in the match. He said, "If any man deserved special mention, he was Kelly, who was playing in the very best form, and had occasionally some grand runs all by himself."

A week on from their victory over Clyde, Celtic met their next Scottish Cup opponents, East Stirlingshire, at Merchiston Park. After a fairly even start to the game, which Celtic had the better of in large parts without managing to score, it was the home side who took the lead just before the half-time break. The following passage from the "Glasgow Herald" tells of Celtic's efforts to find an equaliser and of how this left them susceptible to counterattacks from their opponents: "The second half was begun with great determination, but, play as they liked, the Celts could not find an opening. The second half was at least fifteen minutes old when McLauchlan got the ball at his feet, and made off with it. He ran the whole length of the field, but when about to shoot Kelly made up on him and gave him an ugly charge, for which a foul was given."

However, for all of Celtic's efforts, they could not break through the East Stirlingshire defence, and with only minutes remaining, James Kelly is quoted by "An Alphabet of the Celts" (Eugene MacBride, Martin O'Connor and George Sheridan) as muttering "Isn't this terrible! Isn't this terrible!" under his breath in disgust. Thankfully though, Kelly's worst fears would not be realised, as the Celts produced one of their now legendary dramatic comebacks to win the day. The "Glasgow Herald" continued its story:

"The Celts played very hard to equalise, but could not find an opening. As time approached it looked as if the Celts had seen the last of the ties, and four minutes from time McLaren played left wing instead of Maley. He sent in a long shot across the field, which was caught by McCallum and sent through. This point scored three minutes from time, and a minute later the same player scored a second goal. The game was now over, and a very hard game thus ended in a win for the Celtic by 2 goals to 1."

Somewhat remarkably, Celtic Football Club then found themselves in the semi-final of Scotland's premier tournament within a year of taking part in their first match. They would face Dumbarton, winners of the 1882-83 competition, in mid-January, but several other games had yet to be played before this tie. These included several friendly matches, two of which I shall briefly discuss, as well as the first round of a tournament by the name of the Glasgow North Eastern Cup. Firstly the Celts, with Kelly their leader as was the norm by now, won convincingly by five goals to one at South Croft Park in Rutherglen. Clydesdale, Celtic's opponents, were said to have played "in front of the largest number of spectators that had ever lined Clydesdales' ropes" by one newspaper journalist. The historical significance of this match would become truly clear in time.

Next up for the Celts, only two days after their win over Clydesdale no less, was a charity match against Mitchell St. George's of Birmingham (also known as Birmingham St. George's), played at Celtic Park. St. George's had reached the quarter finals of the F.A. Cup that season south of the border, before being knocked out by the eventual winners of the tournament, Preston North End. At the end of the 1888-89 season, they applied to become members of the newly formed English Football League, but were unsuccessful, taking up the unenviable mantle of the side who received the most votes of all those who were not accepted. In the early 1890s, as Celtic began to truly prosper, St. George's had another such application rejected, and eventually folded in 1892 due to financial problems.

The match itself was well fought, with the Birmingham club taking the lead before latterly going down to the home side by seven goals to one. If one studies Celtic's financial information from their first season in existence, we find that the match itself, minus St George's guaranteed appearance fee of twenty-five pounds, raised over forty-three pounds for charity. This may not sound like much in the modern day, but it provided almost ten percent of Celtic's charitable donations that year, highlighting its importance.

This figure was to be obliterated only days later however, as the Corinthians came to town for one of the most hotly antici-pated matches Celtic had ever been scheduled to contest. This was to be the first New Year's game the Celts had ever played, as they faced their highly thought of opponents on the third of January 1889 at Celtic Park.

As an aside, it is perhaps worth mentioning the origins and principles of Corinthians Football Club, which set them apart from virtually every other side of the day and was nothing like anything we see in the modern game. Corinthians were an amateur club, but unlike a notable Scottish equivalent, Queen's Park, they refused to "compete for any challenge cup or prizes of any description", as this was forbidden in the rules upon which the club was founded. This meant that they would not take part in competitions such as the Football League or the F.A. Cup for the majority of their time in existence, although it has to be said they did begin to enter the F.A. Cup in 1923, having made the decision "to depart from their usual rules and to take part in a contest which did not have charity as its primary object."

The last sentence is truly indicative of what Corinthians of London were all about – charity. The match against Celtic was one of countless ties in which Corinthians took part, all in the aid of good causes. Notably, despite the fact they were amateurs, they were generally considered to be one of the best English sides at that point, hence the large crowds they attracted upon their visit to Scotland in 1889.

As for the match itself, James Kelly captained the side once again, but he was not the only Kelly in the Celtic line up that day, for John Kelly, a goalkeeper who would only ever make two competitive starts for the Celts, also featured. Having made his debut against Mitchell St. George's only days earlier, he would have been out to impress against Corinthians, and so he did. The following passages are from the "Glasgow Herald", recalling not only the events on the field of play, but also the scale of the occasion in the surrounding stands and terracing.

"Continuing their annual tour, the Corinthians met the Celtic on Celtic Park, Parkhead, yesterday afternoon before one of the largest crowds that ever witnessed a game in Scotland. The proceeds after payment of the visiting team's expenses, went for charity, such as the providing of a dinner to poor children and old men and women. Upwards of twenty thousand tickets were sold by the committee and friends of the Celts."

"The Celtic won the toss, and the Corinthians kicked off. The home side at once began to press, and a foul being given against the strangers the ball was taken dangerously near goal, but McLaren shot past the posts…The Corinthians returned to the attack, and kept up a perfect siege at the Celts' goal. Shot after shot was sent in, but Kelly the new goalkeeper, who hails from the Mearns club, saved miraculously. The enthusiasm of the spectators was tremendous, and it knew no bounds when the home team, after about five minutes play scored the first goal of the match. Groves dribbled beautifully down the field, and after eluding the half backs passed the ball to McCallum, who shot it through." [Celtic 1, Corinthians 0]

The game continued upon "soft ground" in a similar style, with both teams throwing themselves forwards whenever the opportunity presented itself, although it has to be said Celtic enjoyed more in the way of success.

"The Celts continued their aggressive tactics, and after some clever passing Coleman scored the second goal ten minutes from the start. At length, [Corinthians] got away, and Lambie was making straight for goal when he was tackled by Gallagher, who conceded a corner. Lambie placed the ball finely, and…Dewhurst headed it through, scoring the first point for the strangers. The ball was scarcely in play [again] when the Celts forwards rushed it up to the other goal. Cooper had to fist out, but Dunbar came up and breasted the ball through, making the third point for the Celts..." [Celtic 3, Corinthians 1]

"The Corinthians were defending well all this time, but their forwards were hardly up to form. On the other hand, the Celtic front division combined magnificently, and out of a scrimmage Maley scored the fourth goal. The interest in the play never slackened, but with the exception of an occasional run by the Englishmen, when Kelly saved, the Celts had the best of it." [Celtic 4, Corinthians 1]

In the end, Celtic would finish the tie as the victors by six goals to two. In doing so, the Celts, who were still less than a year old (in playing terms) had emphatically beaten one of the most famous footballing sides in the world. This was a remarkable achievement, but one which is largely forgotten as it was only a friendly. The "Glasgow Herald" finished their article regarding the match as follows.

"The result was – Celtic, 6 goals; Corinthians, 2 goals. It has been asserted that the Celtic show their paces best on dry ground. Yesterday, the field was in a perfect puddle, but notwithstanding the Irishmen showed great speed and stamina, and altogether fairly surpassed themselves. It is understood that the sum realised by the match amounts to between £300 and £400."

Of course, the final sentence of that passage reminds us once again of the true purpose of this exhibition tie, which was perhaps Celtic's first "glamour friendly". The newspaper's financial assertion was slightly exaggerated. When studying Celtic's official monetary release from their first full season in existence, one finds that the total figure raised by the match was actually just shy of two hundred and eighty pounds, which decreased to a little under two hundred and thirty-five pounds once Corinthians had been reimbursed for their relevant expenses. However, when one considers that this money formed more than half of Celtic's charitable donations in their first year, its significance becomes more tangible.

Nine days after the mammoth match with Corinthians, Celtic returned to competitive action as they faced Dumbarton in the Scottish Cup semi-final. The crowd was less than a third of the size of that which had assembled to see the match against the London club, but the importance of the tie was still clear to see, as "The Scotsman" described the crowd of approximately six thousand as "probably the largest crowd that ever assembled at Dumbarton".

Celtic would win by four goals to one (with John Kelly making his competitive debut in goal), but on this occasion, James Kelly would take the majority of the praise in the newspaper reports of the coming days. The previously referenced "Scotsman" said "Kelly, at centre-back, played a better game on Saturday than he has done this season."

The Scottish Cup Final which followed was to be one of the most intriguing football matches the country had yet seen, with the new kids on the block, Celtic, set to face Third Lanark, who had twice reached the final in previous years, albeit losing both of them. To contextualise the appeal of this match somewhat, I feel I should highlight that the attendance of the 1889 Scottish Cup Final was higher than that of the two previous finals in which Third Lanark had played, combined.

When the day of the fixture arrived, the field was considered by both sides to be "unplayable" due to heavy snow, and thus both clubs lodged protests prior to kick-off, meaning the day's game would be considered a friendly. However, this was not explained to those paying spectators in attendance until after the end of proceedings, causing much displeasure and disdain, to put it lightly. Third Lanark won the match by three goals to nil, although it didn't matter tremendously much. John Kelly's name appears much more in newspaper reports than that of the Celtic captain, thanks partly to Celtic's opponents, who were giving him so much to do. The fact that the first occasion upon which he was beaten that day was met by "a scene of wild excitement" from Third Lanark supporters in attendance on goes to highlight that the paying public wholeheartedly believed this match to be the Scottish Cup Final, not simply an expensive friendly.

The Scottish Cup Final proper was held a week later in better playing conditions, with the same men taking to the field of play and, no doubt, many of the previously aggrieved spectators returning also. Part of me cannot help but feel it would have been a cruel twist of fate for those Third Lanark fans had Celtic won this match, as reports had spoken of deafening cheers greeting their second goal a week prior. It must have been difficult to accept that their side had not won the Scottish Cup that day as they had believed, but it would have been truly gut wrenching for them if the Celts had taken the glory away from them seven days later. However, there would be no celebrations for the new club from the East End that day, for once again Third Lanark would emerge triumphant, winning by two goals to one.

Having had a goal chopped off early on in proceedings, Celtic again went close through Tom Maley, who "missed a remarkably easy chance", before Third Lanark took the lead. Celtic, a goal down at the break, started the second half the brighter of the two sides, putting their opponents under fairly consistent pressure before Neil McCallum "equalised amidst a scene which simply baffles description".

As the match drew to a close, Celtic maintained a "continual bombardment" of their opponents' goalmouth, playing to a level which was described by one journalist as "simply astounding", but no matter how hard they pressed "they could not increase their score." Subsequently, Third Lanark netted late on, sending their followers wild whilst taking the wind out of the Celtic sails. In the few moments which remained, the Celts looked like a shadow of their former selves, and no more scoring followed. Thus, Third Lanark had won the Scottish Cup for the first time in their history, a little more than sixteen years on from their formation as a football club. Celtic would not need to wait as long as their Glasgow counterparts for such success in the competition, but it was not to come in their first season. Still, to reach the preeminent fixture of the Scottish game was an astonishing achievement nonetheless, and one which deserves to be lauded to this day. The Celts were on the rise, and under the leadership of their first captain, this ascent would continue at an admirable pace.

"Tales of Their Time:
"Great Fire at Celtic Park""

Interspersed throughout this book, in an attempt to provide the reader with an insight into the footballing stories of the day, are a selection of newspaper reports related in one way or another to Celtic Football Club. These vary notably in terms of length and stature, but nevertheless each encapsulate a little bit of history. After all, it's not every day one reads of how Celtic almost went on an American tour in 1898 or why there may be two horses buried underneath Celtic Park.

"Aberdeen Journal" – Thursday 13th November 1890

"A contemporary "doon sooth" publishes the following: – "The Celtic Football Club has one worshipper, an Aberdeen resident, who attends every match of the club, wherever played." Now, who is he? There are not a few enthusiasts in Aberdeen, but that there is a man in our midst so far "gone" on the game that he is at the expense and the trouble of journeying to see Celtic play can hardly be regarded as [anything] other than a [traitor]."

"Freeman's Journal" (Dublin) – Monday 14th March 1892

"It is always greatly satisfying to be able to announce the successes of Irishmen in any capacity or in any part of the world, but the triumph which is recorded of our countrymen in our football columns today is unique. It is the victory of the Celtic Football Club over the Queen's Park in the final tie of the Scottish Association Challenge Cup at Ibrox Park, Glasgow, last Saturday. It is no exaggeration to say that the eyes of Scotland were on this match, the Celtic being a club exclusively composed of Irishmen now resident in Glasgow, while their opponents, the Queen's Park, a native team, have won the Scottish Championship no less than nine times. Fully forty thousand spectators were present. In the end, the Irishmen won, amidst great excitement, by one goal to nil. The Celtic are a very charitable club, annually giving large sums to the Catholic charities of Glasgow, and on tomorrow they will hand Mr. Michael Davitt a substantial sum for the evicted Irish tenants."

"Dundee Evening Telegraph" – Monday 21st March 1892

"On Saturday afternoon Mr. Michael Davitt, who was accompanied by Dr. Tanner, M.P., Mr. John Ferguson, and the officials of the Celtic Football Club, paid a visit to the headquarters of the Celtic at Parkhead, and laid the first sod of the magnificent new ground presently under construction for the famous Irish combination. The sod was a genuine Irish one from Donegal, covered with a fine coating of shamrocks. It was well and truly laid by Mr. Davitt, who will carry away with him as a memento of the occasion the fine trowel with which the ceremony was performed. Mr. Davitt afterwards proceeded to the old ground, where he found a crowd nearly ten thousand strong waiting to welcome him."

"Dundee Courier" – Tuesday 25th August 1896

"Overcrowding Tramway Cars – Several tramway car conductors were brought up at Glasgow Central Police Court on Friday charged with having allowed their cars to be overcrowded last Saturday in Gallowgate. Mr. David Wilson, who appeared for some of the accused, urged that it was impossible to keep the people off the cars owing to the rush for the Celtic Football Club sports at Parkhead. Superintendent Orr said that if the surplus passengers refused to leave the car the conductor ought to have stopped, and given them in charge to the police. A fine of 2s 6d was inflicted."

"Edinburgh Evening News" – Tuesday 13th July 1897

"Support for the Hibernians – At a meeting held in Glasgow on Sunday of the members of the Celtic United Brake Club, it was resolved to sever connection with the Celtic Football Club, and support the Hibernians at their matches in and around Glasgow. The cause of severance is owing to the Celtic Club not issuing season tickets and fulfilling a promise of a subscription alleged to have been given. The number of members understood to be affected by the dispute is about one thousand."

"Dundee Courier" – Friday 18th Match 1898

"It is announced that an English syndicate has practically concluded arrangements to take the well-known Everton and Celtic Football Clubs to the United States next season to play a series of six matches in various parts of the States. The games will be exhibition and educative. With reference to this report a Liverpool correspondent says the matter is by no means settled. They would have to play during the English close season, which synchronises with tropical heat in the States, and, though six games only have been suggested, it is considered this last difficulty is almost insuperable."

"Dundee Evening Telegraph" – Monday 26th October 1903

"Footballer's Tragic Death – Famous Internationalist Suffocated – Mickie McKeown of Celtic-Hibs Repute – A tragic discovery was made yesterday afternoon in the bottle works of Mr. Robert Paul, 98 Broad Street, Glasgow, one of the employees coming across the body of Michael McKeown (thirty-three), amongst the ashes in an empty lime kiln. The deceased was seen about seven o'clock yesterday morning in the bottle works, where he usually slept at night, and was not seen again alive. The casualty surgeon, who examined the body, was of opinion that death was due to asphyxia. McKeown was a well-known footballer in his time, having played for the Celtic Football Club. Mick will live in the annals of football for his grand play in the international match at Hampden in 1890. In that game he partnered Walter Arnott, and the pair gave a great display and saved Scotland from defeat, the result being a draw of one goal each. McKeown learned his football at Lugar, Boswell, Ayrshire, where he was born. He afterwards joined the Hibs, and then went to Celtic, in whose ranks he repeatedly showed good football. At the same time he carried on licensed premises in the East End of the city. Blackburn Rovers afterwards secured his services, where he played for several seasons. In 1897 he returned to Scotland, and again played for the Hibernians, and was subsequently seen in the ranks of several Clubs, including Fair City Athletics at Perth."

"Dundee Evening Telegraph" – Tuesday 10th May 1904

"Great Fire at Celtic Park"

"Grand Stand and Pavilion Gutted – £6,000 Damage; Only Partly Insured – Club Likely To Lose £4,000 – The grand stand and the pavilion at the grounds of the Celtic Football Club, Glasgow, were completely destroyed by fire last night. The Central and Eastern Divisions, under Firemaster Paterson, were turned out, and on their arrival in the narrow roadway between the football ground and Janefield Cemetery the firemen found that the stand itself was a mass of flames, and that there was little or no hope of saving the pavilion. The fire had originated near the east end of the stand, and, fanned by a slight wind, the flames were blown westward with terrible rapidity. In an incredibly short time they worked their way through the open woodwork with a loud and ominous cracking which could be heard at a considerable distance. The wind carried the sparks in the direction of the "Grant" Stand, and at one time there was serious danger of it also becoming ignited. Fortunately the breeze was not of sufficient strength to carry the embers such a distance, but the scorched and blackened grass bore testimony to the danger in which the erection was placed."

"A Brilliant Spectacle"

"Before the police arrangements had been thoroughly perfected the crowd in Janefield Street was very dense, and numbers had climbed upon the wall of the cemetery. When at its height the fire shed a brilliant reflection on the sky, which was seen for miles around. As far away as Coatbridge the semi-circular glow showed clear above the horizon. From the other side of the park the spectacle was a fine one, the whole erection with the woodwork of the terracing and the roof all ablaze, the iron struts and girders standing out against the bright background, parts of the corrugated iron roof falling in large sheets into the burning basement of the structure and throwing up great showers of sparks and flames. About half an hour after the Brigade arrived, the large flag staff which stood above at the centre of the stand fell outwards into the street, carrying with it a portion of the structure. The fire at this time had spread to the west of the grand stand, and soon the pavilion was also in flames. The building, being like the stand principally constructed of wood and light and inflammable material, burned rapidly. The upper storey was completely destroyed, and although one or two rooms in the ground floor were not burned out, the building was totally wrecked. By midnight the flames had pretty well spent themselves. All the corrugated iron of the roof had fallen in great twisted masses among the burned and ruined terracing, and the beams and girders lay bent among the other debris, the whole [scene] presenting a picturesque sight."

"The Destroyed Stand"

"The grand stand, which was on the north side of the field, was about one hundred and ten yards in length and thirty yards in breadth. It was constructed after the usual pattern of such erections, with terraced seats rising backwards from the cycling track to the outside of the grounds to a height altogether of about fifty feet. It provided sitting accommodation for three and a half spectators, and had a corrugated iron roof supported on steel struts and girders. The pavilion, which stood a little to the north-west of the stand, was a comparatively small building, being only about forty feet by thirty feet and two storeys in height. It included the rooms of the club, a billiard room, in which was a table which cost about £75; retiring rooms for the players, bathrooms, and other apartments. In the pavilion was a large quantity of what in football parlance is described as "stock", consisting of players' clothing, hurdles and other apparatus, and seats for the track, to the value of about £500. When erected about ten years ago the stand and pavilion cost about £6,000. The erections, however, have from time to time been strengthened and improved to meet the requirements of the Dean of Guild Court. So recently as the International football match, which was played on ninth of last month, the stand was completely renovated, and having been officially inspected by the Master of Works, the liners of the Court declared it to be safe and sound in every respect."

"£4,000 Loss to Celtic"

"The erections destroyed were insured to the extent of only about £2,000; and there was no insurance on the contents of the pavilion. The loss to the Club were therefore amount to fully £4,000. The stand which has been destroyed, it should be understood, is the grand, or north stand – not the "Grant" stand, which is on the opposite side of the field. Notwithstanding the destruction of the stand, the match between Hibernians and the Celtic will be played tonight according to arrangement."

"Edinburgh Evening News" – Thursday 26th January 1905

"New Grand Stand For Celtic Park – Celtic Football Club were today granted [permission] at the Glasgow Dean of Guild Court for the erection of a new grand stand to replace the structure burned down last May. The new erection will occupy the entire north side of Celtic Park, and will, with terracing in front, provide accommodation for about ten thousand spectators. It will be a solid steel structure with a domed roof of corrugated iron. The estimated cost is £5,000."

"Dundee Evening Post" – Friday February 10th 1905

"Football Pavilion Burglaries – Champagne, Boxing Gloves and Developers – Celtic and St. Mirren Clubs Victims – At Glasgow Sheriff Court today two young men...were sentenced to twelve and six months' respectively for housebreaking. [One man] broke into a number of club pavilions, stealing biscuits and ginger beer from Deanside Gold Club; two pistols, boots and a jersey from Clyde Football Club; a clock, a bottle of champagne, and a bottle of brandy from Celtic Football Club; and footballs, boxing gloves, and physical developers from St. Mirren Football Club, Paisley. He also stole a large number of brass articles from Reid's Factory in Cathcart Road, and was associated with [the other man] in stealing clothes and money from the premises of Rowlet Limited, Govan. All the offences were committed in January. Both prisoners pleaded guilty. The Celtic Club's billiard table cloth was cut up, and prisoner, when arrested, said it was to wrap the clock in."

"He's the Greatest in the Land!"

Recently, I had an interesting conversation with a gentleman who made some good points regarding our club's past. His premise, essentially, was that the Club has two notable sections within its history – that which lies within the living memory of the current support, and that which preceded it. Largely, I had to agree with this, but after some consideration I came to the conclusion that personally, I believe there to be three areas of the Club's history; the present day, the consolidated past and true antiquity. The first is self-explanatory, as it is basically any time which can be remembered by any supporter who is still alive. The second, in my mind, relates to any era one generation removed from fans who are still with us. For example, an elderly supporter who was told by their mother or father of players and matches which they had seen would fit this description. Finally, the third is the early days of the Football Club in the truest sense. Nobody who is still alive can remember the events which took place then, nor did they have close relatives who did. Therefore, historical resources and documents form the basis of our knowledge of these times.

Yet, when one considers each of these eras, some striking similarities appear throughout the generations. Of course, great victories, painful defeats and wonderful talents are just some of these repetitions, but on a lesser note, players infamous for behavioural problems do also. From the first years of Celtic Football Club's existence and the likes of Dan "The Wild Rover" Doyle, such individuals have come and gone with varying levels of success. Of course, it almost goes without saying that football supporters are much more likely to put up with less than perfect attitudes and such from players who are in possession of exceptional ability. In this regard, Dan Doyle was no different and neither was the man who is the subject of this short chapter, Tommy McInally.

Critically, as Tommy began his Celtic career a short time after the end of the First World War, his days are not yet within the realms of antiquity like Doyle's, but in the consolidated past. As such, more anecdotal information is available regarding his time as a Celtic player, including the likes of this supposed exchange between himself and then manager Willie Maley, beginning with the words of the latter: "Tommy, you pick up the ball from midfield and run with it", to which McInally replied, "But boss, I'll get sent off for handball if I do that!" In all seriousness though, as we will discover, McInally was a conflicted character capable of amazing feats of skill or frustrating performances hampered by poor fitness or attitude. In that sense, he was most certainly not boring, and in a way, I have a funny feeling he may well have appreciated such a sentiment.

Believed to have been born on the eighteenth of December 1899 in Barrhead, he was the younger brother of centre-halves Arthur (who played once for the Celts in 1917) and John (who plied his trade with Abercorn). The youngest of nine children, McInally's early life may always hold some secrets. The son of Francis and Annie McInally, bizarrely it appears his real name was, at least initially, Bernard (the name shared by his grandfather), as it is found on his birth certificate. However, by the time of his baptism, this has altered to Thomas Bernard, before presumably the Bernard was dropped almost entirely in his later life. Despite all of the excellent work by researchers which led to these discoveries, nobody has ever been able to say with any certainty why Bernard became Tommy, and perhaps never will, but it all adds to the charm of the man's story.

In his early years, Tommy lost his father, who died shortly after his third birthday. Whilst he would not have known it at the time, this event would play an enormous role in McInally's life, as later his lack of a father figure would become abundantly clear. However, returning to his childhood, Tommy was educated at St. Mungo's Academy, where he followed in his brother's footsteps by playing for the school side, before spells with Croy Celtic and St. Anthony's led on to his eventual move to Celtic. Signed on the twenty-second of May 1919, his acquisition was welcomed by the Celtic support for he had previously enjoyed two trials with

Rangers, who considered him a potential target on more than one occasion during his early career.

The happiness within the fan base would only be reinforced midway through August 1919, when Tommy McInally made his debut against Clydebank at Celtic Park – and scored a hat-trick. Incredibly, the Hoops would play at home two days later, this time against Dumbarton, and Tommy repeated the feat, leaving the field at the close of play with another three goals to his name and the adulation of the crowd once more. Of the first trio, the "Glasgow Herald" gave Tommy high praise indeed, likening him to the great Jimmy Quinn of all people (thanks in part, perhaps, to his relationship with Croy Celtic): "The Celts appear to have secured in McInally a worthy successor to Quinn. To score three goals on a first appearance is certainly promising, particularly as no other Celtic forward got the better of McTurk, whose saving of other splendid shots from McInally was the feature of the Clydebank defence."

Speaking of McInally's second hat-trick, the "Dundee Courier" opened their small piece on Celtic's match the following morning with the headline "McInally Again Shines for Celts". Tommy's second goal is also worthy of mention as it hints of what would become one of his trademark abilities – that of leaving defenders in his wake before shooting powerfully – and was described as follows: "Beating both backs close in, McInally scored a second goal with a terrific shot."

It is to his great credit that Tommy McInally was the first Celtic player to score two hat-tricks in his first two competitive matches (considering the Scottish League and the Scottish Cup), whilst becoming only the third man to net three goals or more on their competitive Celtic debut at that point. For the record, the two men to do so prior to Tommy were John O'Connor (who scored five in the Celts' first Scottish Cup tie against Shettleston in 1888) and David McLean (a striker who netted three times against Port Glasgow Athletic on league duty in 1907).

Another hat-trick against Clyde would follow a little over a month later, with other strikes arriving thick and fast in various matches. As such, by the time Celtic visited Ibrox for their tenth fixture of the league calendar, Tommy McInally – still just nineteen years of age – had scored sixteen goals in nine games; a stunning start.

However the Celts, who had not yet dropped any points, would lose that league match against Rangers by three goals to nil, signalling the first occasion upon which they had not scored as a team that season. Subsequently, Tommy would only net once in the next six weeks, but did rally after the turn of the year, scoring another fourteen times before the season was out. Disappointing defeats by the Ibrox side (coupled with a poor draw at home), Clydebank and Dundee as well as several goalless draws gave Rangers the edge come the final day of the season, as they won the League Championship by three points. This would not be the last time that Tommy would struggle to get the better of the Ibrox side, but after scoring thirty-one goals in thirty-three League and Cup appearances in his inaugural season, he could have felt justifiably content with his individual efforts.

Although the following campaign of 1920-21 would start with a goal on the opening day of the season for Tommy, it would not be successful for Celtic, whose one-all draw that day with Hamilton Academicals hinted that not all was well. Tommy would net twenty-eight goals in forty League and Cup outings that year, but again his team's inability to take any points from Rangers, and indeed his personal failure to score against them, contributed to the Celts finishing as runners-up to their rivals once more, albeit by a larger gap than they had done previously. Ironically, Celtic would regain the league title at the end of the 1921-22 season after Tommy's lowest scoring campaign as a Celtic player thus far, although eighteen goals in twenty-seven outings was still a very respectable ratio for any striker.

By this stage however, it was clear Willie Maley's patience with Tommy and his antics – both on and off of the field – was wearing thin. Previously, after a two-one away win against Clyde in the November of 1920 (in which Tommy scored), Maley had taken the team down to Seamill Hydro for a short getaway prior to their upcoming league match with Raith Rovers. However, despite strict orders to the contrary whilst the team resided in the alcohol-free resort, it is said Tommy snuck out to the local town one evening and returned somewhat the worse for wear, only to be caught in the act by his manager. As a result, McInally was dropped for the next match, but having been forgiven for his sins he returned a fortnight after the event, scoring two dramatic last minute goals to hand the Celts an unlikely win away at Falkirk. Early in 1922, Tommy rejected a potential move south after Manchester City had bid for him, later citing his reason as being that his mother did not want him to leave her. Yet, a transfer would be forthcoming in time, as concerns about Tommy's drinking and weight gain led to questions from manager and supporter alike in the weeks and months to come.

Soon thereafter, when Celtic lost to Hamilton at home by virtue of a three-one scoreline to again fall in the third round of the Scottish Cup, Tommy would be the subject of much criticism for the Celts' toothless attack. One Scottish newspaper described the Cup exit as "the sensation of the afternoon" whilst another said it "astounded the football world". Indeed, Maley kept his team [who were three-nil down] out on the pitch at half time and shouted and bawled at them for all of the crowd to see, such was his disappointment at the manner in which they had played thus far. McInally would only feature in the league game immediately following the defeat (wherein Celtic ironically beat Hamilton Academicals convincingly) before being dropped from the side until the end of the season as Maley rejigged his forward line. Tommy McInally would then receive a league winners' medal, but would soon find himself departing Celtic Park regardless, having not been taken on the Club's tour of Czechoslovakia and Germany in May.

Subsequently, despite scoring over seventy-five times in just three seasons, Tommy was sold to Third Lanark during the summer of 1922 for a couple of thousand pounds. McInally would never truly settle at Cathkin Park, as he twice helped to keep them in the top flight of Scottish Football, but failure in this sense would arrive at the end of the 1924-25 season when they finished bottom of the league. Celtic were hardly prospering by their high standards either – two fine Scottish Cup wins aside – as they continually languished in third and fourth positions in the league. By all accounts, it was a well-known fact that Tommy longed for a return to Celtic Park – and his wish would be granted – but only once Willie Maley decided to take that calculated risk. Of course, Tommy had appeared at Parkhead as a Third Lanark player since he left Celtic, but one cannot help but presume it was not his last showing in the East End for the Third's which persuaded Maley to bring him home, because he was sent off for "apparently interfering with the referee" after "temper entered into the contest". Third Lanark finished the seven-nil defeat that day with just eight players on the field, owing to Tommy's dismissal and another two men being injured.

Yet, when the time came for Tommy McInally's return to Parkhead as a Celtic player, he was hailed as a prodigal son of sorts, particularly as he immediately notched up a rapport with the young Jimmy McGrory. Instead of returning to his old role of centre forward, which was now held by the aforementioned Jimmy, Tommy took up a position in the team at inside-left, which he would largely maintain for the next three years. As a result, Celtic positively romped to the Scottish League Championship that season, winning it by eight points from Airdrieonians and Heart of Midlothian, as well as scoring more goals than any other side. In this sense, Maley's gamble had paid off. Very few downsides were present that year, but the most painful was undoubtedly the Scottish Cup Final defeat to St. Mirren which prevented a historic double.

Before returning to the matter of domestic football momentarily, it is noteworthy that 1926 saw Tommy McInally make his only two outings in the colours of his native Scotland. Tommy's debut arrived as Ireland travelled to Ibrox, only to be beaten convincingly by their hosts. Of McInally's showing, "The Sunday Post" mused "It is difficult to size up McInally's play…He was the coolest man on the field and one of the cleverest…His feeding of Gallacher was one of the features of the game. But he overdid the solo stunt, though if he had been able to use his left foot with confidence, I believe he'd have had the Irish defence [in his pocket]…McInally must be given another chance."

This would be the case in a three-nil win over Wales at Ibrox, wherein he was both praised and criticised to some extent by the media for his performance. "The Sunday Post" said "McInally, though he continued to lie a trifle too far back, assumed the role of purveyor in chief. From him to Gallacher went a dozen perfectly judged passes in the first half", whilst the "Dundee Courier" stated "McInally was a signal failure, and never at any time did he reveal his club form or the understanding of the outside man's actions." Sadly, Tommy never had another opportunity to display his talents in a Scotland jersey.

The domestic shoe would be on the other foot the next year, as Celtic lost the league title but did win the Scottish Cup Final, overcoming East Fife by three goals to one. Jimmy McGrory was unavailable for selection that day whilst recovering from two broken ribs, and as such Tommy took up the role of centre forward, although he did not score. The following season would be Tommy's last at Celtic Park, and in truth it would be a sad end to a career which had promised so much a little under a decade previously. Rangers would again win the Scottish League Championship, and a thumping four-nil defeat to the Ibrox side in the semi-finals of the Scottish Cup would mean Tommy would leave Parkhead without any major silverware in his farewell season at the Football Club. However, the Celts did win the Glasgow Cup that year, giving them something to celebrate. His last goals would arrive in the form of a brace during a three-nil win over St. Johnstone at Celtic Park, whilst his final appearance would come in a three-nil home loss to Raith Rovers on the last day of the league season.

Tommy left Celtic Park for the north of England on the twenty-fifth of May 1928 as he was transferred to Sunderland for a fee of two and a half thousand pounds. A little over one year later, he headed much further south to Bournemouth, before short spells with Morton and Derry City followed in 1930. His playing career would eventually draw to a close with a few years spent at local sides Armadale and Nithsdale Wanderers. Post-war, he enjoyed a brief spell as a Celtic scout. A showman both on and off the park, Tommy also spent some time as a singer at various clubs and social establishments in Glasgow. His mother died in

1939 and this, combined with the outbreak of the Second World War and all of the worries it brought with it, must have had an enormous impact on McInally. As a result, he continued to struggle with his alcohol consumption as the years passed and his health deteriorated rapidly, with him developing throat cancer in the early 1950s.

Thomas McInally died at the age of just fifty-five on the twenty-ninth of September 1955. In the days following his death, newspapers across Scotland carried headlines such as "Football's "Clown Prince" Dies" and "What a player and what a man!"

Beginning with the former, which appeared in the "Aberdeen Evening Express", the article which followed said: "Tommy McInally, famous Celtic footballer and internationalist died today in a Glasgow hospital. A fabulous personality of the 1920s, McInally, in addition to gaining fame as a top class player, acquired a tremendous reputation as a football "joker". The man who played football with a grin...the greatest "larker" Scottish football has produced...the Clown Prince of football...any one of these tags would provide a suitable epitaph for Tommy McInally. A natural footballer, and always a boy at heart, he dearly loved to "kid the other fellow." It added a certain relish and spice to his enjoyment of the battle of wits."

The latter headline came from the "Evening Times", praising Tommy's ability whilst making reference to some of his misgivings, saying: "Tom McInally hit football in a big way from the moment he started as a schoolboy, and would have gained greater renown had he cared seriously to go all out for it. He was almost incomparable in his command of a ball. He could do anything he cared with it. Did he not on one memorable occasion in the course of a five-a-side game sit on the ball and invite all [others] to come and get it? What a player and what a man!"

"Tom McInally hadn't two thoughts for what his critics thought. He had his own way of doing things, whether right or wrong, but I wouldn't say that he harmed anyone intentionally. In fact, if he had been able to control his waywardness as surely as he could master and make a football do his bidding, he would not have been Tom McInally."

When looking back, it can often be the simplest option to solely dwell on the faults which people of the past possessed and the problems that they caused rather than to focus on the positives, but I do not wish to fall into this trap. Clearly, Tommy was a conflicted man. Blessed with sublime skill and an attitude which said that life was there to be lived, overindulgences would contribute somewhat to his downfall, but there was much more to the man than that.

Tommy McInally scored one hundred and forty-three goals for Celtic in two hundred and thirty-eight competitive appearances in all competitions – a fantastic return for any striker – whilst winning two Scottish League Championships, a Scottish Cup and two international caps. Achievements such as these must not be taken for granted, nor overshadowed in history by personal problems.

I shall end this short chapter with the words of Adam McLean – himself a Celtic great who played alongside Tommy at both Celtic and Sunderland for many years – and with a song once popular on the Celtic terracing. Adam spoke to a journalist from the "Evening Times" of his departed friend and colleague soon after his death and said, "What can I say about Tommy? First of all he was one of the most kind hearted souls I have ever known. He spent much of his time and means helping other people. I would pay that tribute to him above all else. As a player he was inimitable. He made football so easy, and, when I was his outside-left, I just had to wait for it. No player of my time ever made the pass so easy to take."

"Tommy McInally, he's the toast of ground and stand,
Tommy McInally, he's the greatest in the land!
Even though I get the sack, how I love my Tommy Mac,
Oh, I love my Tommy McInally!"

"Tommy McInally, he's the man that makes us sing,
Tommy McInally, as he charges up the wing!
And when he gets the ball, you can hear the Celtic call,
Tommy, Tommy, Tommy McInally!"

"The Forgotten Goalscorer"

Gallacher (or Gallagher) are surnames which have been irrevocably interwoven into Celtic's past. Of the eight men to have held either name who turned out for the senior side, it is understandable that the tale of one shines far brighter than any other. After all, Patsy Gallagher was a sporting revelation, and to this day, there are still those who consider him to be the greatest Celt, not just the finest Gallagher, of them all. Another notable mention should also go to Charlie Gallacher, the man who took the corner kick which Billy McNeill headed home to win the 1965 Scottish Cup Final against Dunfermline Athletic, but please allow me to turn your attention now to a more obscure figure, that of John "Jackie" Gallacher.

Jackie, born on the seventeenth of May 1924, began his footballing life with Armadale Thistle, from whom Celtic signed the young man in July 1943. Standing a little shy of six feet in height, he had a lot to live up to as a footballer, for he was the little brother of the famous Hughie Gallacher, the Newcastle United and Chelsea star who often kept Jimmy McGrory out of the Scotland side in the 1920s and 1930s. Sadly, despite scoring over four hundred professional goals for various clubs and twenty-three for Scotland (he remains the third highest Scottish international goalscorer ever), Hugh would tragically take his own life on a railway line in 1957.

However, horrific though it would be, nobody would have known of the fate which would befall Hugh back in the days when Jackie was making his own mark at Celtic Park. In his younger life, Jackie was a self-confessed Rangers supporter, but that would become irrelevant as he started to bang in goal after goal for the Celts with regularity, to such an extent that he netted eleven times in his first eight outings for the Club. A debut goal against Dumbarton in a four-one defeat was perhaps disappointing, but a hat-trick to secure a three-two triumph over Albion Rovers (with a certain Jock Stein playing for the Cliftonhill side) and a brace to snatch another victory by the same margin against Falkirk soon helped Jackie on his way.

Some of Gallacher's early success must be attributed to the presence of loanee Gerry McAloon though, a clever inside-forward with whom Jackie seemed to quickly develop an affinity on the field. Upon McAloon's return to Brentford at the end of the season, Jackie would start to struggle somewhat, eventually requesting a transfer out of frustration in 1945. Whilst he would remain a Celt for many years yet, one can appreciate why he apparently claimed to be "unsettled" at the Club. After all, many of his scoring labours must have seemed fruitless when opposition sides could net so easily against a frail Celtic defence.

Around a year later, Jackie would score nine goals in four matches as the Hoops progressed to the semi-final of the Victory Cup, where they were set to meet Rangers. The replay which followed the first contest against the Ibrox side is a match I have discussed at some length in another section of this book, but it is sufficient to say now that Gallacher – as well as several other Celts – were subject to tackles ranging from robust in nature to borderline assault that evening. As a result, Jackie was injured; moved to outside-left barely able to function, and then crocked once more before finally being removed from the field by stretcher. A few days after the match, "The Sunday Post" featured the following snippet.

"Talking of nursing homes, Jackie Gallacher's Hampden injury may turn out to be a bit worse than originally anticipated. The external cartilage is suspect. Jackie was due to re-join his [wartime] unit, but Celtic have submitted a request for a period of leave in order that an operation, if necessary, may be carried out at home."

Gallacher would not feature in another senior match for the Celts until the middle of August 1947, over a year after the previously referenced Rangers fixture, although it must be said McAloon did return to Celtic Park on a permanent basis during the intervening period. Subsequently though, despite scoring a brace against Third Lanark and the first goal in a two-nil win over Rangers at Celtic Park in the weeks which followed, Jackie would not re-emerge in the senior side once again until the summer of the following year, by which time McAloon had departed Glasgow, for Belfast Celtic.

The season of 1948-49 would be the last in which Jackie would have any great involvement in the Celtic team, but to his credit, having not played more than a smattering of matches in the last two years, he rediscovered his goalscoring form, netting twenty-one times in twenty-six appearances in all competitions during that campaign. To highlight the mess which the Hoops found themselves in at this time though, it should be noted that Jackie's sole hat-trick that season came in a four-all home draw with Falkirk, whilst three of his braces came in a four-two, six-three and four-three defeats against Hibernian, Clyde and Dundee United respectively.

Celtic were very poor at this stage, eventually finishing the season in sixth position, barely scoring more league goals than those which they conceded. However, thanks to a three-one win over Third Lanark in which Jackie played but did not score, Celtic did win their first piece of post-war silverware (and Gallacher's only honour in his time at Parkhead) in the form of the Glasgow Cup in 1948. This event must have been quite a thrill for all of the players, as they strutted their stuff in front of a record crowd of eighty-seven thousand people on a Monday evening at Hampden Park, enjoying one brief night of glory amidst an otherwise gloomy period on and off the field.

Jackie Gallacher's final appearance for Celtic would have overtones of his first, for as he played his solitary match of the 1950-51 season, he scored the only goal for a Celtic side who lost heavily – five-one on this occasion – away to East Fife.

Despite the fact he was criticised by many in his era for inconsistency and has been largely forgotten by the majority of modern day supporters, Gallacher's goalscoring record is, in itself, worthy of some admiration. Jackie finished his Celtic career having scored ninety-four goals across one hundred and sixteen appearances, a ratio not too far away from one goal per match. Of course, the majority of these goals were not scored during officially competitive ties, but credit must be given where it is due.

One cannot help but wonder whether these figures would have been higher had it not been for a combination of injury and timing. Regardless, Jackie Gallacher may not have reached the heady sporting heights of his brother Hugh, but for a born and bred Rangers fan, he most certainly did his bit to help Celtic through some of the most difficult footballing days the Club has ever endured.

"John the First"

Most football clubs can be accused of having had the odd diver in their midst at some point or another, but when it comes to Celtic Football Club and our divers (or should I say "Divers"), we find ourselves discussing players who were Divers by name rather than nature. Yes, three Divers have played for the Celts over the years, although I think it is fair to say the latter two – a father and son pairing – are more widely known the first. Born on the nineteenth of January 1874, a little over two months before the inaugural Scottish Cup Final, John Diver entered the world in Glasgow's Calton, an infamously poor area of the city, from which came not only John, but several men who would feature for the Football Club across the generations. Indeed, his parents Michael and Caroline are also said to have had the surname "Diver" on John's birth certificate, so one must presume the family became the "Divers" sometime thereafter as the latter appears on future official paperwork.

Having begun his career with the Vale of Clyde and Benburb before a spell with Hibernian of Edinburgh, the man who would go on to feature across each of the five forward positions signed for Celtic, the rising power in Scottish Football, in September 1893. With his teammates still enjoying their newly found status as the Champions of Scotland upon his arrival, things certainly seemed to be on the up for the Parkhead Club. However, despite an impressive start to the league season of eight wins, one draw and one loss meaning the Celts found themselves top of the table after ten matches, a five-nil defeat at Ibrox, which accounted for the aforementioned loss, undoubtedly rattled the Celtic team. After all, the Ibrox club were their closest competitors the previous season, and despite the fact they would fall away as the 1893-94 campaign progressed, they sat in second place in the league standings (only two points behind the Celts) when the name "John Divers" first appeared in a senior Celtic side.

Whilst John would make his debut in the first round of the Scottish Cup against Hurlford on the twenty-fifth of November 1893, it is noteworthy that Celtic had once again lost to Rangers at Ibrox the week prior – albeit in the Glasgow Cup this time – by a single goal. This must have brought back memories of the previously referenced drubbing the team received there only a couple of months beforehand, and with this in mind, the Celts had to be careful to avoid complacency and another defeat the next week – and so they did.

Although John did not score on his debut as Celtic won by six goals to nil "in front of a very sparse crowd" at Celtic Park, he must have impressed to some degree with his performance, as he started the following Scottish Cup tie against Albion Rovers only a few weeks later, which Celtic won seven-nil. Few other Celtic player's careers will have started with a pair of such emphatic victories, but even after two appearances in high scoring affairs like these, John was still searching for his first goal, something he would likely have been keen to set right.

He continued his quest as he made his league debut only a week later, as another match littered with goals, the likes of which are so rare now that we can often only dream of seeing a handful of them for ourselves, resulted in an away win at Dumbarton for the Celts, who won by five goals to four. As I researched this match, I found the match report in the "Glasgow Herald" to be unusually expansive for this time in history (at a few hundred words in length), and therefore I knew that this must have been a pulsating encounter indeed. Dumbarton, whilst they certainly weren't as good as they had been a couple of years previous, were still considered to be somewhat formidable opponents, and the fact they put four goals past the Celtic defence, who had only conceded fifteen league goals all season (five of which came in the hammering at Ibrox) is testament to this.

However, as I scrolled through the article, I came across a line which reminded me that I was staring into the depths of history when, regrettably, social attitudes were entirely different. This quote, which I refuse to repeat due to the fact that a racial slur was used within it, compared the work rate of Dumbarton to that shown by the slave labour of old. Bizarrely, it seems to have been intended to be a compliment of sorts, praising the home side for their industrious efforts upon the field of play, but I could not help but squirm when I read it. I wonder what the author of the piece would think of Scottish Football nowadays if he were to see players of all nationalities and ethnicities pulling on their respective jerseys across the country on a weekly basis, or if he were to discover that Scottish Football's most expensive export was a Kenyan, the sublimely talented Victor Wanyama.

Returning to the tale of John Divers though, he held down his place in the side following the dramatic win over Dumbarton and on the thirtieth of December 1893, he put his name on a Celtic score sheet for the first time in front of approximately twelve thousand spectators versus Third Lanark at Cathkin Park. Both sides started the match brightly according to newspaper reports, with John Divers and the great Sandy McMahon "looking dangerous". A few lines later, we find a description of Divers' goal: "After thirty minutes play the Celtic scored the first goal of the game, as a result of pressure which nothing could resist. McMahon trickily headed the ball in, and Divers made no mistake, fairly beating Wilson [the Third Lanark goalkeeper]." In the end, Celtic won the match by three goals to one, and as time passed, John Divers began to cement his place in Celtic's starting line-up.

Early in the New Year, on the thirteenth of January 1894, John featured once again in the next round of the Scottish Cup, wherein Celtic continued their high-scoring run, easing past St. Bernard's by eight goals to one at Celtic Park, meaning Celtic were averaging seven goals a game in the competition that season thus far. There remains some debate as to whether or not John Divers actually scored in this match, as one newspaper attributes the fourth of Celtic's goals to a Divers header, but another makes no mention of any header nor goal from Divers, instead describing the fourth goal as being scored by McMahon. I suppose we should appreciate the wonders of television replays and recorded matches nowadays in this sense. Celtic and Divers progressed to the semi-finals regardless, where they would defeat Third Lanark by five goals to three, with John, amongst several teammates, sharing the plaudits in the press following the match.

Thereafter, Celtic lined up for their first Scottish Cup Final against Rangers, on the seventeenth of February, 1894. Despite two decades of attempts, Rangers had never won the tournament and as such, when one considers that the Celts had already secured the Cup once in their few seasons in existence, it is understandable that some regarded Celtic as the slight favourites for this match, (although this view was most certainly not universally shared). After all, they had already scored twenty-six times in four Scottish Cup matches that season and were so far ahead in the league standings that they were Champions in all but name.

Sadly, John Divers was not selected to play in the final tie, despite the fact he had made good showings in all of the prior rounds of the competition that season, and Celtic slumped to a painful defeat as Rangers won by three goals to one. Perhaps it is the romanticism of hindsight, but I believe there to be some truth to the notion that history can repeat itself time and time again, for when I look back at reports written about the Scottish Cup Final of 1894, I feel some of it could have easily been applied to more modern Cup Final meetings between the Glasgow clubs, as Celtic "were unlucky, of that there can be no doubt" among other things.

Essentially, defensive lapses cost the Celts against an organised, resilient Ibrox side and, once they found themselves trailing in the match, their opponents sat back and absorbed everything they could throw at them, regularly breaking away on a counter attack whenever they had the opportunity. Of course, the scoreline rarely lies and Rangers, who had most certainly had the better of Celtic thus far that season (winning the three matches the sides had yet contested), were "hailed as the winners of the Cup for the first time".

The following week, John Divers returned to the side as the Celts finally overcame Rangers in a league match which finished with a scoreline of three goals to two in their favour. This would be the last victory of what must be regarded as a successful year for Celtic Football Club, despite the obviously disappointing

Cup Final result. To sufficiently recover from an early season defeat of such magnitude to win the league was remarkable, as many teams would have had their confidence shaken so much by this event that they would have floundered. As for John Divers, he must have felt things were headed in the right direction – he was making more regular appearances and was now a firm part of the first team to retain the Scottish League Championship, but in the years to come, events would turn his head towards English Football.

As 1894-95 began, there was some speculation as to whether or not Celtic could make it an unrivalled three League Championship titles in a row, but a relatively poor start to the season, coupled with defeats against Hearts both home and away later in the campaign soon put that idea to bed. John Divers did not feature in the first two matches in the middle of August, but did appear in the side once again, owing to other players' injuries, as the Celts lost to Third Lanark later in the month. After this, he was dropped once again, before re-emerging, perhaps somewhat unexpectedly, in the side to face Rangers in the first derby match of the season at Celtic Park, "before twenty thousand spectators".

The following quote from the "Glasgow Herald", which describes the first goal that day, made me smile partly because of who the scorer was but also due to the innocent way in which the ensuing celebrations are referred to: "The game had only gone five minutes when the persistency of the Celts was rewarded, Divers scoring cleverly from a centre [a cross] from the right, and, needless to say, this success was warmly applauded by the home crowd."

As the match progressed, the play was described as "very fast and exciting – by far the hastiest of this season – but taken all round, the Celts undoubtedly had the best of it." Despite this, Rangers equalised sometime around the hour mark, causing the game to "rage faster than ever, if that were at all possible", and numerous robust challenges forced the referee to intervene on several occasions.

Rather than describing the following goal myself, I shall leave it once more to the hands of the reporter who was at the match, over one hundred and twenty years ago: "A couple of minutes play after the Rangers' success, the Celts' supporters sent up a wild shout which must have been heard a long way off, signalling that their team had once more gained the ascendancy. It was a result of some clever go-ahead play by Blessington and Madden, who passed the ball over to the wing. Haddow saved a hot shot, but on rushing out to meet the ball again, the goal was left open, and Divers, making no mistake, scored the second for the Celts."

Eventually, the tie would swing away from Rangers, as the Celts opened up a three goal lead. However, rally though they did, they could not claw back their hosts, who went on to add a fifth goal, and the match finished five-three in favour of the team in green and white. Unsurprisingly, the performance of John Divers (now twenty years of age) was widely praised, and not only his natural talent, but his ability to stand up and be counted in the biggest of games was becoming increasingly apparent. Such attributes would serve him well, particularly later in his career.

A few weeks onwards, when Celtic next made a league appearance, John held his spot in the first team and scored again, helping his side to recover from a goal down to win by four goals to two away at Clyde. Celtic would likely have been rather confident as the Glasgow Cup Final tie, involving themselves and Rangers, neared. Since their aforementioned five-three league victory against the Ibrox side, Celtic had won six of their last seven competitive matches, although John hadn't featured for over a month since the match against Clyde.

However, he was recalled for the Glasgow Cup Final as James Blessington was unavailable for selection, therefore freeing up a spot in the Celts' forward line. Once again, John Divers did all he could to shine when given a chance to play in the first team, playing well in an exciting game, before scoring the second of Celtic's goals in a two-nil victory.

"It was a grand display of stamina, strength, and clever all-round play, and the spectators really had nothing to complain about. Just as half-time was drawing...close, the Celtic forwards came away in a body and the ball being passed from right to the left across the goal-mouth, Divers banged it through and scored the second goal."

At the close of the "Glasgow Herald" article from which the previous quote was sourced, the author describes how several members of the Celtic team were carried from the field on the shoulders of their peers at the end of the match at Cathkin Park. Whilst no names are mentioned directly, I think it is likely one of these men would have been John.

Such a grand performance would see Divers appear in the majority of Celtic's matches over the remainder of the 1894-95 season, missing only a couple of potential outings from December through until May. During this period, Celtic were knocked out of the Scottish Cup by Hibernian, only to be reinstated following an appeal, which I shall discuss momentarily.

Newspaper reports speak of special trains being laid on from Glasgow to Edinburgh for "a considerable number" of away supporters, so much so that, when their ranks were combined with the home fans, the total attendance for the void match numbered over twelve thousand, with several hundred stuck outside having seen gates and turnstiles closed before they had reached the front of the queues.

As I have hinted, after Celtic's initial two-nil defeat to the Edinburgh side, Celtic lodged a protest of complaint with the Scottish Football Association. Interestingly, the following piece from the "Glasgow Herald", published on Boxing Day of 1894, gives us some insight into the details and results of such a protest.

"Scottish Association Committee...The Celtic protested against the Hibernians on the grounds that two of the Hibs team were ineligible to take part in the recent tie. After evidence, Mr. McLean (Ayr), seconded by Mr. Brown (Third Lanark), moved that the tie be replayed at Easter Road, Edinburgh, on Saturday first, on the ground that Neil and M. Murray had violated the professional rules. Mr. Williamson (Mossend Swifts), seconded by Mr. Smith (Hearts), moved as an amendment that the tie be awarded to the Hibernians. On a division, three voted for the amendment and twelve for the motion, so the tie will be replayed."

Subsequently, Celtic reversed the scoreline and edged past Hibernian in the replayed match and so they progressed to the next round, but only after they had survived a protest against them. Again, we must turn to newspaper reports to discover the basis of such a complaint: "At the close of the game, Captain Murphy, on behalf of the Hibs team, formally lodged a protest with the referee on the grounds that McEleny of the Celtic played in a five-a-side for a club other than his own during the summer time and further that Mr. P. Gallacher, the Celtic linesman, coached his team during the progress of the game." Yet, even once this had been dismissed, the Celts' efforts would be in vain as a poor performance away against Dundee would see their Scottish Cup run come to an abrupt halt before the end of January.

As the season drew to a close, John scored in each of Celtic's final three league games, including the fifth in a dramatic six-five away victory at Leith Athletic and another in a final day win over Dundee, exorcising the demons of their Scottish Cup failure to some extent. Notably, John was absent from Celtic's fourth to last league game of the campaign, a one-all draw at Ibrox Park. At first glance, one would consider this omission somewhat odd – after all, John Divers seemed to reserve some of his best performances for matches against Rangers – however, John was not left out of the Celtic side because he wasn't considered to be playing well enough or due to an injury, but as he was set to make his international debut against Wales in Wrexham.

As such, whilst Celtic and Rangers shared the points at Ibrox, Scotland drew with Wales a few hundred miles south. Incredibly, Celtic players scored more goals in Wrexham that day than they did in Glasgow, as both John Madden and John Divers struck to give the visitors a slender two-one lead at half-time. Divers' goal is described as follows: "Divers, with a bit of clever tricky dribbling, got well down on goal, and with a smart short beat Jones."

However, as is previously referenced, Scotland were unable to hang onto their lead for a victory, conceding a single second half goal without reply as the match finished two-each. Sadly, despite a good team performance and a great individual goal coupled with a slightly disappointing result for Scotland, John Divers would never wear the colours of his country again, having earned only a solitary international honour. Of course, Divers wasn't the only Celtic player to be lowly capped by his country. As is discussed in significantly more length and detail in my previous work, his compatriot John Madden, who made his final Scotland showing alongside Divers, scored five goals in two appearances for his country, and was never rewarded with another call-up. This may seem somewhat bizarre and, in all likelihood, there were many contributory factors to such decisions.

Moving on, John did not feature particularly often throughout the course of the following campaign, 1895-96, as Celtic won the Scottish League Championship for the third time, taking the title back from Heart of Midlothian. The highlight of a frustrating season, from Divers' point of view at least, was likely the opening goal in an end to end victory at Boghead in September, as Celtic emerged victorious against Dumbarton by three goals to two.

In truth, although John started both the first and last league games of that season – each of which ended in two-one victories for the Celts – he found it very difficult to break into a relatively established, and more importantly currently in-form, forward line of John Madden, James Blessington, Allan Martin, Sandy McMahon and William Ferguson. Ironically Ferguson, with whom Divers would compete for a starting place over the next couple of years, had only been given his senior debut because John had been away playing for Scotland in Wales.

Having said that, a few games into the 1896-97 season, John was given another chance once again and he impressed, scoring two of the Celts' three goals as they eased past Hearts at Celtic Park without conceding. This result, as well as the return fixture later in the campaign, which was drawn, were oddities of sorts, as Hearts went on to win the title and Celtic slumped to a fourth place finish despite taking three points from a possible four against the eventual champions. Of course, three losses in their final three league games (Celtic only lost four times in the league all season), were what turned out to be fatal in this sense. Notably, John didn't play in any of these three matches. In fact, Celtic won two thirds of their league fixtures in which Divers featured that season, drawing the other third – he never appeared in a losing league side.

Of course, many of you will ask why Divers stopped being chosen for the first team if he was playing well and Celtic were attaining successful results with him in the side, and you would be right to do so. However it is sad to say that, in a large sense, this situation was of his own making. On the twenty-first of November 1896, Celtic lost by two goals to one in the replay of the Glasgow Cup Final against Rangers, having drawn the initial tie one-all a week earlier.

In the first of the two matches, Divers had an uncharacteristically bad game, being described by the "Glasgow Herald" as "particularly weak" before they went on to say that he often "dallied too long" with the ball to be effective. One week later, although Celtic led at half-time, the final finished with Rangers the victors. Again, Divers did not have the best showing of his career – nor did several Celtic players – and the disappointment of such a defeat, when Celtic were considered by many to be favourites, was likely clear to see.

Anyway, in the days which followed the replayed match, much criticism was made of the Celtic team in several sections of the Scottish press, particularly in a publication called the "Scottish Referee". A week on, with Celtic set to face Hibernian in what was then a top of the table clash at Celtic Park, the Celtic team refused to take to the field unless a journalist representing the aforementioned publication, who had been rather harsh in his comments regarding their last performance, was immediately removed from the press box and ejected from the stadium. As a result of some heated discussions with the Club's hierarchy, the team soon agreed to put their personal opinions to one side and represent Celtic Football Club that day – all but Barney Battles, Peter Meehan and John Divers – who simply could not be persuaded to participate.

This debacle caused the game to be delayed by fifteen minutes, and forced Willie Maley out of retirement to fill one of the gaps in the starting line-up. Bernard Crossan, a talented player in his day who featured in Celtic's first ever league match in 1890 was now far past his best, but also accepted a spot in the side. However, even with these adjustments, Celtic were still left with no choice but to start the match with ten men, as nobody could be found to fill the remaining role in the team quickly enough. By the time the second half began, whilst Celtic were certainly not at full strength, they at least found themselves to be numerically so, as Thomas Dunbar (one of the relatively few players to turn out for both Celtic and Rangers) arrived from Hampden, where Celtic's reserve team had been playing. Remarkably, the senior Celtic side actually led their visitors for a time, before an equalising goal denied the Celts an unlikely victory as the match finished one-each.

Unsurprisingly, the Celtic Committee were incandescent with the three voluntary absentees, whom they quickly branded "malcontents", before saying they "would never be allowed to kick a ball again" as Celtic players. For the rest of the season, at least, this proved to be the case. Determined to prove a point of principle, none of the three men made another appearance for Celtic during that campaign as Peter Meehan moved to Everton, soon to be followed by John Divers, and Barney Battles headed to Dundee.

In 2010, Eric MacKinnon of the "West Lothian Courier" penned the following regarding the Celtic Committee's actions following the player strike, quoting from a past issue of the same publication as he did so: "The Courier revealed the trio's fate in an article on December 5, 1896."

"The business committee of Celtic F.C. met last night to discuss the actions of Meehan, Battles and Divers on Saturday in refusing to play against the Hibs. The delinquents were brought in but had no explanation to make, apart from demanding their release from the club. This was, of course, refused and they were told to attend a meeting with the S.F.A. when their case would be brought up. It was resolved that whatever the action taken...the three offenders would never be allowed to play for Glasgow Celtic again. The feeling was that nothing less than a twelve month suspension would be sufficient."

"The Courier continued with the story in their Boxing Day edition, when it revealed that the Celtic trio were not happy to be left receiving a half-crown pension during their suspension from the team and they reported the players seemed in a "sorry plight". The tale continued in the next issue, January 2, 1897, when the Courier ran a story under the headline "The Celtic Suspends", revealing one of the trio may be offered an olive branch by the club."

"It is believed that the Celtic are contemplating taking back Battles and playing him with Doyle at left-half, thus allowing King to move up to centre position. Meehan, it is thought, will go to Everton and Divers is anxious to share his fortunes with Meehan and may accompany him to Liverpool. But Aston Villa are in Glasgow with the avowed purpose of signing the left winger."

Of course, the Aston Villa link came to nothing – as did the potential olive branch – but I consider the previous article to be interesting nonetheless, not only because it details the processes followed by the Celtic Committee, but also because it hints at the problems Celtic soon found themselves facing. Yes, they had stood by their principles and refused to bow to pressure to play any of the three men again, but the team had noticed a dramatic dip in both performances and results since their suspensions had been implemented. After all, Meehan and Battles were vital first team regulars, the latter of whom had not missed a Celtic match for approximately a season and a half prior to the player strike, whilst the former had only been absent for two fixtures in the same time period.

As was previously mentioned, the Celts suffered defeats in each of their final three league matches of the campaign, destroying any hopes they had of retaining their Scottish League Championship, but that was not the most embarrassing event of this time. Not only did these three losses occur, with one result being that the Celts did not win a competitive match from the twelfth of December 1896 until the fourth of September 1897 (a time spanning just a week short of nine months), but they also became the victims of one of the first "giant killings" in the long history of the game, going down by a scoreline of four goals to two in the first round of the Scottish Cup against non-league Arthurlie in January 1897.

To contextualise this event somewhat, I'd ask you to consider the occasion upon which Inverness Caledonian Thistle knocked Celtic out of the Scottish Cup in 2000 in the third round, as it is probably the most similar defeat of recent years to that which the Celts suffered in 1897. With injuries and suspensions leaving only a shell of a Celtic team available for selection, the Parkhead outfit were forced to call up four reserves to the senior side simply to fill their starting line-up. However, even with this handicap, virtually everyone with an interest in Scottish football at the end of the nineteenth century would have expected Celtic to find a way past their amateur opponents, even if it did require a replay at Celtic Park, but alas, for the second consecutive season, Celtic found themselves out of the Scottish Cup after only a single fixture. This was truly embarrassing, both for the team and their supporters, and in many ways it exemplified all which had gone wrong at Celtic Park over the course of the previous few months.

If one positive did come from the defeat to a side who went on to lose by five goals at one at home to Morton in the next round of the competition, it was this – such results, combined with the occasional show of indiscipline – fundamentally led to the appointment of Celtic's first manager, William Patrick Maley, in April 1897.

Whilst this colossus led his team to the Scottish League Championship title in his first full season in charge (1897-98) without the presence of the three dissidents from the previous campaign, John Divers spent his days at Goodison Park with Everton. In all, he would make thirty-two appearances for the Toffees, scoring eleven goals in his spell there, which totalled a little over a year in length. During this time, notable moments included winning goals against Bury and Notts County, as well as playing in front of some crowds which were, for the late 1890s at least, considered to be large indeed (often over twenty-five thousand). At the end of John's only full season with the club, Everton finished in fourth position in the league and fell at the semi-final stage of the F.A. Cup.

North of the border, the Football Club John had left in the midst of a lengthy winless streak was now beginning the 1898-99 season as the undefeated Champions of Scotland, and Maley began to wonder if what would have been considered only a year or so previous to be the seemingly impossible could be done. Having started the new season fairly well, Celtic had now lost three consecutive league matches (against Rangers, Hibernian and St. Mirren) and were in desperate need of a lift, not simply in terms of performance but also morale. After all, for the undefeated Champions to lose four of their first eight league matches was not what anyone had expected nor hoped for. With this in mind, Maley set about bringing back two faces which were well-known to the Celtic support and soon, Barney Battles and John Divers were Celtic players once again. For the record, Peter Meehan moved to Southampton and continued his career there, before an eventual move to Canada in the early part of the twentieth century.

As such, by the end of October, Battles and Divers were playing alongside each other again and Celtic were back to winning ways. Whilst Barney missed the occasional game due to injury, John was an ever-present figure for the remainder of that season, as Celtic won eight of their last nine league fixtures, finishing third in the league table behind Rangers and Hearts. To their credit, the Ibrox side had a perfect season, winning all eighteen of their matches. Now, you may wonder why I have highlighted this – other than the fact it was an impressive feat – but I shall come back to that.

On a personal level, John scored eleven goals in fourteen appearances that season, with particular highlights coming in the form of a hat-trick against Partick Thistle (a match in which he "excelled" according to one newspaper), a double against Third Lanark and a goal in a nine-two victory over Clyde. However, such personal achievements were to be eclipsed by the team performances which would see Celtic taste glory again, as they secured the Scottish Cup for the second time. However, to win the Scottish Cup is one thing – to do it in style, against several opponents, culminating in a final against the first and only side to win every single match throughout a Scottish league campaign is something entirely different.

Having played in every competitive match since his return, scoring in two of the rounds of the Scottish Cup thus far (including a tough victory over Port Glasgow in the semi-final), Divers' selection for the Scottish Cup Final against Rangers was inevitable. Having taken the lead early in the second half that day through Sandy McMahon, "Divers very cleverly got past Crawford, and passing to Hodge, the latter player dashed the ball into the net" to make it two goals to nil in favour of the Celts, putting the Scottish Cup firmly out of Rangers' grasp and avenging the defeat of 1894. Thus, in the space of a little under three years, Celtic had done what they seem to do time and time again, going from the despair of an unexpected defeat against relative minnows with players being pilloried, to an equally surprising victory over the 'perfect' Rangers, as some of the villains of old – and two in particular – redeemed themselves and became heroes once more. Willie Maley too had seen himself vindicated to a large degree by such a result, for the decision to bring back both Barney Battles and John Divers had not been supported by everybody with an interest in Celtic Football Club at the time.

This was not to be the end of such successes for Divers either, as he continued to set right all that had gone wrong in 1896-97, doing his utmost to push Celtic forward and build towards a new century which would bring them success of which he could only have dreamt. Whilst he was unable to help return the Scottish League Championship to Celtic Park during his second spell at the Club, John was very capable of two things above all others, excellent Scottish Cup performances and providing moments of individual magic.

The Ibrox side won the league again as 1899 turned to 1900, but with a derby match scheduled for New Year's Day 1900, just one match was yet to be negotiated in order to achieve another unbeaten season, albeit not a 'perfect' one like that of the previous campaign. Regardless, as Rangers, who were once again regarded as favourites for the tie, travelled to Celtic Park with the new century only hours old, John Divers readied himself along with his colleagues for what would become another historic victory.

Having taken the lead early on through John Bell, the home side conceded their advantage soon after. As the match hung in the balance, John Divers took the initiative over the destination of the points, scoring two goals in quick succession to give Celtic a three-one lead at half-time. Despite the visitors' attempts to mount a second half comeback, the final whistle signalled celebrations of sorts for the Celts who, despite finding themselves runners-up over the course of the whole season, had most certainly won the day. In truth, it could have been even better for John Divers, as he missed a penalty which would have sealed a truly memorable hat-trick. Whilst history will remember John Bell as the man who scored the first Celtic goal of the twentieth century, make no mistake about it, it was John Divers won the match for the Parkhead side.

In the weeks and months which followed, Celtic and Divers would ease past several Scottish Cup opponents, before a date was set for what would be the first of two epic semi-final encounters with Rangers. This match would end with a two-all scoreline thanks to a dramatic late equaliser from the Ibrox side, with two good teams cancelling each other out in large parts, and both forward lines having the better of their opponent's defence. However, when the foes met once again a fortnight later, there was no doubt as to who the better team was, as Celtic trounced the Light Blues by four goals to nil. Despite Divers' appearances in both of these matches, he was not one of the star men, playing competently without ever excelling. He would save such individual prowess for the Scottish Cup Final.

The stage was then set for Celtic to take on the most successful Scottish Cup side ever at this point, the team whom the Celts had first defeated to lift the famous old trophy, Queen's Park. With the benefit of hindsight, we can now see this match to have been the last hurrah of amateur football in Scotland, as the Celts' opponents would never feature in a Scottish Cup Final again (correct at the time of writing), whilst the professional Parkhead Club would go onto to register more Scottish Cup triumphs than any other side.

The game itself was a fiercely contested affair, in which Queen's Park took the lead before a crowd of approximately eighteen thousand spectators. Moments prior to this, "Divers had hard luck with a lovely header which just glanced over the bar". As the game progressed and Celtic searched for an equaliser, "The 'Spiders' goal underwent one very narrow escape after twenty minutes had gone, "the ball from a kick-out by Gourlay being returned smartly by Divers, and only a timely punt by D. Stewart, while Gourlay was out of position, saved the custodian."

A few minutes after this chance had gone awry, Celtic's efforts gained reward, as Sandy McMahon levelled the scores. At this stage, the odd Queen's Park attack aside, the momentum was firmly with Celtic, who won a corner. "Pressure by the Celtic looked dangerous for a time, and [they] gained the lead from a lovely corner by Bell. Judging beautifully for the wind, the ball curved out to McMahon, whose header was converted by Divers, also with a header."

As the Celts continued their relative onslaught, both John Divers and John Hodge wasted opportunities which they "should have scored" according to one sports writer, before the provider of the second goal turned the finisher for the third, as Bell gave his side a two goal lead just prior to half-time.

Both sides started the second period brightly, although it is said that Celtic, who were now playing against the wind, had no hesitation in putting the ball out of play when tackling or clearing in order to waste a little bit of time. Regardless, as the amateurs pressed forward and attempted to gain a foothold in the match once more, Celtic broke away on the counter attack: "A rush by the Celtic left led to bungling by D. Stewart, and Divers, accepting a header from McMahon, scored a fourth point for the Celts, the goalkeeper having no chance to save whatsoever."

To their credit, despite finding themselves four-one down, Queen's Park responded admirably during the remainder of the match, eventually returning Celtic's lead to a single goal, but they were unable to find an equaliser. In truth, these two late strikes from the amateurs certainly gave the scoreline a better reflection of the game as a whole since it was far from one sided in nature. Both teams spurned glorious chances by all accounts and this, combined with some laudable defending and goalkeeping, "restricted" the goalscoring to a mere seven.

A writer for the "Glasgow Herald" remarked on the Monday following the match that Celtic had been lucky to win, feeling a draw may have been a fairer result, and perhaps this may have been the case, but when one examines Scottish Football at this point in time, a few things become abundantly clear. Firstly, as I have discussed, amateur football was falling away from its professional compatriot and secondly, Celtic had the ability to outperform every other side in the country on their day. They did not exhibit the consistent displays of Rangers, who would eventually go on to win an impressive four league titles in a row, but they seemed to have an ability to click unlike any other. In time, Maley would manage to couple consistency with class, but not until the middle of the decade.

John Divers, the man who had just scored the winning goal in the biggest domestic football match Scotland had to offer, would only remain a Celtic player for a little more than a year. During this period, he played in the majority of their league matches and all of those in the Scottish Cup. Along with his teammates, he was unable to wrestle the championship title away from Ibrox, but John did have the pleasure of another run to the Scottish Cup Final to enjoy – which included a last victory over Rangers at Celtic Park for him to savour.

Whilst the Celts had found themselves fortunate to edge last year's Scottish Cup Final by virtue of a four-three victory, they were left disappointed as Hearts reversed the scoreline in early April of 1901, denying the Parkhead Club a third Scottish Cup in a row and John Divers of one last piece of silverware with Celtic. However, in a style somewhat typical of the first John Divers, he did not depart with a loss, instead playing one final time in the first league match of the new 1901-02 season at Celtic Park, saving his side from defeat in the process.

Extensively detailed newspaper reports regarding this match were few and far between, but the "Dundee Evening Post" did say the following: "Taking one consideration with another, the game was full value for a draw, yet at one time Dundee looked all over a winning set, until Celtic in vulgar parlance "bucked up" in the closing quarter of an hour. It was a good game, and deserved a bigger gate. The result will give Dundee any amount of confidence, for it isn't every team that can boast of a draw with the "bould, bould Celts.""

John Divers left Celtic for the second and final time a couple of months later in mid-November 1901, having not featured since the draw with Dundee, but he would return to Celtic Park sooner than many supporters may have thought, joining Hibernian and appearing in a two-all league tie at the ground less than one month later. Having eventually helped Hibernian to a fairly mediocre mid-table finish come the end of the championship campaign, John and his colleagues set their sights on the Scottish Cup, beginning with victories against Clyde and Port Glasgow (in which Divers netted once), before hammering Queen's Park in the quarter final by a margin of seven goals to one (with John scoring an impressive hat-trick). On the Monday following the victory over Queen's Park, the "Edinburgh Evening News" stated joyously "It is no exaggeration to say that the Hibernians have played one of the games of their career. Once having found the net there was no holding them [back]...McGeachan and Divers divided the scoring honours."

In the semi-finals, whilst Celtic visited St. Mirren, Hibernian travelled to Ibrox Park to take on Rangers on the twenty-second of March 1902. That day, John Divers would prove himself to be a thorn in Rangers' side whenever he wore a green jersey, as he scored the first of the visitor's two goals without reply from their opponents, booking their place in the Final. To rub salt into the Ibrox side's wounds, the "Glasgow Herald" described Divers' goal in the following manner: "After half an hour's play, Divers got through though he was most evidently off-side..."

Therefore, Hibernian would take on Celtic in the Scottish Cup Final of 1902 at Celtic Park. Those of you who are familiar with the Edinburgh side's seemingly endless inability to win this tournament in modern times will know all too well when Hibernian last tasted Scottish Cup glory, but for those of you who do not, please do not get your hopes up as I am not about to discuss a victory for Celtic. Yes, despite being notable favourites for the final, not only due to the location of the match but also because of the gulf in league places between the two sides, the Celts stumbled and fell in what was described as "a very poor game" by one sports writer, losing one-nil to Divers' Hibernian.

Upon their return to Edinburgh, the Cup Winners, John included, were greeted by cheering crowds which were so large in scale that they stopped much of the local traffic as the team and their prize were paraded through the city, along Princes Street and up towards Easter Road. For Divers, this victory represented a third Scottish Cup win in four years – an impressive statistic for any player – and an indication of the individual qualities which he brought to the teams of which he was a member.

In the following season, John Divers would win the second Scottish League Championship of his career, as Hibernian turned an eighth place finish in the previous campaign into a convincing six point advantage over runners-up Dundee in 1902-03. During this run towards the title, Hibernian took apart both Celtic and Rangers in Glasgow, scoring nine goals in their two journeys to the city.

With this achievement under his belt, John played one more season with Hibernian before retiring in the summer of 1904. Whilst he will not go down in history as a Celtic nor a Scottish footballing legend, he was most certainly a very talented player who found a fair amount of success and had the privilege of playing with three of the biggest football teams around at the time, both north and south of the border. In all, he scored forty goals for Celtic in eighty-seven league and cup appearances, and finished his whole career with three Scottish Cup winner's medals, two League Championship winner's medals and one international cap to his name, as well as other minor honours besides. This is a proud record worthy of respect and I'm sure John was very happy with that which he achieved.

In a sense, it is a shame Divers was unable to feature more than he did for Celtic, but he found himself competing for places at a time when the forward line was beginning to see the introduction of the likes of the legendary Jimmy Quinn, whilst veteran talents such as Sandy McMahon and Johnny Campbell continued to hold down a place and, in all honesty, few players could have forced those names out of a Celtic line-up.

Willie Maley is quoted as saying the following of John Divers, and although I know none of you reading this nor myself have ever seen him, I feel it helps to quantify the sort of player that he was – frustratingly talented: "He's an artist, I tell you. It's a treat to watch him play. His only fault is, he's too artistic at times. He does too much."

John died on the thirteenth of March 1942, at the age of sixty-eight, having suffered the effects of mouth cancer for a few months before contracting pneumonia. He passed away in his Baltic Street home, just a short distance from Celtic Park, almost thirty and forty years after the deaths of his two colleagues from the infamous player's strike, Meehan and Battles. Whilst this event was undoubtedly a mistake, I sincerely hope that this is not all that the first John Divers to play for Celtic is remembered for. Instead, I feel we should all consider what he brought to Celtic in their formative professional years – a talent many would envy and a rare ability to change a game singlchandedly.

Along with his dear friend Barney, he remains an occasionally maligned Celtic great.

"The Chronicles of Willie Maley:
"The Formation of the Celtic Club""

"By Willie Maley, Celtic F.C. Manager"

"Once Tom and I had definitely decided to join the Celtic we were quickly brought into touch with the "heid yins", and I may say that never since have I met a more enthusiastic body of men than that first Celtic committee."

"At their head they had Dr. Conway, a most popular and kindly East End medical, whose untimely end a few years later robbed the new club of a worthy Chairman, and one who would, if he had been spared, have been a worthy representative of the great club it was destined to be."

"Of the rank and file of that committee, besides John Glass, I met J.H. McLaughlin, H. Darnoch, John O'Hara, James McKay, Frank McErlean, J. McDonald, Joseph Shaughnessy, John and Willie McKillop, Hugh Murphy, Dan Malloy, and Davie Meikleham. It is hard to believe, but of that list of rare good friends only three are left with us."

"The work of the club went on in great style, and the new ground proceeded with greatest keenness. The enclosure was situated at the corner of Janefield Street and Dalmarnock Road, bounded on one side by the Janefield Cemetery. We had, in addition to the playing pitch, a practice pitch. The old pavilion still lives in my mind. The dressing rooms were built underneath the stand, which was built to hold about five hundred people. In addition we had comfortable offices in the little erection."

"Process of Building"

"In the process of building the first team we used to have little practice games even before the ground was completed, and I remember my first appearance on the famous pitch. With several

126

other young players, who had been secured before the big "catches" were made, we stripped under the shadow of the stand in course of erection, and, wearing a white shirt with a hand of green across it from shoulder to shoulder, the pioneers of the great Celtic trotted out before a handful of enthusiasts. We had several of these practice games, and after each we were taken down to the hall in East Rose Street, now the headquarters of the rising club, and here, after a good tea, we used to have harmony provided by our good friends."

"With the inclusion in the Celtic net of Kelly, Dunbar, McCallum, Groves, Coleman, McLaren, McKeown, Gallagher and James McLaughlin, the excitement rose tremendously, and these little gatherings got to be regular parties. In Neilly McCallum, once he got settled amongst us, we had a regular artiste, and his singing was a great treat to us all."

"Before going further into detail regarding the first team, I might be allowed here to venture my opinion on its formation and how it was done. The great deeds of Renton in 1888 and the Scottish Cup victory of Hibs in 1887 had brought both clubs so prominently before the football world that it was certain, with professionalism existing in England since 1885, that many temptations would be put before the leading players in both teams. Knowing this, the Celtic management thought if the players who would suit them were going to be taken away, they might as well have a try for them. The state of affairs in Scottish football at that time was perfectly evident to anyone, and if the S.F.A. didn't punish certain clubs at the time for breach of the professional rules, it was a case of their turning a blind eye to the delinquents. They certainly had some individuals before them, also a club or two, but even a Commission did not find out what lay absolutely on the surface of Scottish football management."

"That being so, Celtic were not the first club to poach on their neighbours preserves, and though the Hibs made a tremendous "song" at the departure of some of their best men to Celtic, Parkhead were only following the lead of others of those days. Kelly and McCallum, of Renton, who joined Celtic at this time, were expected at Easter Road, where Dunbar and Coleman, with their club mates McLaughlin and Gallagher, had followed them from Cowlairs. McLaren, McKeown, McGhee and McGinn, not to speak of Pat Lafferty, had all been brought from the famous Lugar Boswell team to build up the famous Hibs team of 1887. Madden, of Dumbarton, another countryman of ours, had promised his adherence to the Celtic standard, but his defection will form a paragraph later on."

"My point on the formation of our team by players from other clubs being now made, I will say that I regard the Celtic club the luckiest that ever existed, in that they formed a team in their first year which was within an ace of winning the Scottish Cup, and that that team was built up by a set of men whose knowledge of the game was practically nil. Not one of them had any previous experience of football. J.H. McLaughlin's athletic knowledge lay in the cricket field. John Glass and Co. learned their football after the Hibs won the Cup in 1887. I often wonder if the good objects of the new club lent to the first committee a guiding hand in the selection of the wherewithal to attain the success of the undertaking which, by the first rule in the Celtic book of rules, was laid down to be "the maintaining of a fund for providing dinners to poor children in the three East End parishes of Glasgow".

"Professionalism Begins"

"Professionalism was introduced to Scotland in 1893, and it was through the late Mr. J. H. McLaughlin that this step was taken, a movement which in itself was sufficient to wipe out the stain of "pro-amateurism" which existed in Celtic in common with every leading club in Scotland up to 1893, with the one exception of Queen's Park, who, I am pleased to say, have always been true to their traditions in this respect."

"I am often told, nowadays, of certain men in football whose sole aim is the money they make out of it, and how readily this class of player finds an excuse for not playing, but never, of course, for not getting his money. I will just give an example of the very different spirit which pervaded the men in these days, when no one would dream of lying off if he had half a leg to stand on. Gallagher and I were sort of rivals at this time for right-half place in the team. On a tour [of England and Ireland], whilst skylarking in his own sweet way (and he had a great way with him, too, poor Pat), he rushed along a passage into his bedroom, which was a few steps lower than his passage, jumped on to the bed and somersaulted over to land on another bed nearer the window. He went too far, and brought his foot right through the window, cutting the heel very badly. He had been very keen to play against Bolton [Wanderers], and rather than lie off he played with his foot in bandages, finishing up with his boot streaming with blood, and almost finishing his career. Pat had his faults, but he had a big heart."

"The Old Brigade"

"Of the General Committee, the names of William McKillop, James McKay, Hugh Murphy, Davie Meikleham, John McDonald, Joe Nelis, Joe Shaughnessy, Frank McErlean, James Curtis, Dan Molloy and Pat Welsh appeal to me as being the "heads" of those days, and good-hearted, earnest committee men they all were. Of the players of the first years whose names might be inscribed as having done great service both on the field and in the committee room, I would name James Kelly, Michael Dunbar, T. F. Maley and Pat Gallagher."

"I have said in a previous article that I reckoned the Celtic a very lucky lot to have attained success so early in their existence, and I reiterate that emphatically. The reasons, however, are not far to find. The club started with a committee who had before them the incentive of charity, the most noble work of all the world's deeds. Many of them were very closely connected through their parish associations with the St Vincent De Paul Society, in which their work was constant. When the proposal to make football the means to the end of further good to the poor of their districts, our lot once together were a most harmonious band, and their first year's work was marked by a splendid unanimity which laid the foundations of our club solidly and well. In later years, as I will tell, dissensions crept into the fold through personal jealousies, but these did not last long, nor never could, in Celtic circles."

"The Master of the Dribble"

"Fernie, the happy rambler;
Supreme in every wile;
Trailed in his wake, the baffled ones;
The victims of his guile."

For as long as our Football Club has been in existence, there have been particular teams which have stood out for one reason or another in the folklore and history which inevitably surrounds all things Celtic. Regardless of the reasoning behind it, certain playing squads are more widely remembered than others, just as a similar mantra can be applied to individual players or indeed matches. It is likely that debate will rage for the entire lifespan of the Club and beyond as to who was the greatest player ever to pull on the green and white jersey, and equally so it is almost inevitable there will never be a consensus attained. For example, I have read historical accounts of supporters who are no longer with us which attest that it was the magical Patsy Gallagher who was the greatest of them all; or the deadly but unassuming Jimmy McGrory; or perhaps even the enigmatic Charlie Tully. In this sense, I cannot help but wonder whether the majority of supporters simply idolise whoever happened to be the star of their youth. Of course, nothing associated with such attitudes is worthy of criticism, for I hope and pray one day to live to an age where I will be able to tell future generations, "I saw Henrik Larsson you know!"

The purpose of this chapter is not only to tell you the tale of a fine footballer in an attempt to stop it being lost to some extent, but to document in more detail than ever before, the story of this individual as a man with the help of those who were closest to him. It is therefore with immense pleasure I present to you one family's take on their departed patriarch, who just happened to be one of the greatest Celts of his generation – the so-called "Master of the Dribble" – Willie Fernie.

Prior to my meetings with the Fernie family, I must confess that whilst I felt I had a reasonable knowledge of Willie as a player, I knew rather little about him as a man. I doubt I would be alone in this sense, but what would follow would be enlightening and enjoyable, as I sat down with his son Alex Fernie and brother in law Norman Douglas for the first time. As is often the case when carrying out such interviews, I couldn't have received a warmer welcome. They are a lovely family who are rightly proud of the footballing achievements of one of their own. As such, it may come as no surprise to you when I say I was privileged to see many pieces of Fernie related memorabilia which would not be out of place in a museum.

William Fernie was born in the village of Kinglassie in the Kingdom of Fife on the twenty-second of November 1928, to parents William and Jean. The third of five children, Willie had four siblings – Andrew, Thomas, David and Mary. Both Andrew and Thomas followed their father's footsteps by heading down the local coalmines to work (although the latter did eventually escape this to pursue a trade as an electrician), but even from an early age, it was apparent Willie did not wish to do so himself. Instead, he chose to work on a farm when he left school at the age of fourteen.

During my research for this chapter, I spoke extensively via email with Willie's sole surviving sibling, Mary. As the youngest child and only sister, she joked that her brothers may have considered her to be "a bit of a nuisance" in their early years. However, having a little sister did have its advantages, as she explained: "My brothers were always jokers, larking around and inventing new ways in which to enjoy themselves. For example, they made full use of the pram which they were supposed to take me out in for a walk when my mother was busy. Instead of doing what they were told, they would march up to the top of a steep hill near our home, take me out of the pram and sit me by the side of the street whilst they took turns to shoot down the road in it. Bill's [Willie's] finest moment of lovable idiocy came some years later though, after we had all been to see a show in which a magician whipped the cloth from a fully laden table, leaving all of the glasses and cutlery exactly as they were. Of course, Bill was keen to recreate this feat, and soon after when we were home alone, he gathered us all together to show off. My mother had a lovely cake stand which she was very proud of – amongst other things – which sat on the table in question. Bill had us all make a drum roll of sorts for him, before he grasped the table cloth and pulled as hard as he could. Sadly, it didn't go quite as he had hoped, as everything went flying across the room whilst we all ducked for cover. Several items were broken to pieces, including the cake stand, and it would be sufficient to say my mother was not happy when she discovered what had gone on!"

Running concordantly with Willie's progression from a child into a young man was his interest in the game of football, although in later years he told reporters he did not see a top flight match until after his eighteenth birthday when he went to watch East Fife take on Motherwell at the original Bayview Park. According to Mary, "he was a very athletic boy, once being crowned as the champion at his school sports."

A fan of Heart of Midlothian in his childhood he, like so many of the men who would go on to become Celtic greats, had no affiliation or love of the Parkhead side as a youngster. Despite this, even from an early age, it was apparent to those that knew him that Willie Fernie had the potential to become a footballing icon, although nobody would have predicted that Celtic would have been the Club to reap the benefits of his talents for so many years. Firstly, while playing with school teams and latterly with junior side Leslie Hearts, the young forward attracted ever increasing attention from scouts of professional clubs. Early trials with Aberdeen and Raith Rovers around the end of wartime would lead nowhere, but consistently good performances which helped Leslie Hearts to win two consecutive Scottish Secondary Juvenile Cups again drew focus to the star of the team. In an odd twist of fate, whilst many clubs wished to secure the signature of Willie Fernie for his playing abilities, it would be a nasty injury which would ultimately make Fernie himself wish to pick up a pen and join one of them in particular.

During what would turn out to be his last match for Leslie Hearts (against Vale Emmett in a Cup Final at Easter Road),

Willie – who was being watched by a crowd of scouts as had become normal – suffered a broken jaw. As Mary recalled, "It was a big worry when Bill was hurt. He had to have his teeth all wired up for somewhere in the region of six weeks, and liquids fed through a straw was all he could manage then. At that time, we didn't know whether or not he would ever play football again, but that didn't stop my brother from following his dreams."

Naturally, this injury cooled the interests of many clubs, at least temporarily, as they knew the young man would be the subject of an enforced absence. As such, they all went their separate ways after the match, except for a gentleman by the name of Pat Duffy, who made a special effort to visit the young Fernie in hospital. Pat, a man with a reputation for having a keen eye for a player, was one of Celtic's scouts at that point and his decision to make himself known to Willie and ensure he was alright would prove pivotal. According to Alex, "That visit meant a great deal to my dad. Previously, he had no love of Celtic nor any particular inclination to favour them above the other sides who wished to sign him, but the fact that Pat Duffy had taken the time to visit him did not go unnoticed, especially as no representatives from other clubs did so. One man's actions literally made the Football Club which he represented stand out from the crowd, and from then on it was only a matter of time before my dad would become a Celtic player. No other club stood a chance after that incident. My father was the type of man who remembered people's good deeds and respected them for their actions."

Willie Fernie would sign for Celtic on the twelfth of October 1948, a matter of months after he had suffered his jaw break. Having stayed in touch following his time in hospital, Pat Duffy would travel to the village of Kinglassie to visit the youngster, also bringing along a special guest with him. One cannot help but speculate, although I accept there is a large degree of romanticism attached to this presumption, that if Fernie's mind was not already made up prior to Duffy's visit, it would have been when Jimmy McGrory – the Celtic manager – strolled in through the front door with him. After all, it's not every day that one of the greatest goalscorers of all time pops around hoping to sign you for his team. Regardless, Willie Fernie became a Celtic player only three days after the Hoops had conceded six goals at home to Clyde in the League Cup. If nothing else, I hope that scoreline alone will help to highlight that this was not a great period for Celtic Football Club, and it would take many years to recover from the ravages of World War Two. If that is not sufficient, then perhaps making mention of the fact that the Celts had only emerged victorious from one of the six league matches which they had played that season prior to Fernie's arrival at the Club will be.

However, whilst it would be perhaps the easier option for me to tell this chapter's tale from the point of view of the Fernie family alone, I feel I would be doing the story as a whole an injustice if I were to do so, for other events of importance were to happen in 1948. Previously, I mentioned Willie's brother in law, Norman – born in 1940 – and therefore I feel I must also provide you with some background regarding his family. The youngest child of Alec and Eileen, a publican from Campbeltown and a homemaker from Dungannon in the Irish county of Tyrone, Norman held a keen interest in football from an early age. Unlike Willie and the Fernie clan, the Douglas family were avid Celtic supporters. It came as a welcome surprise then when one of Norman's older sisters, Audrey, became secretary to Jimmy McGrory at Celtic Park. This in turn would lead to her becoming friends with many of the people at the Football Club, both staff and players alike, whilst also managing to secure a place as a ball boy for her younger brother Norman in 1952. Critically, Audrey's appointment at Celtic Park also led to her meeting Willie Fernie.

Whilst Norman's first Celtic game as a spectator would arrive at Cathkin Park in the November of 1948 – a day upon which the visitors lost a pulsating encounter by three goals to two – Willie would not see any first team action until almost eighteen months later, spending much of the intervening period on loan at Kinglassie Colliery. Following on from their close shave with relegation in the 1947-48 season, the Celts had steadied the ship somewhat under McGrory's stewardship, but remained no more than a solid mid-table side. Regular hammerings from the champions Rangers, coupled with the occasional heavy defeat against the likes of Heart of Midlothian, Hibernian and even East Fife continued to hurt morale. Undoubtedly, there were some young and exciting talents to be found within the playing squad, with the likes of Bobby Evans, Charlie Tully and Alec Boden all regular and established starters prior to Willie's first senior appearance, but a combination of poor results and an acute distrust of the Scottish Football Association and their referees (which was at one of its highest intensities during this time period) weighed heavy on the shoulders of all those who loved the Football Club. Happily though, good times would come again.

Willie Fernie would make his Celtic debut on the eighteenth of March 1950 as the Hoops won by a single goal to nil away at St. Mirren, with Mike Haughney – a ex-captain from a commando unit in World War Two – netting the crucial strike around twenty minutes prior to full time. Fernie, along with several other team members, played integral roles in the build up to the goal. Whilst some Glasgow newspapers barely covered the match at all, partly due to the fact that the Scotland rugby union side's last minute triumph over England at Murrayfield was undoubtedly the sporting story of the weekend, "The Sunday Post" (a newspaper published in Dundee) discussed the match in some detail in an article entitled "Four Youngsters We'll Hear More About". Within it, they said the following.

"Here was a game in which result was of secondary importance. It was more of a full-dress trial for four young forwards, two on each side. Right thoroughly did those two more experienced defences put them through their paces. And all four emerged with flying colours. On the home side we had teenage debutants at inside-right and outside-left – Kirkintilloch boy, Allan Lawson, ex-Airdrie, and George Brown, from Arthurlie. For Celts we had newcomer Willie Fernie from Kinglassie Colliery, at inside-right, and playing in his third big team game, Irishman Bobby [Bertie] Peacock, from Glentoran."

"Points that pulled out the applause for each: – Lawson – Coolness and slick moving of the ball in the face of the fiercest tackles. Brown – Ability to trap the ball in the air with both head and feet. Fernie – His play when not on the ball – simplifying his colleagues' passing by utilising the open space. Peacock – Revealed himself top-line exponent of the through pass – that McAuley-like precision."

Of the starting eleven from Willie's first Celtic match, six men – himself, Mike Haughney, Bobby Evans, John McPhail, Bobby Collins and Bertie Peacock – would feature in the Coronation Cup Final a little over three years later, whilst five – all of those previously referenced except for Mike Haughney – would also line-up for the famous seven-one victory over Rangers in the Scottish League Cup Final of 1957. Others with whom Fernie would play prior to the end of the 1949-50 season – namely Sean Fallon and Charlie Tully – would also go on to appear in both of the aforementioned matches, perhaps adding credence to the theory that keeping the bulk of a footballing side together so that they may develop and flourish in time is beneficial.

A week after the Celts' win at Love Street, Fernie delivered a superb display – the sort for which he would become renowned – as Celtic dispatched a very solid East Fife side (who would finish above them in the league standings) by four goals to one at Celtic Park. In the fortnight which followed this before Celtic took to the field once again, some newspaper columnists were in their element, not only talking Fernie up as a potentially good player, but as the next Patsy Gallagher. Such statements, especially when coupled with the arrival of an old teammate at Ibrox sowing the seeds for potentially endless comparisons could well have affected Fernie negatively, but Willie didn't allow it. In order to give you some idea of the mood within the press at the time, I shall quote sections of two articles, published next to each other in the sports section of the "Dundee Courier" newspaper in early April.

"Two years ago, two young Fifers played in the same team in the Scottish Juvenile Cup at Easter Road, Edinburgh. On Monday, one of them signed for Rangers. The other is making a name for himself with Celtic. The juvenile side was Leslie Hearts, and the players left-half Jim Pryde and inside-forward Willie Fernie. Pryde, now twenty-one, was capped in all three junior 'nationals in this, his first junior season with Newburgh. Rangers got on his trail, and he signed for them on Monday night."

"Another Patsy Gallagher – When Celtic chief Jimmy McGrory attended that juvenile tie in 1947, he was running the rule over a different player altogether – but it was seventeen year old Fernie who took his eye. Who was better qualified to judge an inside man than the Celtic manager, whose record as a centre forward depended on the services of the men alongside him? Willie Fernie so impressed Jimmy that he, personally, watched him the following Saturday. He had no need to watch him a third time. Here, he was convinced, was a boy who could develop into an inside-right of a calibre not seen at Parkhead since the days of Patsy Gallagher."

"Says Celtic scout Steve Callaghan – "We played him in every position but his own to give him the poise and experience he requires. He is still training with the junior club, but once he starts full-time training at Parkhead that should make a big difference to his play." Willie, now just over nineteen, stands about five feet eight inches and weighs about eleven stones. In his second appearance with Celtic against East Fife, his play was a delight. He fetched, carried and distributed the ball like an old campaigner."

For the sake of record keeping, it will likely come as no surprise to most of you when I say that Willie Fernie had a more successful career within the footballing realms of Glasgow than his counterpart Jim Pryde, who made only fifteen senior appearances for the Ibrox club before being sold to Morton in the mid-1950s.

Willie Fernie would score his first Celtic goal on the final day of the 1949-50 league season, as the Celts drew two-each with Clyde at Shawfield. However, it is safe to assume that the scoreline may well have been one apiece had it not been for Fernie, as one newspaper described how he managed to score at both ends of the field that day: "Almost half an hour after the start, Tully crossed a ball from the right wing into the home goalmouth. Collins got his head to it and sent it to Fernie who, in turn, headed past Hewkins. This was Fernie's first goal for the Celtic first string and he was all smiles. Five minutes later his smiles had almost turned to tears – he had turned a Barclay corner through his own goal."

At the start of the next season, Willie Fernie would play in all but one of Celtic's Scottish League Cup matches, as well as appearing on the opening day of the league campaign as the

Celts lost by four goals to three to Morton at home. However, he would only make one more league appearance until February, with Bobby Collins generally being the inside-forward who kept Fernie out of the side. This was also to be the case during Celtic's Scottish Cup run, which eventually culminated in the Hoops winning the trophy for the first time since 1937. However, Willie would travel with the squad on their tour of North America during the summer of 1951.

The next season saw Fernie make even fewer appearances than he had done the year before, with only a single showing to his name, this time as an outside-forward in a three-one away loss at East Fife in December. However, Willie was still young and his chance to play regular football with the senior team would come in the following campaign, that of 1952-53.

Briefly turning our attention to Norman – or "Norrie" as he is known by the family – he began life as a ball boy at Celtic Park in 1952, with the rewards for his efforts being half a crown per match. Of course, whilst the money was nice, neither Norman nor the other lads did the job merely for the financial reward, but for the proximity to the players and the matches which accompanied it. He said: "I loved my time as a ball boy at Parkhead. Not only to see some of these guys whom you regarded as heroes up close, but to actually get to know them, was quite a thrill for us. It took me a few years of spending my time in the less desirable spots behind the goals and the like, but eventually I managed to attain one of the prime locations for a ball boy in front of the main stand. That was great simply because it meant you were one of the first ones down the tunnel at half time and got your pick of whatever biscuits or cakes had been laid on for us. Speaking of money though, we all loved it whenever Rangers came if it was raining. Inevitably, some of their supporters would throw coins at us or the players when they were taking a throw-in or whatever. Anyway, when it rained you could hear a distinct thud when they struck the wet turf around you, so it was easy to find them and gather a good little bit of change over the course of an afternoon. You couldn't do it so well when the ground was dry. For a brief time, maybe a period of six months or so, a ginger lad by the name of Jimmy Johnstone was part of our team. He was quiet, never joining us whenever we had a kick about inside our dressing area in the gymnasium underneath the old stand, but when I consider it now, he was almost certainly on his best behaviour as he likely knew the club were looking at him as a potential signing of the future."

During the 1952-53 season, Celtic would only manage to rack up one more point in the league than they had done the previous year, this time finishing eighth as opposed to ninth, winning just a fraction more than one third of their matches. Celtic's attempts at both cup competitions showed some initial promise before faltering soon after, but this campaign was undoubtedly important for Willie Fernie as it was the first in which he played in the majority of Celtic's matches in all competitions. It is clear he gained a sufficient amount of experience during this time, which would serve him well. He also scored his first hat-trick on the thirteenth of December 1952, at home to Dundee in the Scottish League. The "Dundee Courier", with the help of a famous old footballing face, recounts the feeling of amazement on that winter day.

"The twenty-five thousand spectators left Parkhead in a daze. They just couldn't believe the score! "That was the most astonishing game I have ever seen." The man who said that to me none other than Jimmy ("Napoleon") McMenemy, probably one of the most outstanding forwards who ever played for Scotland. He was one of the great Celts [between 1902 and 1920], and has twenty-five Scottish and League "caps". Still a staunch Celtic supporter, every Saturday sees him at Parkhead."

Of Fernie himself, the "Glasgow Herald" said: "Then in twelve minutes came the first serious Celtic raid of the second half. McIlroy, in midfield, square passed to Collins, and that delightful little player scampered up the wing past Cowan. [He then] crossed a ball for possession of which McIlroy and Fernie challenged Henderson, and which the inside-right quickly dispatched into the net. Five minutes later Collins and Fernie cut the defence to ribbons after McIlroy had again started the movement from the centre of the field, Fernie finished perfectly...Fernie and McIlroy added fantastic goals in the seventy-seventh and eighty-eighth minutes from almost impossible angles…[Dundee] had no player of the skill and enthusiasm of Collins, Fernie or Stein, three extraordinarily fine players."

Around six months later, having finished their league campaign with only four wins in their last sixteen matches, the Celts remained a mid-table side low on confidence as the one off Coronation Cup tournament loomed large on the horizon. However, Celtic would be buoyed somewhat by success in the Glasgow Merchants' Charity Cup, a trophy which they had only won twice previously since the start of World War Two. Willie Fernie's performances would prove vital, as he netted in each of the three matches which Celtic would play in the competition, the only man do to so that year.

Regrettably, Willie Fernie would miss the first two of Celtic's three Coronation Cup clashes, but he would play in the final versus Hibernian after a sterling display against Arsenal (which saw press commentators calling for the introduction of a "British League" and questioning how on Earth Celtic were capable of producing such a performance after several poor results during the season just finished) and a hard fought win over Manchester United helped the Celts to book their place at Hampden Park. On the day of the final, the "Dundee Courier" made the following reference to one of the prizes awaiting those men who would participate in the match: "Each player taking part in the game tonight will receive a replica of the Coronation [Cup] trophy, valued at £17 10s."

This assertion was correct and the miniature of the Coronation Cup awarded to Willie Fernie is still in the proud possession of his relatives. Many families are not blessed with heirlooms of much note, but then again few have such a famous footballing relation. Regardless, I am certain the replica is worth a lot more than seventeen pounds in the modern day.

As for the match itself, the same newspaper said the following in an article entitled "Rollicking Celts Win Coronation Cup": "The Coronation Cup final was easily the game of the season. Not for many years has a big show game at Hampden produced such thrills, spills, and excitement. The cup fighting spirit shown by Celtic has not been excelled by any of the Parkhead teams through the ages. Right from the word "go" Celts set about their more fancied opponents. The wing halves came storming upfield with the ball – and Hibs' defenders were obviously worried. Fernie was running rings around Govan. Collins was leading Paterson a merry dance. Mochan was causing Howie all sorts of bother in the middle."

"Younger made…miraculous saves before he had, at last, to admit defeat. And what a goal! Peacock and Fernie brought the ball upfield. Fernie squared to Mochan. The ex-Middlesbrough player was about twenty yards out when he whacked a perfect long range cannonball effort into the Hibs' net. There were one hundred and seven thousand people in Hampden's huge bowl at the time [although the official attendance later put the figure at over one hundred and seventeen thousand], and every one of them seemed to join in the general pandemonium which followed this great goal."

Clearly, such a triumph propelled Celtic forward. Suddenly, this side had something which is absolutely necessary for success to be achieved – belief – and they had it in abundance. Willie would miss only four of Celtic's thirty league matches the following season, whilst featuring in all six Scottish Cup ties as the Hoops secured a historic double, their first in forty years. Fernie scored ten league goals that season, including five which came in consecutive matches as Celtic powered towards the title. He would also bag three Scottish Cup goals, one of which would turn out to be the winner away from home against Hamilton Academicals and another in the semi-final replay against Motherwell.

However, it was not simply Fernie's goals which proved crucial to the success of this double winning Celtic side, but his general play, mixing sublime skill with pace and power to which this article from the "Glasgow Herald", published on the Monday following the Scottish Cup Final of 1954, alludes.

"Eighteen minutes after the restart Fernie went off on one of the dribbles that had at once delighted and depressed. In towards goal and along the goal line he went with an Aberdeen player making unsuccessful attempts to tackle him from behind. Just when he seemed to have lost control Fernie recovered magnificently and there was a chipped pass laid on for Fallon to plumb in the centre of the goal and with almost sufficient time for him to turn and say – "This is it now". The winning goal it was, though first Buckley and then Leggat made brave efforts to force a replay. If Celtic think they might have had a couple of penalty kicks in the first half – I thought there were entitled to one when Martin brought down Higgins – they cannot but be grateful to the referee for employing the advantage rule as Fernie made the important goal. Mr. Faultless had a good match."

Now, I would love the opportunity to leave the previous quote without further explanation, purely so that some of you would presume that the reference to "Mr. Faultless" was made as a description of Fernie's performance that day. However, this was not the case as Mr. Faultless was, in fact, the name of a referee called Charlie hailing from Giffnock. One can only wonder what sort of jokes were made at Charlie's expense during his officiating career, but I suppose this is proof that at least one Scottish referee across the years has been Faultless.

During the summer of 1954, Willie Fernie would become one of the first men ever to be given the honour of representing Scotland at a World Cup Finals (his international debut had come just a matter of weeks earlier in a two-one friendly win away against Finland). Great controversy had been caused four years earlier by the Scottish Football Association choosing not to send a team to compete in Brazil despite the fact that they had qualified to be there – much to the players' understandable dismay. Instead, the Association dispatched the squad to tour North America. The governing body, in their seemingly infinite wisdom, had previously announced that the Scottish national side would only travel to take part in the 1950 World Cup if they emerged as the winners of the British Home Championship that year. However, as they did not, the Scots were forbidden to attend.

Fortunately, four years later, attitudes would change – thanks in part to significant public pressure – as Scotland again finished second in the British Home Championship but took up their invitation to attend the 1954 World Cup, which was to be held in Switzerland. However, once again the Scottish Football Association would come in for much criticism as Scotland's involvement in the competition turned out to be somewhat shambolic. Instead of sending a full squad of twenty-two men to the tournament, they instead selected only thirteen individuals, immediately hampering the nation's chances before a ball had even been kicked. Supposedly without a hint of irony, a much larger travelling party, including all of the relevant dignitaries from the Football Association and their wives made the trip alongside the shorthanded team. Also, as Norman pointed out, "All of the other sides had travelled with the appropriate equipment, light shirts and boots cut off below the ankle so that the players would be as comfortable as possible in the summer climate. However, the Scots were sent with heavy woollen jerseys and the big, solid boots which stopped about a third of the way up their shins. They must have been melting as they contested those matches; it was a complete joke."

On the field, the Scots lost their first match by a single goal to nil against Austria in Zurich. The "Glasgow Herald", as well as making several references likening the fixture to the infamous battle of El Alamein fought in the middle of World War Two (which would have still been fairly fresh in the minds of many readers), blamed the defeat not on a great showing from the Austrians or indeed a poor performance from the Scots, but on officials in charge of proceedings, using phrases such as "a monstrosity of a decision" and "nonsensical notions of offside".

However, as one would perhaps expect in post-war Europe, there was also a notable degree of defiance contained within the article, as well as a reference to the play of Fernie himself: "Every Scot who saw the match is proud tonight of his fellow countrymen who nearly succeeded in defying the efforts of eleven Austrians, a Belgian referee and a Swiss linesman, to beat them...Fernie took his fair share of abuse and still was the best forward..."

Yet, in the match report which followed the Scots' second and final fixture in their first World Cup tournament, there were no complaints as to the result, as the press had seen reigning champions Uruguay decimate the Scottish side, winning by seven goals to nil. At the time of writing, this remains Scotland's worst ever defeat.

"Scotland's hopes of qualifying for the quarter finals of the World Cup died a sad death here this evening, and forty-three thousand spectators, the largest crowd that has so far attended a match in the tournament, were present at the funeral. The humiliation of the defeat inflicted by Uruguay was particularly hurtful after the Scots' meritorious display earlier in the week against Austria..."

Willie Fernie was criticised in the wake of this result as it had been his misplaced pass which led to the first goal of the match being scored, but in all honesty there was not a Scotland player who featured that day who was not the subject of some derision. After all, it is a very rare occasion when any player is praised after his side loses a match by a seven goal margin. However, it is the mark not only of a fine footballer but of the man himself when a player bounces back from such disappointment and proves their respective worth. From a historical standpoint, it is clear that the majority of the blame for the nation's poor showing in 1954 must stand with the Scottish Football Association, who themselves have since described the preparation for the tournament as "atrocious". This view can be underlined by the fact that the first Scotland manager, Andy Beattie (himself a player with Preston North End and Scotland prior to World War Two) resigned his post between the Austria and Uruguay matches, claiming he had been put in an impossible situation by the country's footballing hierarchy.

Returning to domestic matters, Celtic were not able to repeat the heroism of their previous season in 1954-55 but they did come fairly close, finishing the league in second place behind champions Aberdeen and losing in a replay of the Scottish Cup Final to Clyde. One of the most disappointing aspects of this campaign will have undoubtedly been the fact that the Celts actually beat Aberdeen both at home and away that year, but too many draws against the likes of Queen of the South, East Fife and Motherwell would cost them dearly in the end. As one would expect, Fernie made a notable contribution, scoring thirteen goals and playing in the majority of matches, despite missing some in the spring. A similar fate would await the Celts in the following campaign, that of 1955-56, as more inconsistent league form saw them finish the season in fifth place and another Scottish Cup Final defeat, this time coming against a rapidly improving Heart of Midlothian, awaited them at Hampden Park in April. For the record, there would be no shame in this, as only two years later the same Hearts side would win the league by thirteen points, having scored an astonishing one hundred and thirty-two goals in the thirty-four fixtures involved, averaging almost four goals per game in the process.

Of course, better times would come in the next couple of years, as Celtic won their first two League Cup trophies and gradually began to climb the league table once again. The Football Club's initial success in the Scottish League Cup would come thanks to a three-nil replay victory over Partick Thistle at Hampden Park. However, more important things would happen for one Celt that week, as Willie Fernie married his fiancée Audrey Douglas between the two fixtures.

The story was such big news that it made the front page of the "Evening Times" on Monday, the twenty-ninth of October 1956. An article with the headline "Willie Has His Name Taken" read as follows: "The biggest event in a weekend of big events for Celtic and Scotland footballer Willie Fernie was his marriage today to Miss Audrey Douglas, secretary to the Parkhead team manager [Jimmy McGrory]. The wedding – in the vestry of Christ the King Church, King's Park – was sandwiched between Celtic's appearances in the Scottish League Cup Final on Saturday, the replay on Wednesday and Fernie's virtually certain selection to play for Scotland against Ireland on Wednesday week…And the couple are curtailing their honeymoon to allow Willie to play in Wednesday's Cup replay at Hampden…Mike Haughney, Celtic's right-back, was best man."

Less than a year later in the summer of 1957, Fernie again travelled across the Atlantic Ocean to tour North America with Celtic. Mary once joked that she "looked forward to these excursions almost as much as her older brother, because he would bring her back pairs of tights which were not yet available in Scotland, much to the envy of her friends."

During the tour, Celtic played Tottenham Hotspur on four occasions, losing the first three of these ties before finally overcoming their opponents in the final fixture which they contested. Writing for one Scottish newspaper of his adventures in North America, Willie made an interesting note alongside his discussion of the second of these clashes, which took place in Vancouver, for a gentleman he had attended school with travelled a great distance purely to see his old friend again.

"And many Scots travelled thousands of miles to see us play. They came by car and plane. It was by road from Prince George five hundred miles away that an old schoolmate of mine came to see me. He was David Rogers, of Dunfermline, who went to the same school in Kinglassie."

Shortly after his return home to Scotland and just prior to the start of the upcoming football campaign, Willie and Audrey's first child Billy was born. Babies are generally the source of some inevitable upheaval for any new parents, but in the earliest weeks of Billy's life, he was not the predominant source of such stress as Newcastle United made a significant bid of eighteen thousand pounds – the highest fee ever offered to Celtic Football Club at that point – for his father's services. Indeed, Newcastle United manager Stan Seymour and Chairman Wilfred Taylor travelled up to watch Fernie play as the Hoops demolished East Fife by six goals to one, staying in a Glasgow hotel and hanging around for some significant time thereafter in the hope their target could be persuaded to head south. Celtic's position was simple, as one newspaper quoted, "We are not prepared to transfer Fernie if he does not wish to leave us." Clearly then, whilst they had rejected the English side's bid, they knew all too well that it would be impractical to keep the player against his will, intentionally leaving the door open ever so slightly for a potential move and large payday to boot should that be the case. However, with the decision left largely to Willie, he made it perfectly clear to the press that he and his wife had a very young son to think of and a new house in Clarkston to pay for, and therefore the move did not interest him. As such, Seymour and Taylor eventually returned home empty handed.

The season of 1957-58 would be notable not only for the seven-one demolition of Rangers, but for the alteration of Willie

Fernie's role in the Celtic side, moving from inside-forward to half-back. The sports pages of "The Evening Times" from the night of Celtic's greatest triumph against their rivals (in terms of scoreline at least) make interesting reading for a variety of reasons. Of course there is the immediate reaction this victory, which only briefly references Fernie's late penalty, but there are also other articles of note. One, which I find to be deliciously ironic in its submission and placement is a question from "Blue Do", a Rangers fan from Govan, writing in to the sporting questions and answers column, with his query – "Let me know the Celtic team which lost eight goals against Motherwell and the date?" This, of course, makes reference to Celtic's worst ever defeat, an eight-nil loss away at Motherwell only days after the Celts had won a gargantuan Scottish Cup Final against Aberdeen in 1937. The identity of "Blue Do" will likely never be known, but I would imagine his or her inevitable misery that day will have been compounded when they picked up their copy of the "Evening Times" to discover their question situated below a headline which read "Rangers Reel… Celtic 7 Rangers 1."

Considering that day at Hampden from a more serious point of view however, it is generally accepted that even amidst a Celtic team within which every player had a great game, one man excelled above all others, and that was Willie Fernie, who scored the seventh Celtic goal from the penalty spot. "The Times" of London exclaimed that Willie was Celtic's "inspiration…[having] started many of the moves which brought goals"; the "Daily Record" said "Fernie was the most distinguished ball worker afield, some of his fantastic dribbling runs at speed tearing the very heart out of the Gers"; and the "Sunday Pictorial" told readers how the "fleet-footed Fernie tore the Rangers defence to shreds." Indeed, Robert Kelly spoke after the match of how his individual performance had been of a similar standard to that shown by Patsy Gallagher at his peak, drawing parallels with the assertions made by some newspaper reporters about the young Fernie many years earlier.

Another article published around the same time entitled "Watch out for the Fernie name" discusses why Willie, now approaching his thirtieth birthday, should be included in the squad for the upcoming World Cup qualifier against Switzerland, a match of crucial importance with regards Scotland's potential participation in the tournament. It reads: "Next Friday, before the S.F.A. offices close up for the night, letters will be sent out…Inside will be the names of the twenty-two Scotland players from whom our team will be drawn for the make or wreck World Cup game with Switzerland at Hampden on November sixth…But the name to watch is "Fernie". On very good authority I am told that there is a big push on to bring back Willie and his wiles and his wanderings. And that despite the fact that Fernie has been a Celtic half-back all season, for the Swiss game at least the feeling is that we should have some brilliant individualist, someone who can throw overboard the stereotyped stuff and produce the completely unexpected. If the selectors do decide to go all out on that policy, Willie Fernie is undoubtedly their man…"

Having subsequently been announced as a squad member for the tie versus the Swiss (his only appearance in a World Cup qualifier), Willie Fernie would banish any ghosts of Uruguayan defeat in mesmerising fashion when the sixth of November arrived, as the same newspaper recounted with the headline "It's Swiss-Bang Fernie – Scotland 3 Switzerland 2". At this point, I would reemphasise the fact that Scotland had to win the match to guarantee themselves a place in the 1958 World Cup, edging out the Spaniards – who came second in our qualification group – in the process. As such, we shall pick up the action at the start of the second half, with the game tied at one apiece.

"If ever a great effort was needed from Scotland it was now. In the first half they had been well ahead in football moves – but only up to the eighteen yard line. The gravest reflection on the forwards was that Willie Fernie was far and away the best shot on the field…"

"…Then general Hampden rejoicing in seven minutes as Willie Fernie made a great goal for Scotland. Fernie beat three men in one of his dazzle runs, moved right over past the eighteen yard line on the right and his chip across was turned neatly into the back of the net by Mudie. But every Scotsman on the field rushed to give Fernie the handshakes – and Mudie was the first to get there."

Scotland would proceed to take a three-one lead before a late Swiss goal made the final moments understandably nervy. This was a critical victory for Scotland, one for which the whole team deserved credit, but it was clear for whom the vast majority of the plaudits had been saved, as "The Verdict" column in "The Evening Times" portrayed: "No day of all-round glory for Scotland – but a wonderful afternoon for Willie Fernie. He was not only Scotland's greatest half back, but greatest forward, too. He literally laid on the Scottish goal for Mudie and with any luck at all would have scored one or two himself. He looked the complete footballer, which was a lot more than could be said for some of the other players. The Scots all round were better ball workers, but generally were poor finishers. Yes, we will have to do much better in the World Cup Finals in Sweden."

Whilst the last couple of lines hinted at the international disappointment which would lie ahead, the fact which should undoubtedly be celebrated is that Willie Fernie made a phenomenal contribution in taking Scotland to the World Cup Finals of 1958. Within the latter years of his footballing prime, he clearly remained one of the most talented and inventive footballers playing the game in Scotland. As I said previously, the mark of a great player is not only how they are able to perform when things are going well, but how they can react and adapt when things do not. Inferior players may have crumbled on an international level post-Uruguay, but Willie did quite the opposite. He dug in and continued to improve, eventually excelling against the Swiss to leave any questions about his ability beyond all reasonable doubt.

However, having proved his point to the Scottish footballing public, Willie Fernie's time as an international football player was nearly at an end. He would travel with the squad to Sweden for the World Cup Finals but would only feature in one of his side's three matches, this time on the wrong side of a three-two scoreline as Paraguay edged out the Scots in the second set of group stage matches. Preceded by a draw with Yugoslavia and followed by a defeat to France, Scotland found themselves exiting the tournament at the first opportunity once again, something which would become a frustrating habit in years to come. Fernie, of which the "Glasgow Herald" said "...apart from a few flashes of his dangerous dribbling form early in the game, [he] was much too easily thrust aside by his unscrupulous opponents", would finish his career as a Scotland player with twelve international caps and one goal to his name. During that time, he played in six different positions in the team, which was very telling not only of his natural ability but of his willingness to adapt when required. Indeed, he was referred to as "Mr. Versatile" in the media in respect of this. In the years which followed, Willie would voice a rare footballing regret with regards his time as a Scotland international. It was that he never had the chance to line up alongside outside-right Gordon Smith, a player whom he admired greatly and a member of the legendary Hibernian attacking line, the "Famous Five".

Willie Fernie would begin to appear more sporadically than he had done for many years as a Celtic player during the 1958-59 season after the previously discussed World Cup, with competition for places in the half-back line now being contested not only by the old stalwarts of Bobby Evans and Neilly Mochan but younger men such as John "Eric" Smith and a certain Billy McNeill. Considering his family's livelihood and feeling that he did not fit in with the Club's policy of starting younger players, Willie proceeded to hand in a formal transfer request. Once it became clear this would be granted, speculation as to where Fernie's future lay became rife in many sections of the news media. Whilst only Aston Villa and Middlesbrough would ever submit tangible bids, Birmingham City, Cardiff City, Leicester City, Liverpool, Manchester City, Newcastle United, Sheffield United and Tottenham Hotspur were all linked with having an interest in the Fife man by one newspaper or another. The Villa Park side's offer, believed to have been somewhere around the fifteen thousand pound mark, did not meet Celtic's valuation of the player and was therefore rejected. However Middlesbrough, their main rivals for Willie's signature, were willing to be more adventurous, eventually breaking their own transfer record to that point by offering to pay Celtic nineteen thousand pounds for Fernie. This was promptly accepted, and before Aston Villa could submit another bid (if that was their intention), a deal was agreed and the Fernie family were off to Teesside.

Willie would bid Celtic Park farewell at the start of December 1958, with what everyone – likely including himself – believed to be his final appearance in the green and white Hoops coming rather aptly on his thirtieth birthday. However, not all was well that day as Partick Thistle returned to Maryhill with the points after winning the match by two goals to nil. Undoubtedly, the Celtic support were sad to see Willie depart as he moved down south where he would take to the field with, amongst others, a young man by the name of Brian Clough. On the day of his arrival in the city, just a short time after alighting a train from Glasgow, Fernie took part in a friendly match with his new side against French club Nîmes Olympique. The home team won the match by three goals to nil, with one newspaper later reflecting: "They're going to love Willie Fernie on Teesside. The brilliant Scottish ball-playing international laid on the second goal for Clough after thirty-three minutes…Clough revelled in the service from the stocky Scot."

Middlesbrough would only achieve a mid-table finish in Division Two at the end of Willie's first six months there, but by the time the following campaign reached its climax, they had risen several places to a very respectable fifth, only two points behind Liverpool and Sheffield United in third and fourth respectively. Notably, they were also narrowly knocked out of the F.A. Cup early on by the other Sheffield side, Wednesday, who would go all the way to the semi-finals of the competition that year. Willie and Audrey's second son, Alex, would also be born during his tenure at the Teesside club, although this would occur north of the border so Audrey and the baby could be close to their wider family.

As for Celtic, the Parkhead side continued to stutter along in Willie's absence, finishing the 1958-59 and 1959-60 seasons in sixth and ninth places respectively, languishing in the realms of the mid-table. Of course, no one would have known then that the decade ahead would hold such great times for the Celts, and as such, the return of a former hero was naturally greeted with much enthusiasm during this relatively bleak spell. Willie Fernie signed for Celtic for a second time in October 1960 (almost exactly twelve years on from his original signing), despite being linked to possible moves to Aberdeen, Hearts and even Rangers in the press. "The Evening Times" captured the mood the following day rather well as it gleefully pronounced "Paradise Regained – Fernie Is Back. Life is sweet again for the thousands who love the green and white of Celtic – they've a top star inside-forward to cheer, Willie Fernie. With one dramatic midnight dash to Edinburgh to re-sign the wandering wizard of the inside-forward world from Middlesbrough, manager Jimmy McGrory achieved three aims: – 1. He gave Celtic the experienced inside-forward they sorely need. 2. He demonstrated to the supporters that Celtic were not fooling when they said they would pay good money for a top grade inside-forward. 3. He gave the biggest boost of the year to the flagging hopes of the Celtic youngsters, who had been steadily losing confidence as the team failed to click. Now with the maestro Fernie to conduct the inside-forward tune, the youngsters will be given a lead on what is wanted, and they'll benefit no end."

The next day, Celtic would welcome St. Mirren to Celtic Park for a league match which saw Fernie make his second debut for the Club against the same opposition whom he had done so initially. Naturally, he was warmly welcomed, as the same newspaper described with an article headlined "That Auld Fernie Touch – Celtic's Attack Hits the Goal Trail." It continued, "To the roar of welcome, Willie Fernie trotted out at inside-right in the Celtic team against St. Mirren. Thirty seconds later the park was a moving mass as hundreds of youngsters swooped down from all corners to pat Willie on the back, and seek the autograph of the man who had returned to lead the expected Celtic revival."

"Magnificent Fernie. After being fouled on his first two runs towards Williamson, he went off on a mazy run in which he beat three St. Mirren men before cutting a great pass to Carroll, whose first-time shot was deflected off the target. That set the tempo for a series of Celtic attacks which brought a fifth minute Auld goal.

Taking up a pass from Divers, Auld cut into the middle of the field and from twenty-two yards beat Williamson with a right foot shot that dropped over the 'keeper's clutching fingers. Celtic had scored their first goal for five games. Their supporters in the thirty thousand crowd were in green and white heaven."

Whilst the return of Fernie was rightly well received, the last line of the aforementioned quote is very telling. In five league games prior to that day against the Paisley side, Celtic had only managed two draws and three losses, scoring just three goals and conceding eleven times, including an embarrassing five-one home defeat to Rangers. The reference to the Hoops scoring "their first goal for five games" included the Glasgow Cup Final from which Partick Thistle emerged triumphant a couple of weeks earlier. Clearly, Celtic were in trouble, but Fernie would help to return matters to a more even keel. Whilst his ability was undoubtedly a great assistance, I wonder whether his presence alone also allowed the Celtic side to gain some confidence. After all, he was undoubtedly one of the greatest figures of his era. It is perhaps also worthy of mention that of the ten men who took to the field that day alongside Willie Fernie, four of them – Billy McNeill, John Clark, Stevie Chalmers and Bertie Auld – would go on to become Lisbon Lions, becoming not only some of the finest players of their day, but of the Club's entire history.

For the remainder of the 1960-61 season, Willie would feature in the majority of the Celts' fixtures, helping them to a fairly respectable fourth place finish in the league and a Scottish Cup Final which, of course, they famously lost via a replay to Jock Stein's Dunfermline Athletic. However, whilst this campaign lacked any silverware, it had given Willie another year in the Celtic Park spotlight, something he undoubtedly enjoyed.

The 1961-62 season would be the last in which Willie Fernie would spend time at Celtic Park as a player, with his second departure from the Football Club arriving towards the end of November 1961. According to Norman, it was around this time that Willie began to air his beliefs that there was "a very, very special youngster" currently at the Football Club – one who had the potential to be "truly world class" – so much so that he would rave about him whenever he and his brother in law spoke. The lad in question was none other than Bobby Murdoch, still many months away from even making his first team debut, who would go on to be called "my complete footballer" by Inter Milan boss Helenio Herrera. Clearly then, Willie had an eye for talent, and this would bode well for later life when playing football was no longer an option for him.

His final match came at Ibrox against Rangers midway through September, and fittingly he netted what looked like the winning goal, before a stunning strike from a young Jim Baxter levelled the scores at two-each in the final moments of the fixture. However, sadly this match is not generally remembered for being Willie Fernie's final appearance in the green and white Hoops, nor indeed is it recalled for Baxter's late equaliser, but for the tragic events which would occur as the crowd exited the Copland Road end of the stadium at the close of proceedings. A barrier collapsed, causing a crush in which two men were killed and more than fifty injured, in a horrible precursor to the dark events which would follow almost a decade later.

Returning to the story of Willie Fernie, he would not move as far away from Celtic Park upon this departure as he had done previously, joining St. Mirren at Love Street for the sum of four thousand pounds. Here, despite not making a plethora of appearances, he did enjoy some success, helping the Saints to narrowly avoid relegation and impressing on his debut, as the following quote from the "Scottish Sunday Express" highlights: "Can one new player transform a struggling side into a well-groomed force? St. Mirren fans will shout "yes", for that is exactly what Willie Fernie did at Muirton [Park] yesterday. Willie, who was transferred from Celtic during the week, gave St. Mirren composure, and they put on a skilful display that made St. Johnstone look a school's outfit...He scored a brilliant goal...had a great shot cleared off the line...then "made" the final goal with a brilliant header."

Willie also reached the Scottish Cup Final once again, his fifth, this time at the expense of his former club Celtic, whom he helped to knock out by scoring the first goal in a three-one semi-final victory. Of this triumph, with the Love Street side reaching only their fifth such final themselves, the "Glasgow Herald" said: "St. Mirren's success against Celtic at Ibrox Stadium in the semi-final of the Scottish Cup was thoroughly deserved. They were the superior team in every way and played with assurance from start to finish. It must be said, however, that this was one of Celtic's poorest displays of the season. They were shaky in defence and most disappointing in attack, of which they had a near monopoly in the second half, when they also had the advantage of a strong wind. In a well-balanced St. Mirren team three players were outstanding – Fernie, Clunie and Williamson. The former Celtic inside-forward was in top form in the first half, during which he frequently outwitted his opponents either by his own skill on the ball or with his carefully measured passes."

When one watches film of this match, it is to be noted that upon Fernie's strike opening the scoring, he simply turns away from the goal and jogs towards the halfway line whilst his teammates rejoice – he does not celebrate against the Football Club which he loved so dearly by this point in his life. Again, this match had ugly overtones associated with it, with large brawls breaking out on the Ibrox terracing which eventually saw spectators spill out on to the running track, causing a cessation of play for somewhere between fifteen and twenty minutes before police gained control of the situation. Disappointingly, Willie Fernie would again be unable to add another Scottish Cup winners' medal to his collection come Cup Final day, when his side lost by two goals to nil against Rangers before a crowd a little shy of one hundred and twenty-eight thousand people at Hampden Park. "The Evening Times" would say of Willie's individual performance, "Fernie was the one St. Mirren forward who looked to have the imagination and the guile to outwit the Rangers defence, but he had few supporters when opportunity arose."

In the next few years, Willie would leave Love Street behind, and brief stints with Partick Thistle (although he never played a match there), Alloa Athletic, Fraserburgh, Coleraine and Bangor would follow. Having celebrated the birth of his third son Andrew, in July 1963 he finally hung up his boots and retired from the playing side of the game about a year later. However, this was not to be the end of his footballing story, as none other than his old friend and teammate Jock Stein came to him looking for a reserve coach in 1967. As one would expect, Fernie happily obliged, and over the next six years helped to progress the talents and careers of many young players, including the likes of Kenny Dalglish and Danny McGrain. As Norman told me, both Willie's personality and his attitude to training made him well liked by those coming through the ranks of the Football Club.

"Willie was popular with the young lads not only because he was an ex-player himself – one of a very fine standing whom they could look up to – but also because he was a very approachable man. He cared deeply about the lads, not just as players but as human beings. If anyone had a problem away from football, he would do his best to listen to their concerns and help to address them. With regards the football itself, his training drills were found to be enjoyable as well as beneficial. One of the things he often did was take the boys out into the car park at Celtic Park and have them face each other on an imaginary field without boundaries. The aim was to play a lot of one touch stuff, as well as encouraging players to try to beat their opponents on an individual basis. As a result, the accuracy of passing and reliability of first touches improved, but above all else, the lads were enjoying their football, and that is a critical factor in the development of any young player."

Equally, Sean Fallon, then assistant manager at the Football Club, had much praise for his colleagues Jock Stein, Neil Mochan and Willie Fernie as he recounted to author Stephen Sullivan in his biography entitled "Sean Fallon: Celtic's Iron Man": "We were one of the fittest teams in Europe and Neilly had a lot to do with that. He also was a great guy to have around the place, liked a laugh, and he was the kind of character who bounced off myself and Jock very well. We needed people like Neilly. It was the same with Willie Fernie, who came back later in the 1960s to help me with the reserves and did a great job. He was another clever coach, a lovely man and a great friend. And one thing about all of the people we had with us: they knew and loved the game…" Also, in another interview with Stephen, Sean said "Willie had been one of the best players I'd ever played with."

Midway through his six year spell as a coach at Celtic Park, Willie and Audrey's fourth and final son, David, was born in 1970. In late 1973, the opportunity to manage a senior side became available, and Willie left his tenure as a reserve coach to try life as "the boss" at Kilmarnock Football Club. Following his appointment, as telegrams and letters carrying messages (some of which I saw myself) arrived from friends old and new, Willie told one newspaper reporter: "I am delighted at this chance. I have always wanted to become a manager. I have tried for jobs before but have found they were filled by invitation. This time I didn't apply – I was invited to take the job."

Thereafter, Fernie would oversee his first match on the thirteenth of October 1973, as the then undefeated Airdrieonians – who had won eight of their nine league matches thus far that season, conceding only two goals in the process – visited Rugby Park. A resurgent Kilmarnock recorded a resounding four-nil victory that day, much to the delight of their new manager and fans alike.

Four years at Rugby Park would follow wherein Willie helped his team to two promotions. The first of these and the reactions to it were headlined as "the nicest story of success", by one newspaper, whose article continued:

"Kilmarnock 2 Stirling Albion 1 – Kilmarnock observed all the properties of promotion at Rugby Park as champagne was drunk in the dressing rooms and fans beat on the doors demanding a sight of Willie Fernie. Instead, the manager stood quietly and spoke modestly about the nicest story of success this Scottish season. "We've worked hard to get back up. Now we must start working all the harder.""

"Fernie, one of Scotland's newest managers, can afford to talk so optimistically, for everyone around Rugby Park on Saturday was anxious to spell out the facts about the effect he had on the team since joining them in October. Then, Kilmarnock were ninth in the second division and the process of decline had set in fast. Since, the side has only lost one of its last twenty-four league games, climbed up the table, and the Stirling [Albion] match saw them safely home."

During the coming seasons, Kilmarnock became one of the most exciting sides to watch in Scotland. At points, their results varied notably, but more often than not, newspapers were rather kind in their coverage of them as many people admired the style in which they tried to play their football. Superlatives such as "excellent" and "heroic" were regularly present in the printed form one week whilst words like "brave" and "unlucky" could be found following the next weekend's matches when a tie had not gone their way. An example of one correspondent's praise for Fernie's side follows.

"If I was asked to nominate the most admired team in Scotland this season I'd have no hesitation in pointing to Kilmarnock", writes Jim Blair. "There is an enterprising, forward-thinking policy about their football that rubs off in conversation with Rugby Park manager Willie Fernie. He doesn't go in for blinding people with clichés or hiding behind half-truths. If he thinks it he says it, and I admire him for it. For instance, Killie, although not yet sure of a 'Top Ten' place next season, have been honest enough to commit themselves throughout the league to open, attacking football and they've used only seventeen players doing it."

Having achieved second place in his debut season as a manager, taking Kilmarnock back to the top flight of Scottish Football, Fernie's side would finish twelfth from eighteen teams at the end of the subsequent campaign. Normally, this would have been considered a success, but due to league reconstruction, only the top ten sides that year would go forward to form the inaugural Scottish Premier Division in 1975-76. Therefore, without being relegated, Kilmarnock found themselves back in the second tier of the league system, but this did not daunt Fernie, who simply led them to the runner's-up spot once again to propel Kilmarnock into the Scottish Premier Division for the first time.

However, despite going on to record the biggest victory of the season in the Premier Division (beating rivals Ayr United by six goals to one at home), Kilmarnock often found themselves losing narrowly whilst occasionally being outclassed and were rooted to the bottom of the table by some distance come the final day of the season. Willie was sacked in the autumn of 1977 following their relegation. He subsequently spent the rest of his working life as a taxi driver.

"His dismissal from Kilmarnock was something which negatively affected my dad, although he never voiced such thoughts explicitly", Alex told me. "I would go and watch Kilmarnock's home matches when he was the boss there, and I thoroughly enjoyed it. Kilmarnock were a part time outfit in those days, and although they had their ups and downs, I do believe my father did a relatively good job on the whole. However, I think an argument could be made to suggest that he was somewhat naïve. Firstly, he continually tried to impart his philosophy to the team that football at its best is played in an entertaining fashion, and although this was admirable in one respect, it did mean that they would often lose high scoring matches by a single goal, going down by three goals to two or something similar [Motherwell beat Kilmarnock by five goals to four in a league match in November 1976, highlighting this point]. Therefore, when things were going well the fans were happy, but when runs of poor results started to mount up, some quickly turned on him. Other managers would have been more prudent – see Bertie Auld at Partick Thistle as an example – grinding out somewhat boring draws in search of single points rather than employing a win or bust mentality, but that was just the way my dad believed football should be played, and I certainly won't criticise him for that. Secondly, he never signed a set contract with Kilmarnock, so he had no protection from the sack. Again, his footballing philosophy was to blame partly, as he thought a club should never be held to ransom by their manager if he is doing a poor job. However, as such, I also think he felt those in control of Kilmarnock would show more faith in him than they did, and when he was thrown on to the managerial scrap heap, it most certainly hurt him."

Thereafter, Willie would never return to any serious involvement in the sport from which he had made his livelihood for several decades. Never one to tout himself around in search of a job, he expected any Football Club which seriously wished to have him on board in the months and years following his departure from Kilmarnock would make first contact, but nobody came. Ironically, he made more money from his taxi driving than he did as the manager of the Ayrshire side. Indeed, he proved popular with many of his customers, particularly those with an affinity for Celtic Football Club, and although the work was hard and the hours were often long and unforgiving, his family roundly believe he enjoyed the majority of his time behind the wheel.

In the middle of the 1990s, as Celtic moved into a newly built stadium and worked towards eventually stopping the threat of Rangers attaining ten consecutive Scottish league titles, Willie bought a season ticket for the first time, taking up a seat in Section 104 on the lower tier of Celtic Park's North Stand alongside his family. Here, he would witness the highs and lows which came with the territory of being a Celtic supporter, and much to the family's collective amusement, he wasn't recognised by fans as often as one might presume. The reason for this was simple, as they regularly attended matches with Alex's best friend – who also has a chapter devoted to him in this book – Gerry Cleary. Now, as Gerry would say himself, he has a rather distinctive appearance. As such, it is said that people would often approach the group whilst they walked up Kerrydale Street or stood outside the ground because they had spotted Gerry, totalling bypassing the fact that he was generally accompanied by one of the finest Celtic players of them all. Of course, Willie found all of this to be very amusing as one would expect. Putting such comedy aside though, the critical point is that Willie Fernie had come full circle by this point. He had grown from the boy with no interest in Celtic whatsoever to become of one of their greatest players, subsequently taken up a coaching role and now found himself as devoted a supporter as any other, and I believe that there is a certain beauty in that.

As he entered his late seventies, Willie's health would take a turn for the worse following on from one of Celtic's more notable domestic victories of the Gordon Strachan era, as Alex recalled: "My dad had always been a physically fit man up until that point in time, thanks in part to the athleticism of his youth and due to the fact he didn't drink alcohol or smoke. I can still remember when all of that changed though, because it came just hours after

Celtic beat Hearts when Craig Gordon infamously put the ball into his own net in the last minute [that was the fourth of November 2006, as two goals in the last five minutes turned a looming defeat into what seemed an unlikely victory for the Hoops at Celtic Park]. The next morning, my mother phoned me to say my dad wasn't well. In all honesty, I thought nothing much of it at that stage. After all, I had spent quite a bit of time with him the previous night, and he was elated at the fact Celtic had come away with the three points. However, when I made the trip to their house and saw my dad, I immediately knew something was wrong, although I must confess I wasn't sure what exactly. His neck was swollen and he was having problems speaking as he normally did, so it wasn't long before he was taken up to the hospital in an ambulance."

In the hours and days which followed, Willie and his family were informed that the elderly gentleman had ruptured his oesophagus [more commonly known as the gullet] and the prognosis was not encouraging. It remains unclear to this day exactly how Willie suffered this, but the best guess of the hospital staff was that he may have woken up to be sick during the night and resisted his gag reflex in an attempt not to vomit. Regardless, the majority of those who experience this die as a result, and it was made abundantly clear as Willie headed for the operating room that he may not survive. However, the doctors and other health-care professionals were slightly buoyed by his overall good health, and felt this gave him a fighting chance. Indeed, as Willie's family told me, had his general health been significantly worse than it was at the time which his illness occurred, the hospital staff may have made the decision not to attempt the procedure at all.

Yet, in a manner typical of the fight and determination he embodied on the football field during his playing days, Willie Fernie came through the operation to repair his oesophagus, and he would survive. However, it quickly became apparent that his life may never be the same again, as the nature of the injury which he had suffered meant that it was believed he would never be able to eat or drink in the conventional manner. He would have to be fed through a tube, but not even this would hold Fernie back, who continued his recovery and would surpass his doctor's expectations in doing so, as Alex continued his story.

"In the months following his operation, my dad started to attend a local day centre for the elderly and infirm one or two days a week. All of the men and women there were looked after and kept entertained – it got them out of the house and gave them the chance to socialise a bit – as well as giving a temporary respite to their carers, which in my father's case was my mother. The staff there had been told my dad wasn't allowed anything to eat or drink, but one day when nobody was watching he decided to take a risk and have a quick cup of tea. This could have been a very bad move, but as it turned out he was fine, suffering no ill effects whatsoever. Subsequently, he told his doctor this, and over the course of time, they tested his oesophagus out by trialling him with tea, yoghurt, soup and other fairly safe things, and my dad was fine. As it happened, he eventually got back to eating and drinking in the same way which he did previously – something we all take for granted in our daily lives – and it made a tremendous difference to him. He even got back to the football, albeit only once."

In later years though, Willie's health would begin to deteriorate once again, particularly after the death of his beloved wife Audrey in the October of 2010. Having been diagnosed with Alzheimer's Disease some years earlier, the effects of this illness began to take its toll. Mercifully, Willie never failed to recognise his family members, even during his final days, but would eventually lose his ability to speak amongst other things.

Willie Fernie died on the first of July 2011 at the age of eighty-two in Glasgow's Victoria Infirmary. His passing was met with a great deal of mourning, something only equalled by the outpouring of praise for the man from those who were fortunate enough to have known him. His funeral was held on the seventh of the month at the Linn Crematorium in the south side of Glasgow, the same venue which saw those of his old teammate Jock Stein and the man whom he once tipped to be a star of the future, Bobby Murdoch. The Celtic squad, as well as their manager and coaching staff, were touring Australia at the time of Willie's death, and were therefore unable to attend the funeral. Otherwise, it is all but certain that Neil Lennon, John Clark, Danny McGrain and several others would have been there to say their goodbyes. However, there was still an array of mourners with Celtic connections present, with the likes of Billy McNeill, Jim Craig, John Divers, Charlie Gallacher, John Fallon and Bertie Auld joining Chief Executive Peter Lawwell in attendance. Representatives from Kilmarnock Football Club were present also.

Fittingly, upon the return of the Celtic team for their first home match of the new Scottish Premier League season – which did not take place until the thirteenth of August due to the Hoops' involvement in the Dublin Super Cup – the start of play was preceded by a minute of applause for Kinglassie's departed son. Two of Willie's children (Alex and David), two of his grandchildren (Andrew and Sean), his brother in law (Norman) and another family member (Abby, Norman's grandchild) were among the fifty thousand strong crowd that afternoon who watched Celtic put five goals past their visitors, Dundee United. Alex described the memorial for his father as follows: "Nobody looking at me amongst the throngs of people during those moments would have known I was any relation to Willie Fernie. The tears weren't streaming down my face or anything, but that's not to say it was not an incredibly poignant experience. I listened to the stadium announcer go through his introduction as the players gathered around the centre circle, with it being said that my dad was "one of the finest players ever to have worn the green and white Hoops", but it was only when the minutes applause began that the hairs on the back of my neck stood up. To see tens of thousands of people at Celtic Park rise as one in acclamation of any player is impressive, but when they do so for your dad it's something else entirely. As his pictures circulated on the big screens inside the stadium, I was filled simply with immense pride. There was nothing sad about that moment, it gave me great comfort and I'm thankful to the Football Club for remembering my dad in that way."

Reflecting on his brother in law towards the conclusion of our discussions, Norman told me: "Willie played football the way that it should be played, fairly but with great determination and an abundance of skill. As an individual player, he liked to entertain the paying supporters and joining Celtic allowed him to do that. Such a footballing ideology likely contributed to his eventual downfall at Kilmarnock as we have said, but no matter. He was quick on the ball and boasted a powerful shot, whilst his ability to dance around players on the byline before passing to a teammate was sublime. Powerful and precise in his tackling and in possession of a fine vision for passing, he was the perfect player in many senses. Honestly, when he returned to Celtic Park for his second playing stint there, some people would actually phone the Club in advance of matches to see whether or not he was going to be playing before deciding whether or not to attend. I genuinely regard him in the very highest echelons of the individuals I have seen represent Celtic Football Club over the years. He was special. That aside, he was a very good husband to my dear sister Audrey and I have a great admiration and respect for him as a man because of that."

During my correspondence with Mary, I asked her finally for her overall thoughts on Willie. She said: "I am truly very proud of my brother for doing so well. The fact that his name is still well known within the ranks of not only the Celtic support, but of Scottish football fans in general, is testament to the fact he was a special player. My parents knew he was going to make it when he joined Celtic, and I know that they, just like my other brothers, shared this pride in him also. We all went to watch him occasionally and quickly became Celtic supporters ourselves, although my eldest brother Andrew followed him more than the rest of us. However, great footballer though he undoubtedly was, above all else Bill was just one of my brothers, and I loved him fiercely for that. He was such a gentle natured man and a true sportsman."

During his two spells at Celtic Park as a player, Willie Fernie made three hundred and seventeen competitive appearances for Celtic Football Club, scoring a total of seventy-four times. In a similar manner to that of some other players from his era, his individual talent really warranted a greater medal haul than the single League winners' medal, one Scottish Cup winners' medal, two Scottish League Cup medals and one Coronation Cup winners' medal which he did win, but let it be known he remained very proud of these achievements nonetheless. From a footballing point of view, his name will undoubtedly be remembered forevermore amongst the ranks of the Celtic legends, but to those closer to him, he will not only be this, but a loving brother, father and grandfather to an incredible family also.

Having provided the assists to the winning goals in both the Coronation Cup Final of 1953 and the Scottish Cup Final of 1954, it was very apt that on perhaps Celtic's greatest day during Willie's era as a player, he was allowed the opportunity to put the icing on the cake by scoring the seventh goal in the Celts' largest victory over Rangers – particularly after delivering such an exceptional individual showing. Speaking personally, it has been a truly special honour not only to be given the opportunity to write about a gentleman of such historical importance as the wonderful Willie Fernie, but to have been entrusted by his family to do so. I am immensely grateful to them and everyone else who assisted me in this regard. With that, I shall leave you with a few words of the famous song recounting that gloriously sunny afternoon at Hampden Park, just miles from where Willie would finally go to his rest.

> *"Another goal for Glasgow Celtic;*
> *Another victory for the cause;*
> *Another reason to be giving;*
> *Another cheer just for the Bhoys;*
> *For if I live to be a hundred;*
> *I'll never have such fun;*
> *As the day that Glasgow Celtic;*
> *Beat the Rangers seven-one!"*

"The Chronicles of Willie Maley: "Why J.H. McLaughlin Hurriedly Left Mass""

"By Willie Maley, Celtic F.C. Manager"

"Of the great and good men whom I was privileged to join with in that famous first year, I would give pride of place to John Glass, whose photo hangs above me as I write, and it seems but yesterday since I heard him invite me to throw in my lot with the Celts. A man of whom Celtic will be ever proud. To have any idea of the work John could, and did, do for the club he loved, one had to live with him to realise it. For years he thought of nothing but Celtic. He was at it from morning till night. In the early days the men brought to town had to get work, and, of course, John Glass had to do that. If a fellow had to be persuaded he was coming to the best team in Scotland Glass could do that in a jiffy, whilst many a fellow's fortune was made right away once he had listened to the voice of the charmer in the person of the burly Celt. As straight as a die, he never hesitated to speak his mind, and I always remember him on the occasion of that first Scottish final, in replying to the toast of the losers, how we who knew him, and, knowing how he felt, understood how much he meant when he told his hearers the Cup was only delayed in its journey to Parkhead. Poor John had his heart set on the Cup that day like many more."

"A Faithful Servant"

"For nineteen years we had in John Glass the most faithful clubman any club ever had, and one who never grumbled at any job as long as it was for the club. He was ever the Parliamentarian, and would insist on everything being done in a constitutional way, but on occasion his temper would burst out at some outrageous proceeding, and the delinquent would know all about it. I remember on the occasion of the Glasgow Cup tie in 1889, when Queen's Park beat us, how he tackled a cash-taker who was reported to him, as one of his nominees, to be the worse of liquor on duty. John L. Sullivan [the first heavyweight champion of gloved boxing] could not have handled this man better than our "Grand Old Man" did on that occasion, and I think eventually it did the culprit good."

"Of the others, we had in James McKay, ultimately to be the treasurer and ground construction manager, another unassuming yet very enthusiastic member. Jamie wrought away quietly yet well, taking the complaints and praise all as one. The present ground was built under his supervision, and whilst we know that too much money was "buried" practically in the now famous pitch, that is lost sight of, in his case at any rate, by the untiring devotion to duty we always had from Jamie."

"The others were all grafters. One John McDonald used to put us players through it with a wonderful bottle of medicine he had which was guaranteed to spring us a yard or two each time we took it. It did. Once some of the boys dodged John by throwing it out of the window and screwing their faces. It only occurred once. After that John saw it go down properly before he had done with each patient. I personally have tender memories of this, my first football medicine."

"J.H. McLaughlin came more into the limelight after he assumed the treasurership in 1890. He was organist in these days at St. Mary's, Abercromby Street. I remember how once, after a big game at Celtic Park, a meeting was held in the offices there after the game, which was prolonged till the late hours. Our treasurer, who always took the money home, forgot all about the cash, which lay securely in this little wooden office unforgotten until, as the treasurer was giving of his best at late Mass, he suddenly remembered the cash, and sudden illness necessitated his retirement from the choir, and a rush up to the field relieved his mind when he found the cash safe and sound."

"Friendship with Dunbar"

"Michael Dunbar was a native of Busby, and therefore a close neighbour of ours. I got to know him in the games between Busby and Cathcart, and the personal friendship made then developed with the formation of the Celts. Wherever we travelled in these early days we two were bedfellows. Always fond of practical joking (of a sensible kind), I have been the victim, with others, of [his] native wit. I remember once on a journey to England in our first year, Mike and I were enjoying the comforts of a good bed after an overnight journey, when a knock came to the door and a voice announced letters for the secretary. I, lying at the front of the bed, was too comfortable to rise and open the door, and shouted out I would get them when I came down to breakfast. My bedfellow, however, insisted on my rising, and when I refused he planted his feet in the small of my back and I found myself dumped on to the floor to the detriment of my bones. Journeying on the next night, we found ourselves similarly placed the following morning, but I had taken the wise precaution of being at the back of the bed and next to the wall. I thought it was the turn of Mike to get up and open the door for the letters. I coaxed him, but he was obdurate. I planted my back against the wall and my feet against his back to give him my dose of the previous morning. Unfortunately the bed was a light one, and instead of shoving him out on the floor, I shoved the bed along with him and I fell down the back of the bed next to the wall."

"Dunbar, as a player, was more of a grafter than the limelight man, and he was of the hardy type so needful in the old days. He was very clever with his shoulder work, and the old-fashioned hip charge had a rare exploiter in the Cartvale man. I remember him in a Glasgow Cup tie with Queen's Park, where McArn, then one of the Queen's strongest halves, and a real strong one at that, opposed to Dunbar had been having our lot out in great style. It had to be stopped, and Dunbar took the job in hand. His solid shoulder "dunts" shook up the sturdy Queen's half, and when the "hip" movement came into play McArn was soon brought to absolute impotence."

"In my football travels I have met very many what I would term real working men, whose foresight and solid thinking powers were most marked, and in this class I place my friend and co-official, M. Dunbar. Slow to express an opinion, he never gives one which he cannot stand to and back up. In many of our tightest corners, where sound advice is needed…he has brought to our counsels a long head and a well-balanced thought which has been invaluable."

"Tom E. Maley's Worth"

"Of the four players mentioned, P. Gallagher, J. Colman, T.E. Maley and M. Dunbar – all four did a lot for the club as players. My brother Tom, in his early days, was a most useful committee man."

"I will be told I omitted my own name from this list of player-committeemen. I did so purposely. I have always considered myself extremely fortunate to have been amongst the elect in these days, and it proves the little bits of luck that come one's way at times. It was Tom the club wanted when I was brought in as an extra, and it was my good fortune that the scarcity of players enabled me, a young, untried colt, to be dumped in amongst a team of the class they were. I may have developed quickly, but undoubtedly the great men I had beside me were chiefly responsible for that. I was keen, however, and I was very proud when I felt I could hold up my end with some of them when my day came along, as it ultimately did. Certainly if I lacked the ability, none of them could beat me in enthusiasm, and when one looks back on the life of our club, it has been this note of enthusiasm that has carried us up to the honours which we have achieved, and in which I am delighted to say, we can stand comparison with any club in existence."

"The Great Dan Doyle"

"Another giant of the game then developing was Dan Doyle, at that time with East Stirlingshire, and latterly with the Hibs, to pass from there to Grimsby Town. Dan, even then, was a great man, and later one to be feared by the stoutest when it came to a tackle."

"My notes may, at times, be forced by circumstances to take me off the sort of beaten track. Like the flowing tide, which first fills in the deep side pools before getting into its long, steady flow, so my tale must, until I have reached the straight run of the Celtic club's yearly doings, be allowed slight digressions. Our official list of games played starts with August first of that year with a tie against Abercorn in the Exhibition Cup, and it is here I want to say a few plain words as to that famous episode in our career."

"Our rise in Scottish football was received by the public with anything but favour. In all the games played off Celtic Park up to this [point] we had been met with scant courtesy, and had been howled at on more than one occasion as "professionals". Time has proved many things, and one is that the taunt might have been more widely distributed with truth. The conditions of the day in football, was in our minds, sufficient excuse for rule breaking."

"The Exhibition Cup was played for by all the leading clubs in the West of Scotland, and in concluding arrangements for the competition we got into loggerheads with the Exhibition Committee, who were inclined to run things with a high hand. Our people, with the strongly marked combative spirit of their forefathers, would have none of this, and were met by a threat of reprisals as to the club's professionalism."

"Well, our people, in the Exhibition Cup case, were just in the humour for a fight, and asked for it, but better counsels prevailed, and we played in the Cup ties. During the course of these games the treatment given our team was a disgrace to the game as they were abused on all sides, and when, at the final game, when we were beaten by a team made up of Cowlairs, Queen's Park, Renton etc., by two to nil, our lot were jeered at and insulted in disgraceful fashion. Our management received then the real stimulus to make the club, which was then so unjustly derided, a power in the land, and one which would make the same class respect them as they now scoffed at them. I think I can safely say we have done so."

"Our lot, strung up for the [next] occasion [on which we faced Cowlairs less than fortnight later in the Scottish Cup], struck what is now a traditional Celtic game of accurate short passing, and after the first ten minutes Cowlairs were absolutely swamped, our boys winning by eight goals to nil, and that with Tom Duff, the Cowlairs goalkeeper, playing a marvellous game.

It was a case of the cat and mouse, right through, and I can still see in my mind's eye the white shirted Cowlairs players running after our lads, who played that day in a specially provided all-green jersey as [an alternative to] the colours which we were playing in that time – white shirt with green collar and a Celtic badge on the left breast."

"The enthusiasm generated amongst our crowd by this victory brought us great gates thereafter and also a new clientele for the game. I have always held that our inception gave an impetus to the game at that time which sent it bounding along afresh when it seemed to be slipping backwards."

"Nothing Else Even Comes Close"

On the first of February 2015, Celtic faced the current Ibrox club for the first time in the semi-finals of the Scottish League Cup. This chapter is not about that match nor indeed that football club, but the story of a man who, thanks to a particular series of events – some of which were out-with his control – saw Celtic that afternoon for the first time in his life. As it happens, I also had some direct involvement in this tale, so whilst the majority of this chapter will discuss our protagonist's experiences, I will chip in with a few of my own memories and reflections when an appropriate moment presents itself.

Matt Donohue (or Matthew Evan Donohue to give him his full name) is a fourth generation American citizen hailing from the borough of Andover, New Jersey. With a population of less than one thousand, it nestles quietly in the hills halfway between New York City and the state border with Pennsylvania. The "Big Apple" is situated about fifty miles away from Matt's home, and with that in mind, it is not surprising to think that the majority of live sporting events he has attended have taken place there.

As we began our interviews, Matt told me: "I've seen the Yankees win the World Series, been to N.B.A. Finals with the Knicks and watched some of the more vicious hockey games, including Stanley Cup Finals supporting the Islanders, but none of those touched what I experienced in Glasgow. It was unlike anything I'd ever seen before. When I look back on it now and compare it to the sports on show over here, it just reaffirms the fact that nothing else even comes close."

Born on the twenty-seventh of March 1980, Matt is not a member of a Celtic mad family. In fact, it was only truly in the few years immediately preceding his birth that his uncle, Robert Donohue, had begun to develop an interest himself in following events across the Atlantic Ocean at Parkhead. Reflecting on his uncle and the significant influence he had on him, Matt said:

"My Uncle Robert was born in Brooklyn in the mid-1950s, but spent the majority of his live as a resident of Breezy Point – a well-known Irish area – over in Queens. He was a typical New Yorker in a lot of ways, but the sports which he held a passion for would have been seen to be fairly atypical back in his day. He liked cycling and racquetball, but the bulk of his devotion was always reserved for soccer."

"I can't say this with absolute certainty, but I presume his love of Celtic really grew out of the connections he had with Ireland and the Irish community in and around New York. During his life, he would travel annually to the old country, and to my knowledge he visited each one of the thirty-two counties on the island at one point or another during his life. He simply adored the place. His strongest family connections were seated in Armagh, and as the years progressed, he would bring back more and more about Celtic in the form of newspaper clippings and the like. I can still remember him excitedly opening up the New York Times every Tuesday in the 1980s, digging about in the depths of the middle pages in search of the tiny text which contained the Scottish football scores from the previous weekend, and the hollers of delight or the wails of despair which often followed tended to be indicative of whatever the result had been. The clippings he would bring back from Ireland were mostly match reports the family had kept for him, so he'd only find out exactly what happened in most games on a yearly basis. Of course, the introduction of television and internet coverage saw an end to these charades, but there was a certain level of romanticism attached to them."

As the years passed, Matt grew to hold a similar interest in this footballing side from Scotland, spurred on not only by his uncle but also by the fact he began to play the sport himself as a child. As has already been referred to, the increasing availability of coverage and news, both via television stations and the internet grew to the point where nowadays Matt hasn't failed to watch any of Celtic's competitive matches in the last six or seven years.

"Well over a decade ago now, I can remember travelling into Manhattan to watch Celtic play European matches. The first one which springs to mind was the four-three victory over Juventus, but that was surreal not only for the scoreline but for other matters besides. This fixture took place at the end of October 2001 and it was the first time I'd made the trip into the city after the events of the eleventh of September that year. There was a very odd vibe about the place. However, watching a match such as that in the Supporters' Club soon took my mind off things, at least temporarily. I can also recall seeing us win two-nil at Anfield en route to Seville – that was a great night, the place was jumping."

Robert Donohue passed away in 2007, but did live long enough to see Neil Lennon, an Armagh man, rise to the role of Club captain at Parkhead, something which Robert took great satisfaction in. Despite spending a significant amount of time over the years in Ireland, he never visited Scotland and did not have the pleasure of watching Celtic play live, something one can only presume he would have enjoyed immensely. Therefore, I feel it is safe to say he would have been very happy that his nephew and footballing protégé Matthew would go on to see the Celts for himself. Matt explains:

"I suppose I knew fairly early on in my life that I wanted to see Celtic at some point, but when you're still a kid or a young adult, dreams like that are restricted by a lack of finance more than anything else, but the desire was there regardless. I'd heard the atmosphere generated at big games on the television, but it was only really when YouTube grew to prominence that I started to get a better idea of what it was really like on location. Nothing can replicate being there in person, but watching a camera held by someone within the crowd as opposed to someone high up on a television gantry does give you a more personal viewpoint on things. Spending hours of my time after big fixtures watching video after video just added to my urge to make the trip someday, and several years later when I found myself able to do so, I made up my mind and quickly decided just to go for it. I sorted out dates which suited my work – and indeed, my wife Meg – and booked up."

When Matt made his travel arrangements in the autumn of 2014, he was set to see Celtic play a league match against Kilmarnock, but as fate would have it, the Hoops' progression to the latter rounds of the Scottish League Cup meant this match would be temporarily postponed and replaced with a semi-final tie from the aforementioned competition. Had Celtic gone up against either of the other two semi-finalists that year, Aberdeen or Dundee United, it likely wouldn't have been too difficult a task for Matt to turn up a ticket for the game. However, as it happened, the draw would put Celtic and the current Ibrox side on a collision course for the first time, making any hopes of going to the match somewhat remote, even by Matt's own admission.

Indeed, the changes in the fixture list also gave Matt one or two other things to think about at home, as he explained: "My wife has never had any great interest in sports, let alone soccer, but she knows I adore it so she puts up with me as best she can. Initially, she was very supportive of the notion of my trip to Scotland – after all, she is aware how much Celtic Football Club means to me – and although this support never wavered, I would be telling a lie if I claimed the prospect of me being in Glasgow for a derby match didn't concern her at all. When she discovered who our opponents would be that weekend, she told me she was a little worried about the prospects of any potential violence, and to be honest, when I consider the way that Glasgow derbies have been portrayed in the media in the past, with the history they have developed, both true and false, I could understand where she was coming from. However, it didn't put me off one bit. Our opponents were almost irrelevant to me, I was going to make that journey to see one team and one team only, Celtic."

Over the years, I have been fortunate enough to speak to many Celtic fans who live around the world, some situated in particularly far flung areas one may not immediately think the Celtic support would be found within. I have had the pleasure of meeting a small number of these men and women in person after they had flown thousands upon thousands of miles to visit Glasgow, with two standing out in my mind above all others. The first of these individuals was Sean McGinlay from Adelaide, South Australia, whose story is told in my previous book, with the second being, of course, Matt Donohue. Now, much links these two men, with their infectious love of Celtic Football Club and their willingness to travel great distances at significant expense to watch them play being the most obvious. However, the other common factor which they share is perhaps not so immediately apparent, for prior to their trips I spent a significant amount of time speaking to each of them, providing them with advice on all the usual queries visitors may have, whilst also offering to give them a sporting tour of Glasgow. Both of the men accepted my invitation, and as such the second common thread that they share is that I spent time with each of them, driving them around the city and showing them many of the footballing sights most tourists simply bypass.

Of course, both of these excursions were tremendously enjoyable from my point of view, and I shall discuss Matt's thoughts on his trip around the city momentarily, but please allow me to make what I consider to be an important point first of all. Prior to my online involvement with the Celtic fan base, I had not had much interaction with supporters based abroad. In this respect, I must confess I did not appreciate them nor their love for our Football Club to the degree which I do nowadays. Indeed, it was the time which I had spent with Sean in a previous year which ultimately led to me making the decision to offer Matt my ticket for the Scottish League Cup semi-final set to be played during his time in Glasgow.

I felt conflicted about the match for a variety of reasons which I would imagine many of you can understand, and I therefore felt it would be best to do something positive with the ticket which I had been allocated, and I am very glad that I made the choice which I did. Regardless, I now appreciate my relative proximity to Celtic Park all the more and that is something which all of us who live within a few miles of our Football Club's home must do. I also consider myself very lucky to own the season ticket which I have now held for over a decade. After all, many supporters only see Celtic Park in the flesh every few years, and the tale of Robert Donohue just proves that there are some never fortunate enough to lay their eyes upon it nor hear the cacophony of noise regularly produced there. We must savour our time watching Celtic, because all things – people included – eventually pass.

Having decided on his holiday for the year, Matt did not only travel to Glasgow, instead flying from New York to Dublin before spending a few days travelling around the island of Ireland. This included a visit to Solitude, home of Cliftonville Football Club, whom Celtic faced in a Champions League qualifier only a few years ago. Thereafter, he flew from Belfast to Glasgow on the morning of the thirty-first of January, probably spending less time in the air than I did in my car negotiating the early morning traffic on the outskirts of Scotland's largest city. However, unlike that which Matt travelled in, my vehicle was not full of men and women travelling to support the other team set to contest the semi-final.

Despite having spoken to Matt at some length prior to his arrival in Scotland, I must confess I was unsure exactly what he would be like as I made my way through Glasgow International Airport's terminal building in search of him. Of course, any nerves which I may have had quickly vanished as I spotted the man in question sitting on a bench outside the domestic arrivals hall and proceeded to introduce myself. Immediately, the warmth of the American gentleman shone through, and it was clear to me that we were going to enjoy the day ahead of us.

Subsequently, having clambered into my car, we made our way past the nearby St. Mirren Park briefly before following the motorway towards the city. It was then that I took a slip road and turned to our left, immediately bringing Ibrox stadium into view. Recalling that moment, Matt said: "As much disdain as I have felt for the clubs which have played at Ibrox over the years, I couldn't justify coming all the way to Glasgow – particularly to then go on a footballing tour of the city – and not take a trip over there. Clearly, the stadium has seen better days, and removing my green tinted spectacles momentarily, a significant amount of investment appears to be required to bring the place up to scratch. We parked the car and went for a quick stroll around, and although it's not somewhere I ever intend to go and watch a match, I appreciate the fact I had the opportunity to see it for myself. After all, it's a site of some historical significance, not only for Rangers, but for the other clubs – as well as international sides – who have triumphed there over the years."

Thereafter, only a short stop at Matt's hotel in the Gorbals interceded before the tour began in earnest, as we headed out to the East End of the city via the Gallowgate. My companion seemed impressed by the plethora of Celtic bars there, as well as the famous sign fronting the Barrowland Ballroom, before we turned into Abercromby Street. Matt recognised St. Mary's immediately, as we proceeded to head inside.

"Visiting St. Mary's Church in the Calton – the birthplace of Celtic Football Club – meant a great deal personally", Matt told me. "It might sound a bit over the top, but really, if my old uncle could have seen me there he would have been over the moon. It was early on a Saturday morning – there was nobody other than myself and Frank around – and as I stood there in the entrance hall, gazing through the glass before me into the grandeur of the chapel itself, it was very apparent there was something special about the place. I don't know whether it was the atmosphere, the history or a combination of both, but being there had quite an effect on me. It was then, after Frank asked me to look down, that I realised I had been standing on the mosaic floor mural commemorating our Football Club's foundation on the church grounds. Seeing that added a certain level of realism to the whole thing – after all, where else could you ever find a mention of football built into a place of worship? It was a great privilege to visit St. Mary's."

Having left Abercromby Street behind us, I drove Matt along the remainder of the Gallowgate, passing north of Celtic Park before making our way down to St. Peter's Cemetery, Dalbeth, on London Road. With the home of Celtic Football Club still visible in the distance, I set about my best attempt at mimicking a Celtic Graves Society style tour of the notable individuals who rest there. This began with the likes of early stars Dan Doyle and Barney Battles Snr., before progressing past the memorial to all those previously involved with the Football Club and coming to an end by the graveside of Celtic's greatest ever goalscorer and manager for two decades, James Edward McGrory.

There was one only place to go next, but with Celtic Park on the horizon to the left, I intentionally headed out the cemetery and swung the car to the right. This may strike some of you as odd, but my thinking surrounding it was really rather simple – I wanted Matt to enjoy the best possible view of Celtic Park as he made his way there for the first time. Therefore, after a quick detour, we turned from Dalmarnock Road on to the Clyde Gateway (which is the new dual carriageway style road approaching the ground from the south, passing the Sir Chris Hoy Velodrome) and Celtic Park appeared in all of its glory. Matt wouldn't contest the fact he was open mouthed at this point, taking it all in as we covered the several hundred yards still between us and the ground itself. However, what Matt did not know at this stage was that I had previously informed a friend at Celtic Park of his trip to the city, but I'll leave Matt to best describe the events which followed.

"Prior to travelling to Glasgow, one of my main aims was to see Celtic Park for myself and to go on a tour of the stadium if this was at all possible. However, when I tried to book a place on a tour latterly, I discovered they were all full. After all, clearly I was not the only travelling supporter present in the city that weekend. With hindsight, I should have asked someone to secure a spot for me much earlier rather than waiting until the week of my trip. Mercifully though, none of that mattered, as Frank had already arranged something else entirely. Now, I won't mention the individual in question, particularly since very few others would know who they are, but they truly have my undying gratitude for the kindness they showed me that day."

"I was given a private tour of the stadium, accessing not only the arena itself, but the dressing rooms and the box which hangs from the roof of the South Stand also. I had the chance to see the trophies in the boardroom and the opportunity to sit in Ronny Deila's seat in the home dugout, but the most memorable moment of what was a very special experience was walking down the tunnel and out into the stadium for the first time. You have to understand, I had seen this place endless times from almost every conceivable angle over previous years via television coverage and the internet, but to actually stand there for myself and drink it all in was something indescribable. I toured several baseball stadiums in North America as a child whenever I was away somewhere with my parents, and although I enjoyed it, almost all of the stadia involved housed teams I had no emotional connection whatsoever to, and with that in mind, you may be able to grasp how difficult I found the task of vocalising what my visit to Celtic Park truly meant to me. I just hope that one day I will be able to see a match there in person too."

Speaking personally, it was very satisfying to see Matt's dream of visiting Celtic Park come to fruition. It was immediately apparent how much it meant to him and, with a glint in his eye, we carried on our tour of the city's footballing sights. Next up on our list of destinations was the eerie Cathkin Park, once the proud home of Third Lanark Athletic Club and, prior to that, the second site of Hampden Park. This gave Matt, as indeed it does with any other visitors, a glimpse into the world of old football stadia. For those of you who may not be aware, Cathkin Park is now a public park in Glasgow. Although the old stand may be gone leaving one side of the football pitch empty, the other three sides of the field – once home to tens of thousands of spectators – are still covered in terracing and crush barriers. Granted, much of this is weathered and indeed some of it is completely overgrown with trees and plant life, but more than enough of the old fixtures remain to make it abundantly clear it was once a football stadium. As such, it is a rare opportunity to stand on a large terrace such as this, and indeed it is an even more exclusive privilege to stroll out on to the playing surface upon which – for example – Celtic defeated Rangers by two goals to nil to win the Scottish Cup Final of 1899. As Matt aptly put it, "When you stand here in this historic place, you can almost feel the ghosts around you."

Following thereon, trips past Hampden Park and to the graveside of Celtic's first manager, Willie Maley, took place before I parked my car in the South Side and both Matt and I took a taxi back into the city centre. Prior to Matt's visit, I had been invited to attend a pub gathering of several Celtic supporters with whom I am dear friends, and as one would expect, when they heard an American Celt was to be in town that weekend, they were all keen for me to bring him along. Over the next few hours, Matt was treated to Glaswegian hospitality at its finest, with a few drinks and a nice meal being heartily enjoyed by all those in attendance. Midway through that evening's festivities, I would say goodbye to Matt Donohue. Clearly, he did not wish to risk having to endure a hangover whilst watching Celtic for this first time, and I applaud him for what was a sensible move. Anyway, before continuing on with Matt's trip to Glasgow, allow me to say this – it was a great privilege to spend a day in my American friend's company, I enjoyed it immensely and I look forward to seeing him again in the future. Like an almost countless number of other men, women and children, he may not be your typical Celtic supporter in terms of his locale, but in every other sense, we are one and the same. Matt recalls his experiences of the next day:

"I decided to leave for the stadium fairly early, maybe an hour and a half or so before the match was due to kick-off. I'd been shown the route to take from my hotel in the Gorbals, so I was confident I knew where I was headed. That said, I have to say that whilst I was never worried for my own safety, I did have my guard up to some extent for the first portion of the journey just in case. After all, I was in a foreign city for a sporting event of some magnitude. Anyway, as I walked by "The Brazen Head" there was a queue of people standing outside waiting on the place opening. An Irishman and his twelve year old son were also walking past the pub, and I got talking to them as they did so. I asked if they would mind heading to the stadium together and I think once they heard my accent they thought it would be a good idea to keep me pointed in the right direction. That aside though, they were really nice folks, and when we eventually went our separate ways I could see Hampden Park a short distance away. At this point, thousands of people bedecked in green and white were headed for the ground, and the crowd soon swelled to such a degree that we all found ourselves walking down the middle of Aikenhead Road."

"Thus far, nothing had happened which I considered to be particularly out of the ordinary, but that would change a few moments later as a small van [which we would refer to as a minibus] clearly destined for the other end of the stadium drove by. I'd seen a few buses carrying blue-clad supporters earlier on my walk, and so this didn't perturb me, until I saw the back door of the moving vehicle swing open. The lad hanging out of the rear hurled what I can only describe as a racial slur at the Celtic supporters walking nearby, and as you can understand, this wasn't met with a particularly friendly reaction. As the van accelerated away and the few people who had decided to give some sort of chase abandoned their efforts, this event simply reminded me where I was and what I was about to attend. After all, it would be almost unthinkable for someone to be able to do such a thing and get away with it outside a major sporting event in the United States."

As he made his way into Hampden Park – up the stairwells which lead to the plateau at the top of the so-called "Celtic end" and down on to the seating areas on the other side of the mound – Matt was one of the first few thousand to take their places in the stands. However, as the teams warmed up and the turnstiles continued to spin, the crowd grew until the stadium was at its modern day capacity of just under fifty-one thousand. At this point, Matt turned around and began to appreciate not only the scale of the occasion, but also the fact that his dream of seeing Celtic in the flesh was about to become a reality.

"A few minutes before kick-off, I stood midway up the stand behind the goal and did a full turn on the spot, drinking in the sights and the sounds before me. Previous to that, I'd spend a lot of time observing the players, spotting all these guys I'd seen on the television on countless occasions and watching them go through their paces with the coaching staff. That alone gave me quite a thrill. It was only when they all disappeared down the tunnel for their final pre-match preparations that the focus of my gaze altered to the Celtic support around me, and to say the sight of them standing there in their tens of thousands was magnificent would be an understatement. In that moment, to realise I was part of them, not simply in spirit but in person, was something really quite special. It meant a lot to me, and once again I couldn't help but think my uncle would have been smiling down on us all."

Describing the match itself briefly from his viewpoint behind the goal at the "Celtic end", Matt continued:

"The game itself was quite nervy for the first ten minutes or so, thanks in part to the terrible condition of the playing surface, but when Leigh Griffiths scored, any air of concern was lifted from the collective shoulders of the Celtic support. Thereafter, Kris Commons almost burst the back of the net with the shot which he struck from just outside the box, and it was party time on the eastern slopes of Hampden Park. I was left breathless hugging the people next to me amidst the celebrations, but I wasn't complaining, it was fantastic. Oddly, I heard very little of the supporters at the other end of the ground that day. One or two outbursts of singing were audible early on, but once their team fell behind they were seemingly silent for large parts, although that may just have been due to the din the Celtic support were making. After all, it would be an understatement to describe it as a racket."

"The singing was non-stop, and louder than anything I've ever heard at a sporting fixture – it was truly incredible, and I lost my voice temporarily. I have to reiterate though, my enjoyment of that day had nothing to do with our opponents nor their fans, but rather everything to do with Celtic – the players, the manager and the supporters. It was special."

"Come the end of the match, I was elated. Not only had I seen Celtic, but they had won. My only regret, small though it may be, is that both goals that day were scored in the first half when the Celts were attacking the goal at the far end of the field, but no matter. I had been told in the pub the day prior to the match that if Celtic won, I'd virtually be able to fly back to North America under my own steam – that's how good it would make me feel – and that turned out to be the case. The adrenaline rush produced by the result lasted for quite some time, but the smile on my face resulting from the whole experience stayed there for a lot longer, I can absolutely assure you of that."

After the fixture, Matt was not one of the thousands of Celtic supporters who went out on the town to celebrate their team's place in the final of the Scottish League Cup, nor did he have time to be, as he was set to fly back to Belfast later that evening. However, he did leave his hotel in the Gorbals briefly in search of a quick meal. Not being a culinary hotspot, his location limited his choices somewhat, and he eventually plumped for a small café which remained open into the early evening. There, he would be treated to a glimpse into a humorous exchange of opinions within one Glaswegian family unit, with stereotypes, swearing and much more rolled into one. Again, I'll leave it to Mr. Donohue himself to recall the events which followed.

"I ordered my food and sat down in the knowledge I would likely have to wait a while for it be prepared, and I was the only customer present in this little café. Three staff members were working, an older gentleman and two young women, whom I presumed to be a father and his two daughters as there was a resemblance between them. Everything seemed to be relatively normal at first, and then, for some reason unknown to me, an argument of sorts started. It seemed to begin fairly sedately over something small, but quickly escalated to another level entirely. Within seconds they were shouting and bawling at each other – you know, really going for it – swearing blindly and calling each other every conceivable name with impressive regularity."

"Of course, I had to contain my laughter and pretend to be staring out of the window as all of this went on – after all, I didn't want to become the centre of attention – but it really was quite amusing. I've worked in catering previously, and I know from experience it's not an uncommon occurrence for tempers to become frayed, particularly if someone has made an error or if something has gone awry. It struck me as if such arguments happened in the café often, as midway through it, the father strolled over with my food, presented it politely, telling me to enjoy as he did so, before returning to his war of words without skipping a beat. Latterly, it all died down and returned to relative normality, and all of them wished me well as I said my goodbyes. Let me tell you, whilst the food was decent, the entertainment was excellent."

Readying himself for the start of his long haul back to the United States via Belfast and Dublin, Matt climbed into a taxi bound for Glasgow International Airport as his time in Scotland came to a close. In an attempt to strike up some conversation, he asked the driver whether or not he had been busy today, and although his answer was "yes", the discussion did not unfold in the way many would expect.

"I think everyone who has ever been in a taxi, be it in Glasgow, New York or any other city, knows that there are some drivers who are far more talkative than others", Matt said. "Anyway, after this guy told me he had indeed been busy, he made some vague remark about the football match which had been played in the city earlier in the day, and he really didn't seem to be too happy about it. Naturally, I presumed that had he been a Celtic fan, the smile would have been covering his face from ear to ear, and so I quickly made the deduction that this gentleman was either a supporter of the other side or didn't have any time for football whatsoever. A few seconds later, once he had taken a short time to consider my accent, he asked me why I was in Glasgow. Not wanting to create a potential for disagreement, I panicked ever so slightly and just said I was here to visit the Kelvingrove Art Gallery. He rolled his eyes a little, presumably thinking I was a just somewhat eccentric American, but I think it was the sensible option on my part. Again, had he been a Celt, I expect he would have spent every conceivable second which remained of the journey in an attempt to indoctrinate me into all things Celtic, as well as rejoicing at the fact his side had made it to the Scottish League Cup Final that afternoon but again, as this did not occur, it suggests my initial suspicions may well have been accurate."

Upon Matt's return home to New Jersey, Meg, understandably happy that her husband had not only enjoyed himself thoroughly but had also came back in one piece, proceeded to quiz him in more detail regarding the logistics of the fixture he had witnessed than the match itself.

"As I said earlier", Matt told me, "Meg has never held any great interest in sport, but she was intrigued to know more about how the tie had been policed and the fans kept apart – that kind of thing. I could have seen the greatest goal scored in the history of the sport that weekend, and it wouldn't have peaked her interest whatsoever, but the event as a whole most certainly did.

Segregating supporters at sporting events seems like a very alien phenomenon to the vast majority of people in North America, my wife included. It's just not something that we do here, thanks largely to the fact there are very few sporting rivalries evenly remotely intense enough here to warrant it. Anyway, she wanted to know all about the relevant police operations, with everything from how the different groups of fans are physically separated through to whether there were helicopters, horse patrols or riot police present in and around the stadium. One could be forgiven for thinking I had visited a warzone rather than a football match based on that stream of questioning, but all of that just seemed to appeal to her. Thankfully, not all of those I have since spoken to about my time in Glasgow have leapt to such conclusions, with many of them focusing solely on the sporting elements."

Nowadays, some months after Matt's trip, those of his work colleagues with an interest in football have long since interrogated him about every aspect of his expedition, as he recounted. "I suppose the best way in which I can quantify how they all reacted to my trip was that they felt I'd been to an exotic, far flung country to see a football match. In a sense, I suppose I had. I guess something comparable would be if someone from Glasgow went to Belgrade to see Partizan face Red Star; or to Buenos Aires to watch Boca Juniors take on River Plate. It just seems so unusual to them. Whilst some Americans are great travellers, others rarely, if ever, leave the boundaries of the United States. After all, if you want to go on vacation, the country is so large it offers plenty of options to suit your individual preferences. Regardless, to have been to Scotland is considered quite a big deal, and to have seen Celtic in person – for those with an appreciation of football anyway – is on another level altogether. When I get reactions like that to my stories, it just reinforces my feeling of good fortune."

"In closing, I can only thank the Celtic support and the people of Glasgow again for their hospitality. Words cannot adequately describe what my trip to Scotland meant to me. It is a great honour to be a Celtic supporter, and even now, I cannot help but smile whenever I consider the fact I have finally seen the team I hold so dear in person. To walk up the Celtic Way, tour Celtic Park, drink in the atmosphere amidst tens of thousands of other supporters and gain a whole new insight into many of the historic places and stories associated with our Football Club was simply sensational. My experiences will live with me forever, and I hope others of a similar vein await me in the future."

During my research for this book, I stumbled across many poems and songs devoted to the subject of Celtic Football Club which were once common sights in newspapers and the like. One stuck in my memory above all others, but having no obvious location in which to place such a piece, it remained a quiet afterthought. However, having written this chapter, I felt I had finally found an adequate home for it. Titled "The Question", it was published in the "Glasgow Observer" in January 1926. As such, its inclusion here is dedicated to the memories of Robert Donohue and all of those departed Celts who followed the Hoops from distant lands in years gone by; and also to his beloved nephew Matt and the rest of the present day Celtic support who continue to wholeheartedly back our Football Club from afar with such distinction and pride.

"The Question"

"By devious ways where the exile strays;
In many a land afar;
Their fancy flies to Paradise;
No matter where they are;
The Green and White, like a beacon light;
Upon their path has shone;
The question slips from Celtic lips;
"How did the Bhoys get on?""

"Tho' seas divide we think with pride;
Of the team we left behind;
We are faithful still, through good and ill;
We bear the Celts in mind.

So memory clings in their wanderings;
To lighten an exile's load;
The tramp of feet down Janefield Street;
Or a vision of London Road."

"Far across the surf we can see the turf;
That came from the Shamrock shore;
The team tripping out, the welcoming shout;
We heard in days of yore.
We read with zest of Britain's best;
And the mighty deeds they've done;
One thought in view when the mail comes through;
"Have dear old Celtic won?""

"Celtic by Numbers:
"The King of Kings and Kris Boyd?""

During the 1892-93 season, the top goalscorer in the Scottish Football League was a Celtic player for the first time – or rather two of them in fact, with Alexander "Sandy" McMahon and John Campbell tied on eleven goals apiece as the campaign drew to a close. By the end of the following term, McMahon would become the first Celt to make the title his own, standing alone with sixteen league goals to his name. In all, the highest goalscorer in the top flight of Scottish Football has been a Celtic player no fewer than thirty-seven times over the years, although on three of these occasions they shared it with players from other sides, and once with another member of the Parkhead ranks as previously outlined.

Notably, since the inception of the league system in Scotland, Celtic have provided the season's top goalscorer more than any other team, but the Club also boasts the individual who attained this position for the longest consecutive period of time – Henrik Larsson – who led the way in goalscoring from the 2000-01 treble winning season through to 2003-04, for four campaigns running. In fact, between 1995-96 (Pierre van Hooijdonk) and 2004-05 (John Hartson), the highest goalscorer in all but one of these ten campaigns hailed from Celtic Park. For the record, the exception to this rule was Marco Negri of Rangers in the 1997-98 season, not that it affected the eventual destination of the Championship title. Equally well, five of the six goalscorers with the highest cumulative totals in Scottish Premier League history – from 1998-99 onwards – played for Celtic at some point during their careers (Henrik Larsson, Derek Riordan, Scott McDonald, John Hartson and Anthony Stokes).

Of course, the individual leading the way in this regard has not and will almost certainly never be a Celtic player, Kris Boyd.

Yes, the Irvine born lad has – as of the summer of 2015 – scored one hundred and eighty-six goals in this competition, twenty-eight more than our super Swede on one hundred and fifty-eight. Now, as one would perhaps expect, this became a notable talking point around the time that Boyd surpassed Larsson's total. After all, it is no surprise that fans of rival clubs will often try to win the bragging rights over each other, and there is nothing wrong with that.

I feel I should take a few moments to consider which one of these two gentlemen was, indeed, the better goalscorer. Of course, in a Celtic book, this answer may seem somewhat clear cut, but for the sake of fairness and neutrality, I shall continue. After all, it was none other than Colin Stein – who himself netted for Rangers in the 1972 UEFA Cup Winners' Cup Final – that said the following to the "Daily Record" newspaper in 2009.

"Kris isn't far short of Larsson's record now and that speaks volumes for what he has achieved in his time with Kilmarnock and Rangers. People seem to look down on Kris and I read recently someone said he wasn't in the same class as Larsson... Don't get me wrong, Larsson was a great player for Celtic and he deserves the praise he got for what he did at Parkhead...[but] Kris has shown himself to be one of the most prolific forwards of his generation and I've no doubt he will overtake Larsson soon enough. When he does, I think he'll prove himself to be one of the best strikers out there – and I'm not just talking about Scotland. Larsson was highly regarded across the world for what he did with Celtic, Barcelona and for a short time at Manchester United and rightly so. But in terms of scoring goals, I don't see why he should be considered to be a better finisher than Boyd. Larsson might have got a bigger variety of goals but I don't necessarily think it makes him a better scorer as such...Every team in Britain will wish they had a player in their side that scored the type of goals Kris does."

Now, whilst some of you allow your laughter to die down and perhaps wipe away the odd tear currently rolling down your cheek, I will do my best to analyse this debate objectively. During his seven years at Celtic Park, Henrik Larsson scored two hundred and forty-two goals in three hundred and fifteen competitive appearances, an average of 0.77 goals per game. Kris Boyd, during two spells with teams playing at Ibrox totalling five and a half seasons, scored one hundred and thirty-eight times in two hundred and thirty-five outings, albeit with a portion of these coming in Scotland's second footballing tier, averaging 0.58 goals per game. Considering their careers as a whole, Larsson registered four hundred and seventy-one goals in total, whilst Boyd, aged thirty-two upon the penning of this book, has scored two hundred and fifty-six.

However, it is only once one digs down into these statistics that their true significance becomes clear. The highest level which Kris Boyd has played at with any consistency is in the top flight of Scottish Football, with a spell in Turkey's "Super Lig" ending goalless, a time in Major League Soccer only bringing seven goals and two years in the second tier of English football only yielding another dozen. Henrik Larsson, on the other hand, has played at the highest echelons of the global game, enjoying periods in five top European leagues scoring barrel-loads along the way, as well as excelling in the European and International arenas which we shall address momentarily. Another domestic statistic of note is that whilst Kris Boyd only ever managed to register a solitary goal against Celtic during his time at Rangers, Henrik Larsson netted fifteen against the Ibrox side.

Whilst Kris Boyd has only managed to score three goals in his twenty appearances in continental competition with Kilmarnock and Rangers (an average of one almost every seven games), Henrik Larsson bagged a colossal fifty-nine goals on the European stage in just one hundred and six showings (an average of approximately one goal every two games), as well as holding the title of the highest cumulative goalscorer in the UEFA Cup/UEFA Europa League to this day with forty – ten ahead of his nearest present rivals, Radamel Falcao and Klaas-Jan Huntelaar.

Some people may argue that Boyd's better international goalscoring ratio hints at his relative prowess when compared to Larsson, but again, under closer scrutiny, this viewpoint can be quickly disregarded. Yes, with seven goals in eighteen outings for

Scotland – and therefore a goals to games ratio of 0.39 – the Ayrshire man does have the better of Larsson, who boasts a record of thirty-seven Swedish goals in one hundred and six appearances, with an equivalent ratio of 0.35. However, Kris Boyd has never appeared at a single major international tournament with Scotland, whilst Larsson's late equaliser against England in the 2006 World Cup meant he became only the sixth player ever to score at three separate World Cup Finals. For the record, he scored at both the 2000 and 2004 European Championships as well. Also, when one considers that his nation failed to qualify for the 1996 European Championship and 1998 World Cup tournaments entirely, this becomes all the more remarkable. Kris Boyd's seven international goals have, on the other hand, come in the form of a brace in the Kirin Cup (yes, that old three team tournament held annually in Japan), goals against the Faroe Islands, Georgia and Lithuania in European Championship Qualifiers, and a single strike against South Africa in a friendly match. Now, that's hardly the same, is it?

Lastly, I feel it would be wise to compare the honours achieved by the two men during their respective careers. For Kris Boyd, his records reads two Scottish Premier League titles, two Scottish Cups and two Scottish League Cups, as well as being a UEFA Cup runner-up, coming on with four minutes left in the 2008 Final in Manchester. Top scorer in the Scottish Premier League on four occasions and player of the month three times, it would be a respectable haul for most players, and he deserves credit therein.

Henrik Larsson's list of career honours is significantly lengthier in nature, so for the sake of relative brevity, I shall stick to the highlights, which are as follows: four Scottish Premier League titles, two Scottish Cups, two Scottish League Cups, one UEFA Cup runners-up medal (despite his best efforts as he scored twice in the Final in Seville), two Dutch Cups, two La Liga titles, one Spanish Super Cup, one UEFA Champions League, one English Premier League title and one Swedish Cup. The highest Scottish Premier League goalscorer five times, he was the recipient of the European Golden Boot in 2001 and was voted to be the player of the year in Scotland on two occasions. Notably though, Henrik only won the Scottish Premier League player of the month award twice, so Kris will always have that over him.

Before voicing my concluding thoughts on this topic, there is one further statistic which I imagine some of you may find rather amusing, and for that alone I feel it must therefore be worthy of inclusion. Now, after Henrik's departure from Manchester United in 2007, he returned to Helsingborgs in Sweden and some of his achievements there prior to the eventual end of his playing career went unnoticed by many Celtic supporters. With this in mind, it is not surprising that Larsson's prowess in the 2007-08 UEFA Cup – the season in which Rangers reached the final of the tournament – is relatively unknown. Yet, here is the kicker. With six goals in eight appearances in the competition that year, not only did Henrik Larsson score more UEFA Cup goals than Kris Boyd that season, he actually netted one more time than Rangers did during their entire UEFA Cup campaign.

Therefore, in bringing this segment to an end, I feel it is sufficient to say that while people can attempt to make comparisons between Henrik Larsson and Kris Boyd just as they can with any other players, the two are incomparable when one adopts a pragmatic approach. To give Boyd his due, he remains a solid, if somewhat uninspiring player, and there is no shame whatsoever in that. However, despite his ranking as the highest Scottish Premier League goalscorer ever, it is likely his efforts may be largely forgotten in future generations. Be that as it may, I feel it is a fair assertion to make that to all but the most deluded football fans, Henrik Larsson was clearly a cut above Kris Boyd and the vast majority of other footballers, as he was truly world class. The Swede's achievements speak for themselves, and it is a certainty that his name will go down in footballing folklore as one of the finest players ever to ply their trade in Scotland. Unlike the previously quoted Colin Stein, I do believe this makes Larsson "a better scorer as such", and perhaps the finest testimony of this fact came from World Cup winner Thierry Henry in the minutes directly after the 2006 UEFA Champions League Final, with the Frenchman having been a member of the losing Arsenal side.

He said in a television interview: "People always talk about Ronaldinho and everything but I didn't see him today – I saw Henrik Larsson...He came on, he changed the game, that is what killed the game...sometimes you talk about Ronaldinho and Eto'o and people like that, [but] you need to talk about the proper footballer who made the difference and that was Henrik Larsson tonight, [with] two assists."

"Our First Captain: "Minor Cups and Major Controversy""

Only a couple of months after the Scottish Cup Final loss to Third Lanark, Kelly would enjoy his first victory as part of the national setup as they faced England at the Oval in London. Scotland came back from a two-nil half-time deficit that day to win by three goals to two. The only disappointment for Kelly was that he was denied his first international goal by the referee's half-time whistle, as the "London Standard" explains: "From a scrimmage Kelly at length kicked the ball through, but the point was not allowed, as half-time had already been announced." The "Dundee Courier" also reflected that "This was distinctly hard luck for the Scotsmen." However, three second half goals would turn the tie around regardless, and curiously the news of the national side's triumph was well met across most, but not all, of their homeland.

Considering this tale, the "Glasgow Herald" said: "All over Glasgow great excitement was manifested as the time drew near for the announcement of the result. The "Evening Times" was the first of the evening papers to publish the news, shortly after the close of the game. In Argyll and Buchanan Streets the boys were surrounded by eager purchasers, and a large number of copies was rapidly disposed of."

"In Edinburgh the result of the match was received with mixed feelings – satisfaction that the Scottish team had won and disappointment that [players from the East of the country] could claim no credit in the victory. This state of feeling was clearly exhibited at Tynecastle [Hearts were playing Dumbarton at the time], where the occupants of the ground gave a hearty cheer at the half-time result. When the final result of the match was made known the news was received with incredulity, and while some vexation – pardonable in the circumstances – was displayed, the result was hailed with satisfaction."

James Kelly had now tasted international victory and he would enjoy Scottish Cup success with Celtic too, but not for a few years yet. A more pressing issue was that of the two remaining tournaments of Celtic's inaugural domestic season, the Glasgow North Eastern Cup and the Glasgow Merchant's Charity Cup. Firstly, Celtic would face Northern Football Club, a side hailing from Springburn, in the former of these two competitions. Despite going a goal behind within ten minutes against "the Northern", Celtic would quickly equalise before pushing on late in the game and eventually winning by a comfortable margin of four goals to one. James Kelly is said to have been the most influential of the half-backs on the park that day, continually feeding the ball upfield to the forward line and keeping the Celtic machine ticking over nicely.

For the next month, Celtic would spend their time playing friendly matches against Scottish, English and Irish opposition. A week after the aforementioned tie with Northern, they headed to England where they were set to take on Newcastle West End (one of the two sides which merged to form the Newcastle United we all know today). However, this was not the Celts' first trip south of the border, for they had travelled to London not long after their Scottish Cup Final defeat to play Corinthians once again, although they lost by three goals to one on that occasion. Returning to the story of the Celts' trip to Newcastle though, it is perhaps interesting to note that as the team travelled down the east coast of Britain by train, they were not the only footballers aboard, for Rangers were also heading to the north east to face their own friendly opponents, Sunderland.

The following passage from one newspaper tells a little of the day in question: "Song and story passed away the time, and one and all were glad when the train drew up at Newcastle. A hurried luncheon, and then, getting into their armour, the Celts set forth to do or die. Well was it for McKeown's nervous system that he was absent, for on the journey to the ground the horses in the brake betrayed a weakness for waltzing, to the great danger of a crowd of onlookers (and a few pots that happened to be outside of an ironmonger's shop), and finally they refused to go on, thus compelling the Celts to get to the field as best they could. A goodly number of spectators turned out to witness the "young and phenomenal team," as the Celts were termed. The field is anything but a football field [referring to the poor quality of the surface]."

"The game I won't attempt to describe, and the result is already known – four to three in favour of the Celts, the three being mainly brought about by capital play on the part of that bane of Scottish footballers whilst in England, the referee. Taking into consideration the weak team of the Celts, the ground, and the twelfth man, the performance is a fairly meritorious one. Kelly gave a capital exhibition, as also did McLaren…"

Having returned to Scotland, the Celts played a couple of domestic friendlies, scoring eight goals at Dalziel Park (home of Motherwell Football Club between 1889 and 1895) and narrowly defeating Cowlairs away, before returning to England to face Bolton Wanders and Burnley on consecutive days. Celtic lost to the former by two goals to nil, before beating the latter three-one. The Celts then travelled to Ireland, where they would face Distillery and United Belfast, overcoming both of them in the process.

Around ten days later, Celtic went up against Renton in the Glasgow Merchant's Charity Cup at Hampden Park. The Celts were invited to play in the tournament, which was limited to four teams at that point, and this was a small honour in itself, especially for a Club enjoying its first full season in the game. To the disappointment of many of the twenty thousand spectators in attendance, and to the jubilation of the others, Renton scored within the first minute of the match, eventually going on to win by five goals to two. Despite the scoreline, James Kelly was described as "doing great things for the Glasgow team at half-back" by one newspaper report, which later went on to say he "was cheered loudly for a magnificent run."

Regardless, Celtic were out, and it would be left to Renton, Queen's Park and Third Lanark (the latter two had yet to play their semi-final) to contest the trophy. A week after Celtic's Glasgow Merchant's Charity Cup exit, the Celts would find themselves in the third final of their short lifetime. However, unlike their previous disappointments, the Parkhead side were not about to let this opportunity pass them by, as they lined up against Cowlairs – the side who had beaten them in the Glasgow Exhibition Cup Final back in September 1888 – in search of some sporting revenge.

Therefore, it would come to pass that on the eleventh of May 1889 in the Glasgow North Eastern Cup Final, Celtic Football Club secured their first Scottish footballing honour, even if it was considered to be somewhat minor in stature, defeating Cowlairs by six goals to one at Barrowfield. As we all know, this was to be the first of many triumphs, and whilst our first Scottish Cup and Scottish League Championship wins will always receive far more recognition than the Glasgow North Eastern Cup, it will always hold a special place in the history of Celtic, as an early and important step on a long and windy road, which began away against Clydesdale in December 1888 and would one day lead to the south of Portugal and beyond.

As the following season got underway, Celtic took part in another small competition known as the Rangers & Clydesdale Harriers Cup, where they beat Renton in the semi-final and Rangers in the final by two goals to nil, maintaining their one hundred percent record of victory against the Ibrox side. Having subsequently featured in a few more friendly ties, one of which ended in a ten-nil victory over Victoria Harp, Celtic returned to Scottish Cup duty, no doubt determined to go one better than their performance of the previous year. However, this task was made all the more difficult upon the announcement of the draw for the first round of the tournament, which paired the two biggest sides in the country, Celtic and Queen's Park, together.

When match day arrived, Celtic Park was swarming with people, such was the attraction this fixture brought with it. The attendance is generally regarded to have been somewhere in the region of twenty thousand, although it may well have been a little higher, allowing for those who obtained free entry in one way or another. The following passage from the "Glasgow Herald" said of the crowd that day: "Association football is the rage, some say the evil, of the day. Without entering into the pros and cons of the question, no one, we think, will have the hardihood to deny that at all events it has become the sport of the people. Saturday was the day on which the ties in the first round of the Scottish Cup competition were down for settlement, and a modest estimate shows that some forty thousand persons attended the various games in Glasgow alone."

"The fates of the ballot necessitated the Queen's Park and Celtic meeting each other this early in the season. The tie took place on the ground of the Celtic at Parkhead, and will long be remembered as one of the most notable events in the history of the game in Scotland. Incredible as it may appear, hundreds of persons were seen wending their way along the Gallowgate en route for Celtic Park as early as noon. The match was advertised to begin at four o'clock, but fully an hour before that time the grandstand, for which an extra charge was made, was packed with spectators, and all around the enclosure there was not an inch of spare room. It is calculated that the field is capable of holding twenty thousand persons, a good many of whom obtained admission free, while a large number [quoted by another source as numbering in the thousands] could not be admitted at all."

"Regarding the game, little need be said. Both teams were in good form, but every fifteen minutes the crowds broke into the field, and play had to be stopped. It was more of a scramble than good football. The Celts scored not long after the start, but the goal was disallowed for offside, and there being no further scoring the game ended in a draw."

Subsequently, this fixture and its result was declared to be null and void by the relevant authorities due to the previously referenced crowd intrusions which occurred at several junctures during the tie. In truth, having seen the match finish in a draw – rather than a victory for one side or the other – this decision was made all the easier and was significantly less controversial than it probably would have been if one team had emerged victorious, only to have it taken away. Of James Kelly's performance, one newspaper report said "Hamilton made a gallant attempt to capture the home citadel, but Kelly was playing such a great game as to be practically impassable."

Clearly, this match was another critical indicator that domestic football was only gaining popularity in Scotland, and ties such as this, coupled with several others, likely played a large part in the Scottish Football League's inception in the following year. Demand for football was higher than ever before and it was clear for all to see that a few teams in particular had the power to pull in crowds on hitherto unprecedented levels. I cannot help but wonder how the reporter who discussed the cumulative attendance of forty thousand people at the day's football matches in Glasgow would have reacted if faced with the Scottish Cup Final of 1937, when educated estimates of the true attendance produce a figure of one hundred and eighty thousand enthusiastic spectators at Hampden Park alone. Equally, I'm sure the thousands of green and white clad supporters who trail down the Gallowgate before European matches in modern times would prove quite the sight to someone who found a few hundred people doing the same thing in 1889 to be "incredible". Of course, times change – we must remember that – but it paints a stark picture nonetheless. Quite simply, many people of the late 1880s were amazed at the level of support this new Football Club garnered in such a short space of time, but as far as I am concerned that's just Celtic; irresistible then and irresistible now.

One week after the void match at Celtic Park, the two sides faced off again, this time at Hampden Park. It was clear that the footballing authorities did not want a repeat of the previous fixture's off field antics becoming on field problems due to encroachment, and so they implemented a plan designed to limit the attendance, as is described by the "Glasgow Herald": "The doubling of the price of admission had its effect upon the attendance at Hampden Park on Saturday afternoon, where the Queen's and the Celtic met to play off their undecided tie in the first round of the Scottish Cup competition. There were only about ten thousand spectators, as compared with the twenty-five thousand the previous week."

The game itself was a competitive one, played on a good surface in nice weather, and despite a magnificent performance from James Kelly in particular (articles speak of him preventing "certain disaster" at one point and showing "the best piece of play of the day" at another), Celtic lost by two goals to one, ending their Scottish Cup dream before it had barely begun. In the weeks which followed, Celtic drew for the first time with Rangers in a friendly match, before easily progressing past United Abstainers in the third round of the Glasgow Cup (despite beginning the latter match with nine men, only for the other two players to appear about five minutes into proceedings).

The Celts then beat Cambuslang by four goals to nil in the Glasgow Cup semi-final, before defeating Clydesdale without any difficulty of note in the first round of the Glasgow North Eastern Cup – which, of course, Celtic were defending – at Parkhead. Bizarrely, James Kelly did not feature in the five-nil win over Clydesdale, and yet Celtic fielded no replacement, instead playing with only two half-backs and ten men in all. This was counterbalanced by the fact that their opponents fielded only nine men for the entirety of the tie, which seems to be a tad farcical when one considers it from a modern standpoint, although such events weren't quite as rare as you might think in the early days of the Scottish game. For the record, "The Scotsman" said, "The feature of the match was the phenomenal goalkeeping of Sydney Ross, the Clydesdale custodian." Considering the fact this goalkeeper was forced to play with only eight men in front of him, I feel the efforts of the gentleman in question deserve some recognition here.

The following weekend, on the fourteenth of December 1889, Celtic met their rivals Queen's Park once more, this time in the final of the Glasgow Cup. Strange as it may sound, one of the few advantages which was presented by the lack of league football was an abundance of cup competitions and the continual excitement of knockout tournaments. Now, whilst the tie was played at Cathkin Park, so as to be a neutral venue, the admission prices were doubled from their normal rates once more by organisers, and thus the crowd, albeit large, was perhaps not quite of the scale which it could have been without such an increase. The "Glasgow Herald" said: "Despite the fact that the Third Lanark had erected a new stand capable of holding one thousand, six hundred persons, the accommodation was taxed to its utmost, and when the game started there were fully twelve thousand present."

The fixture itself, which is still remembered as one of controversy, was not considered to be the greatest example of the sport by one reporter writing another article in the same newspaper, who said: "The game was a disappointment from various causes. The ground was hard beneath, with a soft surface, and this prevented the men showing that accuracy which would have characterised their play with safer footing. Probably from this cause, little incidents occurred which under ordinary circumstances would have been obviated. For the infringement of the rules, probably unintentional, both sides were penalised, and this gave rise to outbursts of feeling and temper by several players during the game. A member or two on both sides had to be cautioned for roughness and, unfortunately, if reports are true, the ill feeling did not terminate on the men leaving the field, as a disgraceful incident is said to have occurred afterwards in the pavilion."

One newspaper report from the time tells of two crucial refereeing decisions, both of which were made when the game was tied at one goal each, before hinting at the resultant aftermath: "From a foul given against Groves the Queen's once more got down to the Celts' charge, when Berry passed the ball over to Sellar, who shot promptly. Many persons thought the ball had gone through, but they were mistaken, and on the ball being kicked off the Celts were again at the other end when Groves slipped the ball past Gillespie. Offside was claimed and given, the decision not meeting with general approval...There was not a goal between them teams so far as the play had gone. After some desultory play the Queen's got another goal, Sellar sending the ball through. The point was appealed, but the referee allowed it, and one of the Celtic players left the field, the game being stopped for a few minutes owing to the unwillingness of the Celts to proceed. At length, the game was resumed."

Therefore, we can see that Queen's Park were given the benefit of an offside decision which prevented Celtic, who were probably playing the better football then, from taking the lead. Moments later, Queen's Park scored, but the Celts alleged "that

Hamilton had illegally charged the goalkeeper" according to another report. These pleas were ignored and the goal given. Clearly, it was not only some of the Celts in the stands and terracing who felt they had been wronged, but at least one of the players also. Two factors which I feel were likely contributory to this anger are also worthy of mention – the first being that Queen's Park were well known to be the establishment club of the time as I have previously stated, and the second being that the Celts had not yet managed to beat the Spiders, this being their fourth attempt (including the void match discussed earlier). Both of these aspects, as well as many other personal battles of which we are not aware, most likely led to the heated post-match scenes which involved some fiery characters. Regardless, by the time the full time whistle sounded, despite all of Celtic's efforts and some fantastic defending by Queen's Park, the Parkhead Club lost by three goals to two.

Celtic subsequently submitted a formal protest to the Glasgow Football Association in the aftermath of this tie, but it was rebuffed. At the turn of the New Year in which Scottish football would take a monumental step forward with the introduction of a league system – Celtic began their footballing efforts in 1890 with a three-two victory over Everton at Celtic Park. The English side had ended their first league campaign south of the border with an eighth place finish from twelve clubs the previous season but, with one Dan Doyle in the role of captain, they were a team on the up who would end the 1889-90 season in second place. Doyle played that day at Parkhead but he was unable to help his side avoid defeat, as it is said the home half-back line of McLaren, Kelly and McKeown dominated the game for large portions. Of course, Dan Doyle would go on to have many happier times at Celtic Park.

A few weeks later, in mid-January, Celtic took on Cowlairs in the second round of the Glasgow North Eastern Cup. This was the second occasion upon which the sides had attempted to play the tie, for an earlier scheduling was declared a friendly prior to kick-off due to the hard nature of the pitch. This was just as well for Celtic, who lost by six goals to one, but thankfully such a poor performance had reared its ugly head in a friendly match rather than one of a competitive nature. This time though, things did not get off to a much better start for the Celts, who soon found themselves a goal behind after only ten minutes amidst howling wind and rain. However, as half-time passed and the minutes of the second period began to tick steadily away, Cowlairs made an error which has befallen many visiting teams to both the old and new Celtic Park grounds over the years. Defending a narrow lead, they gradually began to sit deeper, and soon found themselves hemmed into the area around their goalmouth for a large proportion of the remaining time. This sustained pressure eventually told, as William Groves equalised for the home side late on, forcing the fixture to be replayed.

Subsequently, Celtic would travel to Springburn's Gourlay Park where they won handsomely by five goals to nil, again in unfavourable weather conditions for players and spectators alike – although it has to be said that this did not dissuade any of those in attendance, as "one of the largest crowds that ever visited Springburn was gathered at Gourlay Park" according to one report.

A couple of weeks later, the Celts faced Glasgow Thistle at Beechwood Park as the Glasgow North Eastern Cup reached the semi-final stage, emerging as five-nil victors again, with the previously referenced half-back line again receiving praise for their "grand" style of play. It was then, exactly a month on from this victory that the Celts added the third honour to their slowly growing list of accolades, retaining the Glasgow North Eastern Cup after a hard fought two-nil victory over Northern.

In April, Celtic embarked on another tour of middle England, facing Bolton Wanderers and Blackburn Rovers, as well as playing a return tie with Everton. However, in footballing terms at least, it was not to be an enjoyable trip, for the Celts were well beaten by both Bolton and Everton, only managing a draw with Blackburn before they headed over the Irish Sea to play Distillery of Belfast once again. Notably, James Kelly only featured in the match against Blackburn as he was again busy on international duty (with Scotland drawing one-all with England on this occasion) and therefore unavailable for selection in the two previous fixtures. Celtic were the comfortable victors in Ireland, and they returned to Scotland to prepare for the final tournament of their season, the Glasgow Merchant's Charity Cup.

Despite all of their preparations, the Celts once again crashed out of the competition, without so much as registering a goal, having been bettered by Third Lanark. Interestingly, James Kelly did not take part in this match as he was injured almost two weeks previously in the one-all draw with Blackburn Rovers.

By the time Celtic's next fixture came around, Kelly had recovered sufficiently to be able to feature, as the Parkhead side travelled to Edinburgh for a friendly with Heart of Midlothian. Celtic won by two goals to one, with Kelly getting back into the swing of things. However, there was a rather unique caveat attached to this tie for Willie Maley, who was forced to take part as the visitors' goalkeeper. The Celts' previous stopper, James McLaughlin, had departed the Club after the loss to Third Lanark, and so without a proper replacement, Celtic had to find someone to cover the position, and this rather unenviable role fell to Maley. Never one to shy away from a challenge however, he gave it his best, although as the following quote from one newspaper suggests, he was a little fortunate to only be beaten once by the home team: "Maley's charge might be said to have escaped on two occasions by the merest luck – the ball at one time striking the crossbar, and at another rolling along the line."

By the time Celtic played their next friendly match, they still had not found a new goalkeeper, instead having to ask Duff of Cowlairs to cover for them, which he did for each of the remaining half dozen non-competitive ties which the Parkhead side had scheduled at that time.

Incredibly, some months later, when the Celts lined up for their first match of the inaugural Scottish Football League, they still had not recruited a recognised goalkeeper to their ranks, instead being forced to play full-back James McLaren (a Scottish Cup winner with Hibernian in 1887) in goal. This decision was reflected in the four-one defeat to Renton which Celtic suffered that day, as McLaren was guilty of a couple of mistakes which you would not expect to see from a natural goalkeeper. Of course, he did his best and deserves credit for it, but it was clear for all to see that Celtic needed to find a new custodian, and fast. Thankfully for the Celts, Renton were later expelled from the competition after being found guilty of professionalism, and thus the impact of this disappointing and somewhat ridiculous defeat was nullified.

Subsequently James Bell, formerly of Dumbarton, was acquired and immediately thrown into his first game, as Celtic won by five goals to nil at Tynecastle. However, in all honesty the Parkhead side were so dominant that day that McLaren, Maley or anyone else could likely have stood between the Celtic posts without facing too much to worry them. This was reflected by one journalist who attended the match and later said in his newspaper column, "Bell's abilities as a goalkeeper could not be judged, as he was scarcely ever troubled."

Celtic put their first two league points on the board that day in Edinburgh, but in time they would have them taken away, as they were later deducted four points because James Bell was deemed to have been an ineligible player because he had featured for Dumbarton less than two weeks prior to his first Celtic appearance.

Regardless, this punishment would not make any difference come the end of the season, as the Celts finished in third place, eight points behind joint champions Dumbarton and Rangers. However, prior to the final table being established, there was still a whole season worth of football to be enjoyed, beginning as Celtic welcomed Cambuslang to Celtic Park for the first proper Scottish League tie ever held there. The Celts won by five goals to two, but Bell showed signs of nervousness, gifting the visitors a one-nil half-time lead: "About ten minutes from the finish [of the first half] a combined run by the Cambuslang forwards ended in a shot from Penderleith which Bell failed to catch, and Cambuslang scored the first goal."

One week later, the two sides who would go on to dominate Scottish Football for significant periods of time in future, Celtic and Rangers, met each other in the Scottish Cup for the first time, although James Kelly was unavailable for the match owing to a suspension handed down by the Scottish Football Association. His crime, if you could call it that, was that he featured for Renton in a testimonial match against Celtic at the end of the previous season.

Two newspaper reports, the first from the "Dundee Courier" discussing the thought process of the Scottish Football Association's Committee, and the latter from the "Edinburgh Evening News" focusing on the subsequent decision of the Professional Committee of the same organisation with regards punishment, recalled the events as follows. Please note that the first meeting was held on the nineteenth of August 1890, with the second occurring on the fourth of September, two days before the Scottish Cup tie with Rangers.

"The Chairman said that he had now a matter to bring forward with regard the benefit match which was played for James McCall, of Renton. A game took place on the last Saturday of the season on the Celtic's old ground between the ground team and the Old Renton. Previous to that contest his opinion was asked as to whether the match was legal or otherwise, and he decided that the match was contrary to the Association's rule. Notwithstanding, the match took place. Mr. Kirkwood, of the Third Lanark, maintained that the match was quite legal, and he held that McCall was well worthy of the benefit match. After some discussion, Mr. Sliman, of the Battlefield, moved "That the Association uphold the President's decision"...Mr. Sneddon, in seconding, said the clubs playing the match gave a studied insult to the President [this was followed by some applause]...It was then agreed "That this matter of professionalism be left to the Professional and Business Committee, and that Messrs McCall and Kelly be cited."

"The Professional Committee of the S.F.A. have pronounced their findings on the famous McCall case. For playing with Old Rentonians, McCall and Kelly have been suspended for an indefinite period, and the Celtic, for their share in the transaction, are severely censured. That is all we are given to know, for we cannot pierce the privacy of this committee meeting, and not knowing the evidence...it is almost impossible to say whether even handed justice has been dealt out. It has been roundly asserted that the Celtic infringed no written laws, but only acted contrary to the advice of the president of the S.F.A...Why these two players receive the heaviest punishment the S.F.A. can mete out and the Celtic club escape with censure are two positions that cannot be reconciled but as was remarked on Monday a scapegoat must be provided, and whether a logical course be pursed or not, personal dignity and amateur purity must be vindicated and upheld. After all, in these times of Leagues and other strange things to the old-time footballers and trembling officials, it is probably safer to dispose of two players than to strike a blow at a powerful club. The latter might make a show of resistance, and the present tottering structure of Scottish amateurism might thereby collapse."

The Celts beat Rangers by a single goal to nil at Parkhead that September afternoon without Kelly, thanks to a strike from Willie Groves late in the first half. Prior to this, the Celts had two goals disallowed by the relevant officials, both of which are described below, adding to the general feeling of unfairness garnering strength within the ranks of the Celtic support (which was also catalysed by their captain's enforced absence).

"The Celts, led by Madden, gallantly responded to the shouts of their admirers, the right winger and Groves both missing chances. Still the home team pressed severely, and Groves with admirable judgement passed the ball to Crossan, who sent it out of Reid's reach amid deafening cheers. Crossan, however, was palpably offside, and the appeal...was promptly sustained."

"For the first twenty-five minutes, the game appeared to be anybody's, but the wonderful combination of the Celts' forwards gradually began to assert itself, the Rangers resorting to some very questionable tactics in keeping their opponents at bay. The Celts were rewarded with a foul close to the goal-mouth, when Groves adroitly tipped the ball to Dowds who with a fast low shot sent it through. This second point was also disallowed, to the very apparent chagrin of the Celts and their supporters."

Of course, as is previously mentioned, Celtic did finally manage to score an acceptable goal, described as "brilliant" by one reporter, who proceeded to say that it sparked "scenes of extraordinary enthusiasm." Notably, this was also the first match in which James Bell really displayed some of his true ability as the Celtic goalkeeper, starting off somewhat anxiously before hardening his stance once Celtic opened the scoring. He was determined that he would not let this slender lead to be taken away from his new side, and so he proved as good fortune smiled down upon him, as the following quote highlights.

"Time was now drawing near, and, with almost inevitable defeat staring them in the face, the Rangers pulled themselves together and showed something akin to their true form for the first time during the whole contest. As a result Bell had a very bad ten minutes of it, but he exhibited goal-keeping of an exceptionally high order, shot after shot being successfully negotiated. Once certainly luck was with him, for he only partially stopped the ball, which hit the post and went outside."

James Kelly would miss Celtic's first ever league defeat against Third Lanark the following weekend, owing to his ongoing suspension, but he would return to the Celtic team for the Celts' first round Glasgow Cup tie against Battlefield thereafter. Newspapers refer to Kelly being "received with hearty cheers" from the home support upon his appearance on the field of play, suggesting that, unsurprisingly, the Celtic support had not lost any faith in their leader, instead rallying behind him in the face of adversity. The Celts excelled that day, scoring six goals in the first half and eventually winning by seven goals to one.

Celtic were again without Kelly for the second round Scottish Cup tie against at home. Regardless, after that fixture ended in a two-all draw, the captain returned for the away replay, which his side largely controlled, having scored their opener within only a few minutes of the first whistle, eventually winning by three goals to one. The Parkhead side, buoyed by the presence of Kelly, continued their good form, beating Northern in the Glasgow Cup and Wishaw Thistle in the Scottish Cup, sealing their place in the next rounds of each competition before partaking in a brief return to league duty against Abercorn, whom the Celts overcame by five goals to one.

The month of November would be taken up entirely by more cup duty. Celtic began with a five-nil Glasgow Cup victory over

Clyde at Celtic Park on a day which James Kelly "interposed" on several occasions, breaking up the visitors' play effectively and without too much hassle. Three goals in three minutes helped Celtic to a three-one Scottish Cup success at West Craigie Park against Dundee Our Boys the following weekend, before a fortnight's break allowed them time to rest prior to their Glasgow Cup tie against Partick Thistle. Again, the Celts were by far and away the superior side when this match was played at Celtic Park amidst dreadful weather conditions, which soaked the pitch and the players alike, with the home side winning by five goals to one.

It was then at the end of November that a fiasco which would last until mid-December began, as Celtic continued their Scottish Cup endeavours and travelled to Larkhall to take on Royal Albert. Initially, prior to the first match, it was decided the tie would only be a friendly due to the presence of a heavy ground frost which had failed to lift as kick-off time approached. This was not a unique event, far from it in fact, and thus a two-all draw was played out and a new date scheduled for the sides to return for their Scottish Cup tie proper.

When the two sides met again a week later, the pitch was playable, and thus the game began in earnest. Unlike the previous meeting, the visitors were now firmly on top of their opponents, opening up a four goal lead without reply in the second half of the tie. It was then, with approximately ten minutes of the match remaining that, according to the "Glasgow Herald", "a slight accident occurred, and a rush by the spectators prevented the game being completed." In modern times, such an event would be dealt with dependent on which competition it occurred in, but in some cases (particularly so late in proceedings) – including the UEFA Champions League – it would likely restart another day from the second upon which the clock stopped with the scores just as they were.

However, this was not the case in 1890, as the following passage, which recounts the meeting of Scotland's governing body at which the issue was raised, displays: "A meeting of the Scottish Football Association was held last evening...Mr. T. R. Park, president, in the chair...The protest by the Royal Albert, Larkhall, against the Scottish tie with the Celtic on the grounds that the match was stopped 12 ½ minutes from time was considered. Mr. Park said he was of the opinion that this match was no tie, and the matter, he thought, simply resolved itself into a question of where it should be replayed. By rule seventeen, when it could be proved that spectators conducted themselves in such a manner as to interfere with the players, the Association had the power to order the tie to be replayed. He therefore moved that the tie be replayed. This was seconded."

"Mr. Kirkwood (Third Lanark) said the Association held the ground club responsible for the conduct of the spectators, and therefore he moved that the tie be awarded to the Celtic. His opinion was that all the Royal Albert wanted was another game with Celtic to swell the exchequer. Mr. McCulloch (Our Boys) seconded the amendment. After hearing the evidence of the referee a division was taken, and, by twelve votes to six, it was resolved that the match be replayed. It was decided the tie should be played on Ibrox Park on Saturday first."

Thus, one could rationally say that common sense lost that night. I am sure that not even the most optimistic of ardent Royal Albert supporters could have foreseen a dramatic four goal comeback had the final few minutes been played out as scheduled, but I suppose there is little to be gained from complaining about it, particularly nowadays. One thing was clear though, Celtic, their supporters, and several other figures within Scottish football believed the game had been interrupted and subsequently called off purely because Royal Albert wanted another payday and their supporters hoped for another shot at team often referred to in newspapers as "the Irishmen". The following passage is also from the previously discussed meeting, telling of Celtic's desire to see the gate money raised from the replay donated to charity, and of the timely refusal of such a request.

"In the case of Mr. T. Maley, the Celtic umpire [each Club supplied one linesman for matches at this point], who was reported by the referee for striking a Royal Albert player with his flag, it was decided to take no further action in the matter. On the decision of the committee being laid before the Celtic representative,

Mr. Maley asked the committee, if possible, order that the proceeds of the match be allocated to charity, because the Celtic club considered that the whole matter was a monetary concern. Mr. Park, in reply, stated that the committee had no power to allocate the funds to charity. Mr. Sneddon (Edinburgh University) moved that until the thirtieth of April, no cup ties be allowed to be played on the ground of Royal Albert, Larkhall, but the motion was lost."

Eventually, after one unplayable match and another which was called off only minutes from full time, the tie was decided at Ibrox Park in mid-December, as the Celts won by two goals to nil. However, it would all seem rather pointless for James Kelly and his side as they faced Dumbarton and were knocked out of the tournament only a week later, having been defeated by three goals to nil at Boghead Park. Once again though, this was not the entire story, for a protest was filed to the Scottish Football Association – this time, by Celtic.

To understand the nature of this appeal, one must first consider the weather that day, and the reaction not only of the Celts, but of their opponents prior to kick-off. "The Scotsman" began its match report as follows: "Dumbarton v Celtic – This tie was played at Boghead, Dumbarton, before a large crowd. The ground had been cleared of the snow, and during the forenoon bills were put out intimating that the referee had declared the ground playable and that the tie would be played. Both teams, however, protested before the game started. The Celts kicked off."

Critically, we can see that although the referee was happy for the tie to take place, neither of the participating clubs shared his view of the matter. However, having since won by three goals to nil, the tune of the home side altered dramatically, as was highlighted at the meeting of the Scottish Football Association's General Committee which followed to discuss Celtic's concerns: "…The Celtic's protest was next taken up. The grounds of protest…unplayability of the ground. The referee, Mr. Dunn, Cambuslang, was in attendance, and gave it as his opinion that the ground was playable after the snow had been cleared. On the consideration that both clubs had protested, it was moved that the protest be sustained, and on a vote the numbers were equal – six each. The Chairman gave his casting vote against the protest being sustained and it was accordingly dismissed. Some strong things were said regarding Dumbarton's action in lodging and then withdrawing their protest, but nothing was done."

Whether or not such a decision could be taken as a sign of favouritism is speculative, but it is clear that certain people within the Scottish Football Association's committees over the years have been more likely to vote one way or another on certain matters dependent on which football club happens to be at the centre of any given debate. Notably, I do not always refer to Celtic in this regard, but I often think that a serious study of such votes, their outcomes and those decision makers involved (if it were ever feasible) may make very interesting reading indeed.

Returning to the football itself though, Dumbarton (who surpassed Abercorn in the semi-final) were denied the opportunity to lift the trophy for the second time by Heart of Midlothian, who eventually won the final by a single goal to nil. This denied Dumbarton a historic double of sorts, as they also shared the first Scottish League title with Rangers.

In the New Year, the Celts returned to league duty for a time, winning two matches and losing one. It was then, on Valentine's Day, that they faced Third Lanark in the final of the Glasgow Cup. Celtic would win by four goals to nil, thanks to a brace from John Campbell, one from Peter Dowds and an own goal before a crowd of approximately ten thousand spectators. Whilst in the end the victory was a fairly comfortable one for the Parkhead side, the score sat stagnant at one-nil for a significant period of time, and Third Lanark made every effort possible to find an equalising goal. It is said that "relief came" from such Third Lanark attacks, in particular, "through the instrumentality of Kelly", who delivered, by all accounts, a sterling performance, as the Celts won the Glasgow Cup for the first time.

Once again, phrases such as "wild scenes of enthusiasm" could be seen in the Scottish press to describe the reaction of the Celtic support to this triumph, which was regarded by many to be their first significant victory. This was reflected in the manner in which the trophy was presented to Celtic, as is described below (note, this was in the days before laps of honour and trophy presentations on the field of play): "The Glasgow Football Association's cup was presented last night to the winners – the Celtic. The proceedings took the form of a smoking concert in the Royal restaurant, West Nile Street. The chair was occupied by Mr. A. Sliman, Battlefield; President of the Association. There was a large attendance, nearly all the clubs in Glasgow being represented. In making the presentation, the Chairman congratulated the Celtic on their most honourable victory. Mr. Glass, president of the Celtic responded. The members of the winning team each received a badge, as also did the runners-up – the Third Lanark."

Considering the fact that during only the previous season, Celtic had been at odds with the Glasgow Football Association over the officiating which accompanied their final loss against Queen's Park, their triumph in the Glasgow Cup was likely made all the sweeter. Oh, to have been the proverbial fly on the wall when John Glass, not a man known for keeping his opinions to himself (especially those regarding injustice), addressed the Royal restaurant that night. Following the disappointment of their defeat to the Spiders, the Celts had gone about setting things right in the correct manner, with belief and resilience, and all of their efforts had paid off honourably. Firstly, they had conquered North Eastern Glasgow, and now Glasgow itself, and soon the whole of Scotland would follow.

Throughout the remainder of the 1890-91 season, Celtic enjoyed what was left of their league campaign, a short friendly tour in England, and a charity competition involving themselves, Third Lanark, Rangers and Dumbarton. The three aforementioned Glasgow sides had been asked not to compete in the Glasgow Merchant's Charity Cup that year due to a difficulty finding dates to suit all of the parties, and thus they instead played their own small tournament instead as a one-off. Dumbarton won the competition, beating Celtic in the final, but notably, it must be said that although both Dumbarton and Rangers could call themselves league champions in the summer of 1891, neither of them had managed to defeat Celtic in the Scottish league. In fact, Rangers would not enjoy their first victory over the Celts until February 1893, almost five years after their first meeting in 1888.

That aside, prior to the end of the league season, immense controversy was generated by the Scottish Football Association's decision not to select James Kelly – as well as other top class players – for any of the British Home Championship matches (including the England tie) that season. The premise for this situation was fairly simple, but the actions taken by some were borderline childish all the same, causing great consternation within the ranks of average fans and newspaper journalists alike.

Essentially, at a time when the pressure on the Scottish Football Association to allow professionalism within the game continued to mount with every passing year, the body and those in control of it – some of whom remained desperate to hang out to amateurism at all costs – felt very threatened indeed by the introduction of the inaugural Scottish Football League. As 1890 gave way to 1891, the popularity of this new footballing format was very much apparent, and one must presume concerns within the Association were rife that not only their authority but much of their relevance could be usurped by the new League body. Therefore, with league teams scheduled to play more competitive matches than ever before that season, the Association used the inevitable fixture clashes which followed to fire a warning shot back at the young upstarts and attempt to reassert control over a losing battle.

In those days, players were not chosen for the international team as a result of their respective club showings as they are now. Instead, good performances therein only earned men an invitation to feature in trial matches, which a selection committee would watch before picking their preferred elevens for the coming Scotland ties. Previously, with no league format in place, these trials only caused the relatively odd scheduling headache. However, with the birth of the Scottish Football League and the regimented, demanding structure it involved, fixture clashes became a much more serious concern. As such, whilst James Kelly had been invited to feature in a trial match on the seventh of March 1891, he instead made the decision to play for Celtic in a league tie against Cambuslang, as the following snippet from "The Scotsman" notes: "Kelly preferred playing with his own team rather than participating in the trials at Edinburgh."

Unsurprisingly, this brought the scorn of the Scottish selectors down upon Kelly and others who had made the same choice. As this passage from the "Aberdeen Journal" (published in March 1891) tells, the Association decided to make an example of those who they felt had defied them, whilst the language which the "Dundee Courier" used to describe the ongoing hostilities was indicative of the severity of matters.

"Aberdeen Journal": "The Selection Committee of the Scottish Football Association met in Glasgow last night and selected the international teams...It will be seen that the seven [selectors] have excluded all League players who refused or were prohibited from taking part in the trial matches at Edinburgh last Saturday."

"Dundee Courier": "The teams, however, are less strong than in former years owing to the rupture between the Association and the League."

Scotland won the first two of their three British Home Championship matches in 1891, overcoming both Wales and Ireland by single goal margins, but they would fall to the English in Blackburn come the final day of proceedings. Unsurprisingly, this defeat was not met well by the Scottish public, who felt their governing body had all but handed the championship title to their rivals south of the border by intentionally fieldling a weakened team.

The thoughts of one journalist writing in the "Dundee Courier" after the England match in April 1891 are very telling, and likely echo the thoughts of many footballing enthusiasts nationwide.

"Football in the West" – "The feeling in Glasgow and the West of Scotland at the defeat of Scotland in the international match was somewhat divided. Of course, everyone wished Scotland would win, but it was generally admitted that the result was pretty much a "toss up", the two teams being so evenly balanced. There is no mistaking the flower of Scotland was not in the team, and if the Association had been more amenable to reason in their matter of difference with the League, and had been less disposed to stand upon their dignity, Scotland today would not be mourning a defeat. It was clear from the first that the course pursed by the Association in leaving out prominent League players was suicidal, and had Kelly of the Celtic taken the place of McPherson of the Hearts, and McPherson of the Rangers the inside-right [role] instead of Rankine, the probability is that a different result would have been seen; otherwise Scotland might have been said to have been defeated on her merits. When the news arrived that England was two up at half-time the large crowds awaiting were very gloomy, and the final result – two to one – was received somewhat as a relief, as the worst ideas had been entertained. Scotland's weak point was at half-back, and with half-backs too slow, as were undoubtedly the halves on Saturday, the best set of forwards could not win a match."

The sad reality of this controversy was threefold. Firstly James Kelly, who had played in the three previous matches against England and would do so again in 1892 and 1893, was denied an international cap for having the audacity to represent his Club team rather than feature in a trial fixture. Secondly, whilst one cannot say for certain how the 1891 contest with England would have gone, it is abundantly clear Scotland's chances of success would have been increased had their strongest possible eleven taken to the field. Lastly, and perhaps most importantly, the gulf between the Scottish Football Association of the time and both League clubs and paying spectators was significantly widened. Scottish Football would have to modernise, and Celtic would be at the forefront of the drive for such progress.

"Tales of Their Time: "From Charity Concerts to Football""

In this newspaper segment, we predominantly delve into the thoughts and experiences of Mr. John H. McLaughlin (Chairman between 1897 and 1909) regarding the early days of the Club's existence, prior to considering other matters latterly.

"Edinburgh Evening News" – Saturday 10th November 1906

"The Making of the Celtic Football Club"

"Than Mr. J. H. McLaughlin there is no man better qualified to speak of the beginnings of the Celtic Club, one of the most potent forces in the development of the game of Association football in Scotland. And had the Celtic Club done no more for the game than cast up Mr. McLaughlin it would have rendered a distinct service. Mr. McLaughlin has been one of the outstanding personalities in Scottish sport these last eighteen years. A shrewd man of business, the modern developments of football have given full scope to his qualities of acuteness and farsightedness, and his gifts as a speaker, which at one time, when contention was in the air, earned him the title "the orator of the League", have been supplemented by so close a grasp of affairs as to make him as good at building up as at demolishing. Building up, let us say, legalised professionalism on a sound basis in place of the old arrangement of veiled amateurism and official corruption, which he took a leading part in demolishing."

"From Charity Concerts to Football"

"Mr. McLaughlin came to be associated with the promotion of the Celtic Club in a rather curious way. There had been instituted in the East End of Glasgow a movement which aimed at supplying the poorest children in the Catholic schools with dinner, and the Hibernian and Everton Clubs played a couple of matches for the purpose of supplying the organisation under the control of Brother Walfrid, at that time the headmaster of St Mary's School, with funds. So successful were the matches that Brother Walfrid conceived the idea of a club run with the special object of benefiting the poor schools of the East End. He communicated his idea to Mr. Glass, a builder, and Mr. O'Hara, an insurance agent, and to these gentlemen, both now dead, the origin of the Celtic Club was owing. Glass and O'Hara had been running a series of Saturday night charitable concerts, and had got the assistance of Mr. McLaughlin as accompanist. What more natural than that he should come into the football organisation. "We used," says Mr. McLaughlin, "to discuss our prospects till all hours of the morning. We could not look forward to gathering a very special team together; we did not think a newly started club would attract players. Somebody suggested one day that an approach should be made to Kelly, then at Renton, as it was understood he was anxious to start a business in Glasgow. The idea was pooh-poohed, but ultimately two gentlemen waited on Kelly, and he agreed to throw in his lot with the new club. I count that," continued Mr. McLaughlin, "to have been the beginning of the success of the club.""

"McCallum, the Rentonian winger, intimated his intention of accompanying Kelly and Gallagher, who was needed at home on account of his father's death, and Dunbar, who was working at Busby, found it more convenient to play for Celtic at Glasgow than to travel to Edinburgh to assist the Hibernians. "When the news of these men coming spread," said Mr. McLaughlin, "we had no trouble looking for players, they came to us." Among others were McLaren, Groves and McKeown. In this connection there may be recalled the old story that the Hibernians gave these men 25s to 30s a week, according to the state of the funds, and that the Celtic found 10s a week more, but, whatever the terms were, nobody disputes the payment, though so well were the secrets kept that when an Edinburgh paper hinted that Groves had improved his position by going West a threat of legal proceedings produced a prompt and ample apology."

"The First Celtic Team"

"Mr. McLaughlin dwells, with a not unnatural fondness, on the first year's team of the Celtic. Including men of the stamp of McKeown, Gallagher, Kelly, McLaren, Coleman, Groves, Dunbar, McCallum, and the Maleys, it had plenty of individuality, and so well did it succeed as a combination that it reached the final round of the national competition. As will be observed from the names of the original players, the Irish and Catholic elements were exclusively employed in the composition of the side, but the old Hibernian principle of confining the membership to one sect was never contemplated – and in passing it may be suggested that what had occasioned sectarian feeling in Edinburgh might readily have kindled very bitter feelings in the West of Scotland. By taking a different line than that followed by their compatriots in the East, the Celtic promoters showed a wisdom which bore fruit. Soon the net was cast even wider than at first, and everybody recognises the help that has been to the club. But to return to the early players. Some of them had passed their best, and recruiting had to be prosecuted with unremitting care. A great "wing" came into being in the third season of the club's existence after this fashion. The Hibernians had expired of sheer weariness, and McMahon and others had been cast upon the world of football. McMahon accompanied the Heart of Midlothian to Falkirk on the occasion of a cup tie with East Stirlingshire, and would have played and cast in his lot with them, for the time being, at least, had he not previously committed himself to the Hibernians. As the entire thought of the Hearts was concentrated on winning the Cup they paid less heed to McMahon than they probably would have done at another time. McMahon drifted through to Parkhead and gave the Celtic the greatest wing pair the modern game has produced in Scotland. The Celtic were on tour in England at Easter, and on an emergency McMahon was played inside-left to Campbell, an arrangement which proved a brilliant success and last till it was ended on Campbell's initiative by his two years' stay in England."

"The League Origin – A Trying Time"

"It is beyond a doubt that no club within the sphere of operations of the Scottish League has attained greater distinction in a League connection than the Celtic, and probably no club has benefited so considerably financially. It is all the more astonishing to learn that a section of the Celtic Committee were opposed to the idea, and that it was only after a very close vote that it was decided to send a representative to the meeting of club delegates convened to discuss the proposed formation of a Scottish League. Needless to say, Mr. McLaughlin was one of the majority, and he was sent to the League meeting. The success of the English League had appealed to some of the Scottish clubs, notably Third Lanark, Dumbarton, and Renton, and it was on the initiative of these clubs that the formation was brought about. Half gates were the terms the three Dunbartonshire clubs, Dumbarton, Renton, and Vale of Leven, sought to impose, but the Glasgow clubs, Third Lanark, Rangers, Celtic, and Cowlairs, resisted the claim, and as a compromise, two-thirds to the home club, one-third to the visiting club, was agreed upon."

"From the League formation quickly arose a threatening state of things. The athletic press in the West saw in the new movement something inimical to the Association, and some of the leading clubs took up an unfriendly attitude, notably the Queen's Park and the Airdrieonians. The feeling of antagonism spread to the other side, and when the St. Bernard's sought to get out of their professionalism troubles, Renton, one of the staunchest of the Leaguers, made common cause with them. The hand of the Association fell heavily on the Renton Club, and being in sympathy with their erring brother, the League clubs were taking steps to convene a special meeting of the Association, when Renton went to law. Of course, this stopped the proceedings of the sister clubs, and possibly, all things considered, this was as well, as it was agreed that the League clubs lost their case, they would have seceded. The suggestion of secession offers a wide field for speculation, but having in view of the case of Northern Unionism, the hotheads of the stirring days of 1980-91 may now be glad that Renton cut the knot for them."

"Forcing the Hand of the S.F.A."

"However, it took time for the lion and the lamb to get accustomed to each other's company. The League clubs, with growing financial needs, objected to the Association going in for a more or less extensive and quite unnecessary programme of trial games, and the League came out with an edict directed against participation in trial games. The Heart of Midlothian had won the Scottish Cup, and as several Tynecastle players were anxious after international distinction, they alone of the League clubs' players were loyal to the S.F.A. – or disloyal to the League, as you like it. The Hearts came near to expulsion from the League, their position as sole representatives of the capital doing as much for them as anything else; but the international players were debarred from playing in more League games that season. Meantime the League had begun to show that there was money in the game, and a "gate" which crowded out Parkhead on the occasions of the visit of the Hearts as cup holders, and which yielded the then very handsome sum of close on £400, converted the last of the Celtic committee men to the League principle. The money that was coming into the game made it easier for the clubs to practice underhand dealings, and ugly suspicions began to circulate that club officials were helping themselves as well as paying the players. The need of honesty was beginning to be felt keenly by the men at the head of the moneyed clubs, and Mr. McLaughlin, with others like-minded, began a process of organisation and education."

"A committee of the S.F.A. was appointed to revise the rules, which were a confused mess. How the would-be reformers were for the time being beaten Mr. McLaughlin well remembers. "When at the meeting of the committee," he says, "we came to the rules dealing with professionals. I said I thought drastic alteration was required. We looked at each other, and nobody made a proposal. Then I appealed to our own knowledge of what had happened, and said the best course was to be honest." The committee became unanimous in their recommendation that professionalism be legalised, but at the special meeting of the

Association Mr. Burnett, an Aberdeen purist, took the feet from the agitators by carrying a motion that the Associated be styled the Scottish Amateur Football Association. The advantage was short lived. The threat of secession was again made, and, as the public were behind the professional party, the Association capitulated, and professionalism was "recognised." Some of the most strenuous opponents of legalisation, strangely enough, were among the first to register paid players."

"From a Clay Hole to a Sports Enclosure"

"The original objects of the Celtic Club were naturally too good to last – at all events in their entirety – though direct donations to charitable institutions are still given of considerable amount. At the start of the club members were welcomed, but as the number began to rise, and it became apparent that the privilege of membership was sought as the cheapest means of seeing the matches, restrictions were imposed. By and by difficulties began to crop up, and limited liability was proposed. It was objected to, and the objectors carried their point, eloquent gentlemen declaring that if necessary the members would pawn their blankets to keep the club cut of debt. Later the members were asked to come forward and state how much they were willing to advance on loan to the club. The total sum was [only] £40, and after that there was no more difficulty about limited liability. The £10,000 share capital was subscribed, the 200 members each having allotted one fully paid up share of £1. This is the basis on which the club rests, and it is the single club in Scotland in which the man in the street would take shares as a speculation. As a matter of fact he might take some as an investment if he could get them. For the first five years of their existence the club were tenants of a ground which was the property of a gentleman with mistaken notions of the position of the game. "Being an Irish club," remarks Mr. McLaughlin, "the first thing we did was to have a row with the landlord. He knew nothing about football, but when somebody told him that the average drawings were £1,000 he wanted to double the rent. It was only after a hard fight, and before the club had played a match, that an arrangement was come to. Then when the lease was up he named the modest sum of £500 as a yearly rental of a ground not worth £50." But this was a blessing in disguise. Forced to make a shift the club acquired an extinct clay hole, and proceeded to make "Parkhead grounds" as we now know them. Vast quantities of rubbish had to be put in, and there is a tradition that a cart and two horses are embedded under the ground. They fell in, and it was impossible to get them out again, is, in brief, the story Mr. McLaughlin tells with the gravest of faces of the tragic accident."

"In all, one way and another, probably £20,000 has been put out on the ground, and it is as well that it cannot be alienated. Every farthing got from internationals, Mr. McLaughlin says, went in improvements, but that is what, in municipal work, is called remunerative capital expenditure. And what Scottish club would not take over the fortune of the Celtic Club – and Mr. McLaughlin?"

"Dundee Evening Telegraph" – Thursday 12th August 1909

"Mr. J.H. McLaughlin, Of Celtic F.C., Dies – By the death of Mr. John Herbert McLaughlin, Chairman of the Celtic Football Club, a well-known figure in Scottish Athletics has been removed. Mr. McLaughlin had been ill for eighteen months, and his death did not come in the nature of a surprise. Indeed, about a year ago his illness was of a severe nature. Mr. McLaughlin died at his residence, Strathmore, Hamilton. He was one of the founders of the Celtic Football Club in 1888 and on its formation as a Limited Liability Company in 1897 he became Chairman. He also acted as secretary and treasurer of the club at various times. He took an active interest in the affairs of the Scottish Football Association, serving for a time as its president, and also filled the office of treasurer. He represented Scotland on the Football International Board, and his opinion on football matters commanded much respect on both sides of the border. Kindred sports also claimed a good deal of Mr. McLaughlin's attention, especially bowling, and he was president for three years of the Hamilton Caledonian Club."

"The deceased, who was forty-six years of age, is survived by a widow and family. A native of Glasgow, he was educated in St Mungo's School and finished at Stoneyhurst College, where he took the highest honours and was gold medallist for two years in succession. An accomplished musician, he was organist for many years in St Mary's Church, Abercromby Street, Glasgow, and latterly he held a similar appointment with much acceptance in St Mary's Catholic Church, Hamilton. The funeral takes place on Saturday to Dalbeth Cemetery, and a pathetic coincidence is that on the same day the annual athletic meeting of the Celtic Club, in which the deceased always took a great interest, will be held."

"Dundee Evening Telegraph" – Friday 23rd July 1915

"Moving Incident In Hospital – Rescued Officer Visits Soldier Who Gained the Victoria Cross – Lance-Corporal [William] Angus, to whom the King has awarded the Victoria Cross, continues to make progress towards recovery in the military hospital at Chatham, to which institution he was brought about ten days ago from Boulogne. His head is still swathed in bandages. He has lost the sight of his left eye, and his right foot is badly injured, but the doctors say his foot will come alright. A touching incident took place at the hospital one day this week, when Angus was visited by Lieutenant Martin, whose life he saved on June 12, and for which gallant action he was awarded the V.C. As Lieut. Martin walked up to the bedside of his friend and deliverer and greeted him, both were overcome with emotion for a few minutes, and neither could utter a word. When they had recovered their feelings they had an hour's happy conversation, and both were most solicitous after each other's welfare. This was natural, seeing this is the first occasion on which they have met since they went through their thrilling adventure on the grassy slopes near Givenchy. Her Majesty Queen Mary sent this week to Corporal Angus the gift of a garment. It was accompanied by a card, on which the Queen wished him good luck."

"Celtic F.C.'s Congratulations – Corporal Angus was for two seasons connected with Glasgow Celtic Football Club, and Mr. William Maley, the secretary, has addressed a letter of congratulation to Angus' father. He writes: – "I beg to offer you on behalf of my club and personally our sincerest congratulations on the brilliant achievement of your son Willie. That he may come back to you all safe and sound is now our most earnest prayer, and we trust that you may all be long spared to each other to happy and prosperous days. I can safely say that no club has ever had a more willing or conscientious player, and one who always showed by his cleanliness that fine spirit which has in his army life enabled him to do the deed which has earned him a world's acclamation and, I am sure, brought great pride to the folks at home who have followed his career anxiously. That he may soon be quite recovered from his serious injuries is my earnest prayer. Kindly convey to him if possible our good wishes, and we look forward to personally congratulating him on his return.""

"Dundee Courier" – Monday 29th October 1923

"Police Ambush Charabanc – Forty Celtic Supporters Arrested – Forty followers of the Celtic Football Club were arrested by Glasgow police on a charge of breach of the peace. They had attended the game at Ibrox Park between Celtic and Rangers [which finished goalless], and were travelling to the East End of the city in a charabanc. Just before the charabanc reached the junction of Nelson Street and Bridge Street, a large posse of police emerged from the Southern Police Office, and surrounded it, placing the occupants under arrest. A large crowd immediately gathered, and as the driver obeyed the police order to proceed to the police station a few yards away hundreds of people followed the vehicle. Following up the charabanc at a convenient distance in a private car were Detective Lieutenant McDonald and Lieuts. Stirton and Kirkcaldy."

"Seldom has the bar of the Southern Police Office shown more stir for, besides the forty football enthusiasts, there were nearly as many constables lined up. To take down the names and addresses of the men required considerable time. Immediately thereafter thirty-three of them were searched and lodged in separate cells. The other seven, who were young lads under sixteen years of age, were placed in a side room, and later were sent to the detention house in St Vincent Street. Within an hour all the men had been safely locked up, but the chilly atmosphere in the cells failed to dampen the exuberance of the prisoners. Reverberating along the corridors of the office could be heard shouts of "Good old Celts!" and other "war cries". Fully a dozen green and white flags attached to long sticks were taken possession of by the police."

"The Sunday Post" – Sunday 4th December 1927

"It will come, no doubt, as a surprise to learn that Celtic Football Club may soon decide to let Celtic Park for greyhound racing. But, nevertheless, it is quite true. The matter has been discussed in an informal way. The ground has been examined by experts for the racing people, and I understand the Celtic Directors will have the proposal up for consideration and decision very soon. If they agree to let, this does not mean any interference with the club's football. Celtic Park can be adapted readily and quickly to meet the new craze."

"Demolition Derbies"

"Six-two."

Along with "seven-one", this remains one of the most memorable scorelines for any Celtic supporter, at least domestically. Great victories over any rivals, particularly those which are somewhat unexpected in their nature, are always bound to resonate strongly with most sporting fans and continue to bring smiles to their faces many years later. With this in mind, it is perhaps no surprise that phrases such as "Demolition Derby" were coined following the last "six-two" game, all whilst scarves, t-shirts, flags, videos and even a television sketch involving an actor depicting Pope Saint John Paul II served as reminders of a great day.

However, the twenty-seventh of August 2000 was not the first occasion upon which Celtic had recorded a six-two victory over Rangers, for they also did so in 1895 and once again in 1938. Like their modern counterpart, both previous victories occurred in the Scottish League, but unlike the day on which Henrik Larsson famously chipped Stefan Klos, there are likely very few people left who can remember the 1938 result, and none who had any direct experience of that which occurred in 1895.

At the end of their 1895-96 league duties, Celtic were crowned as the Champions of Scotland for the third time, but earlier that season, this outcome would have seemed far from certain. Whilst the Celts began the campaign well, with a record of four wins and one loss with five games gone (the solitary defeat came against Hibernian), they would face adversity in the weeks to follow. The high attained by winning by four-two at Ibrox in the last of these five matches was soon quashed as the Celts suffered what remains their heaviest home defeat, losing five-nil to Heart of Midlothian. With Hibernian leading the table after Celtic's defeat to Hearts, another loss in the following match against St. Bernard's would not have been what the Parkhead faithful were hoping for – after all, the league season was only eighteen games long at this point.

However, by the time Rangers were due to visit Celtic Park in December, the East End Club were playing better football and enjoying successful results once again, having put together a run of eight victories since their last defeat, which included wins over the three sides to have bettered them previously. The Celts were scoring freely as the day of destiny arrived, having found the net a remarkable fifty-two times in their last ten league and Glasgow Cup matches, an average of more than five goals per game. As the nature of this chapter would suggest, they continued such form, putting six past their opponents on the fourteenth of December 1895 in the Glasgow Derby and, notably, opening up a six point gap over their nearest rivals Hearts in the league table as they did so (although it has to be said Rangers had three games in hand, despite being two points behind Hearts).

"Celtic 6, Rangers 2 – 14th December 1895"

Celtic: McArthur; Meehan & Doyle; King, Kelly & Battles; Morrison, Blessington, Martin, McMahon & Ferguson.

Scorers: Martin, McMahon, McMahon, Blessington, Battles & Morrison.

Rangers: McLeod; N. Smith & Drummond; Marshall, Gibson & Mitchell; Barker, McCreadie, Oswald, McPherson & A. Smith.

Scorers: A. Smith & McCreadie.

Of the match itself, the "Glasgow Herald" said the following (please note score updates have been added for your convenience where they are not already included in the articles themselves): "The return league match between the Celtic and the Rangers was played at Parkhead before twenty-five spectators. The match was looked upon as virtually deciding the League Championship. The weather was dull and gloomy, but the rain cleared off before the start."

"A rush by the right wing took the Rangers [close to] McArthur, and when near that custodian Barker passed to A.

Smith, who had no difficulty in scoring. A nasty cross wind, which blew right across the field, proved very troublesome, while the footing was not of the best. The game however, was of the fastest description, both teams alternately having their share of attacking. A corner off Marshall followed, but try as the home team liked they were unable to score." [Celtic 0, Rangers 1]

"A good deal of feeling was imparted to the game, and the referee gave both teams a word of caution, and none too soon either. The home team at last got their reward, a quick shot from the right beating McLeod, who endeavoured to kick the ball out, but it glanced off of his foot into the net." [Celtic 1, Rangers 1]

"The fortunes of the game were fluctuating in a marked degree, the Rangers taking up the running on restarting...An accident to McPherson on the twelve yard line stopped their progress, and the international had to leave the field, the injury apparently being a severe one. Following on this, McLeod's charge underwent regular bombardment, and the custodian made amends for his previous error. Twice in succession he saved brilliantly, one shot from Martin being cleared in great style. A header from McMahon, after a beautifully-placed corner from Ferguson, was too much for the ex-Dumbartonian, and the Celts took the lead after forty minutes play. McPherson reappeared with a bandage around his forehead...and half-time was called shortly after with the Celts leading by two goals to one."

"After the interval the Rangers...were the first to show up, and Hugh McCreadie had hard lines with a shot which just grazed the uprights...A good sprint by A. Smith left Meechan in the rear, and off his centre Oswald put in a clinker, which McArthur managed to hold. Some quiet play followed and then McArthur had again to throw himself full length at a shot from McCreadie, which he barely managed to tip around the post. The fine display of their goalkeeper gave encouragement to the Celts, and a break away by their right wing resulted in their total being further augmented, McMahon putting on the finishing touch with his head." [Celtic 3, Rangers 1]

"Rain came down heavily and the light became very bad, the players with difficulty being discerned. Although they were two goals down, the Rangers responded in a plucky fashion, but McPherson was practically useless, and his presence was more of a hindrance than anything else...Once more the Celts scored, but offside was claimed and allowed, Ferguson being the transgressor. A legitimate point was not long in coming, however, the Celtic forwards clean beating the halves, and sending the ball past McLeod, Blessington being the scorer. A fifth followed within a minute, Battles scoring from half-back. Not content with this, Morrison got a chance from Martin, which he promptly accepted, McLeod making little attempt to save the shot." [Celtic 6, Rangers 1]

"These reverses would have had their effect on any team, but the Rangers showed surprising pluck. They were rewarded by a grandly taken goal from McCreadie, the score standing six to two in favour of the Celts with twenty minutes to go. The game was well contested to the close."

Thereafter, thanks in part to that historic result, Celtic would become Champions, wrestling the league flag back from previous winners Heart of Midlothian. However, more than four decades on, when the Celts would first repeat such a scoreline, they would be the current Champions of Scotland, with their sights firmly set on retaining that title. Sadly, despite all of their efforts, which included some truly fantastic displays, such as a nine-one win over Kilmarnock on the opening day of the season and a five-one away victory at Tynecastle, the Celts would be unsuccessful in this regard, eventually finishing their campaign eleven points behind new champions Rangers.

However, this is not to say that Celtic's second six-two win over their rivals is not worthy of mention or remembrance, for the Celts of the mid to late 1930s were capable of great things – as displayed by the Scottish Cup win of 1937 and the league triumphs of 1935-36 and 1937-38 – but equally they were also prone to repeated bouts of inconsistency. Great wins, such as the six-two triumph over Rangers, were often followed by poor results (a home defeat to Hamilton Academical being such an example), but I feel confident that more successes would have been enjoyed by the Parkhead side had the outbreak of World War Two not put an end to competitive football in Scotland in 1939.

In truth, the result of the tenth of September 1938 is not only important because of the famous scoreline attached to it, but also as it represented the last competitive league victory Celtic and their supporters would enjoy over Rangers for more than twelve years. Put yourselves in the shoes of a supporter of the time and imagine that for a moment, twelve years without a league victory over Rangers. Such a thought would have been almost unthinkable then, and thus there is a certain degree of poignancy attached to the six-two win in 1938, as for many (both those who went on to fight on the front lines and those who took refuge in fragile bomb shelters), it would have been the last Glasgow Derby victory they ever witnessed, and that is a sad fact indeed.

"Celtic 6, Rangers 2 – 10ᵗʰ September 1938"

Celtic: Kennaway; Hogg & Morrison; Geatons, Lyon & Paterson; Delaney, MacDonald, Crum, Divers & Murphy.

Scorers: MacDonald, Lyon, Lyon (pen), Delaney, MacDonald & MacDonald.

Rangers: Dawson; Gray & Shaw; McKillop, Woodburn & Brown; Main, Thornton, Smith, McPhail & Kinnear.

Scorers: Smith & Thornton.

In the "Sunday Mail" of the following day, a Celtic supporter, a Mr. B.F. Glen of 903 Govan Road, Glasgow, said:

"So the Bhoys have done it again! Great stuff this, Celtic! Three successive victories over their biggest rivals is a mighty proud record. To find words to praise my team would be like trying to paint – shall we say the Shamrock?"

"Poor old Jerry Dawson! He must have been mesmerised. Our forwards were here, there, everywhere, dancing their way to success. They did the Lambeth walk while the Rangers' tune was the Blues! We won in a gallop; no one could say anything different. Paterson was a dandy. I have never seen him play better. Calum

MacDonald [more commonly referred to as Malky MacDonald] was also brilliant, and capped a good afternoon's display by getting a hat-trick. Wasn't his third goal a beauty?"

"We mustn't forget Delaney. He was in tip-top form, and elusive as the Scarlett Pimpernel. Bobby Hogg played hard enough, but just didn't strike it. On the day, Morrison was the better back. Willie Lyon was his usual reliable self, and Joe Kennaway couldn't have been better. What a goalkeeper!"

"We certainly outplayed them in the first half, and deserved the three goal lead at the interval. They played as a team, and that was the secret of their success! Celts weren't so good in the first quarter of an hour in the second half, during which they lost two goals; but after that they pulled up their socks and showed them what for. It was a well-spent bob. Attaboy, Celtic!"

Equally, the same newspaper also allowed an identical column for the view of a Rangers supporter, one Dr. S. King, of 38 Bunessan St, Glasgow. He said the following:

"Kinnear's a dandy – isn't he? Even the Celtic fans must admit that, for he had Bobby Hogg on toast. He played his way into the national team! Friend Davie, however, wasn't supported, and that's why the fat was in the fire. McPhail was the principal sinner in this respect. He preferred to adopt a defensive game, and starved Kinnear, who was just "rearin' to go". The experiment of playing Thornton at outside-right was a wash-out. He's a centre, and that's all."

"Smith was so poorly supported it would be unfair to pass judgement on his play. I think Dawson was a trifle slow in trying to save one of the goals, but once he was definitely unsighted. Gray tired in the second half, and this led to wide open spaces appearing in the right defence. Shaw was grand. Woodburn showed tremendous promise, but his over-keenness led to at least two fouls, which produced goals for Celtic."

"McKillop and Brown were just ordinary. In the second half it looked as if Rangers might have snatched a draw, but a doubtful goal by Celtic knocked this idea haywire. After that Rangers seemed to call it a day, and the final score was an exaggeration of superiority. But let's not cry over spilt milk. I'm disappointed, dreadfully so – but not downhearted. It will be a different story on the Autumn holiday – see if I'm right."

If nothing else, I felt those two articles were rather interesting when I first came across them, as they allowed two supporters, albeit under the jurisdiction of the "Sunday Mail" to put their views of the match across. Whilst I'm sure several holes could be picked in both men's accounts (after all, we each see football matches which involve our favoured side through somewhat tinted spectacles), I will only refer specifically to Dr. King's description of Celtic's fourth goal as "doubtful", for others within the press – even those writing on the same newspaper page – put this theory to bed.

The reporter for the "Sunday Mail", referred to as "Scotland's Greatest Sports Writer", going under the pseudonym of "Rex", said the following of that goal at the beginning of his article, before returning to it in more detail midway through the piece: "Celtic scored six goals. But the golden goal of the lot was the fourth. Delaney scored it. And it brought every Celtic player bar Kennaway tearing up the field with congratulations. Because it came at a time when Celtic were so far out of the game, it looked like they'd never find the way back [prior to this, Celtic had allowed a three-nil lead to slip to only three-two]."

"Then just as the equaliser was looming up, Rangers were knocked as flat as my notecase. Murphy, Crum and Delaney broke through. Crum, near the byline, lobbed across, and the flying Delaney headed the ball practically out of Dawson's hands into the net! A peach of a goal. It didn't only take the wind out of Rangers' sails – it pinched the rudder as well. The game was really finished then. Celts were in the mood that occasionally strikes a racing punter – they couldn't do anything wrong. And Rangers had to pay up. Yet, although MacDonald's two concluding goals were gems, they were actually just the froth on Delaney's beer."

Celtic would have to wait until the dawning of the new century until they enjoyed a six-two victory over Rangers once more, and this was to be the most famous of them all, for it signalled the true revival of a footballing giant under new manager, Martin O'Neill. Although nobody knew it at the time, that win would be the catalyst which would lead Celtic to their first domestic treble since 1969 and ultimately, to their first European final in more than three decades. Yes, Rangers were competitive throughout most of the early twenty-first century, but now much of this can be attributed to reckless overspending which would lead to their downfall and leave many innocent creditors unpaid.

This only underlines the achievements of Martin O'Neill and his Celtic side, spearheaded by some of the greatest Celts in recent memory, who truly burst into life on the twenty-seventh of August 2000, a little under sixty-two years on from their last six-two win.

"Celtic 6, Rangers 2 – 27th August 2000"

Celtic: Gould, Valgaeren, Stubbs, Mahe, McNamara, Petrov, Lambert (Mjallby), Moravcik (Boyd), Petta, Larsson (Burchill) & Sutton. Unused Substitutes: Kerr, Berkovic.

Scorers: Sutton, Petrov, Lambert, Larsson, Larsson & Sutton.

Rangers: Klos, Ricksen (Tugay), Konterman, Amoruso, Vidmar (Kanchelskis), Reyna, Ferguson, van Bronckhorst, McCann (Lovenkrands), Dodds & Wallace. Unused Substitutes: Charbonnier, Malcolm.

Scorers: Reyna & Dodds (pen).

I'll leave it to the words of someone whom many may consider an odd choice to recount such a famous victory, before analysing a little of what he had to say, Jim Traynor. The following is from the "Daily Record" on the twenty-eighth of August 2000.

"Celtic's long-suffering disciples flooded into their place of worship yesterday and left convinced they had just witnessed a remarkable resurrection. They had arrived praying for signs of a possible revival but were given much more than any of them had dared to hope for. They saw their side storm into a three-goal lead after only eleven minutes and although Rangers threatened to recover from a truly awful start Celtic were never going to be overtaken. Their own defence cracked at times but you better believe Martin O'Neill's Celtic are genuine contenders."

"Their new striker, Chris Sutton, scored twice as did Henrik Larsson with Stiliyan Petrov and Paul Lambert adding to the haul which stunned Rangers' supporters, who had become accustomed to watching their side dominate this fixture. They had started drifting away long before the end unable to take any more while Celtic's masses launched into delirium and who could blame them? They had waited a long time to taste victory over Rangers and they were not about to miss the chance to gloat and rejoice."

"It was their turn at last and after this thrashing of the ancient rival, who this morning have the worst defensive record in the Scottish Premier League, they are probably convinced the football world is the right side up again. Indeed, in O'Neill they believe they have a saviour although the manager, who was left breathless at the end of his first Old Firm match, will realise just as soon as his adrenaline stops coursing that there is much work still to be done with the team he inherited. However, no one should be in any doubt about what to expect at the top of the SPL after a pulsating and astonishing match in the East End of a city which remains divided by ancient prejudice. Celtic are back. We have a championship."

Now, without picking apart the opening section of Mr. Traynor's article in forensic detail, we can clearly see a religious theme running within the veins of the previous passage. Whether the presence of this topic was intentional is debatable, but one cannot help but notice words and phrases such as "disciples", "place of worship", "saviour" and "resurrection" when reading it. The use of "ancient rivals" and "ancient prejudice" also hints at a noticeable undercurrent, but this may simply be the author's attempt to make a veiled reference to the religious elements stereotypically associated with this old fixture.

As the article continues, this theme dissipates to a large degree, being replaced instead with one of regret and finger pointing. Of course, Mr. Traynor has since been employed at Ibrox, so perhaps this is not a surprise, but one could well say that the article in question was written from a biased point of view. For example, the author states that the referee was "too harsh" in his treatment of a couple of the visiting players, before saying that "Celtic benefited from peculiar judgements made by [Stuart] Dougal and his assistants." The fact that 'pro-Celtic' refereeing performances were rarities (to say the least) in these games tells its own story, I feel. Mr. Traynor spends more column space criticising the officials for disallowing a Rangers goal for offside (moments after awarding them a goal when many were unsure as to whether the ball had crossed the line) than discussing one of the greatest goals the world famous fixture would ever see, as Henrik Larsson made it four-two to the home side.

Regardless, come the final whistle on that sunny day, Celtic had defeated their rivals by six goals to two for the third and final time in the Scottish League. As with the two previous matches I have discussed, the scoreline could have been more in truth, but I doubt many Celtic supporters would have been bemoaning their team's inability to turn six goals into seven as they celebrated in homes and pubs across Scotland and the world.

To his credit, Mr. Traynor was most certainly correct about one thing in his article which I have previously mentioned – Celtic were back – and back with a bang. The Ibrox side would never truly recover from this defeat, as they attempted to combat a Celtic side clearly on the rise by increasing spending, hoping that throwing money at their problems would make them go away. Eventually, such a reckless attitude would lead to their demise, and I feel it is safe to assume that more silverware would indeed have headed Parkhead's way over the following decade if such spending had not occurred. Fundamentally, from that day onwards, Celtic had Rangers running scared, and despite a five-one victory for the Ibrox side in the return league fixture (thanks in part to the twelve million pound Tore Andre Flo), the Celts went on to secure a domestic treble.

Over the next decade, the proverbial pendulum would swing back and forth from Celtic Park to Ibrox, but it was a rare year in which Celtic were not serious competitors for the League Championship, and thus the sun continued to shine on Celtic Park and the supporters which called the stadium home, all whilst storm clouds gathered on the south side of the River Clyde. Nowadays, there is no question as to who the biggest team in Scotland are, and, in its own little way, we have the last of three six-two victories over Rangers, Martin O'Neill and all of his players, to thank for that.

"I Decided My Health Came First"

The world has witnessed the rise and fall of many sporting figures. Injuries, illnesses, addictions and almost every conceivable scandal have all conspired to end careers at one point or another, but perhaps the most prevalent cause of footballers calling it a day has simply been the unavoidable passage of time coupled with the inevitable loss of athleticism and fitness which accompanies advancing age. In the modern day, mental health issues do not carry the same stigma which they did in the distant past, but negative attitudes are still present in some sections of society. With that in mind, I would ask you to imagine what it must have been like to be affected by such an illness almost a century ago, back in the 1920s.

On the fourth of March 1922, a young man by the name of Hugh Hilley strode out on to the pitch at Cathkin Park to take his place in a senior Celtic eleven for the first time. Signed a little under a year earlier, Hugh – named Healy before the family altered their surname to the less Irish-sounding Hilley – was born in Garngad on the nineteenth of March 1899 and now, almost twenty-three years on, he was set to play as the centre forward of Celtic Football Club. However, he did not have the most illustrious of debuts in a match which finished goalless, despite Hugh testing the Third Lanark goalkeeper with a stinging shot midway through the first half, but success would come in time.

Over the course of the next few seasons Hugh, as hard-working and tough-tackling a player as any football supporter could hope to find in their team, promptly retreated to fill the role of left full-back, held for so long at Celtic Park (but being gradually vacated) by the legendary Alec McNair. In this position, Hugh would flourish, soon winning over fans and pundits alike with the all or nothing attitude he applied to his game. He may not have been the most technically gifted player, but through his work ethic he made up for most of his minor shortcomings.

In a similar manner to several players across the eras, the number of injuries which Hugh endured and returned from proved to be testament to his commitment to the Hoops' cause. Never afraid to put his body on the line, it has been said – in a good humoured but not entirely untrue sense – that Hugh's nose was never anything other than broken during the year of 1925. Famously, after a hard-fought goalless draw against St. Mirren in the quarter final of the Scottish Cup that year, Hilley is reported to have said the following, having had his nose broken for the umpteenth time earlier that afternoon: "I had lost so much blood [during the match], I was seeing half a dozen balls."

However, in his own typical style, he would not allow such setbacks to stop him from playing for Celtic, and as such he featured when the Hoops faced the Buddies in a replay three days later, and subsequently in a second replay which would follow that before the sides could eventually be separated. Victories over Rangers in the semi-final and Dundee in the final followed, and Hugh Hilley was a Scottish Cup winner for the first time, having played in every match during the Cup run. For the sake of this brief piece, it is also worthy of note that between the 1924-25 season and the 1926-27 campaign inclusively, he only missed three league matches (one per year as it turned out) and not a solitary Scottish Cup tie from the twenty-one which involved the Celts. This statistic perhaps demonstrates better than any other his importance to the Celtic sides of the mid-1920s. In the two seasons which followed the previously referenced Scottish Cup Final, Hilley would win his only Scottish League Championship medal in 1925-26, before adding a second Scottish Cup success to his collection when the Celts – with the newly introduced John Thomson keeping goal – beat East Fife by three goals to one.

Only three fixtures into the new 1927-28 season though, Hugh Hilley would play his final match for Celtic, or indeed, any other football team. Whether or not warning signs had been present or if his absence came as a total surprise remains unclear, but following a goalless draw with Hamilton Academical in August 1927, it is said he suffered a nervous breakdown of sorts. Very little reference is made to the exact nature of this in the press of the day, although it is clear he did not enjoy the best of performances that afternoon, being beaten uncharacteristically easily by wingers and the like. Clearly, his focus was not solely on the game itself. A week after the incident, one "Sunday Post" column said "Hilley has been X-rayed recently", but a few months later in December, the "Arbroath Herald and Advertiser" perhaps hinted more truthfully at his issues, saying "Hugh Hilley, the Celtic back, has returned from his Highland Nursing Home. It is not likely, however, that the player will be able to take to the field this season owing to the nature of his illness."

Almost three years later, the same newspaper said "Hugh Hilley, Celtic's left-back, gave up the game two seasons ago on account of ill health. He is all right again, and hopes soon to be back at Parkhead."

Alas, it was not to be. Never capped by his country and without scoring a domestic goal, Hugh Hilley made one hundred and ninety-five appearances for Celtic Football Club, playing a crucial if somewhat unglamorous role for five years with admirable enthusiasm and gusto. It must have been tremendously difficult for a man of such supreme physicality, said to have been "fanatical about his health" by Kevin McCarra's "Celtic: A Biography in Nine Lives" no less, to have had to retire from the game he loved due to a mental illness largely misunderstood at the time, both by the medical profession and the public at large.

Following his football career, Hugh set up a successful ice cream café with his Scots-Italian wife, explaining his reasoning by saying, "Finally I decided my health came first. I gave up playing [football], set up...the business, and never looked back."

Hugh Hilley died on the fourteenth of September 1987, at the age of eighty-eight, after overcoming his illness and living a full and happy life. He remains a fondly remembered and much loved Celt of old.

1. The first Celtic photograph from 1888, with the captain James Kelly sat proudly front and centre. Back Row (left to right): Joe Anderson (trainer), James Quillan, Daniel Malloy, John Glass, John MacDonald (officials); Middle Row: William Groves, Tom Maley, Paddy Gallagher, William McKillop (official), Willie Maley, Mick Dunbar; Front Row: Johnny Coleman, James McLaren, James Kelly (captain), Neil McCallum and Mick McKeown.

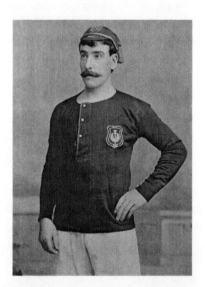

2. Dan McArthur sporting a Scotland jersey, one of his three international caps, and a fine moustache.

3. John Divers (1874-1942)

4. The Celts celebrate their triumphs in the Glasgow Merchants' Charity Cup, the Scottish Cup and the Glasgow Cup. James Hay, the captain who led his team to such success, sits third from the right in the front row. Back Row (left to right): Tom White, James Kelly, Tom Colgan, John McKillop, James Grant, Michael Dunbar (officials); Middle Row: Willie Maley (manager), Jim Young, Peter Somers, Jimmy McMenemy, Davie Adams, John Mitchell, Jimmy Weir, Robert Davis; Front Row: David Hamilton, Donald McLeod, Willie Loney, James Hay (captain), Jimmy Quinn and Alec McNair.

6. Tommy McInally adopts an unorthodox pose.

5. Charlie Shaw

7. Hugh Hilley

8. Celtic Football Club (1930). William Hughes can be seen as the furthest right player in the middle row. Back Row (left to right): William Cook, Peter Kavanagh, Hughie Smith, Peter Wilson; Middle Row: Peter McGonagle, Chic Geatons, Denis O'Hare, John Thomson, Robert Whitelaw, William Hughes, William Quinn (trainer); Front Row: Robert Thomson, Alec Thomson, Jimmy McGrory, Jimmy McStay (captain), Peter Scarff, Charles Napier.

9. George Paterson   10. John Divers (1911-1984)

11. Jackie Gallacher

12. John Divers (1940-2014)

Divers scores Celtic's first goal against
Rangers in the Scottish Cup.

13. John Divers
looks on from
the mud as his
effort finds its
target.

14. Willie O'Neill slides in to dramatically prevent a Rangers equaliser in the Scottish League Cup Final of 1966-67.

15. The Celtic team hail Willie, the hero of the day, after securing the 1966-67 Scottish League Cup.

16. Celtic win it all, 1966-67. Willie O'Neill stands second from the right at the rear. Back Row (left to right): Tommy Gemmell, Stevie Chalmers, Jim Craig, John Fallon, John Hughes, Ronnie Simpson, Bobby Murdoch, Willie O'Neill, John Clark; Front Row: Jimmy Johnstone, Willie Wallace, Charlie Gallacher, Billy McNeill (captain), Joe McBride, Bertie Auld and Bobby Lennox.

17. Gerry and Karen pose with members of the Celtic team on a trip to Rotterdam in 1981. From left to right: Paddy Bonner, Tommy Burns, Roy Aitken, Karen, Gerry, Mike Conroy, Tom McAdam, David Moyes and Danny Crainie.

18. Gerry Cleary, in more recent days, retaining a love for retro shirts.

19. Matt Donohue cannot hide his delight as he visits Celtic Park for the first time.

20. Andrew Cowan with some of the children he met on his trip to Malawi.

21. Pat McManus

22. Willie Fernie, second from the left in the front row, lines up for Leslie Hearts. *(Please note, this photograph and all of those hereafter have been loaned from the Fernie family's personal collection with their permission, before being scanned and in some cases painstakingly restored by the author for your enjoyment).*

23. The young Fernie as the new kid on the block at Parkhead.

24. Fernie shares a moment with Mike Haughney and Jock Stein.

25. Willie and Audrey pose on their wedding day.

26. A few autograph seekers get their man.

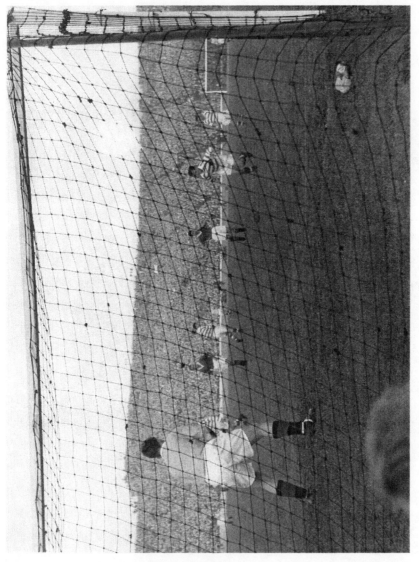

27. Willie Fernie scores the seventh of Celtic's goals in the 7-1 Scottish League Cup Final defeat of Rangers in the 1957–58 season (Photograph 1 of 4).

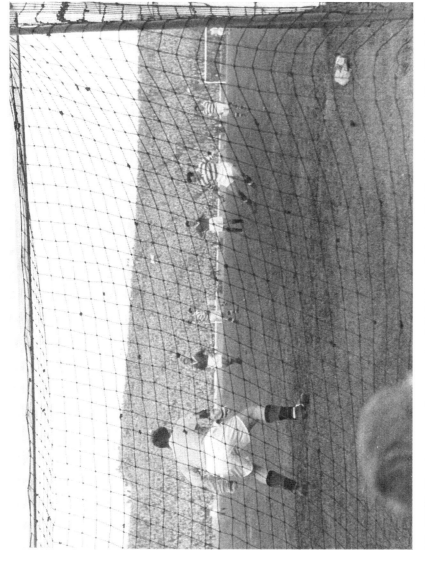

28. Willie Fernie scores the seventh of Celtic's goals in the 7-1 Scottish League Cup Final defeat of Rangers in the 1957-58 season (Photograph 2 of 4).

29. Willie Fernie scores the seventh of Celtic's goals in the 7-1 Scottish League Cup Final defeat of Rangers in the 1957-58 season (Photograph 3 of 4).

30. Willie Fernie scores the seventh of Celtic's goals in the 7-1 Scottish League Cup Final defeat of Rangers in the 1957-58 season (Photograph 4 of 4).

31. The triumphant 7-1 team pose with their prize. Willie Fernie is pictured at the far right in the rear. Back Row (left to right): John Donnelly, Bobby Evans, Sean Fallon, Dick Beattie, Billy McPhail, Willie Fernie; Front Row: Jimmy McGrory (manager), Charlie Tully, Bobby Collins, Bertie Peacock, Sammy Wilson, Neil Mochan and Willie Johnstone (trainer).

32. Fernie, furthest to the right in the front row, is pictured alongside his companions in a Scotland side.

33. Willie admires his collection of Scotland jerseys, with the variance in numbers on show again highlighting his ability and willingness to play in almost any position on the field.

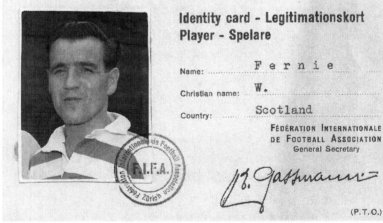

34. Willie Fernie's personal identity cards issued to players at the 1954 and 1958 World Cup Finals.

35. Willie Fernie, pictured second from the left in the front row, sits alongside his Middlesbrough teammates. A young Brian Clough sits directly next to him in the middle of the photograph with a ball at his feet.

36. The police attempt to clear the field of adoring youngsters as Willie Fernie makes his second debut for Celtic Football Club.

37. The Fernie family leave Celtic Park behind them as Willie heads for St. Mirren.

38. Willie holds off the great Stanley Matthews in a seniors' game in later years.

39. Sharing a moment with Danny McGrain in front of Willie's taxi.

40. Willie, his son Alex, and grandson Andrew enjoy a match day at Celtic Park.

"John the Second"

Born on the sixth of August 1911, the second man by the name of John Divers to pull on the famous green and white Hoops of Celtic Football Club signed for the Parkhead side in early December 1932, at the age of twenty-one. Having spent his formative footballing years playing with the likes of Clydebank B.G., Linwood St Conval's, Rothesay Royal Victoria and Renfrew Juniors – the side whom he left to join Celtic – John was evidently a talented lad, but as with the majority of young footballers, he was considered to be more of a raw ingredient than a finished article upon his arrival at Parkhead.

As an inside-forward by nature, John would face stiff competition for starting places at his new Club, with Celtic stalwarts Charlie Napier and Alec Thomson holding down each of the inside-forward positions when John joined the Parkhead side. Of course, neither of these men could go on indefinitely, although when one looks back at their records in the late 1920s and early 1930s – particularly that of Thomson – a supporter of the time could probably have been forgiven for feeling like they had been there forever. Still, as with any well run Football Club, Celtic had a plethora of potential replacements coming through their ranks, some of which John would go on to star beside in future years, although they would see sustained senior playing time prior to him. Such figures included young men of a similar age like Willie Buchan, Johnny Crum and Francis O'Donnell.

John Divers made his Celtic debut alongside the last of the trio named previously against Clyde towards the end of the 1933-34 season. Whilst Francis had seen a significant amount of action with the senior side during that domestic campaign, appearing in the majority of the Club's matches, John was new to all of this, and it may have showed somewhat as he failed to shine in what was, in truth, a poor game all round. Celtic edged past their opponents by two goals to one, with O'Donnell scoring both goals, but the match was largely overshadowed by the injury incurred by the man who would remain Celtic's greatest goalscorer, Jimmy McGrory, who broke a fibula [the bone on the outer side of the lower leg], ruling him out of action for the foreseeable future.

Of course, one silver lining of the aforementioned injury was that it opened up a space in the forward line for the remaining seven league matches that season. John would feature in each of these, scoring his first and second Celtic goals in a tight three-two victory over Dundee at Celtic Park on the twenty-first of April. Of this brace, the "Dundee Courier" said: "The rot started in eleven minutes, when Divers equalised, and the same player in twenty-one minutes put [the] Celts a goal up. Both were scrappy sorts of scores, but there was no denying the cleverness of this young Celt." Regardless, the star of the Celtic show during those final few fixtures of the 1933-34 season was undoubtedly Francis O'Donnell, who capped off an impressive second year at the Club with eleven goals in the seven matches since McGrory's injury. Born in the same month in 1911 as Divers, he was actually the younger of the two men, and I feel it is safe to assume that most Celtic supporters of the time would have presumed Francis O'Donnell would have remained at the Club longer than John Divers.

Come the new season and the return of Jimmy McGrory, combined with the emergence of Willie Buchan and latterly, Johnny Crum, John Divers soon found himself as a firm fixture in Celtic's reserve squad once again. In fact, he would not re-emerge in a senior line-up until around eighteen months had passed, in December 1935, when he featured in two matches before disappearing again until September 1936. However, this is not to say that the time John spent in the reserves was bad for him – far from it, in fact – as Celtic 'A' won the Scottish Reserve Cup in both 1934-35 and 1935-36.

Moving on, John featured another four times for the senior side towards the end of the 1936-37 league season as Willie Maley, knowing that there was no chance of catching Rangers in the league, rested some of his star players in preparation for the upcoming Scottish Cup Final against Aberdeen. John made the most of these outings to increase his profile in the mind of both his manager and the Celtic support, scoring on three occasions.

Whilst this was not immediately rewarded as the 1937-38 campaign began and John appeared only once in the opening ten games, he would soon be given the opportunity to play a few matches in the first team. On the eighteenth of December 1937, Celtic travelled to Easter Road to face Hibernian, and for the first time in eleven fixtures, John would play in the senior side. He made the most of it too, scoring the second of Celtic's three goals in a three-nil victory which was described as follows: "Hibernian… were having more of the game when Divers broke away and, though hustled by Miller, netted with a powerful ground shot."

This was an important day in the course of the 1937-38 campaign for a few reasons. Firstly, it allowed John Divers the chance to maintain a starting place in the side for the following match and, secondly, as bad weather prevented all but three top flight matches from taking place, Celtic climbed past Rangers and moved closer to Hearts – who were also unable to play – at the top of the league table.

Coincidentally, this was also the day upon which Jimmy McGrory was announced as the new manager of Kilmarnock Football Club, with one newspaper article stating: "…his hosts of friends and admirers throughout the football world will wish him the best of luck in his new venture."

This was the culmination of a series of events which made vacant the spot in Celtic's forward line Jimmy McGrory had occupied for more than a decade. Having said that, it is perhaps an appropriate time to cast our minds back towards Francis O'Donnell for a brief moment. Despite scoring an impressive fifty-eight goals in eighty-three senior outings, the big, burly centre forward had departed Celtic and Glasgow in May 1935, moving to mid-table Preston North End in England. One would presume such a decision was fuelled partly by a desire to play more first team football, as though he was a good player, he was unfortunate to find himself as the understudy to Jimmy McGrory for much of his time at Celtic Park.

In fact, some of the Celtic support are said to have criticised O'Donnell for being a little cumbersome from time to time, but

I feel this may have been an excuse to talk down the man purely because he was not quite Jimmy McGrory – whom he often replaced when he did get the chance to play. Of course, one must remember that to all intents and purposes, McGrory was one step down from God himself for many Celtic supporters, and I believe it is likely that, without the presence of the great man, Francis O'Donnell would have went on to become a Celtic great himself, such was his scoring record. Anyway, with an F.A. Cup runner's-up medal, forty-eight goals and one hundred and one appearances to his name, O'Donnell left Preston and went on to play with Aston Villa, Blackpool, Hearts and Tottenham Hotspur, amongst others – all whilst John was still a Celtic man.

Returning to the tale of Divers, he would push on from his impressive performance against Hibernian, scoring a remarkable fifteen goals in eleven league games around the turn of the year, and propelling Celtic, who won all eleven of those matches, up the league table. Of course, as with so many Celtic players who bring a smile to the faces of those who can remember them, John Divers truly made a name for himself and won over any doubters who remained within the Celtic support when he scored twice during one of the eleven aforementioned matches, against Rangers at Celtic Park.

The magnitude of this day, on which John Divers stole the show, was described by the "Glasgow Herald" with the following headlines attached to the two articles from which the quotes are sourced – "Happy New Year For Celtic" and "Ibrox Colours Lowered – Young Celtic Attack Wins The Day".

"Scotland's customary New Year football carnival, with its series of local "derbies" again provided holidaymakers with their most popular form of entertainment. Under favourable weather and playing conditions, the League games...were generously patronised. The big club event of the year, the meeting of Celtic and Rangers, retained its position as the prime attraction, the gates at Celtic Park having to be closed, and it is estimated ten thousand enthusiasts were turned away. The attendance at the game was returned at eighty-three and a half thousand, which is short of the ground record of eighty-eight thousand."

"In the result, as in other aspects, the Celtic-Rangers meeting furnished the outstanding return. Practically throughout, Celtic were the more talented team, and their victory by three goals to nil was fully earned. It was Celtic's first New Year's Day success against their rivals in ten years. With Rangers beaten and Hearts losing another point in a two-goal draw, Celtic now hold the [league] leadership on points basis."

"It was a pity, considering the occasion and the splendid crowd, that only occasionally did Rangers rally their forces and threaten to break down an indomitable Celtic defence at Parkhead. For the most part they were lamentably lax and stereotyped in movement, and were excelled in almost every position by a grand Celtic side. Steadfast in defence, mobile and thrustful at half-back, fast and daring in attack, Celtic reduced Rangers to a sad plight indeed, and in doing so impressed everyone by their wonderful team spirit and apparently endless reserve of stamina."

"What delighted most was the blend of guile and dash in the Celtic attack, where Divers, big and strong with two smartly taken goals to his credit, was much in the limelight."

Whilst the second of John's two goals is not discussed in detail in the newspapers, the first was described as follows: "Divers scored his first goal before the interval when, following a Carruth corner, he controlled the ball cleverly, side-stepped an opponent, and shot into the net." That aside, his overall play was praised throughout the country, with publications such as the "Aberdeen Journal" saying Divers was "outstanding in a field of great players", before referring to him as "indispensable".

It is abundantly clear that such a day was tremendously important not only for Celtic with a view to winning the Scottish League Championship, but also for John in terms of building his status as confident, in-form, forward player.

Only a few months later, with two games remaining in the league calendar, John joined his teammates as they took to the field against St. Mirren, knowing that a victory would secure their place as the Champions of Scotland. Whilst John Divers did not score that day (a bit of an oddity that season considering the vein of form he found himself in), he was, along with many others, instrumental in leaving Paisley with two points in the bag. The following quote from a very brief newspaper report gives us some insight into the teamwork which helped to win the title for the Parkhead Club: "They were given an excellent start, Crum scoring in the first minute after a combined movement in which Lyons, Geatons and Divers took part."

As the league season came to a close a week later, Celtic finished the campaign three points clear of their nearest challengers, Heart of Midlothian. John had scored twenty league goals in twenty league games as April turned to May and Celtic looked forward to a one-off tournament which would allow them to compete with the best of the sides from south of the border as well as their domestic rivals from Scotland, the Empire Exhibition Cup.

Again, both Celtic and Divers would shine as the Hoops added a famous trophy to their increasingly lengthy list of silverware, beating Sunderland, Hearts and Everton along the way. Whilst I shall not discuss the tournament as a whole nor the individual matches in much detail, as I have done so before in my previous work, I feel I must highlight the excellence shown by Divers during the tournament.

The Hoops' first match in the knockout competition (against 1937 F.A. Cup Winners Sunderland) ended goalless and Celtic immediately found themselves with a replay to contend with. Sunderland took the lead in the subsequent clash after testing Celtic's goalkeeper on several occasions, before Johnny Crum levelled the scores prior to half time. Midway through the second half, John Divers took the tie by the scruff of the neck, scoring two goals and sealing Celtic's place in the semi-finals of the tournament. John's strikes are described as follows: "The first was very well conceived, rapid interchanging with Crum and MacDonald leaving Divers, at the inside-right position, with a clear view from ten yards' range. In the second instance, Sunderland clearly considered they had set an off-side trap for Divers forty yards out, but he took the risk and raced clear ahead. Mapson dashed out. Divers was almost on the byline when he delivered his shot, but the ball carried past Mapson to the far post, off which it bounded into the net."

The newspaper article which I have quoted in this instance said the following in closing, which only goes to highlight and exemplify the instrumental impact upon which John had on the match as a whole: "The unorthodox meandering of Divers non-plussed the Sunderland defence and he frequently paved the way for his smaller colleagues to follow up."

In the semi-final, Celtic faced Heart of Midlothian who had, of course, finished as the runners-up in the league season which had just came to a close. Having beaten the Edinburgh side on the two occasions they had played them in the league, the Celtic supporters, and perhaps the Celtic team, were probably fairly confident of their chances going into this match. However, if complacency had led any of them to think that the test posed by Hearts would be an easy one, they would subsequently be proven to be naïve indeed.

Although Celtic would ultimately triumph and win the day, all the accounts of this match tell us that the Celts were very fortunate to progress into the competition's final, owing their place there largely to a truly magnificent display from their goalkeeper, Joe Kennaway. To contextualise this, if you were to read newspaper reports which describe the events of the match itself, it would not be long before you found references to Celtic being "lucky" or even "fluky", whilst mentions of Kennaway saw superlatives such as "marvellous" used in almost every sentence.

As the following quote describes, John Divers played a critical role in Celtic's only goal, scored by Johnny Crum, which would prove to be enough to see the Hoops progress to the final: "Midway through the half Celtic rallied, and after a cross from Lynch had been diverted towards the centre by Divers, Crum, from six yards, hooked the ball in and from off Waugh's hands it went into the net. It was a well-taken point…"

On the tenth of June 1938 Celtic, the Scottish Champions, would face Everton, the team who had finished fourteenth in the English league in the season just gone, but would go on to win the English Championship of 1938-39. Whilst the match was hotly contested, it generally accepted that Celtic had the better of the play in large parts, and it would not be unreasonable to say

Everton were fortunate to maintain a clean sheet through to the final whistle which signalled the end of normal time. In fact, John Divers did have the ball in the Everton net towards the close of regulation play, but to the disappointment of the majority of the crowd – which totalled over eighty-two thousand – the goal was ruled to be offside and therefore disallowed. Extra time proceeded and soon Celtic had their breakthrough, scoring through Crum, never looking back and becoming everlasting champions of the British Empire. In the days which followed, the whole Celtic team were praised widely in the Scottish media, with Divers being described as "particularly prominent" by "The Scotsman", amongst others.

In the season which followed, that of 1938-39, John Divers continued to hold on to his place in the Celtic line-up for the most part, scoring twenty-two goals and only missing a few matches. Whilst Celtic would relinquish their status as Champions to rivals Rangers, who won the league by some distance in the end, John Divers did have the pleasure of playing in the Celtic team which beat the Ibrox side by six goals to two at Celtic Park early in the campaign.

It would also be during this season that John would receive his one and only call up to the Scottish international team for an away match against Ireland. The visitors would win the tie by two goals to nil, recording their forty-first victory over the Irish in the process. The "Glasgow Herald" told the story of the day, and of John Divers' involvement, as follows.

"Divers failed to reproduce his club form, and his club mate, Crum, as well as Gillick, was adversely affected. Divers for twenty minutes at the start played up to reputation, but faded out afterwards, and it is reasonable to assume that he had not completely recovered from the seasickness that claimed him and the others on the stormy passage to Ireland."

Clearly then, John did not perform as well as he could have that day at Windsor Park in Belfast, but as the same newspaper noted, the weather conditions in which the tie took place did not provide the more technical players with the best canvas on which to produce their respective art. "For an hour the game was played in a deluge of rain, and play did not reach the highest standard. Scotland throughout never looked like losing and only masterly goalkeeping by Breen and faulty shooting, largely owing to the conditions, denied Scotland a substantial winning margin."

Back on the domestic front early in 1939, Divers would also score all four goals as the Celts eased by Albion Rovers in a four-one victory at Parkhead, before John had what would turn out to be his last serious hurrah in a Celtic shirt against Hearts in the third round of the Scottish Cup.

Having drawn the first match two-each on the eighteenth of February at Tynecastle, players and supporters alike arrived at Celtic Park on the twenty-second of the same month for a replay which, it was hoped, would settle matters one way or the other. Eventually, it would, but not before thousands of fans had left the match early – a phenomenon which is clearly not new – and Hearts had put up one hell of a fight, taking the lead before letting it slip, as is described by the following quotes, first from "The Scotsman" and latterly the "Glasgow Herald".

"The Scotsman": "Divers, whose late goal saved the football public from spending another £5,000 on Monday, took his first point very well. The covering by Hearts' defenders was very loose at this stage, and a probing pass from Delaney saw Crum in a position to turn the ball towards goal. Divers raced on unchallenged to score at a time when a goal was scarcely deserved. Divers' two goals made him the Parkhead hero, but the real match-winner was Delaney, a positive terror to the Tynecastle defenders, while Lyon was a sheet anchor in defence."

"Man for man, Hearts, as is so often the case, were the better equipped side but never reached any heights in teamwork. They had not the ability to press home their advantages to the stage of disorganising their opponents. Celtic, on the other hand, persevered with their plans until they were practically perfect. They also rose to the occasion with great spirit, and preserved their wonderful record of never having lost a replay under present football conditions. The attendance of 80,040 was a record for a midweek match in Britain, excepting Scottish Cup Final replays and Glasgow New Year holiday matches... Some thousands of people were turned away, including late arrivals from Edinburgh... [Hearts bringing at least ten thousand to the crowd]."

"Glasgow Herald": "Many thousands of people did not see the goal which carried Celtic into the fourth round of the Scottish Cup at the expense of Hearts after a tremendous struggle for supremacy at Parkhead, Glasgow, yesterday. There were only three minutes of extra time left, and everyone's mind was made up that a third match would be required to settle the issue, when the vital blow fell. With his right foot, Murphy placed an accurate corner kick, and as the ball sped across two figures were seen racing in liked streaked lightning to connect – Delaney and Divers. Delaney, too far forward, jumped in vain, but Divers met the ball squarely with his forehead and straight it went for the corner of the net."

"That was reckoning without Waugh, however. With a herculean sideways dive Waugh clutched the ball, but to the consternation of the Hearts defenders and supporters...the referee pointed forthwith to the centre of the field, indicating that a goal had been scored. The ball must have been over the line. To satisfy everyone the referee consulted a linesman, who backed up the decision, and the score stood. That was the dramatic climax to as exhausting and entertaining a match as one could wish to see."

Having finished the 1938-39 season in second position in the league (the Celts were beaten by Motherwell in the quarter finals of the Scottish Cup), Celtic began to ready themselves for a new campaign which would never be completed. Celtic fulfilled just the first five fixtures of the 1939-40 Scottish League season, winning three matches and losing two, both to Aberdeen.

In what would turn out to be the last of these ties the Celts edged past a Clyde team, who had started the season poorly, by a single goal to nil. Only a day earlier, the armed forces of Nazi Germany had invaded Poland, and in all likelihood the looming prospect (read as nigh on certainty) of war would have been far more prevalent in the minds of players and supporters than football, but regardless, a match was there to be played and won.

The "Glasgow Herald" said the following of the tie, hinting at the fact all was not well in Europe: "The humid atmosphere and the small crowd obviously affected the players at Parkhead, and it was not until the second half of the game that Celtic and Clyde were really able to concentrate on the match in hand... Celtic only enjoyed spasmodic raids towards McArthur's charge, and in these only Divers was a real menace."

"The Scotsman" described Divers' winning strike: "The deciding goal, which came two minutes after the re-start, was a simple affair. Murphy, gaining possession, gave to Divers, who, eluding three opponents, drove for the outcoming McArthur's left-hand post. The shot was not a strong one and the goalkeeper erred badly in not getting down to it, as the ball passed over his out-stretched foot – to be helped into the net by Hickie in a desperate attempt to clear... Kennaway, Hogg, Geatons and Divers were best..."

Thereafter, on the third of September 1939, the United Kingdom and France declared war on Germany, and World War Two began. In the very same edition of the "Glasgow Herald" previously mentioned, one can find articles detailing items such as air raid procedures, school closures and petrol rationing (all of which had clearly been prepared in advance and were awaiting publication), as well as the daily crossword puzzle and the reports from the weekend's football matches.

I feel it is apt at this point to take a few moments to consider the impact this had on the city of Glasgow, as well as the bravery and naivety with which the war was considered in those earliest of days. For example, one article speaks of the "City's Calm In The Face Of Conflict", saying "In Glasgow and district the declaration of war was heard to a background of thunder. The sky was overcast, and rain fell in a downpour, as Mr. Chamberlain's message was unfolded. Almost on the instant of his conclusion, there was a vivid flash of lightning and a loud peal of thunder. But the import of the message and the grand manner in which it was heralded by the elements failed to break the general calm. The unspoken thought seemed to be: "Now we know where we are." The long tension had broken. As if to demonstrate that, there was an almost immediate reaction to the Government orders which followed the Prime Minister's statement."

Yet, just a couple of pages later, another article entitled "No Bombing of Civilians – Declaration by Allies and Germany" was visible. In this piece, Adolf Hitler said, "That it is the precept of humanity in all circumstances to avoid bombing non-military objectives during military operations corresponds entirely to my own attitude, and has always been advocated by me. I therefore give my unqualified agreement to the suggestion that the Governments involved in the present hostilities should publically make a corresponding declaration. For my part, I have already publically made known in my Reichstag speech that the German Air Force has received the command to confine itself in its operations to military objectives. It is a natural condition for the maintenance of this command that the opposing air force should keep to the same rules."

Now, to say whether or not the British public believed any of this would be speculative on my part, but I know any of them who did would have quickly changed their minds upon the commencement of "The Blitz". As an aside, the words "if you know your history", which circulate amongst the Celtic support regularly, must apply to more than football on occasion.

As thousands upon thousands volunteered for roles in the armed forces, the fate of football in Scotland was thrown into disarray. It had continued with a semblance of normality during World War One, but this war was to be a different beast altogether, thanks in part to the advancement of technology seen over the previous couple of decades. In the same edition of the "Glasgow Herald" which has been quoted, a small footnote said: "Sporting Gatherings – Included in the closure orders are indoor and outdoor sports gatherings where large numbers of people might be expected to congregate. In this connection, the Scottish Football Association and the Scottish League are likely to meet this week to consider their position."

The following day, as the newspapers ran stories of a Nazi torpedo attack on a civilian cruise liner off the coast of the Hebrides and the postponement of the Ryder Cup, another small article signalled the end of competitive Scottish Football for the foreseeable future.

"The Scottish Football Association informed enquiring clubs yesterday that in the view of the Government Order closing all places of entertainment and outdoor sport, football players' contracts are automatically cancelled. Several clubs, including Rangers and Hearts, have accordingly informed their players that they were free to accept employment elsewhere or undertake other duties. The Scottish League, it is understood, are of the opinion that contracts are merely suspended. But the question chiefly concerns the S.F.A., who at four o'clock tomorrow afternoon will meet to discuss the situation."

The results of this meeting were then published a couple of days later, confirming that all of the contracts held by professional football players in Scotland had been suspended rather than cancelled. Also, it was made abundantly clear that no league competition would take place for some time, until those in charge of the Scottish game received instructions regarding what was allowed from the government and had an opportunity to organise matters, with it being said that "Competitive football is not contemplated."

As for John Divers, he would continue to play with Celtic once the regional tournaments and friendlies began, but football was simply a pastime now, for his real work lay in the shipyards where he promptly found employment. For this reason, it was not an uncommon sight for John to arrive at Celtic Park for a match in his overalls, still covered in grime and dirt from the shift which he had just finished.

In time, this line of work would lead to Divers being sent on loan to Morton, as it was easier for him to combine his endeavours in the shipyards with his favourite sport there due to the relative proximity of the football club geographically. Upon his return to Celtic, thanks partly to a slight slowing one could attribute to age and also to the bulk he had developed due to large amounts of manual labour, John Divers found himself being asked to play as a full-back for the first time in his career, although on occasion he would return to more offensive duties.

At the age of thirty-three, John was released by Celtic as World War Two drew to a close and they began to look towards the future and competitive football once more. Unsurprisingly, Morton were very interested upon hearing this news and soon snapped him up. In all, John Divers made one hundred and ninety-seven appearances for Celtic, scoring ninety-two times. Of these goals, almost half came during wartime and, when one takes a step back and considers the rich vein of form he was in as the 1930s drew to a close, I cannot help but come to the conclusion that war robbed him – and several other talented Celtic players of the time – of his best years. Whilst I feel the Club would have seen more success in the early 1940s and strengthened had war not broken out, instead Celtic were left with a shell of a team upon the end of the conflict, when the rebuilding process began. In footballing terms, this was a great shame, but it pales in comparison to what many people lost during those dreadful years of war.

Anyway, whilst such a move between clubs would have been considered a step down now, results at the time may have suggested otherwise, for John Divers and Morton defeated Celtic by two goals to one home and away during the 1946-47 campaign. The earlier of these matches was held at Parkhead on the opening day of the first proper league season in almost a decade, and the "Glasgow Herald" described it as follows, alluding not only to the poor Celtic performance, but also to the fact Divers was still a very capable footballer.

"Disappointing Celtic, from a special correspondent, Celtic 1 Morton 2 – The famous green and white colours and a goalkeeper to be compared with the late John Thomson are all that Celtic seem to have left of the glories of the years before the war. The silence that greeted the final whistle at Parkhead on Saturday, when Morton won as they liked, was expressive – the crowd that had welcomed the start of a new season so enthusiastically had exhausted their powers of criticism and had thinned to an extent almost unbelievable in a match that had only one goal of difference between the sides."

"It was even more galling for Celtic's followers to have seen one of their former "stars" (Divers) so frequently outwitting his opponents in almost every branch of football skill. Here was the complete inside-forward, accomplishing most with the least possible effort, and in addition he dictated the type of attack that would let his superiority in the art of heading have full scope."

"During one part of the second half Celtic seemed to be completely bewildered by Divers' audacity. Three times in succession he chose to take a throw-in himself, got the ball back – as he originally intended he should – proceeded to "wangle" a corner-kick, and then almost scored with searching headers when the flag-kick came over. Twice Miller's brilliance foiled the scheme, and a third time Milne kicked from the goal-line when the goalkeeper had dived in vain."

"If Celtic could not anticipate the cunning that led up to these menacing efforts they could have at least hindered Divers by marking him closely (with their tallest defender, Corbett), when the corner kicks were taken."

Subsequently, Morton would go on to finish higher in the league table that the Parkhead side. At the end of the following season, that of 1947-48, the Celts would manage to reverse this statistic and register their first post-war victory over the Cappielow club, but it is noteworthy John Divers did not play on that occasion as he had left to join Oldham Athletic for six months (with whom John had previously been on trial in 1945), before returning to Greenock around the New Year. However, to say Celtic had the better of Morton as an individual team that year would be a lie, for once again "The Pride of the Clyde" inflicted two defeats on the Celts, once in the league and once in the Scottish Cup and, in truth, it is difficult to determine which one would have been the more painful of the two.

Firstly, on the seventeenth of January 1948, Morton would roll over their opponents with ease, winning by an impressive margin of four goals to nil, with John Divers opening the scoring in the first half. The following day, "The Sunday Post" described the action, John's goal, and also the terrible conditions in which the match was played.

"Had Mr. Strachey [this is a reference to The Right Honourable John Strachey, then Minister of Food] been at Cappielow yesterday, he'd have been convinced our rations were definitely adequate. For he would have seen ten thousand heroes, begarbed in everything from wellington boots to a handkerchief over the head, endeavouring to keep out the bitter driving sleet, giving a display of endurance that would have put the best-fed countries in the world to shame."

"And he would have seen twenty-two players display stamina that had to be seen to be believed. On a strength sapping pitch they kept at it and had the crowd roaring themselves hoarse and forgetting all their discomfort. Morton won because they carried the greatest strength and tenacity, and because they soon realised the only way to make progress was the aerial route. How different with Celtic who persisted in keeping the ball low – and found it skidding out of control on the wing and sticking in the middle."

"But maybe Morton's greatest asset was the ability of John Divers and Tommy Orr and those "niblick" shots. They could loft the ball just where and how they liked... [Morton] carried not a single weakling. Celts will want to forget this game. Their form was too bad to be true, only Miller, Corbett and McAuley reached their opponents' class. Down on his knees, Divers opened the scoring. A cute head flick from a Liddell cross and he had Miller beaten."

Celtic were at serious risk of relegation that season, and so receiving such a heavy defeat from fellow league strugglers Morton must have been very disheartening indeed. Of course, the Celts would ultimately avoid the threat of dropping to Division "B", but Morton weren't through with the Parkhead side yet, as they were drawn together in the semi-finals of the Scottish Cup in March.

John Divers would not play as his current club edged past his old side after extra-time at a packed Ibrox Park, and nor would he play in the Scottish Cup Final or the resulting replay, which Morton eventually lost to Rangers by a single goal. Instead, he went on to become the Chairman of the Players' Union, whilst dabbling in coaching with Morton and management with Portadown for short periods of time.

In his later life, he would have the privilege of seeing his son, also John (whom we shall discuss at a later point in the book), follow in his footballing footsteps and play for Celtic, something he is said to have enjoyed immensely, as I'm sure any proud father would.

"John the Second" died on the eighth of June 1984 at the Western Infirmary, Glasgow, at the age of seventy-three. His story is somewhat better known amongst the modern-day Celtic support than that of "John the First", thanks partly to his son going on to play for the Celts, making them part of a rare breed – that of the few father and son pairings to have ever pulled on the famous green and white Hoops of Celtic Football Club.

"The Chronicles of Willie Maley:
"We Never Looked Back""

"By Willie Maley, Celtic F.C. Manager"

"Our eleven, after its greatest display against the Cowlairs "team of all the talents" never looked back, and right through season 1888-89 proved themselves the team of the year, despite the fact that Third Lanark beat them in the final of the Scottish Cup. The coming of Celtic meant a lot to Scottish football at that time, and so the continued good form of our team spelt good gates all round."

"Cup ties in these days were played right away in August, the Scottish Cup taking pride of place, and the Glasgow Cup coming on in October. Our next opponents in the Scottish ties were Albion Rovers, then a power in the land. At home we won easily by four to one. We had a couple of spare Saturdays then for friendly games, and we met Dundee Harp, winning by seven to one, and then faced the lion in its den – the Hibs on Old Easter Road."

"To realise what this meant I must bring the readers' mind back to the [transfer] of Groves, McKeown, McLaren, Gallagher and McLaughlin from the Easter Road team to the Celtic ranks. Just at the beginning of the season, my old friend John McFadden, the Hibs secretary, had written, under an assumed name of course, an open letter to the Hibs, in which the story of the Celtic's poaching had been told in flowery language. He prophesised for the Celtic a bad time in the future in view of their poaching proclivities, and had very hard words for the men whom he had poached from other clubs before the Celtic copied his example. All this had roused the Hibs following, but that did not prevent our lot facing the music."

"I was a member of the Celtic team which played for the first and last time on Old Easter Road, on October twentieth, 1888. The Hibs had out a very strong team, and the reception we received on coming out of the pavilion was a stormy one. Our men were jeered."

"Despite one of the roughest games I have ever seen we won by three to nil, our fellows sticking to the game under terrible provocation, and earning their win meritoriously. Of course we had a scene on the field. A [group] entered the enclosure to deal out to McKeown what the East thought he deserved, and Gallagher, ever hot, defended his club chum in real fighting fashion. The mounted police, whose presence on a football field I saw that day for the first time, soon cleared the pitch, however, and the engagement proceeded. A nasty dust-up between Neilly McCallum and McPhee, the latter drafted for the day from the Perth Erin Rovers, finished up the game, which did not last the full time."

"This ill-feeling between the two teams existed for many years afterwards, and we have had many hot times with the Hibs since. But in later days, the influence of Phil Farmer, a Hibs president, and latterly of his brother, John Farmer, has brought all these silly misunderstandings to an end. The Hibs still dearly love to down us, but I don't know any club that doesn't."

"Following our safe return from Easter Road, where our graves had been metaphorically dug by certain sections of the Press, we met the Rangers at Ibrox in the Glasgow Cup. A glorious day found us in Cowlairs form, and the "Light Blues" tasted their first Cup tie defeat by the Celts by six goals to one. Donald Gow played that day for the Ibrox team, and a sorry time he had of it at the feet of McCallum and Dunbar, who kept him running all the time."

"When Willie Berry Scored and Queen's Whacked Us"

"[A few weeks later], we took part in that great [Glasgow Cup] tie in which we engaged the Queen's Park. Berry scored for Queen's right away, Dunning letting a long shot slip through at the corner of the post. This gave the Queen's a confidence they never lost, and they banged into our lot in great style all the time, never letting us settle to our proper game, which was difficult enough to play under the awful conditions of rain and mud.

Bob Fraser laid McKeown out, the first and only time I had seen the sturdy back beaten in a fair and square charge, and this upset the Lugar boy completely. Coleman broke down just after half-time, and with ten men we had to struggle on. But our best efforts went for nothing, and we sustained our first real Cup tie defeat by the team we grudged it least to."

"The enthusiasm that day was tremendous. Our gate arrangements were very primitive. All moneys in these days were taken by ticket gates, and as the time wore on for a start a waiting crowd, blocked at the gates, would not be content, and three large exit gates were laid flat, and the crowd in hundreds rushed in free. The Queen's team, too, could not get near the members' entrance, and had to be brought in through the garden of a private house next to our pitch."

"A Hot Reception Which Awaited an Agent"

"We were pestered at this time by agents of English clubs, and McKeown actually travelled to Burnley to sign, but changed his mind and returned in a couple of days. A wag in an athletic paper of the day had this notice inserted:- "Hard as the devil's was the kick, That sent the ball on high, Och, why did you go, Micky; Why did you fly?""

"It is a strange turn in the wheel of fate that a football agent of these days, P.D. Allan, late of Dundee, is now one of our very best friends. I remember one day we received secret information that Peter was to visit Parkhead to take Neilly McCallum away from us. An engagement was made with the wily Dundonian, and preparations had been made to tar and feather him; but he must have been a bit of a thought-reader, as he did not keep that engagement – a wise decision on his part."

"Tackling the Vale"

"Before meeting Dumbarton [in the semi-final of the Scottish Cup, with the Celts having progressed through several rounds not specifically referenced here] however, we played our first game against the Vale of Leven at Alexandria, where I [played]

284

right-back, and here was taken the first official photo of the team, a splendid copy of which still adorns our "not" up-to-date pavilion."

"This, however, only bucked us up stronger for the great game at "fatal Boghead" on January twelfth 1889, when we faced up to the terrors of that famous pitch. Madden, it will be remembered, had deserted us at the time of the Exhibition ties, and consequently there was no love lost between us at that particular time."

"The Real Celtic Game"

"The game went off at a furious pace, and with our men striking a real Celtic game the strong Dumbarton team was well held. Madden made great efforts to get through, but he had opposed to him, in McLaren, as heady a half as has ever played, and the old Lugar man's work in the first half that day finished Madden's best efforts and rendered him absolutely useless. Our lot, working well, scored first, and from that score never looked back, winning by four to one. George Dewar, as fine a centre-half as ever played, was toyed with by Willie Groves, who played the game of his life that day. The third goal was taken by Groves thusly. Dumbarton had worked their way down to our goal, and from a punt out by Kelly, Groves fastened on to the ball. He dashed down the field with Dewar hanging on to him, but gradually left him, to dodge between the two backs, who came up to meet him, and he practically ran the ball through past Bell. Celtic stock rose high at that time, and we were at last duly admitted to be a great side."

"Later on that season it was pointed out that we had done that year what no other team had ever done, and that was to beat all the four Dunbartonshire teams, Dumbarton, Dumbarton Athletic, Renton and Vale of Leven in one year, two of the games being played at home and four away, so that we were early amongst the records. And now I come to the first Scottish Cup final played by the Celtic, and that was at Hampden Park on the second of February, 1889. The fact of our reaching the final in our first year of existence was in itself, I think, quite a feat."

"When we found ourselves faced with the chance of gaining the blue ribbon of football in our first year, I need hardly say that no step to make ourselves thoroughly fit for the great day was missed. Special training and other assistances that need not be mentioned here were ours, and we all turned out fit and well, bar McCallum, who had been laid up with a poisoned leg for a week or two."

"The weather, which had been fairly good until the Friday, developed through the following night into a regular winter storm, and when we faced up at old Hampden it was on a field three inches deep in snow, which had almost all fallen after the opening of the gates and the reception of about sixteen thousand shillings! The greatest consternation ensued as to whether the game would go on as a tie or as a friendly, but eventually both clubs agreed to protest against the game being counted as a tie. Mr. Campbell, the referee for the day, would not take it on himself to declare the game a friendly one, and so the game went on under protest."

"It was a trial of strength I had no great taste for. As the snow, still falling, hung to our clothing, and, sticking to our boots, clogged our movements badly, the ball too, being at times like a huge snowball. However, both teams lay into their work – and it was work. We clung to our close passing game, giving ourselves too much work, whilst Third played the good old Dumbarton game of long, swinging crosses and fast dashes up the field, their defence meantime banging our lot about all over the shop."

"Our Foolish Game"

"Their game paid [off], [but] our close game, in the circumstances, was foolish. We were constantly charged down just at the finish of good work. Third won by three to one that day. Our fellows undoubtedly played with the idea that they would have another day to decide the Cup, but the Thirds' team were evidently of the opposite notion, and so strongly did some of them feel that later on when the Association decided to replay the game three of the Third Lanark lot struck and refused to play in the replay, but before the match better counsel prevailed. The teams that day are worth recalling: – 3rd L.R.V. – Downie (Thornliebank); Thomson (Arthurlie) and Rae (Rutherglen); Lochhead (Arthurlie), Auld and McFarlane (Thornliebank); Marshall, John Oswald, James Oswald, Johnstone and Hannah. Of that lot, the four forwards, barring Marshall, had been secured by Third from the Junior ranks, Hannah actually being taken from a juvenile team that season. The Celtic team was: – John Kelly; P. Gallagher and M. McKeown; W. Maley, J. Kelly and J. McLaren; N. McCallum, M. Dunbar, W. Groves, J. Coleman and T. Maley. Of our lot, J. Kelly and myself were the youngsters in experience, but I don't think we were in the least nervous on that great day."

"It was a very keen game, full of hard knocks, in which our ex-Chairman, Mr. James Kelly, shone. He was the hero of these two games, and played himself into the International that year by his displays. Our lot again failed by reason of their clinging to the ball and playing the game too closely."

"An Exhibition of High Class Custodianship"

"Who is in goal then?"

This is a turn of phrase which I'm sure many of you will have heard at some point during your life, regardless of whether it arrived on a school playground with jumpers for goalposts or on a 'five-a-side' pitch in later years. By their very nature, goalkeepers are a funny breed, and many of them would likely agree with that sentiment. After all, whilst they play an integral role in the success or failure of any football team, be it at the highest or the lowest level of the game, they are fundamentally different from all of their companions on the field. Unlike your average full-back or winger, who tend to come in pairs, goalkeepers are loners, doing all they can to defend their charge from whatever the opposition may throw at them. In fact, you could say that the only person who truly understands what goes through the mind of any given goalkeeper during a match is his counterpart at the other end of the park. Of course, opposing goalkeepers may not always like each other, but there is generally a mutual respect to be found between the two, and this can often be seen when they shake hands and exchange a few words in the tunnel before a game, or swap shirts afterwards.

One could suggest that it takes a particular type of person to become a successful goalkeeper. Stereotypically, members of this fraternity tend to be a little bit eccentric to say the least, but that is not always the case. Again, modern goalkeepers are generally very tall with hands virtually the size of dinner plates but, once more, that is not always necessary. However, there are three things which are truly critical if a goalkeeper is to prosper – mental toughness, natural ability, and a competent team and defence in front of them. Without these three contributory factors, it is very difficult for a stopper, at any level, to succeed.

Over the years, Celtic Football Club have had some truly special goalkeepers and in truth, one could likely write a book discussing which of them was the best and why. In recent times, we have been privileged to enjoy watching the likes of Polish stopper Artur Boruc and the record-breaking Englishman Fraser Forster, while presently a resurgent Craig Gordon guards our goal.

However, it is safe to assume that the majority of Celtic supporters would say that our greatest goalkeeper was John Thomson, who died in a horrific accident at Ibrox Park in 1931. Whilst there has undoubtedly been some level of romanticism attached to John's memory due to the tragic nature of his passing, it does not detract from the fact that he was an incredibly talented individual, who played almost two hundred times for the Club despite never seeing his twenty-third birthday. With a celebrity status due in large part to his renowned ability for spectacular saves, one can only wonder what John would have gone on to achieve had he not suffered such a fate. He would likely feature as one of the men with the most appearances in a Celtic shirt, that much is certain, but whether as many people would know his name nowadays is debatable, callous as that may sound.

To contextualise this somewhat, one of the very few Celtic goalkeepers whom I believe could have rivalled John Thomson for the title of "the greatest" has a very impressive record – I speak, of course, of one of John's predecessors – Charlie Shaw. Coincidentally, Fraser Forster surpassed some but not all of his records, which had stood for almost a century throughout several high and low periods for Celtic Football Club. Whilst his name is not totally lost to the Celtic support, I feel that he should be more widely remembered for his service to the Football Club than he is presently in some quarters.

Born in the East Dunbartonshire mining village of Twechar on the twenty-first of September 1885, Charlie Shaw would begin his footballing career with junior sides Baillieston Thistle and Kirkintilloch Harp before moving on to Port Glasgow Athletic on the eighteenth of April 1906, aged just twenty. By modern standards, he would probably be considered to be a rather small man, standing at only five feet and six inches tall – certainly too short to be a goalkeeper nowadays – many would think. Of course, back at the turn of the twentieth century, men weren't as tall as they are now and yet, whilst five and a half feet was not considered to be particularly small within the general population, it was still considered to be rather slight for those pursuing a career as a goalkeeper, rough as the game was back in the day. Yet, over the course of his football career, Charlie Shaw would prove all of those who doubted him wrong, by pulling off fantastic saves, keeping an incredible number of clean sheets and collecting an array of winners' medals.

Only three days after signing for Port Glasgow, Charlie took to their home field, Clune Park, for his first senior outing against the relatively high flying Airdrieonians. The visitors had scored forty-nine league goals in twenty-eight showings during that campaign thus far, and so a betting man of the time would likely have backed them to fire several past Port Glasgow and their new goalkeeper as part of a comfortable victory – but they did not. In fact, they left Clune Park with only a point after a two-each draw played out in awful weather, before a stubborn crowd of over fifteen hundred people.

Newspaper reports from the time say that Shaw was first beaten by a "high, simple looking shot", before Port Glasgow levelled and then took the lead prior to half-time. Subsequently, Airdrieonians equalised in the final minute amidst a goalmouth scramble, much to the hardy home crowd's dismay. Without the benefit of television cameras or match highlights, it is impossible to say this for certain, but one wonders if the first shot which beat Charlie Shaw was blown by the wind, and the nervous young goalkeeper was simply caught out. Having said that, putting aside the manner in which it was achieved, a point was a point, and Port Glasgow edged closer to survival in the top division.

By the end of the season, which came less than a month after Charlie Shaw had arrived at the football club, Port Glasgow found themselves tied with Kilmarnock for fourteenth place in the league table. Subsequently, the two sides were forced to contest a play-off match so as to decide who finished third bottom and second bottom respectively. The latter would not be automatically relegated, but they would have their place in the division questioned by the Scottish Football League, who had the power to demote up to two sides per season if they saw fit. However, the decision to expand the league to eighteen teams that summer meant neither of the bottom sides would be relegated.

Regardless Port Glasgow, with the young Charlie Shaw again in goal, won the play-off match convincingly (by a scoreline of six goals to nil) in front of a small crowd at Cathkin Park. The following excerpt from the "Glasgow Herald" describes the situation which led to the arrangement of the fixture, as well as mentioning to how little Charlie Shaw had to do: "These teams having tied for fourteenth place in the Scottish League competition…met last night on Cathkin Park to decide which club comes up, along with Queen's Park [who finished bottom], at the annual meeting of the League next week for consideration as to the teams which will comprise the First Division next season. There was a poor attendance, only thirteen pounds being taken at the gate…Kilmarnock forwards on several occasions tried to get away, but they were never allowed to trouble Shaw, who had a pretty lazy time of it."

The following campaign, that of 1906-07, was to be Charlie Shaw's only full season with Port Glasgow, whose top flight fortunes – alongside those of fellow amateurs Queen's Park – seemed increasingly fragile. The Clune Park side finished the season third bottom once again, attaining only one more point than they had done beforehand, but having played an additional four league games in doing so. For Charlie's part, he kept six clean sheets and helped Port Glasgow to survive the threat of relegation once again, as a final day one-all home draw with runaway league champions Celtic brought them level with fellow strugglers Kilmarnock and Hamilton Academical. However, it must be said though that whilst Port Glasgow's defence were far from perfect, one could conclude that their main area of concern was at the other end of the field with the forward line, as they managed to score only thirty times in thirty-four matches, ten less than any other side in the league.

Charlie Shaw left Scottish Football behind him in the summer, heading south of the border to join Queen's Park Rangers.

In London, he would rack up the first of his notable records as he featured two hundred and twenty-three times for his new side, only missing three matches in the six years which he spent there. Queen's Park Rangers would win the Southern League title twice during Shaw's tenure, before he returned to Scotland in 1913. However, a statistic which I consider to be rather interesting would be lost to the vast majority of readers if I left Charlie's career in English Football at that.

Throughout Charlie Shaw's time at Queen's Park Rangers, from 1907-08 through to 1911-12, regardless of their final league position (which fluctuated quite notably), the west London side conceded fewer league goals with every passing campaign (from fifty-seven in 1907-08 to thirty-five in 1911-12). In fact, the only exception to this rule was that in Charlie's final season, 1912-13, Queen's Park Rangers conceded the same number of league goals which they had done the previous year – thirty-five. Notably, in the two years of English League football which followed Charlie's departure (prior to the cessation of the Southern League until after the end of World War One), the number of goals which the "The [London] Hoops" conceded rose considerably, to forty-three and fifty-six respectively. The fact Charlie was widely missed by the London side's supporters would be highlighted a little over ten years later in April 1924, when he returned to the English capital with Celtic for a charity match against West Ham, during which he was loudly cheered by many of the locals in attendance.

Charlie Shaw signed for Celtic on the second of May 1913, for a fee reported to be in the region of two hundred and fifty pounds. As was the case years earlier with Port Glasgow, Charlie was immediately thrown into first team action, although this time he was not tasked with helping his new side to avoid relegation, but rather to assist their progress to the final of the Glasgow Merchants' Charity Cup. Along with his new teammates, Charlie Shaw was successful in this aim, as they Celts beat Third Lanark by two goals to one in the semi-final at Cathkin Park. From the outset, Celtic were on the back foot, as the following quote from the "Glasgow Herald" explains: "Playing against the wind Celtic were early forced on the defensive, Shaw having to save from

Speirs and Flannery…the home side took the game in hand, but although Shaw was repeatedly tested, a couple of corners was all the Cathkin side could show for their labours."

As the match progressed, Celtic began to find their rhythm, and by the time Charlie Shaw conceded his first goal as a Celtic goalkeeper, the Parkhead outfit had already built up a two-nil advantage. For the record, the same newspaper quoted earlier said of the Third Lanark goal: "Following this, the home lot were seen to better advantage, and shortly before the close Flannery, the latest recruit on trial from Brighton & Hove Albion succeeded in scoring, Shaw having no chance with the shot. Celtic, however, were the better side throughout, and thoroughly merited their win."

Subsequently, Celtic would go on to secure the trophy in front of approximately thirty thousand people at Celtic Park, as the Hoops welcomed their opponents, Rangers. Despite going two goals down within ten minutes – thanks to a defensive mistake from the Celtic backs for the first and a stunning strike for the second – Celtic would fight back to win the match by three goals to two, and so Charlie Shaw, the man who had only signed for Celtic eight days earlier, obtained the first of what would become a numerous collection of honours with the Club. However, that is not the only reason this match should be remembered by those within the Celtic support for it was also the first time the names "Shaw; McNair and Dodds" began a Celtic line-up, a sight which would become more common than not for almost a decade. In the years to come, this trio would earn legendary status, to such an extent that many older fans used to refer to them as the "greatest ever". Even now, whilst their names are not as prominent as they once were, they are still well known, over a century on from their first success together.

Charlie Shaw would keep the first of an astonishing number of clean sheets with Celtic against Falkirk at the end of August 1913. Celtic won by four goals to nil that day, and whilst Shaw may not have been one of the Celtic support's main focuses of attention after that match, he certainly would be when he kept his sixth league clean sheet that season, as Celtic defeated Rangers at Ibrox on the twenty-fifth of October. Celtic were the best of the two teams in the first half, opening up a two-nil lead, but after the interval, the shoe was most certainly on the other foot, with the home side relentlessly peppering the Celtic goalmouth with shots and headers. The relative frenzy of the situation was only increased when Rangers had a goal chopped off for "some infringement not perceptible to the spectators". Subsequently, the home supporters believed their side had scored when a shot evaded Charlie Shaw, only for Alec McNair to clear it off the line before it passed between the posts. As time began to ebb away from the Ibrox side, they were awarded a late penalty which, had it been converted, would have given them the slenderest hope of perhaps mounting one final attack in the little time remaining and salvaging a point – but Charlie Shaw had other ideas, saving ably from ex-Celt and Ibrox favourite, Alec Bennett.

Later that season, the new Celtic keeper would go on to set records many would have previously considered to be simply impossible. Beginning with a somewhat disappointing goalless draw versus Motherwell on the twentieth of December 1913, Celtic – with Shaw in goals – would not concede again until Falkirk finally breached their charge on the twenty-eighth of February 1914. During this time, Charlie Shaw kept thirteen consecutive clean sheets, including matches against strong opposition such as Rangers and Morton. In all, if one includes the minutes after the goal which he conceded in a two-one win against Raith Rovers on the thirteenth of December 1913 as well as those prior to that which he lost against Falkirk, one can determine that Charlie Shaw did not concede a goal for somewhere in the region of one thousand, two hundred and eighty-seven minutes in all competitions – highlighting that the claim which some made that Chris Woods of Rangers held the British record in this regard was nothing other than arrant nonsense.

In the modern day, we have seen Fraser Forster go one thousand, two hundred and fifty-six minutes without conceding a league goal, enough to break Charlie Shaw's achievement with regards league games, and I cannot praise him highly enough for doing so – he is an incredible goalkeeper who will undoubtedly continue to improve with time. However, as I write this in 2015,

Shaw's Scottish record of consecutive minutes played (in all competitions) without conceding still stands. It is a great credit to Charlie though that his league record held firm for almost a century, and it took a goalkeeper of Forster's calibre to better it. After all, some astonishing talents, such as John Thomson, Ronnie Simpson and Packie Bonner have been unable to do so in their times with Celtic Football Club.

As many of you will know, the current record holder for consecutive clean sheets in all competitions in the United Kingdom is Edwin van der Sar, the Dutch stopper who went approximately one thousand, three hundred and eleven minutes without being beaten south of the border. Having conceded in the Scottish Cup against Aberdeen, Fraser Forster did not surpass that total as a Celtic player. Remarkably, impressive as Edwin Van Der Sar's efforts undoubtedly were, the aforementioned goal from Raith Rovers was all that stopped Charlie Shaw from holding this honour by an incredible margin, for had he not conceded that day, his clean sheet tally, which began just before Christmas 1914, would have ran all the way back to the fourth of October 1913 – adding up to a cumulative total of over two thousand, two hundred minutes unbeaten in all competitions, but alas Raith Rovers did find the net, although that takes nothing away from the class and talent of Shaw.

As the 1913-14 season drew to a close, Celtic lined up against Hibernian in the replay of the Scottish Cup Final, which they subsequently won by four goals to one at Ibrox Park. This would be the last time the tournament was held until the 1919-20 season due to the outbreak of World War One, and the Hibernian goal, which was scored by William Smith, was one of only two Scottish Cup goals which Charlie Shaw conceded that season.

By the time that the league campaign was finally complete, around a fortnight after the destination of Scottish Cup had been decided, Charlie Shaw had set another record, albeit a Club one. Having won the league title comfortably by six points from closest rivals Rangers, one only needs to look at the championship table in order to spot the record breaking statistic which positively jumps off the page. Whilst Celtic only scored two more goals than the Ibrox side over thirty-eight games, the Hoops conceded less than half the number their rivals did, finishing the league campaign with Charlie Shaw only having been beaten fourteen times (a little less than once every three games, and only half as often as his predecessor was the previous year). Also, it is notable that three of these were conceded in the final week of the season, when Celtic were already the Scottish Champions. In fact, over the course of the 1913-14 season, no side managed to score more than two goals against Celtic in a single match, and of the twenty teams the Celts faced competitively (in either the league or Scottish Cup), nine of their twenty opponents (including Rangers) didn't manage to find the net at all.

Anyway, whilst the Scottish Cup was postponed for the duration of the First World War, the Scottish League continued as normal and Charlie Shaw, along with many other players like him, were able to continue their career on a serious level. Therefore, on the fifteenth of August 1914, Celtic lined up at Tynecastle for the first league game of the new season, where they were comprehensively beaten by underdogs Heart of Midlothian. Four of the players on the field that sunny day would die during the fighting in the ongoing World War which intensified as the years passed, a poignant reminder not simply of the footballing talent lost during that era but more importantly, of all those killed and the devastated loved ones who were left behind to pick up the pieces and attempt to rebuild their shattered lives.

Although Celtic's league form would improve as the season progressed, they did concede seven goals – half of the total number which they lost in all thirty-eight ties the previous year – over the course of the first four league of fixtures that campaign. Five of these were lost against St. Mirren and Morton, but the trio of "Shaw; McNair and Dodds" was broken up during these two matches, as Thomas McGregor replaced the latter man at full-back. This is not to say that McGregor was a bad player, far from it, but he was not of the class of McNair and Dodds – after all, very few were. Neither of the famous full-back pairing played in the one-nil loss to Falkirk which ended Charlie Shaw's clean sheet record, and the differences between the Parkhead side's fortunes when one or neither were playing, compared to when they were both present in the starting line-up was obvious.

Towards the end of the 1914-15 season, Celtic put together an impressive run of form which secured their second consecutive Scottish League Championship title. "Shaw; McNair and Dodds" started all but two of the Celt's final ten league matches, in which the Hoops won nine fixtures and drew only once, on the final day, away at Motherwell. During this period, Charlie Shaw conceded only three times, and helped his side to maintain their status as champions. When one compares this statistic with that which I previously mentioned regarding goals lost early in the campaign, this was quite the achievement. After all, had that earlier trend been allowed to continue unhindered, the Celts would not have conceded only twenty-five times in all finishing the season in first place, but somewhere over sixty, presumably finishing in the lower to middle end of the standings at best.

The following campaign saw the Celts pull away from their competitors, winning the league by nine points – the most comprehensive margin any champions had concluded the season with in almost two decades. Such supremacy becomes clear when one looks at Celtic's results from that particular campaign, for instead of making a shaky start, the Hoops won their first ten matches in all competitions, including a Glasgow Cup Final victory over Rangers. With regards league fixtures, eight wins from eight gave the Celts a four point lead in mid-October, and some may have already speculated that the destination of the championship title was a foregone conclusion even then.

However, a trio of defeats (interspersed with only a solitary victory in a month) to Rangers and Hearts in the following few weeks – kick-started by a dreadful, mistake ridden loss to St. Mirren at Celtic Park – soon caused this lead to evaporate. Subsequently, as the Celts travelled home from the last of three ties at Tynecastle, they found themselves in second place in the league table, equal on points with Rangers, but with an inferior goal average and having played two games more. Hearts also sat alongside the two Glasgow giants on eighteen points, though they had played two games more than Celtic, and therefore four more than the Ibrox side. Regarding the St. Mirren defeat, the following report from the "Glasgow Herald" shows how even the best of us are fallible.

"St. Mirren will not look for praise where none is deserved; they will rather treasure something more tangible in the shape of two points presented them by their opponents who excelled in doing everything they ought not to do. When a player with McNair's experience mistakes an opponent for a comrade he is making trouble for his goalkeeper, and when Shaw finds himself at midfield and loses the ball there he is adding to his troubles and also to his opponents' goal record...It was simply a case of nothing coming off for a team, of every mistake in defence being punished, and of forwards being sent away empty handed through faulty shooting or from other causes. The result will mean little to the losers and a great deal to other clubs. An unbeaten club is as much a blemish in a competition as one without a victory to its credit, and St. Mirren are due congratulations for being the first to restore equality."

Celtic had certainly endured a poor spell, but a quartet of comprehensive league wins in December, when the Hoops never failed to score more than four goals and only conceded two throughout the entire month, set them up for the run which would continue to the end of the season. Having lost to Hearts at Tynecastle, the Celts would win eighteen of their next nineteen league matches, only drawing against Rangers at Celtic Park on New Year's Day. Over the course of the entire season, Charlie Shaw, who was ever present in the Celtic goalmouth, kept twenty-two league clean sheets out of a possible thirty-eight. Post-Tynecastle, this ratio read seventeen from a possible twenty-six, as Shaw successfully protected his charge during two of every three games, a remarkable record for any goalkeeper. In the spring time, from February through to mid-April, Charlie only conceded one goal in ten league fixtures (and the subsequent goal came on the day Celtic played two league games in one day – winning both – in the evening tie against Motherwell). Be that as it may, come the end of April, Celtic and Charlie Shaw would be champions once more.

As the following season came to a close Celtic had won the league again, this time by a record-equalling margin of ten points from their nearest competitors, Morton. The number of goals which they conceded dropped by almost half also, from thirty-two to seventeen, something which Charlie Shaw and his defenders must take significant credit for. However, despite this success, it would not have gone unnoticed that the Parkhead side had been unable to defeat their Ibrox rivals in the league for almost three years, with their last victory coming at the end of October 1914. Of course, the Celts had enjoyed some success in the Glasgow Cup, but any praise which followed this was eradicated when the Ibrox side won three-nil at Celtic Park in the semi-final of the same competition in September 1917. It is often said that League Championships are won by the best team in the country, and this is true, but this ever lengthening league statistic would certainly have been on the minds of many Celts, players and supporters alike. After all, it was clear to see they were the better side on the whole, but for some unfathomable reason, they had been unable to show this definitively for almost three years.

However, footballing solace and relief would come to every Celtic supporter on the day that the Hoops travelled to Ibrox in October 1917. Having been so comprehensively beaten in the semi-final, Celtic were suddenly considered to be underdogs for this league match, but as the Celts so often do, even in the modern day, they relished this role, especially after Rangers took the lead early on. This event suited the script which everyone was expecting to read, but this only bound a determined, tenacious Celtic side together, as the "Glasgow Herald" recalled.

"The result of the League match at Ibrox was scarcely more surprising than the dimensions of the crowd. Upwards of forty thousand enthusiasts witnessed Rangers achieve such a decisive victory at Parkhead a few weeks ago as made the Celtic visit to Ibrox on Saturday appear to be in the nature of a forlorn hope. That at any rate is how a second trial of strength appeared to the average outsider. But to the seasoned supporter there was always the prospect of the unexpected happening, and it was the hopes and fears of the rival sections that caused the attendance at the

League match to be a replica of the Cup tie…Everything pointed to a very different result. Rangers were at home and at full strength, buoyed up also with the confidence begotten by success; Celtic were asked to do on their opponent's ground what they had failed so abjectly to accomplish on their own territory and this without two players of international reputation and wide experience of these inter-club duals."

"When Bowie scored for Rangers early in the game believers in the unexpected received quite a shock. Those who had faith in Celtic as non-favourites and uphill fighters were rewarded by seeing McColl equalise, and chagrined at his failure to give his side the lead close on the interval. The latter feat was eventually accomplished by McAtee at a stage when a drawn battle was in sight, and then it was Rangers turn to figure as stormers in what was indeed forlorn hope. The home forwards established themselves in their opponent's penalty area, and could not be dislodged; the Celtic defenders, equally obdurate, barred the way to goal, and a titanic struggle followed, and the outcome of much strenuous play was the survival of Shaw's charge after many hairbreadth escapes."

With that, Celtic had finally gotten the proverbial Ibrox monkey off of their backs, and many would have wondered whether they would then proceed to push on and secure a fifth Scottish League Championship in a row, but alas, it was not to be. A disappointing loss against Airdrieonians in the autumn, coupled with drawing four of their five league games in January put them on the back foot, and from this poor spell they could not recover. Interestingly, three of the draws in January were goalless affairs. This highlights the fact that whilst Celtic's defence were still performing well (conceding twenty-six that season, as opposed to seventeen previously), the primary reason for Celtic's failure to win the title was a relative lack of goals scored.

Rangers would not be the champions of Scotland for long though, as a gritty, determined Celtic side took back the league flag only a season later. By now, the Ibrox side were probably the better of the two teams, as they scored far more goals and conceded fewer than their Parkhead rivals, but character and experience helped the Celts to the 1918-19 title, even after Charlie Shaw missed his first two league games since signing for the club due to illness (an early season draw against Kilmarnock and three-nil defeat to Rangers).

As time passed, Charlie Shaw would be forced to take leave from his goalkeeping duties more often, but generally it was only for a game here or there. He was still Celtic's first choice stopper, as he would be until the 1924-25 season, and such minor absences would have little impact until Charlie was almost forty years of age. Upon his return to action on the twenty-sixth of October 1918, Celtic ran out five-nil victors against Dumbarton and, from this point in the campaign onwards, the Hoops would lose only one league match in twenty-five outings, eventually ending the season as the Champions of Scotland.

The following October, almost a year to the day from the Celts' three-nil defeat to Rangers which Shaw missed, Celtic met their rivals once more – this time at Ibrox Park – and lost three-nil again. On this occasion, Charlie was the Celtic goalkeeper, and just like the previous year, Celtic had been on an impressive run of form going into the match, winning all nine league matches which had been played until that point in the campaign. Shaw too seemed to be in good fettle, conceding only five goals in his first eight games of the season. He had lost three to Hibernian the week prior to the derby match, but as his outfield compatriots had put seven past the opposition, this was largely overlooked. However, following the Hoops' loss against Rangers, which is described in some detail momentarily, Charlie Shaw's name would disappear from the Celtic team sheet for almost an entire month. Speculation would suggest that this absence could be attributed to the "simple fashion" in which the first two of Rangers' goals were conceded, but officially Shaw was unavailable for selection due to "injuries and a cold".

"Upwards of seventy-five thousand people saw Rangers defeat Celtic at Ibrox, a rather unexpected result taking the recent city cup tie as an indication of merit. But over a long series of years teams representing these clubs have frequently flouted past achievements and current form to such an extent as to almost prepare one for a League victory following closely on a Cup defeat. It is the inconsistency of Rangers and Celtic when opposed to each other that invests all of their encounters with such engrossing interest, so was evidenced on Saturday, when all records for a League match at Ibrox were broken."

"The Celt lacked every physical attribute to create or utilise opportunities when his side held a commanding lead on play in the first half, and should have been leading on goals as well. An early goal enabled the Ibrox forwards to relax their endeavours and view with complacency the futile attempts of their opponents to equalise. A second success, implicating Shaw, obtained shortly after the interval, proved to be the turning point of the game. To the finish Rangers monopolised the attack, gradually wore down their opponents and finished by three goals the better team."

Thereafter, for the next three league matches, it was not Charlie Shaw who would appear in the Celtic goalmouth, but a youngster by the name of William Lawrie, whom Willie Maley signed from Clydebank Juniors only two days after the previously discussed loss. At this time, Lawrie was described by one journalist as "a lad of promise...full of enthusiasm, confident and hopeful", before referring to him as "another excellent capture by Mr. Maley." He featured only three times for Celtic and would later go on to play with Aberdeen in 1921 before joining fellow Aberdeenshire side Peterhead in 1924.

Shaw's comeback appearance against Ayr United was a somewhat frustrating one. Celtic drew one-all, but it must be said some people actually expected Celtic to lose this match, such was their drop in form over recent weeks. The "Glasgow Herald" said that "Shaw had an onerous task. But it was in attack that the city team really failed." The last sentence is perhaps indicative of Celtic's issues during this time period, as Rangers won the league once more. Whilst both teams conceded a similar number of goals over the 1919-20 season, the Hoops were barely averaging two goals scored per game, whilst their Ibrox rivals were averaging closer to three. Too many winnable matches ended in draws for the Celts, many of which arrived around the turn of the year, and this cost them their chance to retain the title.

The Scottish Cup campaign of 1919-20, Celtic's first since the outbreak of World War One, was also to end in disappointment in the third round, as Rangers edged past the Hoops at Ibrox Park in early March by a solitary goal. It was a tale of two refereeing decisions, as Rangers scored a header from a free kick which never was, and Celtic had an excellent goal (described as the "the best shot of the match") chopped off harshly, after the referee "penalised one of the visiting side for an infringement."

The following season would not prove to be any more successful for Celtic, as they once more finished second in the league and exited the Scottish Cup at the third round stage (this time to Heart of Midlothian). Quite simply, Celtic were now the second best team in the country, comfortably superior (at least over the course of the league campaign) to every side in Scotland, other than their Ibrox rivals. Several draws were replaced by numerous losses, as some of the elder statesmen continued to age and Maley searched for appropriate youthful talent to replace them. One of these veterans, Joe Dodds, would depart the Club a fortnight before Celtic's opening match of the league season, leaving Willie McStay to attempt to fill the void which he left behind. It would be some time before the last of the team who played during the First World War would bid farewell to Celtic Park, but it was clear the new decade would bring new challenges and many fresh faces with it.

One small success of 1920-21 was a two-nil New Year's Day victory over Rangers – Celtic's first league win in the Glasgow derby since their 1917 triumph at Ibrox Park. Whilst Joe Cassidy scored both of the Celtic goals, it is noteworthy that Charlie Shaw made an important contribution also, coping ably with all that was directed his way on that cold day, as the following short quote suggests: "Rangers [who were two-nil down at this point] made a praiseworthy rally in the closing stage, when Shaw had more work thrust upon him that his rival Robb in the other goal had all through...but their inside-forwards lacked the incisiveness or confidence in finishing..."

Looking back, one cannot help but wonder whether any of the Celtic supporters in attendance that day pondered whether this victory was a sign of things to come; an indication that the pendulum of power was swinging back towards the East End of the city. In all likelihood, there probably was some who did so, and their hopes and dreams would have seemingly began to come true, at least temporarily. Celtic would win the 1921-22 Scottish League Championship by a single point from Rangers, having scored the exact same number of goals as their rivals over the course of forty-two matches, but crucially conceding six fewer. With both sides boasting a remarkable total of twenty-three draws between them that season, it was Celtic's regained ability to turn potential losses into draws which helped to bring the title back to Parkhead. The knack of pulling something out of the proverbial fire has long been associated with Celtic Football Club, especially in league winning seasons, and this was to be no different. Celtic registered one less win than Rangers that season, but the Ibrox side lost twice more than their Parkhead counterparts, and their failure to beat the Hoops in the league would prove fatal to their ambitions.

Before proceeding to discuss a couple of these late escapes, it is noteworthy that this season would be the last in which the famous trio of "Shaw; McNair and Dodds" would feature together in the famous green and white Hoops, for Joe Dodds, the irresistible full-back who had left for Cowdenbeath in the summer of 1920, returned home to Parkhead for one more year – and what a year it was to be. Four wins from their first five league encounters signalled a good start to the campaign for the Celts, but narrow away defeats against Hibernian and Kilmarnock, as well as a Glasgow Cup Final loss to Rangers were early low points for the Club and its supporters.

As one would expect though, it was the derby matches which played a large part in the final destination of the Scottish League title. Yet, it was not just these results, but the manner in which they came about which is the source of much interest.

The first of these mammoth encounters came only three weeks after the Glasgow Cup Final when the Hoops travelled to Ibrox Park, along with approximately fifty thousand expectant supporters of both sides. As the following passages from the

"Glasgow Herald" describe, this was to be a good day for Celtic and an excellent afternoon for goalkeeping stalwart, Charlie Shaw.

"Since the season opened football has been played under highly favourable weather conditions, alike from the players' and spectators' point of view, but on Saturday the long spell was broken, and heavy sleet showers in the early part of the day, followed by rain and the accompaniment of a cold north-east wind, formed a complete contrast to the conditions of the past two months. It was unfortunate that the change set in on a day of special importance in the Scottish League competition. The meeting of Rangers and Celtic was the event of the afternoon's football, and the continued attractiveness of the match was attested by an attendance of fifty thousand at Ibrox Park, notwithstanding that rain fell unceasingly throughout the game. Probably an additional twenty thousand would have been present, under normal weather conditions. Fortunately enthusiasts were rewarded for their hardihood in facing the rigours of the weather by witnessing one of the finest contests these illustrious opponents have provided."

"The turf at Ibrox Park had evidently been specially tended, and, to the general surprise, the sleet and rain had made little impression upon it, so that at no time in the course of the contest was play in the least adversely affected. The conditions indeed were suitable for a fair test, and the verdict was a drawn game – one goal each. Celtic were quite pleased with the result, and have reason to be, as they were without the services of at least two of their regular players, McMaster and McLean, and their deputies do not yet possess the skill of their principals."

"Whether the visiting team were due a share of the honours is another question, and one that will provide much controversy but no certain answer between now and the next meeting of the clubs on the second of January. So far as exerting pressure on their opponents' goal is concerned, Rangers undoubtedly held that advantage, but the fact remains that with all their attacking they succeeded only once in defeating Shaw, and McInally had, prior to that, snatched a goal for his side."

"The vigilance of Shaw and his backs can scarcely be overestimated. Rangers attacked with energy, daring and judgement practically during the whole of the second half, and the manner in which Shaw cleared at least half a score of shots of power and direction was an exhibition of high class custodianship. Rangers may feel aggrieved at being deprived of the full reward, solely on account of a display of super goalkeeping, but Shaw stood as one of the units of the opposition to be overcome, and having failed to succeed in doing so, Rangers take the consequences. As a contest, the game will go down as one of the best in a long list of encounters; it was brimful of good class football, attack on one side, defence on the other, and the players' conduct and spirit amidst all the excitement were admirable."

Inevitably, the return fixture between the two sides, the New Year derby match, was also to prove pivotal. The tie, watched by sixty thousand spectators, was played in "bright and bracing" weather and ended in a goalless draw. Once again, Charlie Shaw was to come in for much praise from supporters and individuals within the media alike, although this time he was to share some of the spotlight with his counterpart in the Rangers goal, William Robb, a man who, like Charlie Shaw, would go seasons at a time without missing a single match for his Football Club. "The outstanding personalities were the respective goalkeepers, Robb and Shaw" said one newspaper.

One could be forgiven for considering two draws against Rangers to be somewhat mediocre, especially when their experiences of modern matches between the two sides occurred four times a season in the league, but when one reflects on the Celts' derby record at that point in time, we can see that the Hoops' supporters, players and management would have been wise to celebrate their two draws as a success. After all, Rangers had generally had the better of the Parkhead side since the war, and tying these matches, essentially nullifying Rangers' opportunities to directly take points from Celtic, had a great impact on the title race. As for Charlie Shaw's performance, with the pairing of Alec McNair and Joe Dodds in front of him for the final time in a derby match that day, "The Scotsman" added: "The Celtic held a slight balance in the first half, but the Rangers had the best scoring chances, Archibald, Cairns and Henderson all missing easy openings. After the crossover, Rangers were often in front of Shaw, who had many clever saves."

As the season continued, Celtic would go from strength to strength in the league, saving some of their best performances of the whole campaign for the eventual title run-in. Despite a reasonable start to their Scottish Cup adventure, with a convincing home win against Montrose and a narrow away victory against Third Lanark under their belts, the Hoops would fall unexpectedly in the third round of the tournament (for the third year running no less), as they lost by three goals to one against Hamilton Academical at Celtic Park in late February.

This was, of course, very disappointing for the Celts as it had now been almost a decade since they had lifted the Scottish Cup and, whilst I have no doubts all of those at the Football Club would have understood the severity of the World War which halted the tournament's proceedings, an outsider such as myself can speculate that, had the First World War not taken place, Celtic would probably have won the Scottish Cup at least once during that period, such was the relative quality of their side. Whether this notion would have crossed the mind of any Celtic players in the years after the war (especially those who had played before and through it) is entirely speculative, but one cannot help but wonder if it was indeed a source of frustration for some.

Better times were to come again in the nation's premier knock-out tournament, but before such thoughts could cross the minds of anyone associated with Celtic Football Club, they had the little matter of a Scottish League Championship to win on the final day of the domestic campaign. The Hoops were unbeaten in the league since mid-November and Charlie Shaw had kept thirteen clean sheets from a possible eighteen since the New Year, therefore the Celts most certainly warranted their position in the league table going into the final round of fixtures – one point ahead of Rangers with a slightly superior goal average.

As Celtic and Rangers travelled to their respective away games, against Morton (the new Scottish Cup holders) and Clyde, everyone held their breath and awaited whichever possible outcome would become reality. To contextualise this event somewhat, I would ask you all to consider a situation whereby the destination of the league title hangs in the balance in the modern day – all of the matches being contested kick off at the same time; all are televised; score updates are relayed constantly not only to television viewers but also the supporters in the stands and management teams on the bench via mobile and radio technology. However, none of this was available in 1922, and so questions such as "What was the Rangers score?" and "Have we done it?" must have been rife come the full-time whistle.

At Shawfield, Rangers started brightly, peppering the home side's goal with shot after shot but to no avail, with Clyde attempting to launch counter attacks whenever the opportunity presented itself. At Cappielow though, things were not going so well for Celtic, who were quickly put under heavy pressure as "Shaw was called on early in the game, but had no difficulty in saving from McKay." The Hoops did their best to push forward and take control of the tie in the period which followed this early chance, but failed to create any clear cut opportunities of their own, instead being forced on to the back foot by the home side once again before Joe Dodds, who was making his final outing in a Celtic jersey, cleared the ball and allowed the Celts defence to push out. Prior to half-time however, Shaw would be beaten – only for the nineteenth time in the league that season (Francis Collins, the backup custodian, conceded the other) – as "Morton reasserted themselves and A. Brown opened the scoring" and the visitors went into the pavilion a goal down at the half-time interval.

Now, whether or not this news reached the Rangers team at Shawfield is unclear, but regardless, having been unable to beat Clyde's goalkeeper Anderson thus far, their nervy game remained goalless at the break. The tension in the air at Cappielow was certainly clear to see at half-time when, according to "The Scotsman", "there was an ugly scene on the ground, free fights being engaged in. The playing pitch was invaded, flags were seized by police, and a number of people were arrested."

As the teams re-emerged for the second halves, the situation was thus – a goal either way would likely determine the destination of the Scottish League Championship. This was one of the closest finishes to any league season and, had it occurred in the modern day, supporters' attentions would have been focused intently on both matches at once, with a media frenzy encompassing every event of the day, be it a goal, a missed chance, a debatable offside decision or a fortuitous piece of officiating from either referee.

Anyway, as the games progressed, both Celtic and Rangers pressed forward in search of their first goal. At Shawfield, the second half opened quietly, before Clyde threatened on one occasion and forced Rangers' defence to spring into action. The Ibrox side then began to mount attack after attack only to be repeatedly foiled by the Anderson. At Cappielow, Celtic became increasingly offensive in the nature of their play, throwing caution to the wind and forcing examples of daring defending and gallant goalkeeping aplenty.

With around ten minutes of time remaining, and the other match still goalless, Celtic won another corner kick, from which Andy McAtee scored one of his most important goals in the green and white of Celtic Football Club, causing great celebration from the travelling supporters in attendance.

As the full-time whistles sounded across Scotland signalling the end of the 1921-22 season, both Celtic and Rangers had drawn, and therefore the Celts had won the league by a solitary point. The resilience and determination shown by Celtic during that campaign cannot be praised highly enough, for when it mattered most, they were able to find a goal or two here or there when their rivals could not. Whether it was at Morton on the last day of the season, or away at Motherwell in late November to cite another such example, it was steel as much as skill which won Celtic the Scottish League Championship that year. The "Glasgow Herald" discussed Celtic's triumph in the days which followed in some detail, making specific reference to this Celtic side's sterling defensive prowess, the Club's overall record as the most famous team in Scottish Football, and the rigours of the last of three league seasons which required teams in the Scottish top flight to play as many matches as was ever seen in such campaigns.

"Celtic the Champions – Celtic won the Scottish League Championship on Saturday after one of the keenest struggles yet waged for that honour. The competition for some months, so far as the Championship was concerned, had practically resolved itself into a dual between two Glasgow clubs, Rangers and Celtic, and so close had been the struggle that the issue actually rested upon the [final] games played by the two rivals. Each club was engaged on opponents' ground, Celtic opposing Morton at Greenock and Rangers visiting Clyde at Shawfield Park, and singular to say, both games were drawn."

"As a consequence Celtic, who held a lead of one point, retained that advantage and won the Championship, their record for the competition reading:- twenty-seven games won, two lost, thirteen drawn; points, sixty-seven…The merit of Celtic's achievement cannot be [overstated], and their ultimate success in what was throughout an uphill fight against formidable opponents, revealed those qualities of grit, skill and enthusiasm that have invariably characterised great Celtic elevens of the past…The newly instituted system of promotion and relegation…made the League competition more strenuous and exhausting than it had ever been, and in winning under such conditions Celtic scored a victory worthy to be ranked with their great triumphs of the past."

A few months later, as the new season kicked off, the number of league matches would be reduced to thirty-eight, the same figure which is currently in use once again almost a century later. Of course, there were twenty teams in the top flight back then, with each side playing every other team home and away once only, and there was no league split to complicate matters. Sadly, Celtic would fail to retain the Scottish League Championship title during the 1922-23 campaign, despite beginning the season with three victories, as the new trio of "Shaw; McNair and Hilley" took shape.

Seven games into the league season, with Celtic now having lost twice – already equalling their total number of defeats in forty-two league outings during the previous campaign – Charlie Shaw was dropped from the Celtic side by Willie Maley in favour of the youthful John Hughes, having conceded ten goals during this period as well as four in a disappointing first round Glasgow Cup exit against Queen's Park.

One wonders whether Maley was beginning to search for a potential replacement for the great Charlie Shaw who, despite having a lot yet to offer, would not be around forever. However, despite keeping a clean sheet on his debut in a one-nil win against Motherwell, John Hughes would not become Maley's first choice. He did play five consecutive league matches, including a morale sapping three-one derby loss to Rangers at Celtic Park, but that was to be Hughes' lot as a first team player. Shaw would return approximately six weeks after his last appearance, once Celtic had suffered an unexpected, and perhaps unacceptable, four-one home defeat to Ayr United. Such was the anger felt by the home supporters that day that a small minority began to throw stones from the terracing late in the game, and Willie Maley was forced to approach the area himself in order to placate some of the perpetrators. This topped off what was a dreadful day for Celtic Football Club.

It was not to be a happy return to the squad for Charlie, as Celtic lost to Airdrieonians by a goal to nil, despite the fact the home side had played the majority of the match a man light after one of their side suffered a dislocated elbow and was forced to retire. In all fairness to Shaw though, there was very little he could have done about the goal which he did concede, for it was a last minute penalty which turned out to be the final kick of the entire game. Another home defeat to Kilmarnock a couple of days before Christmas would only make matters worse.

By the turn of the year, Celtic had lost six league matches from nineteen, hardly the form of champions. Of course, how much of this was Charlie Shaw's fault can is debatable, but I feel it would be very unfair to place the majority of the blame on him nor any single individual. After all, constant changes to the line-up cannot have helped the defence to gel, and as any football fan knows, even the best goalkeepers can only do so much if those outfield players tasked with their protection are playing poorly. In all, the Hoops would lose eleven of their thirty-eight league matches that season, finishing in third place in the table, nine points adrift of champions Rangers. However, few within the Celtic support would have been too disheartened by such an outcome, for the trophy cabinet would not lie empty during the coming summer, thanks to an almighty Scottish Cup run, which began with a three-two away victory over Lochgelly United.

Subsequently, in the round which followed the Celts would ease past Hurlford by four goals to nil at Celtic Park in front of only three thousand people, whilst across town thirty thousand spectators joined the Duke of York as a member of the Royal Family took in a domestic Scottish Football match for the first time when Queen's Park took on Bathgate at Hampden. Narrow victories over East Fife and Raith Rovers would follow, before Celtic took on Motherwell in the semi-final of the competition at Ibrox Park before seventy-five thousand people. Whilst the Hoops would take a very early lead thanks to Joe Cassidy, Motherwell proved themselves to be tricky opponents, forcing Charlie Shaw into several saves and clearances before the Celts managed to find another goal through McAtee midway through the second half. They then missed the chance to put themselves out of sight with a poor penalty late on, but it mattered little as Celtic's defence held out resolutely and the match finished with the Celts the victors by two goals to nil.

Thereafter, Celtic would go on to meet Hibernian in the Scottish Cup Final. The Edinburgh side had not won the tournament since their triumph over Celtic at Parkhead a little over two decades earlier and as such Celtic, not unreasonably, were widely considered the favourites to win the Scottish Cup. They'd finished above Hibernian in the league by five points and boasted a slightly superior goal average, but most importantly of all for some was that Celtic had history on their side. Only Queen's Park had won the competition more often than they had, and on the thirty-first of March 1923, Celtic had a chance to equal the Spiders' record of ten cup wins.

Approximately eighty thousand spectators attended the tie, some thirteen thousand of which the "Glasgow Herald" credits as travelling Hibernian supporters. The same newspaper said the following of the match itself, and although Charlie Shaw does not warrant too many references (thanks partly to Hibernian's generally poor shooting).

"The Edinburgh contingent derived much encouragement from the early stages of the contest, which favoured Hibernian to such an extent that their supporters at the interval were justifiably confident that their team held a winning chance. The Edinburgh side set a fast pace, and their forwards made rapid raids on the somewhat slow Celtic defence, which for a time wavered, and had the shooting of their forwards been of the quality of their outfield play the game would have been settled in Hibernian's favour in the first half."

"Celtic took longer than usual to settle, the quick and resolute tackling of the opposing half-backs allowing little scope for studied play, but towards the interval they seemed to find their game…The exchanges continued to fluctuate in the most interesting fashion, first the one goal, and then the other being strenuously assailed. About this stage Hibernian were the slightly more dangerous side, but though hard pressed, McNair and McStay never wavered. A long pass from Ritchie gave McColl and Dunn a scoring opportunity, chiefly owing to McNair failing to get in his kick. A scrimmage close in and a high shot from Dunn which went over the bar were, however, the only outcome."

"Subsequently a fine pass from McFarlane to Connelly allowed Celtic to secure a footing in their opponents' half of the field, and it was only after a defender had stopped a hard shot from McAtee that Hibernian gained relief. Ritchie and Dunn then cleverly beat McFarlane, but the Celtic left-back with a timely tackle averted trouble, while Shaw fisted out a corner kick taken by Walker… Half-time – No scoring."

"On resuming Hibernian attacked strongly, Shaw in the first minute saving brilliantly from Dunn. They continued their pressure on the Celtic goal, but there was not sufficient subtlety in their attacks to combat the crafty defence of Shaw, McNair and McStay. Three more hard shots were intercepted by Cringan before McStay with a long kick let Cassidy away, the move ending in McGinnigle kicking into touch. From an awkward position,

McLean shot over, and a little later McGinnigle charged down a great shot from Gallagher, who in course of his run in to goal, beat several opponents."

"Twenty minutes after resuming, McAtee sent across a long pass to McLean, who immediately centred, and Cassidy, getting the ball after it had bounced, headed into a vacant goal, Harper having left his charge in an effort to save the situation. During the next ten minutes Celtic were the more aggressive side, but in the last quarter of an hour the Hibernian forwards dominated the exchanges, and but for the craftiness of McNair, the dash of McStay and the soundness of Shaw, they would have drawn."

It is clear then that Celtic's sure defence, of which Charlie Shaw was an integral component, played a significant role in securing Celtic's first post-war Scottish Cup, but it has to be said that some luck was also involved, as the following conclusion to the article shows. In all honesty, perhaps this was well warranted for Shaw in particular who, after so many years of physical battles, regularly throwing himself into the mud all across Scotland, was now coming towards the end of his career.

"They [Hibs] came very near to equalising when Walker surprised Shaw by kicking past a clearance from the goalkeeper, the ball striking the side of the net. Close on time Hibernian had a strong appeal for a penalty disallowed, the referee ruling that the handling of the shot from McColl by Cringan was accidental. Full time – Celtic one, Hibernian nil."

At the age of thirty-seven Charlie Shaw, the little goalkeeper from the mining village of Twechar, won his second Scottish Cup with Celtic, his last honour as a member of the Parkhead side. Over the course of the tournament, he conceded only three goals in six games. Shaw did not allow his charge to be breached in either the quarter final, semi-final or indeed the Scottish Cup Final of 1923, a laudable achievement which undoubtedly helped his side towards their triumph.

The following season would be Charlie Shaw's last full campaign as a Celtic player, as he featured in every single Scottish League and Scottish Cup game they contested for the seventh time in his Parkhead career. The Hoops would finish in third place and, having relinquished any chance of retaining the Scottish Cup upon a two-nil home defeat in the first round of the competition against Kilmarnock, few would have considered 1923-24 a success.

Over the course of the entire league campaign, Celtic would concede less than a goal per game, as their opponents only managed to score on thirty-three occasions in thirty-eight outings. Whilst Rangers eventually finished the league thirteen points clear of Celtic, it is noteworthy that Celtic only conceded only four more goals than the Ibrox side. However, the margin of sixteen less goals scored was very telling. Regardless, a steady Celtic defence, which blended youth and experience had finally emerged from the relative selection chaos of the previous year. Veterans Charlie Shaw and Alec McNair passed on much needed guile and know-how to their younger counterparts, Hugh Hilley and John McFarlane who, although more mobile than the two stalwarts were still learning their trade. There was also the McStay brothers Willie and Jimmy who, despite being in their late twenties at the start of the season, would remain Celtic players for several years to come, benefitting much from the experience of those who went before them.

The next footballing year, 1924-25, would see Charlie Shaw's final appearances for Celtic Football Club. He was thirty-nine years of age when the Hoops began their campaign with three drawn matches against Dundee, Partick Thistle and Airdrieonians. Around a month later, only a few days after Shaw had turned forty, his side rewarded him with an emphatic four-nil victory over Motherwell at Parkhead. This was to be the fifth of seven consecutive league wins, the last of which culminated in a one-nil triumph over Heart of Midlothian which was to be Charlie Shaw's final appearance for the Hoops at Celtic Park.

It was then, on the eighteenth of October 1925, that Peter Shevlin, who had just signed for Celtic from St Roch's for a transfer fee of one hundred and twenty pounds a week earlier, took over Charlie Shaw's place in the Celtic goalmouth for a goalless draw with St. Johnstone. It would not be an easy start for Peter, who would see his side lose eight of their next twelve league matches. Of course, once he had time to settle, Shevlin would go on to show what he could do, becoming a popular figure within the Celtic support. It is also safe to assume that Charlie Shaw would have offered the man who he would have known to be his replacement a few pointers whilst he was still at the Football Club, and Shevlin would have undoubtedly benefitted from his predecessor's wealth of experience and knowledge of the game.

Shaw would feature again for Celtic only once, as the Celts lost one-nil away to Motherwell on the seventeenth of January 1925. He would not see first team action again for the Hoops, but in the time before his summer departure Celtic, with young Peter Shevlin between the posts, would go on another run to the Scottish Cup Final which culminated in the dramatic two-one victory over Dundee with famous goals from Jimmy McGrory and Patsy Gallagher (via a somersault).

When Charlie Shaw finally left Celtic Football Club behind him on the second of June 1925, he did so with some fantastic memories and a legendary status amongst the Celtic support. I wholeheartedly believe that had it not been for the remarkable John Thomson, many would still consider Charlie Shaw to be the greatest Celtic goalkeeper to have ever lived, and when one acknowledges that it took someone of Thomson's unique calibre to take this accolade away from Shaw, this is truly indicative of just how talented Charlie really was.

In his thirteen years at Celtic Park, Charlie Shaw played in four hundred and thirty-six matches, maintaining a clean sheet on two hundred and forty occasions – a shut-out ratio of fifty-five percent. In the Scottish Cup, Shaw played twenty-three times, again keeping this ratio above half, as he conceded in only nine of these matches. In his time at Parkhead, he won six Scottish League Championship titles, along with two Scottish Cups, making him one of the more decorated goalkeepers in the Club's long and illustrious history. Incredibly, he never received an international cap. Despite this, he remains a legend in every sense of the word, and an example to young and aspiring goalkeepers everywhere to this very day, as well as those currently between the posts at Celtic Park.

Subsequently, he would be tempted across the Atlantic Ocean, where he enjoyed a spell with New Bedford Whalers Football Club in Massachusetts, eventually becoming their player/manager. Charlie Shaw died of pneumonia on the twenty-seventh of March 1938 at the age of only fifty-two in New York, where he is buried. Regardless of the unending debate as to which stopper was best, it is certain that Charlie shall always hold a place as one of the greatest goalkeepers ever to guard the posts at Celtic Park.

"The Chronicles of Willie Maley: "The Wearing of the Green""

"By Willie Maley, Celtic F.C. Manager"

"At the time we played our first final the gates were divided between the teams and the S.F.A. and the three shared to the extent of the four hundred and fifty pounds after the expenses were paid...A poet of the day burst into rhyme over our defeat in the final thus":-

"From Parkhead's classic, precincts came a wail of discontent;
The air was filled with sounds of woe, with lamentations rent;
Right gallantly the Celts did fight, Alas! 'Twas all in vain;
Old Erin's heroes bit the dust – they never smiled again!
Long will that fight remembered be, and ages hence will stand;
In bold relief the victory gained, by Cathkin's Warrior band;
The Celts, although defeated, still their prestige did maintain;
But till the Scottish Cup they win – they'll never smile again!"

"We must have been sorrowful a long while if the poet was correct in his prophecy, as it was 1892 before we actually did win this Cup. Looking back on this Final after all these years, I am fully convinced we were better without the Cup at that period of our existence. It gave us something to work harder for, and a victory then might have lessened our ambitions considerably, with the feeling of success so easily and quickly gained. That was the feeling of the older and headier men of the club of that time, but did not quite express the feelings of our defeated team that day."

"Paying the Penalty"

"The finalists both paid the penalty of greatness very soon after that famous game, as the teams were at once well tapped by the ever busy English agent, and departures came thickly, as I will later tell with regards our lot."

"We ran counter to the S.F.A. just at this time by reason of our fixture with the Corinthians, which, unfortunately, had been fixed for the same date as the Association trial games owing to the London team being able to get the Oval only for certain dates. Five of our lot had been selected to play in these trials – Groves, Kelly, McCallum, McLaren and McKeown. Kelly and McKeown applied for and received leave of absence, as their merits seemed to be better known than the others, but the other three travelled to London with us. They would not miss such a trip for the chance of a cap, which they argued was very remote. Luckily, the Association took a lenient view of matters, and let the delinquents off. Kelly and McLaren were that year selected to play against England at the Oval, of which I will speak later."

"The social after a game is now a thing of the past in football, a fact, I think, to be regretted, as it enabled players (who had to meet in contest on the field repeatedly) to make up their little differences over the hospitable board."

"The pleasantest feature of the old day socials to my mind was the harmony, and in this particular one referred to we had the referee, Mr. Charles Campbell, who sang, for our special benefit (I fancy), "The Wearing of the Green." We also had big burly Jamie Crerar (who with Andrew Kirkwood and wee Billy Brown, were the Third's strongest men in these days), giving us "Off to Philadelphia"; Andrew Hamilton, of Queen's Park, with his favourite "Bonny Wee Thing", and A. B. MacKenzie, of Rangers fame, in "The Four Jolly Smiths." As a famous Scottish football scribe used to say – "Them wis the days.""

"Our trip to London, which followed on our defeats in the Scottish final, helped to drown our sorrows over the failure to lift the "pot", and we had a rare good trip, this being my first real football outing. These trips, in the days referred to, were really pleasure excursions, and very much different from the ones we make nowadays when we do venture into England to play friendly football. People nowadays would not stand for the free and easy football that in the main was played by the Scottish clubs touring twenty-five years ago. The high jinks in the hotels were affairs entered into as a matter of course. The damage done was freely met by the Club managements, and I may say it was sometimes much more than a joke. Eventually certain hotels over the border would not touch a football team at any price."

"A series of defeats [around] that time were not to our liking, and caused consternation amongst our following. The story is told of an old bowl wife in the Gallowgate who, when "grinding" the bowls to call her customers' attention on a Saturday night; on being told "the Celts are beat again," dropped the bowls to utter smash with the exclamation, "My God!""

"The first cup we won was the North-Eastern, which was played for by the Clyde, Thistle, Northern, Cowlairs, Shettleston, Clydesdale and ourselves. We played the first round that year with the Clydesdale, and the game was played on the present Glencairn pitch. After winning we were sumptuously entertained to pies and ale. Later we qualified for the final by beating Northern, then a strong team, by four to one. In May of that year, we beat Cowlairs in the final at Barrowfield by six to one."

"We had started on an Easter tour on the Friday before the International, and after playing at Bolton on Good Friday, and at Burnley on the Saturday, crossed to Belfast for our first visit to the Green Isle. McLaren and Kelly travelled from London immediately after the International to join us at Preston, from whence we travelled by Fleetwood to Belfast."

"Nearly an Hour Late"

"Our game at Bolton – we got beaten by two to nil – was quite a good one, but we were at a big disadvantage, as through a breakdown on the railway we were nearly an hour late in starting the game – in fact, the crowd had just about made up their minds to have their money back by rushing the payboxes when we drove up, having dressed in the train to save time."

"Burnley gave us the roughest game of our season, and one quite up to the standard of our most recent meetings with the same club. Several Scotsmen played against us in the team.

Lang, of Third Lanark, played for Burnley, but got his collar-bone broken, and on being taken off we allowed a substitute to come on. He proved to be Danny Friel, late of Vale of Leven, and ultimately, to be our trainer. We got very bad treatment from Burnley that day, being even refused water to wash ourselves after the game – not like the present conditions at Burnley."

"Our journey to Belfast via Fleetwood is still a theme of merriment amongst those left to tell the tale. After a week on a fish diet (it being Holy Week), we went down to supper on the steamer at 12.15 [after midnight] to a rare feed of cold meats, which we did justice to. It told an awful tale later, when…we encountered a gale in the Channel, and out of the party of twenty-six, only four escaped the terrors of mal de mer [seasickness]. Poor John Glass, of happy memory, was, with myself, almost the "record breakers" for that journey, and John used to say that in my few spare moments I would tell all around that when I got to Belfast I would walk back. James Kelly was given out as saying to Mr. Glass – "Give my purse and my watch to ma faither." We survived the terrible night, and Belfast with its hearty welcome soon cheered us up and put us quite fit again."

"Mr. Cowan, I Presume?"

Born on the nineteenth of March 1813 on the banks of the River Clyde, the name of David Livingstone is perhaps not one which anybody would expect to find in a book predominantly based around the subject of football. After all, more than fifteen years prior to the first match which Celtic Football Club ever played, the man still famously recalled via the "Dr. Livingstone, I presume?" quote supposedly uttered by another explorer, Henry Morgan Stanley, died in the country now known as Zambia at the age of sixty. It is said that he succumbed to a combination of malaria and dysentery, and whilst his followers would bury his heart under a tree, the rest of his remains – along with his handwritten journal – were transported over a thousand miles to the shoreline so that they could be returned to Britain by sea.

Although Livingstone, who came into the world in workers' quarters next to a cotton factory in Blantyre, is regarded as one of the first great African explorers, he was most certainly not the last, as more and more people visit the continent nowadays on their own journeys of discovery. In 1859, Livingstone – then on his second expedition to Africa – reached an inland lake known by the name, "Nyasa", and selected a nearby area which he dubbed the "Shire Highlands" as a potential home in which Europeans could settle in future. Within forty years, the British government had done that which they did best (and I use the word "best" with an unmistakable tinge of sarcasm) with this area – as well as a significant portion of surrounding land – and claimed it for themselves. After all, it transpired the Portuguese also had their eye on the land in question, and they couldn't let them have it.

Of course, the locals had no say in any of this, and by the time Celtic won their first Scottish Cup in 1892, the area was officially part of the British Central Africa Protectorate. Approximately twenty years later, this mouthful was abandoned and replaced by the name "Nyasaland", but of course it remained part of the

British Empire all the same. For the sake of record keeping, the country then became part of the "Federation of Rhodesia and Nyasaland" in 1953 before finally, under increasing pressure from various parties, the United Kingdom abolished the Federation a decade later and Nyasaland finally gained its independence in July 1964. Now, I would expect that when I refer to the country by its modern name, it will suddenly seem more familiar to you all, for what was once Nyasaland is now Malawi.

Approximately one and a half times the size of Scotland in terms of area, Malawi is one of the smaller countries in Africa, being dwarfed by the likes of South Africa and Algeria at approximately ten and twenty times its size respectively. Equally, with a population of almost thirteen million, there is not an enormous difference in terms of population density between Malawi and Scotland. In terms of shape, it is a long and narrow country sandwiched between Mozambique, Tanzania and Zambia, with Lake Malawi itself accounting for almost thirty thousand square kilometres of its entire area (equivalent to a quarter of the nation as a whole). From the country's most northerly point to the opposite mark at the south is a little over five hundred miles, but most of the landmass therein is a little more than one hundred miles across. Despite this, the country has two distinctly different climates, as the northern uplands are generally considered to be much cooler and wetter than the southern half of Malawi, which is significantly warmer and dryer. Also, in a similar manner to Scotland, the most populous city is not its capital, Lilongwe. Instead, we shall focus on the busiest city in the country, Blantyre, named after the birthplace of David Livingstone.

At the end of 2014, the Celtic Charity Foundation, the official charitable arm of the Football Club, took a group of volunteers to Blantyre with the aim of helping to fix up local schools and improve sanitation in some of the slums in the city. Amongst this group, there were people of different ages from all walks of life. This is the story of one of them, a young man who left Scotland behind him to experience his own, modern day, expedition to Africa.

Andrew Cowan, until recently a resident of Rutherglen (and still a regular of sorts on the Rutherglen Vogue Celtic Supporters'

Club Bus), turned twenty-five earlier this year. He was a fellow pupil in my year group at St Bride's Secondary School (latterly renamed St Andrew's and St Bride's upon a merger with another local school) in East Kilbride, and therefore I knew him prior to his trip. At school, we spent a significant amount of time playing football together, though I must admit that Andrew (or Andy as he was more commonly known) was a far superior player to myself. After all, I was only really ever good at winning headers and clearing the ball away as a determined, if somewhat crude central defender, whilst Andrew possessed a touch more guile and poise. Even at school, it was clear that Andrew was as big a Celtic fan as I, and thus that topic tended to make up the bulk of the conversations we would have in and around classes.

However, since leaving school, I had only bumped into him a handful of times at Celtic Park and spoken occasionally online in the intervening years. Andrew then contacted me hoping that I might help to promote the Rutherglen Vogue C.S.C.'s upcoming supporters' night, which of course, I was more than happy to. I decided to attend the function myself where I met Andrew and the conversation soon turned to his trip. Thus we started the long and winding road which has finally led us here, to a chapter in which I hope I can do not only Andrew justice, but all of those who ventured to Malawi alongside him, as well as the people who call the country their home.

When I conducted my first interview with Andrew, he had just moved into a new flat with his fiancée, Colette, and for that alone, I owe both of them my thanks for finding time for me during a period of inevitable upheaval. Anyway, returning to the story at hand, Andrew began to take me through the process which saw him set to travel not to Malawi, but to Kenya, as he explained.

"In all honesty, it came about in a completely unexpected manner. I suppose I'd been vaguely aware of the fact a group of Celtic supporters had went out to Kenya the year before, but I had no plans to go myself at that stage. Several months later, I logged on to the Celtic website in search of news or fixture details or whatever, I can't really recall, but whilst I was there, something about another trip to Africa caught my eye, and I just clicked on the link without thinking. Before I knew it, I found myself becoming increasingly interested, and eventually I located the relevant email address and sent off a message enquiring as to whether or not there were any remaining places for the upcoming trip."

"Quickly, the people at the Club got back to me and said there were still a few free slots, and if I was interested all I had to do was lay down a deposit to secure my place, with the knowledge I would have to raise a minimum of two thousand pounds prior to departure to cover my journey. I took some time and spoke to Colette and my parents, and although I'm sure there must have been some levels of trepidation on their part for me, they could see this was something I wanted to do and it could well be a once in a lifetime opportunity, so they were very supportive and I really appreciated that. This was the summer of 2013, with a travel date set for January 2014, so although I know it would require a bit of effort, I thought I'd be able to raise the money in time. I owe a lot of people my thanks in that regard, particularly my family, friends and everyone involved in the Rutherglen Vogue C.S.C., I think it's safe to say I couldn't have done it without them. All in all though, I was rather excited, as you would expect."

However, such levels of anticipation would soon decrease rapidly, as a series of terrorist attacks carried out by the extremist organisation Al-Shabaab in Kenya, the most infamous of which was the assault on the Westgate Shopping Mall in Nairobi (in which almost seventy individuals were killed and another one hundred and seventy-five injured), forced the British Government, via the Foreign Office, to advise against all but essential travel to large areas of the country. Unsurprisingly, this left the Celtic Charity Foundation, as well as their volunteers – all of whom had raised significant amounts of money by this point – in a serious quandary. As such, an emergency meeting was called at Celtic Park to discuss the matters at hand.

"Everyone scheduled to go on the trip was very aware of the ongoing problems in Kenya before the meeting was called, and I suppose we all knew, at the back of our minds at least, that if things didn't change, the trip might be cancelled", Andrew told me. "It's important to point out at this stage that the majority of the group scheduled to travel had done so during the previous year as well, whereas debutants like me and a few others were in the minority. I felt that was a positive though, because these people had been there, done it, and were coming back for more. That eased my fears that whilst it would definitely be tough, it would also be very worthwhile."

"To give them their due, the Club were great during that period of time. They laid out our options at the meeting that night, and allowed us to make our own decisions and then vote for whichever path we felt was right for us. The four choices open to us were: 1. To hold off indefinitely in the hope of the situation in Kenya improving and the Foreign Office lowering its travel restrictions; 2. To cancel entirely and return the money to the donors; 3. To abandon our travel plans but to still send the money raised over to the relevant organisations; or 4. To disregard the Kenyan element of the trip and instead search for a suitable replacement elsewhere on the African continent.

A significant amount of debate followed this, with some people in favour of simply calling off the journey and sending the money over, whilst others were keener to change our destination but carry on as best we could with our original aims. Eventually, the decision was taken to find an alternative place to visit, but we knew our schedule would be pushed back by several months as a result. However, looking back on it with the benefit of hindsight, I'm actually quite content that was the case, because I honestly don't believe I was mentally prepared at that point for what would have lay ahead had we gone to Kenya. I don't want to sound lackadaisical about the whole thing because I certainly wasn't – I took the trip very seriously – but I didn't truly grasp the enormity of it all at that time."

Therefore, presumably after many logistical headaches, Celtic announced another destination – Blantyre in Malawi – and set a new date for travel, October 2014. Subsequently, Andrew and all of the other people set to make the trip were given inoculations and medication, protecting them against everything from malaria and yellow fever to typhoid and hepatitis. Alongside this, the group – which numbered twenty-three in total (twenty volunteers, one representative from the Celtic Charity Foundation and two media people from the Football Club) – received details of their travel itinerary. Initially, a bus ride of almost four hundred miles would see the party make their way from Celtic Park to London's Heathrow International Airport. From there, the first of three flights would take them over three thousand, seven hundred miles to the African aviation hub of Addis Ababa, the Ethiopian capital. A second flight would transport them almost another fifteen hundred miles to Lilongwe, before a final hop over to Blantyre – this one just one hundred and sixty miles in length – would complete the outward leg. In total, the trip accounted for a little over five thousand, seven hundred and sixty miles, with a grand total of eleven thousand, five hundred and twenty miles travelled there and back. That is a longer distance than travelling – one way – from Glasgow to Wellington on the south island of New Zealand. It was a gargantuan journey, particularly for a man who had a smile on his face when he recounted looking at a map at one point to see exactly where Malawi was, before noting that he – like many of us I would suspect – had never even previously ventured into the Southern Hemisphere.

The stark reality of this prospect would become clear to Andrew at an unlikely point, standing in line to board his flight to Africa. Firstly though, for the sake of the record, the group gathered for a photo opportunity at Celtic Park before they headed south by bus. Perhaps I am seeing something which isn't there, but when I look back at the photographs from that day, the volunteers look a mixture of enthusiastic and apprehensive standing outside the stadium, about to embark on an adventure unlike any the majority of us will ever see. Anyway, by his own admission, as Andrew stood in the queue of passengers waiting to board their Ethiopian Airlines flight to Addis Ababa, the realisation that he was about to step into the unknown gripped him.

"Don't get me wrong", he recalled, "I obviously knew where we were headed, but as I stood in that line and looked up at the gate monitor which displayed the flight details and destination in big, bold letters, a combination of nerves and excitement hit me. I couldn't help but wonder what I'd find in Ethiopia and beyond. I had no first-hand experience myself to base it on, so there was certainly a slight feeling of tension, but once we were on the plane and in the air, it turned into a typical long haul flight like any other."

Andrew continued, expanding on his own preconceived ideas regarding the journey itself: "The flight wasn't bad. The food was the same sort of stuff you would be given on any other airline, and as we began our descent many hours later, the landscape which greeted us wasn't that which I had been expecting. Stereotypically speaking, I presumed that large parts of Ethiopia would just be desert, but in actual fact the areas around the capital and its airport were lush with vegetation. Some of the views were spectacular, but sadly the same could not be said for the airport itself, which was – without doubt – the worst I've ever visited. The designated smoking areas and the toilets were absolutely filthy, and if any airport is ever to take this unwanted title away from Addis Ababa, it'll need to be truly shambolic."

As Andrew later said, his naturally tired state likely did not make him notice any redeeming qualities which the airport may have had, but he also highlighted the fact that after such a long journey, the last thing he needed was for life to be made more unpleasant by the state of the facilities available. "Obviously, I was a foreigner in their country, so it's inevitable that some things would have seemed odd to me, but the airport was just completely strange. Weird shops sold a bizarre selection of items, it was tricky trying to find things to buy which you would normally expect to be readily available in other airports, and water was leaking through the roof all over the place. I couldn't help but wonder, with a slight hint of dread, about whether or not things were going to get worse than this when we went further into Africa – and if so, to what extent – but thankfully those fears wouldn't come to fruition. Thereafter, we never even got off the plane after flying from Addis Ababa to Lilongwe. We just sat on the tarmac whilst about half of the passengers got off and some new people made their way aboard, soon finding ourselves airborne again."

Upon the group's arrival in Blantyre, Andrew's memories are slightly hazy, and for this, no one can attribute any blame to a man who had just spent more than a day travelling a significant distance. One recollection which he did have was that upon landing, the landscape which awaited him looked a lot more like that which he had expected to see back in Ethiopia, with the heat and dust both factors which any outsider would notice immediately. Details of the subsequent bus journey to the place in which they would be living for the next fortnight are also sketchy, as he passed in and out of an uncomfortable sleep, thanks in part to the rather large holes present in the road surface giving him a jolt every now and then. One thing which he did recall, however, was that the roadside vendors seemed to sell everything and anything imaginable to other locals. Of these items, the most prevalent seemed to be couches (all of which appeared to be almost identical replicas of each other), sticks, pieces of wood and, regrettably, coffins and tombstones.

The group's place of residence in Blantyre was a hostel of sorts, contained within a large, old house surrounded by high walls topped with razor wire. Andrew may not have been greeted by someone saying "Mr. Cowan, I presume?" upon arrival but as he recounted, he was rather happy with what he found there regardless.

"The accommodation we stayed in was actually much better than I expected, although I have no doubts that if someone was to reside in an identical place back home they would consider it to be pretty basic. I presume the neighbourhood in which it was located must have been fairly well off, as all of the houses were situated within gated complexes surrounded by huge fences and walls. For that very same reason though, it made it difficult to judge exactly how wealthy the residents actually were. As for our building itself, it had all of the basic amenities which many people largely take for granted – running water, electricity, and proper beds. It appeared to be a hostel, but I think we'd booked most of it out during our stay so it was only on a rare occasion that we saw any other guests there. The only minor issue I had was that my bed's mosquito net fell off during our first night, so I just had to pull it up and over me like a blanket every evening, but that just goes to show how good our living quarters really were since that's the only concern I had there."

Echoing these sentiments, Andrew and the other members of the group making their first excursions to the African continent would come to appreciate just how precious the aforementioned amenities were the next day, when the group ventured out into Blantyre properly for the first time. Both during and after the bus journey from their residential compound to a school situated some distance out of the city, it became very apparent to everyone involved that these conveniences – access to running water, electricity and a bed for the night – were not niceties to many of the people of Blantyre or the surrounding countryside, but luxuries which many of them had never seen. Despite this, the men, women and children of the local area came out in their hundreds to welcome the group of Celtic supporters in memorable fashion.

"As soon as the children caught sight of the bus approaching", Andrew told me, "They started running from all around, some from quite a distance away, probably up to around a quarter of a mile, just to greet us. It happened out on the larger roads to some degree too, with kids who knew they had no hope of seeing the bus come to a halt doing their best to catch up with it just in the hope of getting a smile and a wave from the people on board. That meant a lot to me personally and I'm sure I wasn't alone, making me feel oddly at home in a place which was, in some aspects at least, so very alien. The welcome at the school itself was fantastic too. Obviously, having only arrived the day before, we were all still very tired – particularly as we had yet to become accustomed to the heat – but the people of Blantyre gave us such a boost, and it just added to our determination to help them as much as we possibly could during our time there."

"Nobody really seemed to have any knowledge of who or what Celtic were – I think we were just seen by the locals as foreigners above all else – but they were tremendously kind all the same. The adults in and around the city centre had a relatively good grasp of English as their second language [the first being the local Chichewa], but the majority of people living in the slums could only manage broken English, which made detailed conversations a rarity. This mattered for little though as I've said, because the people were so nice to us. Considering football, the

English Premier League sides, as well as Barcelona and Real Madrid seemed to be the most popular, but when I saw someone wearing an Arsenal shirt with a Chelsea badge sewn onto it in place of the Gunners' crest, I was again reminded that almost all of the football shirts we would see there would be second, third or fourth hand."

However, one event sure to stick in the memory of any outsider but which would likely be considered as innocuous by a local did catch Andrew's eye on that first day. This did not make him feel out of place or unwelcome, but did highlight again the fact that in some aspects, the people of Malawi have totally different approaches to their lives to us back home. This may also be an opportune moment to discuss the charitable basis for much of Scotland's connection to the African country.

"To cut a long story short", Andrew said, "We had spent some time at the school with the children and were beginning to get familiarised with the jobs which we would be performing in the days ahead. We were also given an insight into the work which Mary's Meals do over there, providing all of the children who attend their schools with a guarantee of one meal a day in order to incentivise them to attend classes. The food which they serve is called "phala" [which, according to the "B.B.C." is a form of "vitamin enriched maize porridge"] and is specifically designed to provide them with as much nutritional benefit as possible, supplying enough energy to allow them to focus on their studies. I believe it was the strong presence which Mary's Meals – a Scottish charity – has there which led to Celtic's decision to choose Malawi as an alternate destination once our trip to Kenya was cancelled. The work which they do in an attempt to battle malnutrition and improve education in the process is inspiring."

Before continuing, it is very noteworthy that by chance, as I write this, it has recently been announced that Mary's Meals now feed more than one million children per day across the world – an achievement the importance of which cannot possibly be overstated. For this, they deserve an endless amount of praise. Returning to Andrew's story, he continued as follows.

"The kids were great. Initially, several of them were very impressed by the modern technology which ourselves and the media pairing had at our disposal. For example, they would be overjoyed when you took a picture of them on your phone and then showed it to them on the screen. Presumably, they weren't as accustomed to seeing their own image as much as we are back home, so it just goes to show that small things like that could give them a real thrill. Anyway, after some time had passed we were invited to take part in an impromptu game of football. I've never been the best at estimating numbers, but I'm confident there must have been close to one hundred kids involved in the match, most of whom were boys. It might sound clichéd, but the ball which they used was impressive, if for no reason other than ingenuity they must have possessed in order to construct it, because it was made out of loads of plastic bags, all wrapped tightly together and bound up. As a group we really wished we had a proper ball to present them with as a gift, but we hadn't brought any with us."

"As you would expect, the kids were playing in their bare feet, and as they all tore around this sandy playing field, you could see the dust rising up in the air. They were so enthusiastic about the game and showed what seemed to be boundless energy chasing the ball around, and then I noticed a small pig had appeared at the side of the field. In all honesty, I thought nothing of it, as we had already seen a few animals wandering around during our short time in the country, but then the kids spotted it and promptly abandoned the football match entirely. A few seconds later, they were all off in pursuit of the animal, and after a minute or two they caught it and quickly beat it to death. I presume they saw it as a food source, but it was certainly an eye opener for me, even though I watched this all unfold from a fair distance. Amidst the welcoming nature of the people, it was easy to get lost now and again and forget where you were, but seeing that definitely reminded me I wasn't in Glasgow anymore."

The next day, the party's efforts began in earnest. Split into three smaller groups of five or six people each, the bulk of the volunteers had the collective task of renovating six local primary schools over the course of a fortnight (two schools per group).

Whilst these projects were ongoing, another trio of volunteers would work outside, continuously exposed to the elements to build the first functioning double latrine to which an entire neighbourhood would ever have access. According to Andrew, who was a member of one of the school renovation teams, the first site which he visited was situated a short distance out of the city, whilst the second was only five minutes or so from the centre of Blantyre within a slum. Both schools consisted only of one room, with the latter boasting a tiny storage cupboard for what few supplies they had. The conditions in each building were poor, with brittle and decaying walls helping to add to their seemingly permanent dark and dingy state. Certainly, these were not places conducive to attaining a good education, nor were they the sorts of facilities which would encourage young children to attend classes, but that would all change over the course of the group's visit to Malawi.

As one would expect, the volunteers soon settled into a regular pattern, which I shall allow Andrew to describe to you in his own words: "Quickly, we developed a routine which we all stuck to for the majority of the trip. We would get up early in the morning, sometime around the 6 a.m. mark, before washing, eating and boarding the bus to our destination. Aiming to be there and begin work by 8 a.m. or so, we hoped to get as much as possible done in the morning so that we could rest and eat our lunches whilst the sun was at its strongest around midday. Thereafter we'd carry on until the early evening, before travelling back to our residence – occasionally stopping off at the local supermarket en route – having some food and a couple of beers then heading to bed and repeating the whole process all over again."

"There was a little bar inside our hostel, consisting predominantly of a single fridge filled with bottles of beer, which were colder at some points than they were at others. We could have bought beer for less at the supermarket, but we were keen to invest in the place which we called home for two weeks. We'd each brought a couple of hundred U.S. Dollars or so with us, which we promptly changed into between eighty and ninety thousand Malawian Kwacha. In the hostel, a beer cost somewhere in the region of two hundred Kwacha, so nobody was complaining about the price, particularly after a long day of hard labour. Every now and again we'd sit outside at night for a while, albeit within the walls of our compound. One thing which will stay with me was the stars – without much access to electricity, there was barely any light pollution in Blantyre – so much more of the night sky was visible than it is in Glasgow, and it was spectacular."

Whilst we are on the subject, I feel I must expand somewhat upon what I was told regarding the previously referenced local supermarket. By all accounts, when the group were inside this large structure, it would actually have been rather easy to forget they were in the heart of Africa, for many brand names and products on sale there carried an air of familiarity about them. Brightly lit, clean and otherwise slightly uninteresting, in many aspects it could have been any supermarket in the world, save for some of the more unusual items on sale here and there. However, it was not this which astounded Andrew – nor the fact that a bottle of vodka retailed for around three pounds sterling or beer for as little as thirty pence – but the contrast between this environment and that in which he had been spending his working days.

"Looking back on it now, one of the things which surprised me the most was how close areas with dramatically varying standards of living were situated in relation to each other. For example, across the road from the supermarket was a large football stadium, but only minutes away from there were some of the slums in which the conditions were simply appalling."

The "Kamuzu Stadium", named after the first President of Malawi upon its independence (Dr. Hastings Kamuzu Banda), has a total capacity of approximately fifty thousand people. Home of one of the foremost domestic sides in the country, "Big Bullets Football Club", it is a bizarre looking arena, which features several different terraced stands, equally separated by large, flat, empty spaces. These stands, which could be likened to being slices of a normal football stadium separated by areas of open ground, are located behind one goal and along one side of the field, with the other two sides marked only by tiny terracing in comparison. With this in mind, I cannot help but wonder what sort of gargantuan crowd the stadium could hold if such work was replicated all the way around the playing field. Whilst all of the members of the national side currently play for African football clubs, it may be of interest to note that two of the players – Limbikani Mvaza and Gabadinho Mhango – who boast over thirty international caps between them, represent the South African side Bloemfontein Celtic, named after their Glaswegian counterparts.

During the group's visit to Blantyre, the Malawian international side were set to face Algeria at the Kamuzu Stadium, a match which the volunteers wished to attend but were prohibited from doing so due to security concerns. The home team were defeated by two goals to nil, although there was no shame in this owing to the much loftier place in the present footballing world which Algeria hold over Malawi.

Returning to the previous point, Andrew continued, "I couldn't help but feel that the proximity of some seemingly more upmarket areas to the various slums in the city was ironic. I suppose it's difficult to describe, but I just found it odd. At points you would be driving down a pleasant residential street with nice cars on show, and then a matter of seconds later, the scenery would change to that of a slum with no running water or sanitation. I was disappointed I wasn't able to attend the match in question, because I think it would have been an interesting glimpse into a different footballing culture, but that was just the way of things."

Moving on, I feel it is important that we focus on the work which was carried out by Andrew and the other volunteers inside the schools during their stay in Malawi. "At times, the heat bordered on unbearable", he told me, "particularly when you were working anywhere near the roofs themselves. They were made of cheap tin, and so whenever the sun shone the whole building heated up very quickly. There were times upon which it honestly felt as if you were trying to work inside a large oven, but we persevered. Our jobs were, basically, to fill in any cracks and holes in the walls as best we could before preparing them adequately for painting. Once we had then painted these surfaces and brightened the rooms up, they were still very plain and uninteresting, so we added items such as the alphabet and numbers to them using as many vibrant colours as possible. Several locals aided our work also as they wanted to help the children of their communities, and their efforts were enormously appreciated."

Typifying this generosity of the local population, Andrew continued: "There was Malawian man who appeared and helped another group with their painting work, but because nobody could communicate with him in any great detail, one or two people were a little concerned in case he thought he was going to be paid at the end of the project. However, this wasn't to be a problem as it transpired that he was a local artist who had chosen to help simply in the hope that someone might purchase one of his paintings. To give you an idea of this man's natural talent, he was able to paint large Celtic crests on the internal walls of the school freehand, simply by copying the badge on the jersey which someone happened to be wearing. By the time they said their goodbyes to him, the group had bought every single one of his paintings between them, giving him the equivalent of a few months' wages in a week or so. Naturally, he was delighted, but the others said it really was a great privilege to meet someone like him, and the pleasure was all theirs."

Upon the completion of the renovation work at the second school, the finished article was met with great joy by the teachers and children alike, just as it had been when Andrew's group had accomplished their work on the first of the two schools. The immediate reaction of the adults when they first ventured inside the completed building perhaps sums up better than I can the importance which music and dance have in Malawian culture, for according to Andrew, within seconds of walking through the door they began to sing in jubilation. During the next few minutes, varying levels of reluctance were overcome as the volunteers were persuaded to join the subsequent dances. As Andrew reflected though, such exuberant reactions were no bad thing, as "they highlighted just how much they appreciated our efforts, which was heart-warming to witness."

Having finished the work required on all of the schools and the latrines, the volunteers had successfully completed their overall objectives with a day to spare prior to their return home to Scotland. To celebrate this feat, and indeed to see some more of the African continent than the insides of school buildings or a toilet, they were taken on a safari style excursion to one of the nearby National Parks. Ironically, according to Andrew, this part of their African expedition correlated far more closely to the stereotypes we are often subjected to at home than, for example, anything he had seen in or around the cities previously, as he outlined to me.

"The safari trip aligned with our preconceptions of it to a much more notable extent than anything else we experienced in Malawi. We drove out of the city by bus, clambered into the backs of green, open top Jeeps and proceeded to make our way into the National Park proper. We saw baboons, crocodiles, elephants, giraffes, hippopotamuses, lions and many of the other animals people back home would automatically associate with a safari. It was a fantastic way to spend a few hours, seeing all of them in their natural habitat, particularly when you come from a country where the wildlife tends to consist mostly of foxes, badgers and maybe the odd deer."

As the group returned to Blantyre, they pulled into a roadside market, aiming not only to pick up a few souvenirs for home, but also to part with any remaining Kwacha they may have had. As Andrew described, this was a step above your average holiday stalls which sell key rings, postcards and baseball caps. "The market which we visited on our way back to the city was fantastically mad. As you'd expect, as soon as the vendors saw a bus full of foreigners pull up, they were understandably enthusiastic in their attempts to make a few sales, promising each of us the "best prices". However, some of them didn't seem to understand the difficulties which come with, for example, trying to get a metre long model sailing ship, complete with masts and sails, through several airports, flights and a bus journey back home. All joking aside though, some of the items on offer were remarkable. The vast majority of them were handmade, so a lot of skill must have been involved in their production. In the end, I plumped for an elephant, a giraffe and a hippopotamus – all wooden, of course – and to my surprise I actually managed to get them all home in one piece. Some of the others bought larger items like drums, but there were no takers for the huge scale model jeeps or indeed the sailing ship I mentioned."

Ultimately, the time would come when the group of volunteer Celtic supporters would depart the city of Blantyre and the African continent. Having spoken to Andrew at great length about this trip and having watched the videoed accounts of other volunteers who were present, it is abundantly clear to me that whilst they may have left Malawi, the impact which Malawi had upon them as individuals will always remain.

Andrew said: "We were all sad when we had to return home. I would have stayed for another fortnight had I been offered the chance, and I get the impression many of the people within the group would have done so without a second thought. Now I understand why many of the people who went to Kenya on the first trip returned for the next journey. If I were ever offered the chance to return to Malawi, I would jump at it, and I'd encourage anyone else with an interest to do the same. Work and family commitments may well prevent me from doing so, but that aside, it was a true privilege to have made the trip, regardless of whether I will again. The country is home to the warmest people I have ever met, with the biggest smiles and most welcoming personalities imaginable. The enthusiasm which they have for life is infectious, and I honestly believe that we could learn a lot from them."

"The trip definitely changed some of my attitudes towards life back home in Scotland. In all honesty, I felt a bit numb for the first week or so after I returned, because it's difficult to automatically revert to normal day to day life when you've been entrenched in that of another culture which is dramatically different. This may sound slightly strange, but at first I actually found some individuals to be more annoying than I had done previously. To see people moaning about the most mundane things as if they were matters of life or death, whether it was on television or on social media, was tremendously frustrating, but gradually I accepted the fact that whilst my views had been altered, these people had not borne witness to what I had seen. To give you a tiny example of a change which I have made in my own life, it is that I have only used the phrase "I am starving" once since I returned home, and when I did so I immediately cursed myself and felt quite bad about it. Whilst life in this country may not be perfect, and it certainly carries its own challenges for each and every one of us, most people really don't grasp how lucky they are."

Towards the end of our discussions, I felt it was appropriate to ask Andrew what advice he would give to any other Celtic supporters, or indeed volunteers not affiliated with any particular football club, who were considering making a trip to Malawi to help the people there. His response was both honest and realistic, attributes truly brought about in this sense by personal experience. He said: "Although it may sound crass, the first thing which any potential volunteer travelling to Malawi has to realise is that no matter how intensively you work or how long you stay, there is always going to be a limit as to what you can achieve during any given time period. I actually felt a bit guilty as our return journey approached, as whilst I was very proud of what we had done, it was abundantly clear that there was so much more which needed doing. However, the reality of it all is that to be as efficient and successful as possible whilst there, you have to accept that you can only do so much. That mind-set enables you to focus wholly on what you're attempting to do and to complete your tasks to the best of your ability."

"On a more positive note, the other mainstay of any advice I would give would be to try not to be too nervous prior to your trip, as a fantastic experience awaits you. Never at any stage in Malawi did I think "I wish I was home", and that is indicative of my feelings whilst there. Yes, the work was hard and some of the things which we saw were not pleasant, but you know your primary objective is to do as much as possible to improve the lives of the local community, and that definitely focuses the mind. Of course, it's much easier to say all of this than it is to embrace it prior to any initial departure, but I know that if I were to return now I would not be nearly as nervous as I was previously, and I think as a consequence I would enjoy it more."

In closing, I feel I must pay tribute to the good people of Blantyre, Malawi; the Celtic Charity Foundation, for enabling members of our fan base to achieve magnificent things in the name of helping others; and most of all to the volunteer Celtic supporters, who travelled so far to assist people they had never met and may never meet again.

Finally, my thanks must go to Andrew Cowan. By his own admission, he is not the type of man to talk much about his journey to Africa, nor his labours therein. Almost every one of the conversations he has had about the trip since he returned to Scotland has been started by somebody asking him about it, rather than him initiating such a discussion. Like the rest of the volunteers who accompanied him to Malawi, he did not do so for personal recognition nor for material gain. I am of the belief they are all a great credit not only to themselves and their families, but to Celtic Football Club also, as they embody the very spirit of selflessness which rallied a community behind a fledgling sporting organisation over a century and a quarter ago. Given that I attended secondary school with Andrew, I know that if someone had come to both of us in the middle of our teenage years and said that one of us would travel to Africa in the future and the other would write a chapter in a book about it, we would have laughed it off as a virtual impossibility. Therefore, I feel this is a rather fitting sentiment with which to conclude – never presume that anything in this world is beyond your abilities, particularly when charity is the beneficiary of your actions. After all, as David Livingstone once said, "If you have men who will only come if they know there is a good road, I don't want them. I want men who will come if there is no road at all."

"Celtic by Numbers:
"Managerial Records""

At this point, I feel it is appropriate to turn our attention to the nineteen men who have had the honour of managing Celtic Football Club full time (for the sake of this analysis, we can rule out caretaker managers and the like). It will come as no surprise to you all to discover that Willie Maley, manager for forty-three years, leads the way in terms of the number of competitive matches which he oversaw, with one thousand, six hundred and fourteen under his belt (please note only Scottish League, Scottish Cup, Scottish League Cup and European matches are included in these statistics, not Glasgow Cup, Glasgow Charities Cup ties etc). However, some of the younger readers may be slightly intrigued to note that it was not Jock Stein but Jimmy McGrory who finished second behind Maley, with eight hundred and forty-one fixtures to his name. However, one must remember that McGrory did hold the managerial role for twenty years to Stein's thirteen. Jock, for the sake of the record, officially oversaw seven hundred and forty-three, but due to his enforced absence following the serious car accident in which he was involved in July 1975, the true number is lower, at six hundred and ninety.

One fact which I believe to be of much note is this – and it is one which is very often overlooked or indeed ignored – of all the matches which Celtic Football Club have played in major competitions, the Club has been managed by Willie Maley, Jimmy McGrory or Jock Stein for more than sixty percent of them. Now, when one realises that statistic includes almost the first decade of the Club's existence, during which there was no manager at all, the impact which these three men had upon the Football Club becomes even more significant in nature.

When one examines the statistics relating to various managers though, further points of interest appear. Firstly, with a win ratio in all major competitions of seventy-five and a half percent, we find that Martin O'Neill is, in fact, the Celtic manager with the highest total in this sense. Behind him comes Neil Lennon, edging out the mighty Jock Stein by around one third of a percentage point. Current boss Ronny Deila follows Stein, albeit after only one season in charge (only the 2014-15 campaign is considered for the Norwegian). Bizarrely, John Barnes is next in the list, ahead of Gordon Strachan, Willie Maley and Wim Jansen respectively. However, it is of course absolutely essential to note that it is much easier to achieve higher win percentage ratios when your managerial career involves less games.

For example, Barnes beat Maley by less than one percentage point, but Maley oversaw more than fifty times the number of fixtures the Englishman did. The troubles which Celtic endured in the post war era also become apparent when we find that Jimmy McGrory, with a win percentage of ever so slightly less than half, has the second worst record, with Lou Macari, who won less than one third of his matches whilst in charge bringing up the rear by some distance. Interestingly, two of our three caretaker managers – Frank Connor and Billy Stark – never saw one of their sides suffer a defeat whilst they were in temporary charge of the playing squad. The other man, Sean Fallon, who of course was appointed as acting manager for the 1975-76 season, won a little more than sixty percent of his matches therein.

Periodically, I am asked whom I believe to be the greatest manager Celtic Football Club have ever had. Many people, perhaps with some justification due to the name of the website I run, expect me to answer "Willie Maley". However, despite that fact my answer remains "Jock Stein", though it is an interesting quandary to consider from an analytical standpoint. Sadly, due to the lack of European Football during Maley's era, it is impossible to compare the two categorically, as I personally believe there were one or two points in time in which Maley's Celtic sides may well have been the best footballing sides on the planet. Be that as it may, we shall progress whilst keeping such caveats in mind.

As we have previously discussed, a quick glance at the relevant win percentage statistics give Stein the edge over Maley, with his sixty-nine percent being a few points higher than Maley's sixty-five. Breaking these down into those from the relevant competitions, we see Stein enjoyed more league wins, by a margin of about seven percent, whilst Maley had the better of the pair in the Scottish Cup, winning seventy-three and a half percent of his matches, just a couple more than Stein.

The facts that I believe award Jock Stein the crown are those of his average honours per season. Willie Maley won sixteen league titles and fourteen Scottish Cups in forty-two seasons (excluding his last as manager when competitive football was suspended after only a few matches due to the start of World War Two), averaging one league title every 2.62 years in charge and one Scottish Cup for every three years. Stein however, with ten league titles and eight Scottish Cups in his thirteen years (twelve if you discount his year of absence in this case) leading the Football Club averaged one title every 1.2 years and one Scottish Cup every 1.5 years.

Whether such averages would have been sustainable for Jock Stein enters into the realm of speculation, for had he continued to manage Celtic for the same period of time which Willie Maley did, he would only have given up his post in 2008, less than one decade ago. He would also have been in his mid-eighties, whilst Maley was in his early-seventies when he retired. Yet, such comparisons between the two, naturally occurring and interesting though they may be are futile to a large extent, for they were managers of a Football Club in two very different time periods. Whilst it is my belief Stein was the finest Celtic manager of them all, I also feel that the Club would never have been able to rise to the stature which it did under Stein without the influence of Maley throughout the early years of the Club's development. They are both managerial behemoths whose names will live in the memory more for their time in charge of our squads than their individual playing careers, and both wholeheartedly deserve the undying credit which they continue to receive. They are in a league of their own, and it is my belief that it will take the appearance of a truly incredible Celtic manager in the future to transform this duo's party into a trio's crowd.

"Our First Captain:
"Champions of Scotland""

The 1891-92 season would be one which would go down in Celtic folklore as being the first year in which the Celts really stepped out on to the big stage. The league campaign started well for Parkhead men as aside from an away defeat against Hearts, they enjoyed victories over Rangers, Clyde, Renton and Dumbarton (to name but a few) before the year of 1891 was out. In knockout competition, they began their Glasgow Cup campaign with a home match against Kelvinside, emerging the victors by eleven goals to one (although the game was declared to be a friendly as Kelvinside scratched [withdrew from the competition] prior to kick-off). The Celts then defeated Partick Thistle and Northern in the next two rounds, before being paired with Linthouse for the upcoming semi-final tie.

Although Linthouse had less than ten years of footballing life left in them at that stage, they were still respectable opponents, as they would be crowned the winners of the Scottish Football Alliance (another new league competition) come the end of the season. However, on the day they were overwhelmed by the Celts in the East End of Glasgow, losing several goals in quick succession in a match which eventually finished nine-two in favour of the home side. For the record, Linthouse, who increasingly struggled to attract people to their matches at Langlands Park as the century drew to a close, thanks partly to the proximity of Ibrox Park, became defunct in 1900.

Celtic were set to face Clyde (whom they had already beaten by seven goals to two in the league) in the Glasgow Cup Final in December. Remarkably, the Celts would repeat this feat, scoring another seven goals – with only one in reply on this occasion – retaining the Glasgow Cup in the process. Back in Scottish Cup action, the Parkhead side would then overcome Kilmarnock

Athletic by three goals to nil before 1891 was at an end. It had been a good year for the Celts, of that there is no doubt. In fact, you could well argue it had been their best year thus far, but it would pale in comparison to the achievements which lay ahead in 1892 and beyond.

However, one cannot say that 1892 began positively for Celtic Football Club, for on the first of January, with the New Year only hours old, the Celts were beaten by eight goals to nil at Celtic Park by Dumbarton in a friendly tie, possibly thanks in part to the presence of a few hangovers. To make matters worse, three additional goals from the visitors were disallowed (thankfully), only reinforcing the dominant display put on by the Sons. James Kelly did not play that day – perhaps if he had his defensive wherewithal and disciplined attitude would have limited the magnitude of the defeat.

Undoubtedly, this result would have hurt Celtic's confidence, as well as a few egos both on and off of the field, but by the time the next round of the Scottish Cup came around in the middle of the month, the Celts were playing much more like their usual selves, having since defeated Third Lanark and Rangers in friendly matches, both by a margin of two goals. In the quarter finals Celtic met Cowlairs, a team with which they now had some notable history as I have previously described. James Kelly returned to the side that day, having not featured since the Celts' final match of 1891, a Boxing Day victory over St. Mirren in the Scottish League. The Celts defeated Cowlairs by four goals to one at home, and went on to set up a mouth-watering semi-final tie against Rangers at Celtic Park.

Thus followed one of the highest scoring matches ever played between the two sides, with the final result eventually reading as five goals to three in favour of the Parkhead club. Celtic led by four goals to nothing at half-time, but a combination of complacency and Rangers' unwillingness to submit to such a heavy defeat led to a much more competitive second half. It was then confirmed that Celtic would face Queen's Park in the Scottish Cup Final, a side they had never beaten and then the most successful club in the history of the Scottish game. This was to be another mammoth tie, and it would be reflected in the equally large number of spectators who flocked to Ibrox Park to see the game in the middle of March.

The following newspaper report may well highlight the extent to which this crowd, which stood at approximately forty thousand people, was rather unique for its day: "Without parallel in the history of football was the interest excited over this year's Scottish Cup Final, which was regarded as in some sense a trial of strength between the principal League club and the leading club outside that body. Looking to the large following which both the Celtic and Queen's Park – the finalists on this occasion – command, as well as the interest taken in the fixture by football followers generally; it was confidently felt that the attendance would constitute a record for Scotland, if not also for Great Britain, the record previous to Saturday having been established in England under the Rugby code. Bearing this in mind, the most elaborate arrangements had been made by the Executive of the Rangers' Club, on whose ground the match was played, for the accommodation of a vast crowd. Extensive stands had been erected all round the ground, the sides and the corners of the field of play had been banked up so that all could obtain a view of the game, and additional entrances had been provided. As early as twelve o'clock – four hours before the time advertised for the start of the game – the gates of Ibrox Park were thrown open for the admission of the public, and even at that early hour dozens put in an appearance at the ground."

As the passage continues, we find this vast interest, coupled with the inability of Ibrox Park to cope with the crowd (not that this is a criticism, for no Scottish stadium could have dealt with such a crowd at that time), ultimately led to the nullification of the tie: "From one o'clock the crowd poured in...and when half-past two o'clock arrived the spacious ground seemed packed to its utmost capacity. Thousands, however, still continued to pour in, and as a consequence, the only thing to be expected took place – the crowd in front were forced over the barricade on to track, and having got this far, a regular stampede took place from the entrance gates right over the field of play, till on both sides of the ground the spectators encroached on the touchline. During the stampede, the crowd made a vigorous attack on the old stand on the north side of the ground which was already tightly packed, but the occupants succeeding in beating them off. The police arrangements were totally inadequate to stem the rush, and it was not till some mounted police arrived on the ground that the crowd was [forced] back so as to be clear of the touch line. At ten minutes past three it was found necessary to close the gates, and large numbers tried ineffectually to gain admission. Before the game started the attendance was calculated to number close upon forty thousand, representing over £1,450 [an enormous sum], and the scene which then presented itself was one never to be forgotten. Every few minutes the rush on the part of the enthusiastic followers of the game was renewed, and in view of the increased excitement which would ensue when the game was started, it was felt that the match would not be allowed to proceed as a cup tie. This turned out to be correct, as several times the game had to be stopped, and by mutual agreement the teams at length decided that the match would not rank as a cup tie, and a protest was accordingly lodged by each with the referee, Mr. Sneddon, President of the Association."

Typically, in the chaos of the day, other newspaper articles are somewhat contradictory with the previous report at several points, as other such journalists mentioned "thousands" managing to attain "free entrance" whilst highlighting that they "believed that thirty-six thousand could be accommodated comfortably". It was also said that "The crowd was a good-natured one, and during the interval sang snatches of popular airs", for not everyone in attendance tried to force their way into another part of the ground. Regardless, if one thing was crystal clear above all other matters that day it was that the Scottish people truly adored football, which was still, in the grand scheme of things, a relatively new sport at that time. They would pay their hard earned money to watch it and they would travel increasingly far and wide to do so, and perhaps it was this seemingly insatiable desire which eventually led to the gradual commercialisation of the game over the generations.

As for the match itself which was, of course, declared to be a friendly (although not everyone in the ground was aware of this), Celtic won by a single goal to nil thanks to a strike around the hour mark from John Campbell, a notable feat on difficult ground, even if the result did not decide the destination of the Scottish Cup. According to one report, "the point" was "the signal for an extraordinary outburst of enthusiasm."

However, to say that Celtic's victory had no consequence whatsoever would be somewhat foolish. One must remember that until this stage, Celtic had never managed to defeat Queen's Park, having only ever managed one draw from four outings against them previously in all competitions, losing the other three. This was not to say Celtic could not compete with the Spiders, for they had most certainly showed they could do so in the past, but the one-nil win in front of the huge crowd at Ibrox must have given them an enormous psychological lift nonetheless.

If anyone would like any evidence of such a confidence boost, then I would simply point them to the scoreline which would follow when the two sides met once again, for the Scottish Cup Final proper, almost a month later. It was the ninth of April 1892 on which Celtic Football Club truly joined the ranks of the Scottish footballing elite, an echelon from which they have never departed, as they beat Queen's Park by a remarkable five goals to one at Ibrox Park. This was a monumental victory, as "The Scotsman" recounted in the days which followed:

"Queen's Park v Celtic – After a series of postponements and delays almost without precedent in the history of the competition, the question of the custody of the Scottish Cup for the next year was finally settled on Saturday, when the Celtic capped their brilliant season's form by defeating the Queen's Park by the large majority of five goals to one. The Parkhead men have struggled manfully for the honour, which they thus secure for the first time, and there can be no dispute as to their right to secure the custody of the national trophy. Since the occasion of the first match the teams...public interest in the contest had in no way diminished, though, as a matter of fact, the attendance on Saturday did not reach the extraordinary limit attained on that occasion. Though prior to the first match the Queen's Park were favourites with the general public – partly by reason of the fact that they had time after time shown themselves to be possessed of the knack of rising to the occasion, and had, as a matter of fact, never been defeated in any final tie for the cup in which they had figured [a remarkable nine wins from nine prior to this match] – the situation was reversed before the start of Saturday's game."

"Several causes contributed to bring about this altered state of matters, but the principal was the weakened state of the Queen's Park team. Nothing but uncertainty prevailed before the match as to the eleven which would do duty for them, and, as will be seen from the teams annexed, the combination which ultimately took to the field for the popular Hampden Park club was of a poorly balanced nature. Still, with the resistance of the wind in the first half, they gave the Celts any amount of trouble, and actually crossed over with the lead of a goal, but in the second period the Irishmen turned the tables, and there was then only really one team in it."

The magnitude of this accomplishment simply cannot be overstated. As the following quote from "The Scottish Referee" highlights, the impact which such a victory had on the Irish immigrant population in Scotland was significant. Yes, many of them may have been poor, and yes, many of them may have been looked down upon by others within society, but purely because of the achievement of a football team – their football team – they would walk that little bit taller for the year to come, buoyed by the fact that although they may not have food in their bellies or shoes on their feet, they had been gifted some pride for their hearts and joy for their souls.

"Coatbridge was en fête on Saturday over the victory of the Celtic. In the second half, when it was intimated that the Celts had scored three goals in ten minutes, you might have heard the cheers at Ibrox...When the intimation came that our team had won in such a handsome manner almost everybody who could muster a cheer and a grin at once put them in evidence. Even the women lent a hand, and helped in no small measure to make rejoicings hearty. But it was when the boys came marching home again from the aristocratic Ibrox that the fun began in earnest. As the evening wore on, the whole East End put on an air of alleged gaiety and a colour of deep carnation that would have given an unenlightened stranger the severe knock of astonishment. Bands, you ought to have seen them! They perambulated the whole district until well on in the evening, and with the aid of a liberal use of party music helped to make things hum along merrily. Of course this caused the risk of a ruction with Billy's men. But what of that? Truly the East End was a perfect turmoil until the very early hours of Sunday, and many of the crowd won't be able to get over the rejoicing racket for days to come."

Almost twenty-five years on from this victory, Willie Maley, who had since managed record breaking Celtic sides, recalled that day (when he played) and the post-match celebrations which followed for a Glasgow newspaper, "The Weekly Mail and Record". He said, "Our lot stamped themselves that day as the champions of Scotland without a doubt, and their football was delightful to watch. What a happy lot we were that night when the Cup was taken up to St. Mary's Halls by John Glass of happy memory. Poor Glass looked as if his chief end in life had been attained, and there was not a happier man in the universe than he that night."

"In his speech...he reminded the bearers of his prophecy when we were beaten by the Third [Lanark] in 1889, and told them he knew then we would do it yet. Cups won nowadays like the Scottish carry with them bonuses of very substantial size; but, I may tell those interested, that the bonus for that cup was a new suit of clothes for each man. I had then attained one of the greatest honours of a footballer's career in winning my Scottish Cup badge."

As spring progressed and the league season drew to a close, Celtic won five of their eight remaining matches, but losses against Dumbarton and Leith Athletic, combined with a draw at Ibrox proved to be fatal with regards their hopes of attaining a first Scottish League title. As with campaigns even in the modern day, one can, with the benefit of hindsight, look back across a list of fixtures and results and be left wondering "what if?", but such is the nature of the sport. The season itself would end on a high of sorts for Celtic and their fans, as they faced Rangers in the final of the Glasgow Merchant's Charity Cup, having taken a modicum of revenge over Dumbarton (who won the league by a narrow margin), beating them by three goals to one in the prior semi-final.

The cup final itself, which was contested at Celtic Park on the first of June, drew a fairly mediocre attendance of around seven thousand spectators. Of course, with the tournament being in the cause of charity, the gate money generated from such a turnout, despite the fact it was lower than the average league meeting's respective crowd, would have been much appreciated by the relevant beneficiaries. Celtic went on to win a match which could easily have gone either way, with both sides threatening each other's goalmouth from the start and the Ibrox side having a goal disallowed in the first half, before Celtic themselves suffered the same fate early in the second period. Eventually though, headers from John Campbell and John Madden won the day, and added to Celtic's trophy haul, which ended the season at three – the Glasgow Cup, the Scottish Cup and the Glasgow Merchant's Charity Cup – an unprecedented feat, hinting at the Club's future prowess for knockout football.

The following season, 1892-93, began on the sixth of August for Celtic, who played Dundee Harp in a friendly match which finished with the scoreline of five goals to two in favour of the Celts. A week later, the new Celtic Park opened its gates for the first event ever to be held on the ground so lovingly known as "Paradise", an athletic meeting dubbed "The Celtic Sports". The following passages come from the "Glasgow Herald" on the weekend prior to the athletics meeting, discussing with anticipation the fervent interest in the event as well as the new stadium itself.

"Enterprise has always been a characteristic of the Celtic Club, and never was this so apparent as in the case of their athletic meeting which comes off on Saturday first. Last year they introduced C.Bradley, the great English sprinter, to the Glasgow public, and the recollections of that runner's performances must still be fresh in the minds of those who visited Parkhead twelve months ago. Bradley is coming north again, and as his form is even better now than it was a year ago, we may confidently look forward to as fine a display of sprinting as has ever been witnessed in Scotland. Besides Bradley, the Celtic have been successful in getting D.D. Bulger, the Irish champion, to grace their meeting. In hurdle racing, Bulger is pre-eminently the first man in Britain at the present time..."

"But the enterprise of the Celtic is not merely confined to foot events. It extends to the wheel races, in which Harris, Polytechnic C.C.; McCready, Dublin; and O'Neill, Dublin, will try their luck against R.G. Vogt, J. McLaren, D. Lacaille, E. Campbell, J.G. Torrance, and others well known in Scottish cycling circles. It will be seen from the mention of these names that the Celtic meetings of Saturday and Monday will form a fitting climax to the athletic season in Glasgow – a season, in many respects, the most memorable in the records of our national sports. In another respect the coming meetings of the Irish club constitute an interesting event in local athletics; we refer to the opening of the new Parkhead grounds. When completed, these will be second to none in Scotland. The cycle path is said to be in good order, but the running one is soft, and to some extent this will militate against good performances. However, time will mend any defects that may be visible on Saturday, and it may be taken as certain that the Celtic will spare no expense in making their new field, with its running and cycle tracks and other equipments, the best, or at all events, equal to the best grounds we have in Glasgow."

On the Monday after the beginning of the sporting events, the same newspaper which I have previously quoted said the following, and the parallels between this event in 1892 when the stadium first opened and the modern day hosting of the opening ceremony of the 2014 Commonwealth Games are clear to see.

"The opening of the new ground of this powerful athletic organisation marks a new epoch in the athletic progress of Scotland. This meeting will long be memorable from the fact that the programme and influence of the club attracted the finest array of competitors of distinction from all parts of the British Empire."

Whilst it is fair to say that not every Celtic supporter would have been happy to have seen the opening ceremony of the 2014 Commonwealth Games held at Celtic Park (for a wide ranging array of reasons), the fact that such an event was held there is an indication of how far the Football Club has come from its earliest days. In years gone by, Ibrox and Hampden have generally been used for large special events such as the Empire Exhibition Trophy and the Coronation Cup, and so it is notable Celtic Park is now considered to best choice for such a ceremony. It may sound clichéd, but it would have seemed impossible throughout a large portion of history for the head of the royal family to visit Celtic Park, or the area in which it stands, which housed some of the poorest and most downtrodden people not only in Scotland, but within the continent of Europe for well over a century, whilst their ancestors enjoyed untold splendour. Returning from that slight tangent, the thirteenth of August 1892 was stormy, with heavy, unrepentant rain falling for most of the day.

"There was an attendance of fourteen thousand spectators, and very few left the ground during the storm, a testimony to the excellence of the programme. In one respect it was fortunate that the thunderstorm broke over the ground just as the crowd assembled, otherwise either a postponement would have been rendered an absolute necessity, or the attendance, had the meeting gone on, would have been considerably reduced."

Once the fun and games of the athletics event was over, the new Celtic Park would be introduced to its primary purpose, top class football, as Renton (who were also the first league visitors to the old Celtic Park, although the result of the tie was later nullified) travelled to the East End of Glasgow on the twentieth of August 1892. Fittingly, the match was to be a memorable one which would be worthy of any new stadium, as the home side won a pulsating encounter by four goals to three, thanks in large part to John Campbell, who scored all of the Celtic goals including two spot kicks (the first of which is said to have been the first competitive penalty ever awarded to a Celtic team). Earlier, with the game tied at three goals each, two men – John Madden and Archibald McQuilkie, were ordered from the field by the referee after they "came to blows" – so with seven goals, two dismissals, two penalties and approximately fifteen thousand people in attendance, it is fair to say that Celtic Park's opening day had it all.

Indeed, during its inaugural season, the new Celtic Park would not see its home side suffer a competitive defeat until the final match of the league calendar when the Celts had already secured their first Scottish League Championship title. Third Lanark were the first away side to triumph there competitively, whilst Sunderland hold the accolade of being the first team to beat the home side in a friendly tie – each by a margin of three goals, it must be said. The new stadium would begin to earn its reputation as a fortress during the 1892-93 season, as several of the country's top clubs visited only to be conquered.

One of these opponents, Hearts, had already defeated Celtic in their first away match that season, and so when the Edinburgh side travelled west to Glasgow, the Celts were ambitious to set the record straight and right the wrongs of the past. The previous fixture at Tynecastle was one of enormous proportions for the capital at that point, highlighting the fact that although they were not currently the league champions, triple cup winning Celtic were the team every Scottish football supporter wanted to see for themselves. The following passage is from "The Scotsman" in the days after the first meeting of the two sides in the 1892-93 season.

"A brilliant opening in their home engagements in the League competition was made by Heart of Midlothian on Saturday, when they defeated such a powerful combination as the Celtic, the holders of the Scottish Cup, the Glasgow Association Cup, and Glasgow Charity Cup. Probably no club match at Tynecastle has been productive of such an extraordinary amount of interest as the match under notice evoked, and the reason for that was not far to seek, as it was generally expected that the game would give a very good indication of the chances of the teams in the important competitions in which they will figure throughout the season. Naturally, therefore, a great attendance of spectators was looked for, and such proved to be the case, for when the game started there could not have been fewer than sixteen thousand persons within the ground, which was generally regarded as a record gate for Tynecastle."

"Within the city, long before the hour of start, it was amply apparent that a match of paramount importance was down for decision, every [horse and cable drawn tram] car travelling Tynecastle-wards being literally besieged by an excited and expectant crowd, and filled to overflowing within the space of a few seconds. Notwithstanding that extra cars had been brought into requisition, the service provided was quite inadequate for the amount of traffic, and as a result all sorts of vehicles were pressed into service, while hundreds of people proceeded to the ground on foot. Inside the ground it was apparent that a fair proportion of spectators hailed from the west, the trade holidays there having afforded many an opportunity of travelling east to see the match."

Before the Celts had their chance to take on Hearts once again on the fifth of November 1892, a few things of interest would occur. Firstly, Celtic would win all of their competitive fixtures except for two, one of which was a two-all draw at Ibrox and the other was a Glasgow Cup win against Partick Thistle which was declared void. The reason for this nullification was that Michael Mulvey, a twenty-three year old Shettleston man whom Celtic had signed that same month from Carfin Shamrock, was ineligible for the fixture as he had already played in a Lanarkshire tie. Subsequently, the Celts would eventually beat Partick Thistle by eight goals to nil in a second replay, but not before Michael Mulvey made his Celtic debut proper, as Hearts came to Parkhead.

Therefore, I shall leave it to the able hands of a writer from "The Scotsman" to describe to you the events of that day, as well as Mulvey's debut goal: "Quite an exceptional amount of interest centred in the return contest between these teams, which took place at Parkhead, Glasgow, on the new ground of the Celtic Club. Fully ten thousand spectators witnessed the game, including a considerable number from Edinburgh, who had journeyed west with special trains which the North British Railway had provided for the purpose. Though the weather was fine, the ground was soft and treacherous, and altogether unsuited to the Tynecastle players, who had to retire defeated by five goals to none. An accident to

Hill, which eventually necessitated his retiring from the game altogether, also considerably handicapped the Eastern Men. At the same time there could be no doubt of the capabilities of the winners, who at every point of the game showed themselves to be superior to their opponents. The first match between the teams, it may be interesting to recall, resulted in a victory for Hearts by three goals to one; so that on Saturday the Irishmen had ample revenge...Nearing half-time, the Celts broke away as a body, with the result that Mulvey, with a clever effort, defeated Fairbairn for a third time."

As the previous article drew to a close, the author made mention of the fact that "The shining lights on the Celtic side were Campbell, Madden, Kelly and Reynolds", again hinting that whilst his performances may not have always been as extravagant as someone like a centre forward, James Kelly continued to play an integral role in the Celtic team of the day. As for Michael Mulvey, he would lose his first team place upon the return from injury of Sandy McMahon, eventually leaving Celtic the following summer for Dundee Harp, having scored four goals in four games, all of which Celtic won.

As the year of 1892 came to an end, the Celts kicked off their defence of the Scottish Cup, a tournament which only Queen's Park and Vale of Leven had ever successfully managed to retain. Also, it could be said that such a feat became increasingly difficult as the end of the nineteenth century approached, for more and more teams were taking part in the competition and the average quality of the sides involved was improving as well. A three-one win over Linthouse and a seven-nil victory over 5th Kirkcudbright Rifle Volunteers later, the Celts found themselves in the quarter finals, set to take on Third Lanark in mid-January.

Having beaten the Cathkin Park side (and scored five goals) two weeks previously in their first competitive tie of the New Year, the Celts would have been justifiably confident as they travelled across the city a fortnight later for their Scottish Cup duel. Once again, the Celts eased past their opponents, scoring five goals and conceding one less than on their previous visit. However, a season which had the potential to be the greatest in the Football Club's history at that point in time, was not to be quite as historic as it could have been, as Celtic would soon lose both the Glasgow Cup Final and the Scottish Cup Final, to Rangers and Queen's Park respectively. Major domestic doubles were unheard of then and so to think that the Celts weren't far away from securing all four trophies that season is rather remarkable.

Still, before these two defeats were to come, Celtic scored five goals in the Scottish Cup once again, defeating St. Bernard's in the semi-final, before losing only their second league fixture of the season against Abercorn. The latter result was the source of much contention, as the following quotation taken from "The Scotsman" shows: "A letter was read from the Celtic complaining of the conduct of the spectators at Paisley during their match with Abercorn. The conduct of the spectators, it stated, was about the worst their team had ever experienced. The oaths and blasphemies yelled by the crowd were simply indescribable. At the close of the game the spectators rushed on the field, and the Celtic players were assailed with all sorts of vile epithets by the crowd, and were otherwise severely assaulted."

For Celtic, this would signal the beginning of the month long slump which would stop a great season from becoming a legendary one. Firstly, the Celts faced Rangers in the Glasgow Cup Final, as the "Glasgow Herald" describes.

"The final tie for the Glasgow Association Cup was played at Cathkin Park, the contestants being Celtic and Rangers. The day was mild, and except for a slight drizzle during the progress of the match, the weather conditions were favourable, and the ground of the Volunteers was probably in better condition than that of any other club in the city…The Celtic were the first to appear, led on by Kelly, and a minute afterwards the Rangers appeared, headed by Mitchell, both teams being heartily received."

Rangers led one-nil at half-time, despite the fact several goals could have been scored in the first half by both sides had it not been for some praiseworthy goalkeeping and a little bit of good fortune on the custodian's parts also. Several shots, such as one James Kelly struck from distance, narrowly missed their intended targets. The game eventually finished three-one in favour of the

Ibrox side, and in truth, on another day, Celtic would have likely been the narrow victors, as their luck simply was not with them at Cathkin Park on this occasion.

A week later, Celtic and Queen's Park met for the shambles which was Scottish Cup Final of 1893. To sum matters up relatively briefly, so they make some sense to those who are not aware of the events of that day, I must mention that due to the poor condition of the field, it was agreed that the first meeting between the sides, which Celtic won by a goal to nil, would be declared a friendly tie, with the final itself being rescheduled for a later date. This was a normal scenario back then, but the decision of the authorities not to tell the paying crowd which numbered somewhere in the region of fifty thousand people of their choice prior to them handing over their money at the gates was to prove costly, as the day ended with many supporters feeling they had been conned.

However, if that seems senseless, then the events of the Scottish Cup Final proper may seem to be wholly ridiculous. With Celtic trailing one-nil, a Queen's Park player shot past the post, but due to the lack of goal nets in those days, the referee, who may have been tricked by an optical illusion of sorts and any crowd noise which followed awarded a second goal. This left the Celts furious, as they remonstrated with the official and opposing members of the crowd exchanged insults and accusations. Despite a late Celtic goal which would have tied the game otherwise, the phantom score stood and Queen's Park won the old trophy again. Subsequently, goal nets would be introduced to Scottish Football thanks to a motion forwarded by Celtic Football Club during the summer.

On the twenty-fifth of March 1893, a great honour would be bestowed upon James Kelly, as he awarded the captaincy of his country for the visit of Ireland to Celtic Park. Less than two years had passed since he was left out in the cold by the national selectors, having only featured once for Scotland since (a four-one home loss to England in 1892), but clearly old wounds had healed with time. Kelly's Scots won emphatically that day, by a margin of six goals to one, with the captain netting what would be his solitary international goal, all whilst Celtic registered a two-nil success away at Renton without the presence of their usual figurehead. The "Glasgow Herald" reflected on James Kelly's performance against the Irish: "After some fine work Sellar passed to the left, and in return Campbell sent the ball back to Kelly, who scored the fifth goal, a grand one, indeed, for Scotland. Kelly fairly distinguished himself, and there was absolutely no doubt after his display that he is still Scotland's premier centre-half."

Only a week later, Kelly would captain Scotland again, this time in the prestigious England match, held at the Richmond Athletic Ground, London. The Scots would lose by five goals to two, but prior to the tie, Kelly would be introduced to someone who would become rather famous, as a correspondent from the "Dundee Courier" describes after complaining about the manner in which he and many other media representatives were positioned at the fixture.

"A word has to be said about the press arrangements, which were most defective. The reporters were accommodated on benches on a level with the field of play, and rows of spectators were allowed to take up in positions in front, thereby obscuring to a very great extent the general movements of the game."

"Royalty was represented in the [four] persons of their Royal Highnesses the Duke and Duchess of Teck [a castle in a region of south-west Germany not far from Stuttgart], Princess May and Prince Francis of Teck…Prior to the start of the game the Scottish captain had the honour of being presented to the Royal visitors. Led on…Kelly advanced modestly to the Royal stand, and vigorously shook hands…He re-entered the field amid the plaudits of the crowd."

Now, without going off on too much of a tangent, I felt this merited some brief discussion as the third individual mentioned, Princess May, would later go on to become Queen Mary. Yet, the irony of all of this is where my interest lies. James Kelly, the man idolised by countless poor and impoverished men and women in the East End of Glasgow, met the future Queen, very much a rarity for a Scottish Catholic of Irish descent in the early 1890s. Kelly was not one to discriminate, he would shake hands and speak to anybody regardless of their supposed place in society, but the same could not be said for the royal family, who would likely have baulked at the idea of spending any time whatsoever in the Glaswegian slums. Regardless, it was another indication of how the game football could propel people into situations they would previously never have thought possible.

With this, James returned to league duty with Celtic, who responded in an admirable fashion to their Cup Final defeat, winning the next eight league matches (the second of which came against Renton as is previously mentioned), beating Rangers, Hearts and St. Mirren along the way. Of all, the Rangers match was perhaps the most crucial, and has since gone down in history as it was exactly one hundred and nineteen years to the day from the Ibrox side's first visit to the new Celtic Park that they made their last trip before liquidation in 2012, leaving on each occasion having suffered a three-nil defeat by the Celts.

The match was also memorable as it featured a collector's item of sorts, a goal from captain James Kelly, which the Celtic supporters who loved him so had never had the privilege of seeing in league football prior to this. According to "The Scotsman", he "scored the first goal of the match with a splendid shot", whilst the "Glasgow Herald" said "A fine shot from Kelly twenty yards from the Rangers' goal was cleverly fisted out by Haddow; but Kelly, this time nearer goal, landed the ball clean in the net inside fifteen minutes from the kick-off." Two goals from Sandy McMahon on either side of the half time interval added to the visitors' misery, and thus Celtic emerged the comfortable victors. To their credit, both goalkeepers (particularly Haddow) had good games, and stopped the scoring from being significant higher than it turned out to be.

Critically, after this match Celtic – with three games in hand – found themselves only three points behind the Ibrox side who had only one league tie yet to play. This meant that three victories from their remaining four fixtures would be enough to seal their first Scottish League Championship title.

Thereafter, James Kelly would lead his side into three games in which Celtic would concede goals but triumph regardless, outscoring their opposition on every occasion thanks to a combination of luck, skill, and unstoppable determination. Thus, after the last of these wins, which came against Leith Athletic at Parkhead, Celtic Football Club – a side who played their first match less than five years previously – had risen to the top of the Scottish game in consecutive seasons. One could debate whether or not winning the League Championship was considered to be as big an achievement as winning the Scottish Cup back in the 1890s, and in truth, it may not have been, but having won each of these tournaments now in successive years, Celtic were stamping their mark as the biggest force in the Scottish game. I wholeheartedly believe that the significance of the ninth of May 1893 will be apparent as long as Celtic Football Club continues to exist, for it proved that Celtic could not only be a great knockout team, but a consistent and occasionally gritty league side, who were able not only to produce positive results when they were playing well, but also when, for one reason or another, things were not unfolding as they would have ideally liked.

Looking back at the league table from the 1892-93 season, we can see that the Celts' victory over Rangers at Celtic Park towards the end of April was vital, as they won the league by only a single point from their rivals. Of course, Celtic may not have slumped to a five-two defeat to fourth place Third Lanark in the final game of the season if it had mattered, but that is speculative on my part. Celtic's superiority in the league that year is perhaps best epitomised in their goal difference, which stood at more than double that possessed by any other side, as the Celts scored thirteen more goals than Rangers in eighteen matches, conceding a couple less also. To rub salt into the wounds of the Ibrox side, the Celts proceeded not only to defeat them in the Glasgow Merchant's Charity Cup Final a week after the league season had ended, but to hammer them, winning by five goals to nil and reemphasising their newly attained place as the Champions of Scotland.

"Tales of Their Time: "The Same Old Celtic""

Now, we hear the recollections of Thomas Maley as he discussed the Football Club's foundation, as well as reading of the retirement of his brother Willie and other points of interest.

"Motherwell Times" – Friday 27th April 1928

"Story of the Celts – Interesting Lecture"

"Lecturing...in the Empire Theatre, Camp Street, on Friday evening, Mr. Tom Maley, one of the original players of the Celtic Football Club, told a deeply interesting story of the history of the Celtic Club. Mr. Wm. Duffy presided over the gathering, accompanied by Mr. Maley, Tommy Milligan, Jimmy McGrory, Mr. Joseph Turner, and Mr. McQuillan, Bellshill. Mr. Duffy, in the course of his Chairman's remarks, said that since the days of Jimmy Quinn there was no more popular member of the Celtic team that Jimmy McGrory, whose goalscoring feats were the talk of Scottish football. They were delighted to have Jimmy McGrory with them that evening, and also their friend and townsman Tommy Milligan. (Applause)."

"Mr. Tom Maley, lecturing on the history of the Celtic Football Club, said that forty years was a long cry, and it was that time since the Celtic Football Club was inaugurated. People today looked on the glories of the Celtic Club, and on what they had achieved, and they knew not of the hard road that had to be trod before the heights of success could be climbed. He would try to tell them some of the difficulties that had to be encountered, and he hoped that those of them who took an interest in the Celtic Club and rejoiced at its success would give a passing thought to the earlier days. As he already remarked, it was forty years since the club had started, and many of those who had taken an active part in its formation had passed away one by one to the great beyond, but there were a few of the old brigade left who still retained the old enthusiasm, the same old Celtic spirit, [even] if they could not retain the youth of those far off days. The Celtic Club, he was proud to tell them, had its beginnings in the mind and heart of a good old man, one of the Marist brothers, named Walfrid, who laboured in one of the poorest districts in Glasgow."

"Times were very hard with the poor in those days, much harder even than today when so many are hard hit, and it troubled this old man's heart to see children coming to school ill fed and not properly clothed. There was no beneficent Education Authority in those days to undertake the feeding and clothing of necessitous children, and anything that was done was by voluntary effort. This brother of the Marist order had recourse to several means for obtaining the necessary funds to carry on his work, and the idea occurred to him that it might be possible to obtain funds through the agency of football clubs. The football clubs responded very well, and none better than the Hibs. At that time the Hibs had a great following in the west and it struck many of them [in Glasgow] that they should start a club that would compare favourably with the standard the Hibs had attained. There was already even in those days a multiplicity of Shamrocks, Emmetts and Harps, but there was no Celtic, and when the new club was proposed to be formed, the name of Celtic found unanimous approval. It was about time that the Hibs succeeded in winning the Blue Ribbon of Scottish Football, and the Hibs said to the Celtic proposers – "If we in the east can do this, why cannot you do the same in the west?"

"The Celts Answer "Yes""

"The Celts answered that with a most emphatic "Yes." If determination could achieve it, the thing would be done. The old brother of the Marist order commenced to work on the idea, and there were many schemes, many suggestions, but it had the appearance of being a well-nigh hopeless task. At last they got together the nucleus of a team, and they were determined to make the Celtic team a success. So well was the team moulded together, that in their very first season as a club the Celtic appeared at Hampden as finalists for the Scottish Cup. They were finalists often again, and cup winners too – indeed, the Celtic had won the cup much more frequently than any other team. In that first Celtic team they only had thirteen or fourteen players to man the club for the season, and they managed it very well indeed. In their first final the Celts were beaten, and they admitted they were beaten fairly. Once having admitted defeat, they set out to reverse the decision next time, and sure enough "the boot was on the other foot." Any trophy that was worth winning had been won by the Celts, and wherever football was played throughout the world now, there was sure to be a Celtic club. (Applause.)"

"The Foundation of Charity"

"When the club was first started, funds were contributed for a children's club scheme and other charitable purposes, and not only did the Celtic play matches for this purpose, but they also gave handsome donations out of their funds. During the years that followed the Celtic club had kept to its traditions, and to many institutions it contributed generously. Notwithstanding that it was forty years since the Celtic club was started, they had never lost sight of the charitable objects they began with, and even today one found the Celtic playing matches here and there in order to assist some deserving cause or another. The Celtic, without doubt, were what they were by sticking loyally to each other, by playing with the proper team spirit, and, whether winning or losing, playing with the Celtic spirit that never lost heart. The old spirit never failed, and after forty years had come and gone, it was the same old Celtic. (Loud applause)."

"Mr. Maley also remarked that it might as truly be said, "Once a Celt, always a Celt." Some Celtic players had gone out to assist other clubs, but they were still Celts at heart. In this connection he told of how, on the day of the recent cup final at Hampden, his brother introduced him to an old Celt who had played in the team thirty-six years ago, and who after many year's absence from football fields had turned up to see another final. The Celts might go east or west, but they were sure one day to find their way back to the old club and their home. (Applause.) Following Mr. Maley's introductory remarks, limelight views were thrown on the screen, showing many interesting photos of Celtic teams and players from the earliest days up till now, and showing also the changes that had taken place in Celtic Park during the same period. Stories were told of famous Celts like Dan Doyle, Peter Somers, Bernard Battles, Jimmy Quinn, and a whole host of other Celtic notables."

"At the close of the lecture Mr. Duffy, in the course of a few remarks, said he was one who remembered the start of the Celtic club in 1888, the years of the great Exhibition in Glasgow. He had followed their fortunes with interest and admiration year after year from the earliest times down until now. At intervals during the evening a splendid concert programme was given by Mr. Gus McManus's Concert Party from Hamilton. Votes of thanks were heartily accorded on the motion of Mr. McQuillan, Bellshill, and an interesting and enjoyable evening was brought to a close by the singing of "Auld Lang Syne"."

"Dundee Courier" – Friday 29th March 1929

"Celtic Football Club's Loss – Pavilion Burned to Ground – Team's Gear and Valuable Photographs Destroyed – The pavilion of Celtic Football Club at Parkhead, Glasgow, was destroyed by fire yesterday forenoon. Not only was the whole of the club's equipment burned, but many photographic records were destroyed. The valuable old pictures cannot be replaced. The outbreak was discovered shortly after nine o'clock by some workmen engaged in the demolition of the grandstand, which is on the opposite side of the field. So rapidly did the flames spread that within an hour all that remained of the erection were some iron beams and supports."

"On seeing the flames coming from the windows of the pavilion, the workmen burst open the door, with the intention of doing all they could pending the arrival of the [fire] brigade. So dense was the smoke, however, that they were unable to get to the seat of the fire. The pavilion was composed almost entirely of wood, and little could be done to save it."

"Trophies Safe – It is understood that the team's cups and shields were not involved in the conflagration. Viewed in the afternoon, the pavilion was a sodden mixture of burned wood, out of which were standing the club's safe and the remains of an easy chair. Many hopes centred around that particular safe. It contained valuable old records of the club, going back to the days when a few enthusiasts in the Parkhead district set out to obtain a field on which to play football and raise what money they could on behalf of the Sisters of Charity in Parkhead and other deserving institutions."

"The loss of these books would have amounted almost to a club calamity. The safe appeared to be intact. At the same time, many fine old photographs went up in smoke. These included a group of the original Celtic team, the first Celtic team to win the Scottish Cup, the first Celtic team to win the League Championship, and single photographs of men who were prominent in the early days. In consequence of the fire the league game, Celtic v Third Lanark, fixed to be played at Celtic Park tomorrow, is to be played at Shawfield."

"Aberdeen Journal" – Tuesday 1ˢᵗ May 1934

"Gang Terrorism in Glasgow"

"Witnesses Afraid to Appear – Stiff Sentence for Rioter – Revelations regarding the activities of gangs in Glasgow were made at the Glasgow High Court today, when John Traquair was sentenced to four year's penal servitude for mobbing, rioting and assault. It was stated that he was a member of a gang known as "The Billy Boys," who followed the Glasgow Rangers Football Club and provided protection for Orange processions. Many supporters of the Celtic Football Club are Roman Catholics, and on March 3, when a special train conveying Celtic supporters to the Scottish Cup tie with St. Mirren at Paisley, stopped at Bridgeton Cross, Traquair and about a hundred members of the gang, armed with banners, sticks, a bayonet, and a hammer, attacked the train, two passengers being injured before order was restored."

"Porter's Evidence"

"A porter at Bridgeton Cross Station had just started his evidence when Mr. Cameron, Advocate-Depute, said – While you were at Bridgeton Cross last Saturday night did anything happen to you? – Yes; a chap told me to keep away from the toll because they were going to get me. Was that because you were here as a witness? – Yes. Detective Lieut. Paterson stated that when anyone appeared in the Bridgeton Cross area with a green coloured scarf or favour (the Celtic colours) it was the signal for disorder."

"Special Policemen"

"As a matter of fact, said the officer, special policemen often have to be posted at certain spots in the street when the Rangers play Celtic. The police have actually to keep the supporters separated as far as they possibly can…adding that it was practically impossible to secure witnesses in cases such as that before the court that day. Mr. Cameron – Is it your experience that you have difficulty in getting witnesses to speak in the Bridgeton district? – Yes. What is the reason of that? – Pure terrorism. The jury, after a brief adjournment, returned a unanimous verdict of guilty in regard to all the charges. Lord Moncrieff, in passing sentence, said that if gang terrorism had reached such a state in Glasgow, then it was the duty of the court to protect witnesses and mete out appropriate sentences. In this case, Traquair would receive a four years' sentence with penal servitude."

"Dundee Evening Telegraph" – Monday 1ˢᵗ January 1940

"New Year Shock for Parkhead – Mr. William Maley, who, for fifty-two years – since the inception of the club, in fact – has rendered magnificent service to Celtic, today announces his retirement. His decision will doubtless come as a shock to not only the friends of the Celtic Club but to practically everyone connected with or interested in football, especially in Scotland."

"Although when it is remembered that he is now in his seventy-second year, it is not altogether surprising that he desires to spend the evening of his days in a more peaceful atmosphere. There is no need to dwell upon Mr. Maley's reputation as a manager. He is too well-known. Not only in Scotland but wherever football is played the Celtic chief is regarded as the greatest the game has known. The history of the Celtic club is a standing memorial to his ability, his knowledge and judgement in the art of rearing, building and blending – to him alone must be given the credit for the succession of honours which have been won."

"The Sunday Post" – Sunday 29th August 1943

"Willie Maley is now out of the nursing home, where he under-went three operations on his eye following a chill contracted on the night of the Paterson-Kane fight. There was a doubt at one time whether the eye could be saved. His friends throughout Scotland will be glad to know that danger is past. Mr. Maley is progressing satisfactorily. Although he must have suffered intense pain, I heard a story which proves how plucky a patient he was. With his eye bandaged he took part in an impromptu concert and gave eight songs. With a fellow patient he sang a duet which had the staff from all over the building down to listen. I am told he "brought down the house" with his rendering of "I'll Walk Beside You".

"Four Days in the Dam"

On the twenty-ninth of August 2013, the draw for the group stages of the 2013-14 UEFA Champions League took place in Monaco. Home to perhaps the most famous Grand Prix in the Formula One calendar, this principality oozes glitz and glamour, thanks partly to its reputation as a prominent tax haven, no doubt. In a sense, it is a sad reflection on the state of modern football that the attention of the world (myself included) periodically falls on this little state, which boasts the highest GDP per capita on Earth and comes in at less than one square mile in terms of size. When one thinks of the great football cities of the world, Monaco would not cross the minds of many – Madrid, Manchester, Milan and Munich, yes – but not Monaco.

Yet every year, this draw takes place there, rather than at UEFA's headquarters in Nyon, Switzerland, where those for other stages of the two major European Club competitions are held. In recent times, I must confess that my dislike for the choice of Monaco has only been strengthened by the emergence of the principality's main footballing outfit, A.S. Monaco, as one of the biggest spending clubs on the planet. Having last been crowned French Champions in the year 2000, the club was relegated in 2011, before Russian billionaire Dmitry Rybololev bought them over whilst they sat bottom of Ligue 2 later that year. Rybololev then invested hundreds of millions of pounds to propel them to the highest echelons of French football, although they have yet to win another top flight title.

The Club's stadium, the "Stade Louis II", has a capacity of only eighteen and a half thousand, meaning it is not dissimilar in size to Rugby Park, whilst being dwarfed by both Pittodrie and Easter Road, but it is a rare day upon which it is filled by spectators. If nothing else, I feel A.S. Monaco are simply a sad example of the influence money can have today.

With all of this in mind, many supporters of European Football, both Celtic fans and others alike, allowed their thoughts to drift back to simpler times as the draw was made. It was remarkable as for the first time, four European Cup winners of old were drawn together in a single group. Unsurprisingly, the Scottish tabloid press soon branded this as the "group of death", but thankfully, the Italians and A.C. Milan soon penned a title much more befitting of the European records of the four football clubs in question (F.C. Barcelona, A.C. Milan, Ajax and Celtic), "Un Girone Nobile" ("The Group of Nobility").

Having overcome Cliftonville comfortably; Elfsborg nervously; and Shakhter Karagandy dramatically in the qualifying rounds, Celtic had reached the promised land of the Champions League group stages once again and drawn some big opponents. In the Rafters household, we had a decision to make following the draw because we were planning to journey to one away game. Those of you who have read my previous work will know that I travelled to Barcelona in 2012-13, and as we wanted to go somewhere different, that left us with two options, Milan or Amsterdam. With the first match day scheduled to take place in Italy only a fortnight or so after the draw and the hassle of arranging time off work in mind, our two options soon narrowed to one and we set our sights on the Netherlands.

On this occasion, my father and I would be joined by my cousin John, whom some of you may remember from my writings regarding the away day in Liverpool on the run to the UEFA Cup Final. Having quickly booked ourselves on an early flight out of Edinburgh, there was just the little matters of accommodation and tickets to attend to. Neither of these were sorted promptly and before we confirmed either, Ajax came to Glasgow.

Now, as a man in my mid-twenties, I must say that my only memories of playing Ajax competitively prior to this fixture came in 2001 when, of course, Celtic went to Amsterdam and trounced their opponents, proceeding into the Champions League group stages for the first time despite losing by a single goal to nil in Glasgow a fortnight later. Personally, I do not remember any of the violence reported to have taken place in the Netherlands in

370

2001, but then again I was only eleven at the time. Regardless, headlines such as "Fighting Fans Mar Celtic Success" from "The Guardian" indicate that whilst such incidents were sporadic, they did occur.

Having said that, in the decade which passed between this meeting of the two Clubs and the scheduled ties in 2013, such stories had long since faded from the memories of many. As a result, I feel the behaviour of some Ajax fans in Glasgow shocked a fair number of people within the Celtic support, although there was a historical precedent of sorts. Personally, whilst I had read of Ajax's problem with hooligans, I must say that I did not expect the atmosphere at the match itself to be quite so vitriolic in nature. Having brought the largest away support Parkhead had seen in some time, the noise being generated inside Celtic Park that night was astonishing, but in many ways the atmosphere was more similar to that of an old Glasgow Derby than a normal Champions League tie. Subsequently, tensions were only heightened as Ajax fans tried to break through the police lines separating them from the home support following Celtic's opening goal, whilst seats, coins and other missiles were thrown by away supporters into the family section of the home support. This was unacceptable, and the lack of arrests which followed somewhat perplexing in nature.

Again, despite all of this, as thousands of Celtic fans prepared themselves for a trip to the Dutch capital, we did our best to find accommodation. Having seriously considered the notion of renting a houseboat on one of the city's canals (a minority of which also came with small motorboats residents could cruise around in), we eventually plumped for a more sensible option and booked an apartment loft space in the middle of one of the city's central districts.

Many of you will know that I have been running Twitter accounts advising other Celts of travel information for a few years now. In this time, I have found that there are several topics which tend to come up over and over again, regardless of which city is in question. Generally, these revolve around tickets; how to get to and from the stadium; and where is good to socialise – fairly rudimentary issues to any travelling supporter. However, one notable difference in the enquiries I received in the run up to Amsterdam was that many of them were tinged with varying levels of anxiety. Yes, some supporters were a tad blasé about the idea of violence in the city, and others worried about it more than they perhaps should have, but the anxiety was certainly there. People wanted to know where was safe to congregate, especially after Celtic, in conjunction with Ajax and the police, released travel information detailing areas to avoid around the stadium only days before the match itself.

Now, as you may have guessed, I had not travelled to the Netherlands, let alone Amsterdam, prior to my visit in the autumn of 2013. It is one thing to tell someone which metro line to take in a city you've never visited, but it's something quite different to try to advise them on where is safe to drink or stay when, in all seriousness, you're not entirely sure yourself. Other than suggesting people should stay in groups and avoid wandering off by themselves, there really wasn't much more I could add. It was a certainty that the travelling Celtic support was going to be enormous in scale, and I feel this reassured many people prior to beginning their trip.

Anyway, as the day of our departure arrived, we were up bright and early and soon found ourselves on the foggy motorway heading east towards Edinburgh for our flight to Schiphol International. Having enjoyed a couple of airport pints and flown across the North Sea on a plane full of fellow Celtic supporters, we disembarked and began to wander through a maze of corridors and moving walkways which seemed to go on forever. We continued to follow the airport's illuminated signs before finally, after a substantial trek, we arrived in the baggage hall where pandemonium ensued as the Celtic team and staff (who had just arrived on another flight themselves) collected baggage. In the scrum, Emilio Izaguirre posed for photographs, Neil Lennon signed some quick autographs, and several other famous faces made their way towards the waiting team bus.

Once we made it through this hall and out into the main terminal, we boarded a double-decker train from Schiphol to the centre of Amsterdam, and as it eventually made its way out of the subterranean tunnel system into the open air, two things became clear. Firstly, the Netherlands really are as flat as stereotypes suggest, because there is genuinely not a hill to be seen anywhere for as far as the eye can see, and secondly, most of the Celtic supporters whom I was with had never seen a double-decker train before, as it seemed to be the topic of much conversation on the way into the city.

Anyway, whilst the atmosphere on the train was fairly subdued, it was all to change when we pulled into Amsterdam's "Centraal Station" (with two a's), a vast structure built in the late nineteenth century which presently serves more than a quarter of a million people per day. In a manner not wholly dissimilar to Glasgow's equivalent, the station has a high, almost cathedral like roof made of huge iron trusses, meaning sound travels far and wide within the building. Each of the fifteen platforms is situated above the station's concourse itself, with stairs leading downwards into a long, central corridor full of shops and eateries. It was here, as we left the platform, entering the passageway below and beginning to head towards the main exit, that a cacophony of sound hit us from one of the other stairwells, as "The Celtic Song" rang through Amsterdam for the first time on our visit. "Hail! Hail! The Celts are here!" was met with looks of both amusement and bewilderment from many of the locals, and in all honesty, the exotic location aside, there were so many Scots and Irish present that at a glance it could have been a domestic away game.

With a wall of noise at our backs, we walked out onto the streets of the Dutch capital. Again, some of the stereotypes everyone is aware of became immediately apparent, with a canal only metres away and narrow houses with sharply pointed roofs on the other side of the water. Eventually, we reached the building which housed our small apartment. However, before we could get into the loft itself, there was the little matter of the stairs leading up to it which we had to navigate first. I presume many of you who made the journey to Amsterdam will know exactly what I am talking about, but for those who did not I shall elaborate. These were called "typically Dutch, very steep, ankle-twisting flights of stairs" by Anne Frank, one of the city's most famous residents, whom I shall discuss later in this chapter. With regards the stairways, these were the narrowest and steepest steps I have come across in my lifetime, often more akin to climbing a ladder than a flight of stairs. Imagine your average stairwell, triple the degree of incline and half the width of the passageway also. These were tricky sober, let alone once you had consumed a few pints and were carrying luggage. With no banisters or barriers to be found, only a keen eye, good balance and about thirty feet of fresh air separated you from the top landing outside our apartment to the front door of the house, four flights down at street level. It is sufficient to say they focused the mind whilst you traversed them.

Having arrived safely and dropped off our things, we headed out into the city centre and soon found ourselves passing through the Dam Square. Surrounded by a mixture of old and new buildings, notably a large Gothic Church and a Royal Palace, it was everything you'd expect from the main square in any European city, with shops and restaurants located around the perimeter and a large war monument erected in the middle. Atypically, however, there was a tram line running straight through the centre also.

Whilst much would be said of the Dam Square in the days, weeks and months to come, it was all quiet on Tuesday afternoon, as we went in search of somewhere to quench our collective thirst. A short walk away, we soon found ourselves strolling along what appeared to be a prominent shopping street which was fully pedestrianised, and quickly, John spotted a small pub by the name of Café Oporto down an adjoining alley. Now, it is critical that I highlight we had the best of intentions upon entering said pub – we were genuinely just going to have a quick one, then head back to the flat for a sleep before going out later on.

As you will have guessed, the fact I have made a special effort to mention this intent alludes to the fact that, through no fault of our own of course, our plan went out of the proverbial window, and things began to get a bit out of hand, but Amsterdam seems to have that effect on its visitors. Anyway, upon entering the small bar, which in truth most Celtic supporters would have probably walked past without even noticing it at that stage, we found it to be relatively busy but far from full. Most of the patrons were locals, and some stereotypically Dutch music was playing quietly in the background.

Knowing it was my round, I left my father and cousin to sit at the only free table in the pub and ventured to the bar without thinking anything of it. There, I found the man in front of me to be another Celtic supporter, boasting a notable Irish accent and wearing a flat cap. As he wandered off with two pints of Magners in hand, I gave him a quick nod and waited to be served. Once I had paid, I arrived back to our table to find my father and my cousin sitting with the flat-capped Irish gentleman and his female companion.

I soon discovered my two relatives had offered to share the table with this couple in my absence and what an offer this turned out to be. As you can imagine, the usual conversations were soon struck up about who was who, where we all came from, how we had travelled, whether we had match tickets, and so on. Still, with reasonably priced beer (a rarity close to the Dam Square) and some great company, there were far worse ways to spend an hour or two.

Unsurprisingly though, "an hour or two" quickly morphed into several hours as more and more Celtic supporters started to filter into the city and, in particular, this pub. Within a couple of rounds of our arrival, the singing started, and like flies to a flame, more and more fans began to appear and the songs began to get louder and louder. As the final few locals vacated the pub in the early evening, a large tricolour of the "Dunmore Town Celtic Supporters Club" was hoisted up onto the wall, and a truly great time was had by all.

Having eaten virtually nothing since our arrival in the city, the three of us eventually left the pub and took a trip to a nearby Burger King for a typically nutritious meal which sobered us up somewhat. It was then, as we went for a stroll through the nearby streets, we found ourselves entering "De Wallen". To those of you who may be unaware, "De Wallen" is the largest of Amsterdam's three Red Light Districts, and I think it is fair to say it is a bit of a culture shock for many of its visitors. Anyway, as we made our way through the narrow streets and alleys of the old city, we strolled past a pub called the "Old Sailor", which was, like an increasing number of local drinking venues, full to the brim with travelling Celtic fans. We stood outside for a few moments, debating whether or not to go in for a beer, but soon decided it would be best to head back to somewhere closer to our apartment in order to have a nightcap so as to nullify any risk of us later being unable to find our way home through the labyrinth of streets, canals and alleyways.

In hindsight, our decision that night was a very fortunate one indeed on our part, for less than half an hour after we had stood outside the pub, the "Old Sailor" and its occupants was violently assaulted by Dutch hooligans, resulting in several injuries and some damage. This incident will most likely be remembered by many in the form of the infamous YouTube video, which shows the attackers approaching from a nearby alley on CCTV, before attempting to invade the pub, and soon turning on their heels to run from understandably furious Celtic supporters within. However, for me, I shall always remember reading about this incident online the following morning, before seeing the video and soon realising we had been very lucky to miss the events which took place. At this point, it is noteworthy to mention that once word of this event circulated, both on the internet, through the local media and via word of mouth, the first real elements of bad feeling in the city became noticeable, and Celtic supporters began to watch their own backs, as well as those of their friends and family around them. Prior to this event, any such emotions were much less prevalent.

With this fresh in the minds of many Celtic supporters, thousands more streamed into the city as match day arrived. Having been given the minimum allocation permitted by Ajax for the game, only a little over two and a half thousand Celtic fans actually had tickets for the away area at the Amsterdam Arena, with some others having purchased briefs for the home sections of the ground. However, at least half of the travelling support were ticketless, and therefore we knew that finding people to watch the game with would not be difficult. Normally, we would have ventured out to the stadium on the day of the match in order to try to gain entry to the tie, but in full knowledge of the fact that away tickets were like gold dust and considering the events of the night before, we had made the decision not to go to the game itself. To some people, that concept may seem somewhat alien, but the Celtic support have a history of travelling to foreign lands ticketless, so we certainly weren't pioneers in that sense.

Having woken up with a slight hangover, we got ready and went for a walk around the city, before heading back to the Dam Square as noon approached. To say that it looked totally different from how it did the previous day would be an understatement, as already around a thousand Celtic fans filled the square, with more entering by the minute and flags going up left, right and centre. A street performer, who appeared to be a North American magician of some sort, was just finishing up his act as we passed on our way to find a pub.

It was then, across from the "Bavaria Bar", which would later become the site of much contention, that we discovered how expensive your average beer was on the Dam Square – six Euros. As we almost choked on our pints at the thought of how much they had cost, we stood outside the pub in the street, watching the world go by. At this point, a blue van pulled up on the kerb a few yards away from us, and a pair of men began to carry crate after crate of Heineken into a small, touristy shop next door. The back of the van was full of the beer, from the top to the bottom and the front to the back, and soon a sign went up in the shop window – "Six Heineken, Nine Euros". Having spotted this, I went inside and bought a six-pack, before returning outside and beginning to lift the remnants of my hangover through the wonders of icy cold lager.

In time, this called for a trip to the gents, which was located at the top of spiral "ankle-twisting" stairs at the back of the pub with the expensive pints. Atop the stairs was a landing, no more than a few feet square, with doors on either side to the male and female lavatories. Exiting the toilet, I opened the door out onto the landing, which was so small the person waiting there had to step down on to the top stair so I could get out, and then I was met with a sight that will probably never leave me. As I stood,

I heard a voice from the bottom of the stairs shout "coming up" in a broad Glaswegian accent. Deciding to be polite, I called back "on you come" – or something to that effect – as the narrow stairs were so tight that it would have been impossible to pass someone once on them. It was then, as I glanced down to the curve in the stairwell, that I saw a man with sunglasses – bedecked in a Celtic hat, scarf and shirt – climbing the stairs with a white stick in his left hand. Now, whether or not the man in question was totally blind I will never know, but the admiration I have for him is endless, because those of us blessed with sight had enough problems navigating the stairwells of Amsterdam.

Having left the visually impaired supporter behind me, I ventured back out into the street, where the crowd of Celtic supporters continued to grow. I found my father and cousin just where I had left them, standing outside the shop with lager in hand. It was at this point that I had an epiphany of sorts, coming to the conclusion that I may be able to get us some discounted, or even free, beer to drink throughout the course of the afternoon. Once I had explained my idea to my companions, they laughed it off as having "no chance" of success, but I continued regardless, walking into the little shop which had been selling the Heineken and asking to see the owner.

A few moments later, a Turkish man with jet black hair and broad shoulders appeared looking somewhat puzzled as to why a Celtic supporter had asked to see him. As I introduced myself, I pulled my phone from my pocket, and showed him my Twitter account. Quickly, we came to an agreement whereby if I were to tweet the location and name of the shop, highlighting the fact it represented an opportunity to buy some cheap beer, he would give us a free slab of Heineken as thanks. Having fulfilled my end of the bargain, I strolled out of the shop with our free cans, much to the amazement of my father and cousin.

Anyway, once the resulting back slapping was over, we continued to stand outside, intrigued to see if the tweet would actually bring the shop an increase in business or not. Initially, the rate of customers continued to be somewhat slow. However, after around twenty minutes or so, the thirsty began to come in search of beer. I must say that this was mildly amusing at first, particularly as we watched the first group of guys wander down the street visibly looking at the signs above the retail units before pointing at the shop behind us and shouting "that's it there!" However, as the minutes and hours passed, a stream of customers became a relative torrent, as word spread – not only via Twitter but through word of mouth – that the shop was one of the few local establishments selling reasonably priced beer. More and more supporters emerged from the middle of the square, and it gave us all a hearty laugh as we stood and watched people look at their phones, point at the shop to confirm the fact they had found it, before going inside and emerging a few minutes later, often with as many cans of Heineken as they could physically carry.

As time passed, the owner of the shop appeared periodically outside his store with more and more free beer for the three of us, saying "As long as they keep coming, I will keep giving you beer my friends", visibly delighted at the business he was now doing. At this stage, we decided we were actually rather hungry, and soon wandered down the street in search of somewhere to eat.

Thereafter, we decided to head into the middle of the square, but not before passing the beer shop one last time to say our goodbyes to the owner, who shook our hands, told us again how much business we appeared to have brought in and gave us yet more Heineken to take away. Upon our return, the festivities in the Dam Square were at their peak, with thousands of people milling about, singing, dancing, doing the huddle and setting off the occasional smoke bomb, causing the volume of the singing to increase when they did so. As we stood, I could not help but notice a few Ajax fans amongst the crowd, drinking with some of the Celtic support and generally having a good time. We soon had a photo taken with a few home supporters, and my dad swapped scarves with one of them. Of course, the Dutch recipient didn't know that my father had only just bought the scarf which he swapped about fifteen minutes beforehand from a street vendor, but he seemed happy enough all the same.

A short time later, I caught sight of a hat which I immediately recognised and had last seen at Firhill in the north of Glasgow – it was Frank Mullen – more commonly referred to as "Franny". Many of you will likely remember him as one of the small group of Celtic supporters mentioned in my previous work who travelled to the away game against F.K. Suduva in 2002, our first trip on the road to Seville. Franny and his companions have followed Celtic here, there and just about everywhere since the mid-1960s, and therefore I wasn't particularly surprised to find them in Amsterdam. As ever, it was a pleasure to spend a few minutes talking and, having wished them all the best for the remainder of their stay, we went our separate ways.

It was at this point, as everything appeared to be going rather nicely, that several police riot vans pulled into the square-without any observable cause of note. Whilst nothing happened – the police simply sat in their vehicles – it was a notable show of strength from the Dutch authorities, and I doubt we were the only ones who decided it would be best to head away from the square upon seeing this. After all, it was beginning to get dark, and we needed a bit of a rest before going out again to watch the game at night, so we headed back to the apartment.

Therefore, as all hell broke loose at street level only a few hundred yards away from us, we were inside the loft of an old house, chilling out before another night on the town. During this time, we had no idea of what was going on back in the square, despite being quite close to the action geographically. This was not a case of streets and streets being engulfed by violent mayhem (see Manchester 2008 for a prominent example of that), but a relatively isolated incident, albeit a horrible and wholly unnecessary one.

As we re-emerged from our temporary home, we visited a nearby restaurant for dinner. As an aside, I couldn't help but notice the truly vast number of Argentinian steakhouses in the city, which were such a common sight one would often see two or three of them in the same row of shops. To be fair, once I had sampled the food which they served, I began to understand the love the locals hold for these eateries, as the produce on offer was truly superb. Inside the restaurant, dark wood adorned every possible feature and fitting, from the walls and floors, to the tables and chairs, and even the roof. It was busier than I had presumed it would be on a Wednesday night, as locals, Argentinians, and a few Celtic supporters filled it from front to back. Pinned on to the walls, a seemingly endless array of paper money from countries all around the world had been left by past patrons, and this reminded us somewhat of Amsterdam's status as a tourist hotspot, and not just for visiting football fans.

Anyway, once we had finished our meal, we made our way straight through the Dam Square as we headed back to the same pub which we had visited the previous day. As we did so, a police cordon, with large pieces of metal fencing and a group of officers was being maintained next to the Royal Palace. The square itself looked like a different world from that we had experienced only hours before. Night had fallen, and the crowds of thousands had been replaced with a fast moving clean up team, attempting to part the sea of cans and bottles in their path. Whatever violence had occurred had ceased by this point, although we still did not know the true extent of it, with a lack of internet access not helping matters. As we strolled up the small alley in which the pub was located, we were met by a doorman telling us it was full. Granted, whilst there was still an hour or so until kick-off, he seemed to have a point. After all, when I glanced over his shoulder, there didn't look to be as much as a few square feet of room inside, let alone any chance of getting to the bar anytime soon. However, just as I readied myself to turn heel and head off in search of another establishment, John said, "Ah sorry, we were in here yesterday and the bar staff asked us to come back for the game."

Unexpectedly, the doorman's attitude seemed to totally change when my cousin said this, and quickly he stepped away from the door and said "No problem. I'm very sorry, please come in and enjoy your night." Having seen similar things happen on a couple of occasions before, I do wonder if my relatives have a way with words when they've had a few beers, or whether they simply grow in confidence, but as we pushed our way through the crowd and "Let The People Sing" shook the foundations of the old Dutch building, this wasn't something I was going to ponder seriously at the time.

As the teams ran onto the park, with Ajax in their iconic red and white shirts and Celtic in our, well, less than famous yellow and green number, "You'll Never Walk Alone" rang out as it did in countless other bars and restaurants across Amsterdam and the world. As the match began, the pub was now packed to such an extent "standing room only" would have been an optimistic phrase.

The teams went in goalless at half time, after what had been a fairly dull and scrappy first half of football. Early in the second period, Beram Kayal blazed a shot high over the bar and then, only a minute or so later, Ajax took the lead via a well worked passing move finished off by midfielder Lasse Schöne. In truth, whilst I do not doubt their efforts, Celtic largely failed to rise to the occasion in Amsterdam, and having only improved slightly after going a goal down, were unable to find an equaliser, losing by one goal to nil in the end. Throughout much of the second half and sometime after the final whistle, the collective mood was remarkably subdued. It was almost as if everyone had that same, somewhat gut-wrenching feeling that it just wasn't going to be our night. The positivity that the performance (rather than the result) in the San Siro brought with it was gone, and for a time, it was replaced with that feeling that is all too familiar for Celtic supporters, that of painful away defeat in Europe.

Having left the pub and strolled around for a while, we found another bar with a few Celtic fans present and sat down outside at a covered table underneath some patio heaters. For those of you who may not know, the night of the match was a poor one with regards the weather in the city, as heavy spells of rain frequented the Dutch capital. Mind you, if you watched the match on television from home, you wouldn't have been aware of this as the roof of the Amsterdam Arena had been closed prior to kick-off.

We sat for a short while, reflecting on a poor performance on the field and, once again, my father and cousin were more upbeat than I. Perhaps age brings with it a degree of wisdom when it comes to the prospect of accepting defeats, or perhaps one simply grows more resistant to such events, having seen it all before, but they always seem to take Celtic's losses better than me. In one sense, I was nowhere near as downhearted as I had been the previous year when Celtic lost by a single goal at the Camp Nou – after all, I hadn't expected Celtic to get anything other than a hefty defeat there – but I was still tremendously disappointed in the hour following the game in the Netherlands because I had believed Celtic could achieve a positive result beforehand.

Anyway, as we listened to the rain battering off of the awning above us, the first bars of "The Celtic Symphony" rang out of the speakers inside the pub and a group of Celtic fans within began to sing. Soon, we realised that the bar staff had agreed to let one supporter hook his iPod up to the sound system, and we ventured inside.

As time passed, more and more Celtic fans appeared, including those who had now safely made their way back into the city from the game. At this point, I actually bumped into a gentleman whom I had last seen with his son at a Celtic Graves Society event in the South Side of Glasgow. Typically, I've never met him in or around Celtic Park, but we happened to stumble across each other in Amsterdam. Anyway, having been at the match, he expressed his dismay at the result and the performance, but praised not only the noise generated by the travelling fans in the stadium, but the restraint they had shown in the face of the home support, some of whom were far from welcoming in their nature.

For example, I had no idea of the presence of a racist banner within the Ajax crowd until this point, and it was only as I spoke to my friend that I began to get some idea of what had happened in the square earlier that day. However, with music blaring and continuous singing, it was hard to attain any level of detail as he shouted in my ear, so much of this remained lost to me until I finally reached Glasgow again. Anyway, sometime later, we returned to the flat and my dad went up to sleep. At this stage, it was only around half past midnight, and so John and I decided to go in search of a couple more drinks. After all, we weren't flying out until Friday morning, so a late Wednesday night wouldn't be an issue.

Soon, we returned to the bar we had just been in to find it was closing up for the evening. Undaunted, we continued to wander around, looking for somewhere to have a drink but, bizarrely, everywhere seemed to shut at one o'clock sharp. Having asked about a bit, we chased up a few suggestions to find bars closed or closing, until a taxi driver said we should try an Irish pub on the edge of the Red Light District which had obtained a late licence for the week. Eventually, this would turn out to be successful, but as we walked in the rain searching for a pub, with distant Celtic songs ringing through the narrow streets of "De Wallen", I couldn't help but laugh about the fact that it was proving to be so difficult to find somewhere to drink late at night in a city famed for debauchery of every sort. This seemed somewhat strange, but so did much of the Dutch capital to an outsider.

Sometime later, we finally found the Irish pub we had been told about. With a lengthy queue, bouncers on the door and a five Euros entry fee, it maybe wouldn't have been our first choice but the place was open, so it would do. Inside, the bar was packed to within an inch of bursting. Having got a couple of beers, we eventually managed to grab two seats when some folk left for the night, as a few yards away, someone spilt a pint down a flight of stairs.

In truth, there was a distinctly odd atmosphere in the pub. Whilst several people were still singing their hearts out, they seemed to be split into disjointed pockets, with more and more individuals sleeping between them or simply sitting staring straight ahead trying to stay awake. I suppose it is worth remembering that many of these supporters had likely been awake for twenty-four hours or more by this point, having flown into the Netherlands on an early flight, with the plan of staying out all night in the city (therefore saving on accommodation costs) before returning home on one of the first flights out of Schiphol.

As we readied ourselves to head back to the flat having had our fill, I stood up and led the way. By this stage, I had totally forgotten about the spilt pint sometime beforehand and, as I strode down from our small seating area on to the main floor of the bar, my feet went from underneath me and I flew up in the air, banana-skin style, before tumbling down the small staircase in front of over a hundred people. The fact that there was no ironic cheer only highlighted that this was a somewhat exhausted set of supporters and, with my pride hurt more than my physical self, we finally made our way to bed.

The following day, we did our best to act like normal tourists and actually take in the sights of the city in which we found ourselves. Typically, this involved simply going for a walk in large parts, but there was one landmark in particular, all joking aside, which we did want to see.

It is perhaps somewhat ironic that, albeit from the other side of a canal, we managed to walk by our destination without noticing it was there initially (and we were actively looking for it), just as hundreds, if not thousands of Nazis would have done during World War Two. The Anne Frank Museum in Amsterdam, built around the house which hid the members of the Frank family, as well as a handful of other Jews during the conflict, is not a big or a grand building. It is not flashy nor distinctive from the outside, but that is not its reason for being. In this case, it is most definitely what is inside which matters.

As we walked through the museum, which was busy with Celtic supporters, one could have heard a pin drop. Before we even entered the old house itself, the haunting atmosphere of the place was palpable, with pictures of the Frank family, as well as other members of ethnic minorities around Europe, adorning the walls. People spoke in hushed tones and in the first few moments of that visit, the rest of our trip to Amsterdam faded out of our minds. As we walked up a set of "ankle-twisting stairs", upon which we were now fairly adept, I saw the bookcase which concealed the entrance to the so-called "secret annex" appear before me.

Moments later, as I ducked my head and clambered through the small hole in the wall, I found myself in a different world. There is no furniture left in the old annex which hid a family from genocide, only empty rooms. Unlike the rest of the museum, there are no exhibits, nor any explanatory speaker telling a story over the tannoy system – only silence. The windows remain blacked out to the world, with a few of the original fixtures and fittings still in place. In truth, it was difficult to take it all in as I stood in the room where Anne Frank wrote much of her diary. Looking back on it now, I feel the magnitude of the visit only truly struck me when I left the creaking floorboards of the old house behind me and returned to steel and concrete of the modern museum.

As I passed a window overlooking the annex, I finally grasped how it had remained hidden for so long, and it is likely Amsterdam is one of the few cities where it would have been possible. Of course, I have already described the maze of streets, alleyways and canals, but what I have not discussed is an aspect of the city which my father aptly compared to "a rabbit warren". Like many tenements in Glasgow, the houses of old Amsterdam are joined together in huge rows, often spanning the length of a whole street. However, what sets the buildings in the Dutch capital apart is that entire blocks are generally joined together in a manner which, seemingly, makes absolutely no sense at all. Houses and buildings have, in the past at least, been stuck together in a rather bamboozling way. This means that, for example, houses which tilt notably to one side – held up by the straight houses built on either side of them – are not an uncommon sight in the city.

Floors in each individual building do not always match up, so half floors are created, and soon, with the presence of deep, narrow houses, bizarre layouts, tight staircases and a lack of any standardised building plans, the "rabbit warren" analogy becomes increasingly clear to behold. Essentially, only the locals truly understand the way in which their city is laid out. To outsiders like ourselves, it would have been very easy to miss a few rooms in any building, presuming instead they must have been part of another structure, and thus we can begin to see how the annex remained concealed for so long.

As I moved away from the window and into the last part of the museum, where some of Anne Frank's handwritten notes still rest to this day, I could not help but shudder as the final destinations of each member of the family were laid bare. The Frank family were split after someone gave their location away to the Nazis, and after trips to different concentration camps, only one of them, Anne's father Otto, survived the war. Anne, who was born in Frankfurt, died at the age of only fifteen in one of the most infamous camps, Bergen-Belsen, in Germany. Only a few months later, World War Two came to an end in Europe, and this camp was liberated.

In a sense, I imagine Auschwitz – which I have not visited – to be one of the few places on Earth which could have such an impact on those who go there. The Anne Frank Museum was just as terrifying and depressing as it was inspiring, for in a city which is famous for its wild side, it has the capacity to make even a travelling football supporter take a step back and think about larger things. To exemplify this, a group of young men of a similar age to me went into the museum at the same time we did. With thick Glaswegian accents and even the odd green and white scarf, it was clear they too were Celtic fans. When they entered the museum, they were relatively jovial, talking away and obviously enjoying their day in the city. However, when they left alongside us, they barely uttered a word, and as they walked away down the canal side, their hands shoved deeply into their pockets, the impact which the experience had upon them was very apparent.

As for my companions and I, we too took some time to reflect on what we had just seen, sitting down outside a local cafe after a long walk. Momentarily, I shall return to the story of our trip as a whole. However, before I do so, I shall leave you with one quote from Anne Frank to ponder: "No one has ever become poor by giving."

Having enjoyed our final night in the city and travelled home the next day, we emerged in the arrivals hall at Edinburgh airport in good spirits. Yes, Celtic had lost, but we were home and had relished the time in each other's company. As I strolled past a newsagents, a headline from a tabloid newspaper caught my attention – "The Battle of Amsterdam", it read – with a large picture of a Celtic fan and several police accompanying it on the front page. At this point, I did something which I very rarely do and actually bought a copy, purely to discover more.

As I look back on these few moments, I cannot help but notice the irony of the fact that whilst I was actually in the city of Amsterdam, I had little idea of the true scale of the violence which erupted and yet, having been back in Scotland for less than half an hour, I found it plastered across the front of several newspapers and, later, featuring on television news. In a certain sense, it seemed somewhat surreal, as I glanced through the pages of the paper in the back seat of the car en route to Glasgow. I recognised not only the locations in which the photographs had been taken, but even one or two of the people whom I had spotted in the Dam Square during the day. To see them running away from police or clustering together outside the "Bavaria Bar" in search of safety in numbers was scary and to think that we could easily have been caught up in all of this had we not left the square when we did was equally frightening.

What followed in the days after our arrival home was a battle for the truth, as it became increasingly clear that the actions of the Dutch police, combined with those of football hooligans who affiliate themselves with Ajax, had been the primary causes of the violence at the heart of the Netherlands.

Even now, as I sit in front of a computer and do my best to recall the events of our trip, one point overrides all others in my head, and therefore I feel I must reiterate it now. On the day of the game, the Celtic supporters in the Dam Square were their usual friendly, sociable selves. Yes, some people had drank a little too much and maybe a few had indulged in other substances, but there was no stench of violence in the air. Celtic fans stood in groups drinking and singing – some even brought musical instruments – and Ajax supporters mingled in the square without fear. I have never been a fan of the term "party atmosphere", but in all honesty it describes the match day mood rather well.

It would have been very easy with the events of the previous night in mind for the Celtic support to totally close ranks that day, putting up an unwelcoming front, but we did not. Regardless of what you may read or what prosecutors may have claimed, the Celtic support was not the guilty party in Amsterdam – the Dutch police and hooligans were – although at times it was difficult to differentiate between the two as they acted so similarly.

Without delving into these issues too deeply, I shall repeat what I said initially after my return to Glasgow. If a group of men in plain clothes broke through police lines and began to attack people (including your family or friends) apparently at random, would your first thought be that these individuals were police officers or hooligans? Would your immediate reaction really be to ask the attackers for identification, or would you simply do all you could to protect your family, friends and yourself? I think we all know the answer, and the fact that neither the Dutch police nor the relevant authorities seemed to come to the same conclusion is rather concerning.

The actions and attitudes which were displayed by the police and authorities, not to mention the hooligans, will undoubtedly discourage many Celtic supporters, including myself, from travelling to Amsterdam for a football match in the future, unless it is for a fixture of such critical importance that it simply cannot be missed. In several senses, this is a pity, because many of the residents of what is a vibrant, unique city were lovely people. They were shamed by a minority, but when you risk assault and arrest (or both) without being guilty of any crime whatsoever, why would any football supporter take the risk of travelling there?

It goes without saying that fans of any nationality or persuasion should be able to travel to matches in any foreign country without worrying about injury or incarceration without cause. They should not have to fear for their safety or that of their loved ones and, should any trouble occur, they should be protected first and foremost by the local police, not vilified by them. In truth, it is lucky that nobody was seriously injured in Amsterdam. I, for one, hope Celtic avoid Ajax for a long time to come, but do thank the numerous good people of the city for their kind hospitality.

"Keeping His Story Alive"

There are many players – particularly those who featured many decades ago or longer – whose names and deeds have been largely forgotten by the modern day Celtic support. William Hughes is such a player. However, unlike many of those I mention from time to time who have featured in a handful of games here or a smattering of matches there, Hughes actually registered more than one hundred competitive appearances for Celtic, a feat which several players more prominent in the minds of many have failed to achieve.

In the past, it has proved tricky to track down William's exact date of birth with any certainty, although it was known he was born in Winchburgh (a town which lies approximately ten miles west of Edinburgh) sometime in 1909. Following some research on this subject, I believe I can now say with a relative degree of assurance that he was born on the seventh of July 1909, to parents James and Elizabeth. My reasoning for this is simple, as the previously referenced date is the only one corresponding to a registered birth of a William Hughes in Winchburgh that year.

William's father James was listed on his birth certificate as a shale miner, and as such, I do not feel I am being particularly speculative by presuming a similar life may have awaited William had he not shown such a knack for football. William began his career with Bellstane Birds, a junior football club based in South Queensferry who – according to Wikipedia – were formed in 1882 and became defunct in 1891; therefore it was quite a feat for someone born in 1909 to play for them. Yet, as it turns out, with some further digging one discovers that there were actually three incarnations of clubs playing under the name of Bellstane Birds over the years, all in South Queensferry and each separated by several years. William played for the third and final Birds club in the Midlothian Junior League, eventually departing the east coast and moving inland to Division Two side Bathgate in the spring of 1927.

However, Bathgate were a football club with a bleak and altogether finite future. Despite reaching an all-time high of third place in Division Two after the 1923-24 season – when they finished well above the likes of Dunfermline Athletic and Dundee United – serious financial issues soon came to the fore and their league position plummeted. Over the next few seasons, they were saved from relegation to the third tier of the Scottish game on two occasions thanks entirely to the fact the decision had been made to scrap the third division, a competition which would not return until after the Second World War, after the 1925-26 campaign. Regardless, Bathgate were forced to resign from the Scottish League in March of 1929 as they could not fulfil their fixtures, and as such, all of their players immediately became free agents. Within days, several individuals received interest from other clubs looking to bolster their playing squads without any significant financial outlay. William Hughes was one of these men, putting pen to paper and signing for Celtic before the month was out.

Midway through March, the "Dundee Evening Telegraph" published the following snippet to this effect: "Bathgate Players Fixed Up – Celtic and Rangers Sign Forwards – Celtic Football Club have fixed up with William Hughes, who for two seasons has played outside-left for Bathgate. Hughes went to Bathgate towards the close of season 1926-27, and on several occasions was sought after by other clubs, but the terms offered were never tempting. Last Saturday, Alexander Macpherson, the Bathgate outside-right, was fixed up by Rangers. Both these players, by the decision of the League, have free transfers, and the Bathgate club will not benefit."

Thereafter, William Hughes would make his debut for Celtic on the nineteenth of March 1929, as the Hoops took on Motherwell at Celtic Park. The home side won by two goals to nil that day, with the new lad stationed at outside-left. Of his performance, the "Glasgow Herald" said "Hughes, who was making his first appearance for Celtic, created a favourable impression."

In the weeks which followed, William would feature in seven more of the Celts' eight remaining league matches, although he would not play at Celtic Park again until the following season. This was not due to a lack of home matches – after all Celtic played four during the period in question, each of which Hughes took part in – but to the fire which had engulfed Celtic's pavilion and damaged part of an adjoining stand ten days after the Motherwell tie.

The twentieth of April would see Falkirk and Celtic face off at Shawfield whilst construction work continued up the road at Celtic Park, and although the match would make no difference to the destination of the league flag (with Rangers so far ahead in the standings that they had already secured the title), there was still second place to play for. It would be memorable for William Hughes, as he netted his first goal for the Hoops. Of this strike, which opening the scoring that day, the "Falkirk Herald" said the following: "It was seldom that the Falkirk forwards got the length of [John] Thomson, but it appeared to be Ferguson's [the Falkirk goalkeeper's] day, and all manner of shots were dealt with by him in confident style. Hume and Mackrell gave him splendid support and broke up many dangerous attacks, but after thirty-five minutes' play they had to admit defeat, Hughes taking the ball as it came from the right and shooting hard into the net."

A week later, Celtic travelled to Rugby Park to take on Kilmarnock, knowing that only a win would guarantee their place as runners-up that season without them being reliant on Motherwell slipping up. Motherwell beat Airdrieonians by a convincing five-nil margin that afternoon, and with only a couple of minutes remaining at Rugby Park, Celtic looked like third place would be their final position, as they trailed the home side by two goals to one. It was then, that a "spirited attack" from the visitors saw Celtic equalise with only moments left, before William Hughes struck the winning goal with seconds remaining to give the Hoops "an exciting last minute victory".

The following season would not be a particularly successful one for Celtic, as they fell to fourth place in the league standings and crashed out of the Scottish Cup at the semi-final stage thanks to a one-nil defeat against Kilmarnock. William Hughes would be used somewhat sparingly, but his prowess as a utility player began to emerge as he filled in at left-back, right-back, left-half and outside-left over the course of the campaign. Still a young man, he would have likely been content biding his time, confident that an opportunity to establish himself solidly as a first team player was bound to present itself at some point soon. However, as 1930 became 1931, such an opportunity was yet to arise. Hughes played less often that season than he had done previously, featuring mostly at outside-left but notably deputising for Jimmy McGrory at centre forward in the second round of the Scottish Cup as Celtic overcame Dundee United by a margin of three goals to two. He also appeared as the Celts avenged the demons of two seasons past by defeating Kilmarnock in the semi-finals of the Scottish Cup, with Hughes scoring in the process. Therefore, although he was not fortunate enough to play in the Cup Final itself, which Celtic won by overcoming Motherwell in a replay, William Hughes could proudly consider himself a Scottish Cup winner, having contributed notably along the way.

As every Celtic supporter is aware, the next season, that of 1931-32, would be forever predominantly associated with the tragic death of John Thomson. Undoubtedly, this had an enormously negative impact on the squad of the period, and in truth it would take them all some time to truly return to any semblance of normality. Again, Hughes deputised for his colleagues that season, generally appearing at centre forward, scoring the odd goal here and there when he did so.

The Celts won the Scottish Cup again in 1933, a fitting tribute to John Thomson's memory, and not a result to be underestimated when one considers the strengths of the Motherwell side whom Celtic defeated in the final by a single goal to nil. Once again, William Hughes did not feature at Hampden Park, but did appear at left-half in many of the Scottish Cup matches which Celtic played during the run which took them there, deputising for Chic Geatons. Therefore, with a second Scottish Cup winners' medal to his name, Hughes may finally have thought his time had come as the 1933-34 league season began, as he featured in all but three of the Club's thirty-eight league matches that year. Interestingly, Celtic only won one of the fixtures in which Willie did not play, drawing one and losing another. Equally well, Hughes played in three of Celtic's four Scottish Cup matches that year, with the only one he did not participate in being the tie in which the Celts fell to St. Mirren.

During the summer break of 1934, Hughes would have much to celebrate on a personal level, as he married his fiancée. Now, this may not seem to be particularly interesting at first, but with further examination its relevance becomes apparent, as we find William married into one of the most important families then related to Celtic Football Club. The following report, taken from the "Dundee Evening Telegraph" towards the end of June, explains in more detail.

"Celtic Player Weds – Miss Bride Agatha Kelly, second daughter of the late Mr. James Kelly who, at his death, was Chairman of the Glasgow Celtic Football Club, and Mrs. Kelly, of Thornhill House, Blantyre, was married in St. Joseph's R.C. Church, Blantyre, this forenoon. The bridegroom was Mr. William Hughes, of Winchburgh, the popular half-back of the Glasgow Celtic Football Club. The bridesmaid was the bride's sister, Miss Nancy Kelly, and the groomsman was Mr. D. Clark, M.A., of Edinburgh."

"The bride was the recipient of many handsome presents, amongst the donors being Mr. William Maley, the manager of the Celtic Football Club, who gave a china coffee service. Mr. Calder, a Celtic director, gave a crystal dressing service; Mr. Patsy Gallagher; late of Celtic, a solid silver tea service. A walnut grandmother clock, with Westminster chimes, was the gift of the employees of the Blantyre Engineering Co. Ltd., of which the bride's two brothers [one of whom was Robert Kelly, who would later become the Chairman at Celtic Park] are directors."

Despite his now strong ties to one of the families running the Football Club, the season of 1934-35 would see any hopes William Hughes had of absolutely solidifying a place in the starting eleven dissipate, as the emergence of the young George Paterson quickly forced him out of the side for the first time in over a year. However, prior to that occurrence in the October of 1934, Hughes would enjoy perhaps his finest individual moment as a Celtic player as the Hoops welcomed Rangers to Celtic Park on the eighth of September. The "Glasgow Herald" described this event wonderfully.

' "Celtic Surprise their Ibrox Rivals – Unexpected Goal by Hughes – Levels the Scores – Celtic 1, Rangers 1 – Celtic rather confounded the prophets at Parkhead on Saturday when they forced a draw with their more fancied rivals from Ibrox in a game in which honest endeavour was more obvious than football skill. Both teams had chances to win the game; but a draw was the most fitting result. Play throughout was hard and keen, and there were two incidents which will long be remembered by the forty-thousand spectators. The first was the equalising goal scored by Hughes just on half time. The Celtic half-back succeeded at the second attempt in getting the ball under control about the half way line, and immediately set off in the direction of Dawson [the Rangers' goalkeeper]…Rangers fell back to cover up, while Craig tried to overtake the half-back. On went Hughes until he reached the corner of the penalty box and then, instead of passing, he sent the ball strongly towards goal. There was a second's silence, and then such a roar; to everyone's surprise the ball was lying in the net behind Dawson."

Disappointingly, the second of the two incidents referenced previously was that Chic Geatons missed a penalty to win the match, but nonetheless it was a fine way for Hughes to bow out of the Glasgow derby fixture. He would never appear in another such match, but for one day, he was the hero who prevented Celtic from suffering a home defeat to their fiercest adversaries. In the long run, it meant little in one sense – Rangers still progressed to another league title – but on a much smaller, more isolated level, it was critical importantly, if for no reason other than the fact Celtic had refused to be beaten on their own turf. Undoubtedly, the side garnered some level of belief that they were gradually closing in on Rangers. Grit and determination such as this was then, is now, and forever shall be appreciated by the Celtic support, irrespective of the individual ability levels of the team on the park.

William Hughes would only make a handful of appearances thereafter for Celtic Football Club, with a trio of victories at the end of the 1934-35 campaign being followed by some sporadic showings the following season. Fittingly, although the endeavours of 1935-36 would be William's last as a Celtic player, he would be rewarded with a Scottish League winners' medal, the first and only one of his career and also the first which any Celtic side had achieved for a decade. His last outing in a Celtic shirt would come on the twenty-ninth of February 1936 in a four-nil away win against Clyde, and aptly he got himself onto the score sheet also.

In September 1936, William Hughes left Celtic Park behind him, moving the short distance to Shawfield to join Clyde. His record as a Celtic player reads as follows: one hundred and four League and Cup appearances, twelve goals, one Scottish League winners' medal and two Scottish Cup winners' medals – a fine haul. In the twilight of his footballing career, spells at Bo'ness, Arbroath and Hamilton Academicals would follow, whilst in his later life, he would run a grocer's shop in Blantyre, Lanarkshire, and enjoy time with his wife.

Bride Hughes would pass away on the seventeenth of December 1960. Whilst I made reference at the start of this chapter to the difficulty involved in confirming William's date of birth, this was easy in comparison to the issues which arose whilst attempting to discover when and where his life came to an end. Indeed, until I visited St. Patrick's Cemetery in New Stevenston, where much of the Kelly clan rest, I believed it to be likely he would be buried alongside his wife. However, having found Bride's grave, I discovered this was not the case.

Subsequently, it was only the help of fellow Celtic supporters William Sinclair and Kevin Chalmers which allowed me to uncover some details regarding Hughes' later life. It appears he remarried in 1962, wedding Marie Gunn in Blantyre, before moving to the north east of Scotland. There he remained, residing in Nairn and Fochabers, even after his second wife's death in March 1995. William Hughes died on the first of January 1996 at the age of eighty-six in a care home in Keith, and now lies at rest in St. Ninian's Roman Catholic Cemetery in Chapelford. Like many good servants to Celtic Football Club, his name may not be the most widely celebrated, but this does not devalue his achievements. I hope that this short chapter, if nothing else, will keep his story alive in the minds of today's Celtic supporters.

"John the Third"

In the summer of 1956, Celtic would sign the third individual with the name "John Divers" to play for the Club. At the age of just sixteen, John had a lot to live up to, for he came with a family history few could match nor ignore. After all, as the son of "John the Second" he was also the great-nephew of the legendary Patsy Gallagher. The modern day equivalent of this would likely be an example whereby Celtic signed Jordan Larsson (son of the great Henrik) a couple of years ago, and before the lad was even old enough to be served in a pub, a hefty weight of expectation would be laid upon his shoulders.

Having begun his career with his school side, that of St. Patrick's High in Dumbarton, John then spent a spell with amateurs Glentyan Thistle, whom he would subsequently leave to join the ranks at Parkhead. A forward player, like his father, great-uncle and even "John the First" (albeit no relation) before him, Divers came to Celtic Park not only with a promising reputation, but a solid affinity for the game of football, with attributes including a powerful shot and an impressive eye for a pass.

He made his senior debut midway through the 1957-58 season at a very exciting time for everyone at Celtic Football Club. Of course, a little less than a month earlier, the Celts recorded the immortal seven-one League Cup Final victory over Rangers, but that was not the be all and end all of positive events at the Club. With notable young talents such as Billy McNeill signing for the Hoops around that time, not to mention an impressive, if somewhat unpredictable first team, many would have felt that Celtic may have been on the verge of finally emerging from the shadows of World War Two and re-establishing themselves as the best side in Scotland once again. Of course, this wouldn't come to pass for several years yet, but we are now blessed with the benefit of hindsight.

Anyway, with Bobby Collins – the great inside-forward who starred with Celtic, Everton and Leeds – unavailable for selection due to an injury which he picked up on international duty, John was called up for his senior debut as Celtic faced St. Mirren at Celtic Park on the sixteenth of November 1957. At seventeen years of age, his selection did warrant some note in the Glaswegian newspapers of the time, who were all quick to mention who this young player was – "Divers, son of the former Celtic inside-forward" (The "Glasgow Herald") and "John Divers – son of the famous ex-Celtic man – at inside-right" ("The Evening Times") being two examples of this.

John did himself proud during his first outing in the Hoops, scoring the opening goal in an entertaining match which would eventually finish in a two-all draw, played in "a pall of mist", which made Celtic Park "look anything but Paradise" according to one newspaper observer. John's goal was described by "The Evening Times" as follows: "Come the twenty-second minute and it was a hap-hap-happy Divers Bhoy. McPhail trailed a ball to the right, and when he sent over a hanging cross Divers used his head to score his first ever Celtic goal."

A few minutes later, whilst Celtic were still in the ascendancy – although this would not last as the visitors fought back for a draw – John went close once more: "Divers was [exhibiting] good inside-forward play and was only inches out with a twenty yard shot from a McPhail service."

Having put on a good showing on his debut, John would not reappear in the first team until almost a year later, in the autumn of 1958. With the departure of Bobby Collins to Everton in mid-September, a slot opened up in the Celts' forward line and John was determined to grab it. Whilst it would take some time for him to fully secure his place in the first team, he did make four consecutive appearances in October that year.

At this point in Celtic's history, there was a clear blend of experience and youth in many of the teams the Club put out on the park and, now we can look back on these years as a whole, it is clear to see that this was the beginning of a transitional period which would eventually be brought to fruition when the catalyst that was Jock Stein returned in the mid-1960s to take charge as manager. This was exemplified as John Divers lined up for his second senior appearance, a two-one League Cup defeat to Partick Thistle, when he stood alongside the likes of Charlie Tully and Willie Fernie, two old stalwarts approaching the end of their days at Parkhead, as well as Bertie Auld and Billy McNeill, two youngsters set to become integral cogs in the side which would rise to become the greatest in the world.

Following that loss, Celtic faced Queen of the South three days later on league duty, with Pat Crerand making his league debut for the Hoops. John Divers opened the scoring for the Celts, finishing off an "all-in Celtic attack" and "giving the goalkeeper no chance" as he did so. Later, John would miss a good chance to appear on the score sheet once again, but he would subsequently make amends by setting up Bertie Auld for the final goal a few minutes before full time, securing a three-one win for the Parkhead side.

One week later on his next outing, John Divers would go one better and score twice for the Parkhead crowd against Falkirk. However, whilst the Hoops would end another league match with three goals to their name, a last minute winner for the away team would painfully snatch the points from a game which any neutral would have enjoyed greatly. It is never nice to dwell on such sore losses, but they are an undeniable part of football nonetheless.

The following is from "The Evening Times": "Dashing Divers – His headers rock the Bairns – Every flag in Celtic Park was at half-mast in memory of Pope Pius XII. Bertie Peacock and Charlie Tully had failed to pass fitness tests just before lunchtime…The Celtic players wore black armbands as a further mark of mourning for the Pope. Inside a minute fans on the terracing were acclaiming one of the slickest goals seen at Parkhead for many a day. Colrain beat Hunter near the corner flag…and his chip cross was met flush on the forehead by Divers and was in the net before a soul in the ground realised what was happening."

Later in the same article, once the author had detailed another three goals which left the score at two-all with the half-time break approaching, they went on to tell of Divers' second – and Celtic's third – goal of the day: "The pace was fast, the game full of entertainment – and Falkirk looked anything but a bottom of the league team. Nevertheless, Celtic had the goal-hungry look and when in the fortieth minute Auld sent over the perfect corner kick, Divers hurled himself through the air and headed the ball inside Slater's right-hand post as he flew past the outside. Another first-class goal."

Thereafter, a stunning piece of goalkeeping denied Divers the chance of a first hat-trick, before some poor defending coupled with impressive, determined forward play swung the game in Falkirk's favour. The following weekend, John scored again as the Celts eased past Airdrieonians at Broomfield. With this, John had netted in four consecutive league games – every one in which he had played in his Celtic career thus far – but was dropped from the team after the Airdrieonians match for six games due to injury, before re-emerging against Motherwell on the sixth of December at a frosty Celtic Park.

I shall leave it to a newspaper article written at the time to explain the events which followed: "Every one of the Celtic players checked into Parkhead a full hour before the 2.15pm start on Saturday – and that is one reason why they "beat" Motherwell. As each player came into the dressing room he was told – "The going is going to be shocking – so go out there now, test it carefully and decide what type of boots will give you the best grip." When the Motherwell team bus rolled up captain Bert McCann and Willie McSeveney also walked out and tested the "rink" for ice. But Celtic won the first round by the length of London Road. Before kick-off anyone with an eye to turning a quick gambling penny would have laid more than a mere shade of odds that the Motherwell forwards, who are not only bantam-weights but built very close to the ground, would trip a dainty and sure-footed way to victory, while giants like Colrain, Divers and Jackson were skidding and stumbling to humiliation."

"The evils and the financial wrongs of betting were proved beyond dispute inside a couple of minutes, for although there may have been frost on the outside of the Celtic boots, there was also magic inside them. While the big men were pounding along on the ice as though this was perfect holding ground, the wee men o' Motherwell were giving a non-stop demonstration of Charlie Chaplin taking a corner at high speed in his old days in the silent cinema."

"From now on they can talk of the Luck of the Rangers or the Luck of the Irish, but the "Old Firm" fans will have the retort perfect when they say "Maybe – but mind that day when Motherwell were saved by the fog?""

Yes, despite a splendid Celtic performance in difficult weather conditions with goals from Auld and Divers giving the home side a virtually unassailable two-nil lead, the referee in charge of the match called the game off with just eight minutes remaining at Celtic Park rather than seeing it through to the end. In the subsequent replay, which I shall discuss in a moment, the Celts could only manage a draw, and thus the combination of poor weather and a referee with a clear lack of common sense cost the Parkhead Club a point come the end of the league season, not that it would have made a tremendous amount of difference, other than to lift them from a sixth place finish to the fifth spot in the league, knocking Airdrieonians down a peg.

Before the two sides would meet in the rearranged fixture though, Celtic would face Stirling Albion (a seven-three win in which John would score twice), Hearts (a one-all draw, the first league game in which John would fail to find the net), Clyde (a three-one win) and Rangers. Not only would this be John's debut appearance in the biggest derby in Scottish football, it would also be his first trip to Ibrox as a senior player.

However, the outcome of this match, which was a tale of two penalties, was a farce due to the horrific weather in which it was contested. The decision making of Scottish officials also played a significant role and this would be queried by supporters and media alike in the days following the game. Anyway, Celtic did actually manage to take the lead through Bertie Peacock early on in the match – before conditions worsened from bad to truly awful – and a quick equaliser levelled the scores and a converted penalty allowed Rangers to gain the upper hand.

The following quote comes from the "Glasgow Herald" and discusses the official's choice to play the game until its finish and an agonising moment for the young Bertie Auld: "After thirty-five minutes play in the second half at Ibrox stadium the referee halted proceedings for a consultation with his linesmen. No one had the slightest doubt about the subject matter; indeed abandonment seemed certain to be the outcome for a dreadful gale of wind and rain was sweeping over a pitch [which had] long since become a quagmire. Not a vestige of the goal line marking could be seen and more than one player appeared sure to collapse from exhaustion."

"After the officials' huddle, however, play was resumed as it had ceased with Celtic making tremendous efforts to neutralise Rangers' two-one advantage. Rangers, despite the fact the ever-strengthening wind had been [blowing] in their favour in the second half, were already more than ordinarily fortunate to be leading; on at least half a dozen occasions their midfield defence had been outplayed and the sea of mud in the goal area had baulked the final shooting foot. Niven too, had made several superb saves...Celtic were committed to centre field thrusts and skilfully and enthusiastically as Colrain and Divers conducted them, the mud was a deadly enemy...then five minutes from time a penalty kick for Celtic... One felt sorry for Auld as he and a colleague searched for the penalty spot in the morass: Caldow, who had converted his side's penalty at the same end of the ground, had the much easier conditions. Auld in the end made a nearly perfect strong shot – no one could have risked trying to side-foot the kick – but the ball struck the crossbar."

Celtic would play the following day, on the second of January, as their rescheduled tie against Motherwell was held at Celtic Park. The fact Celtic had led comfortably by two goals to nil with less than ten minutes to play was irrelevant, as the scores and the match clock were reset to zero. Typically, as fate would have it, Celtic proceeded to draw with Motherwell three-each after two goalkeeping calamities in the final few moments of the tie robbed the Celts of a point. John Divers scored once that day, and it was described in a match report as follows: "Divers, from one of several clever unorthodox back-heelers by Colrain, completed the best of the many attractive attacks of the match."

The rest of the 1958-59 season was to be one of encouragement and expectation mixed with dejection and disappointment for Celtic, something which reflected the state of the Football Club at that point in time rather fittingly. After all, it was not the manager, Jimmy McGrory, who was picking the team on many occasions, but those within the boardroom who possessed a liking for fiddling in footballing matters which should not have concerned them.

Anyway, having drawn with Motherwell, the next couple of Celtic's league matches were postponed and therefore a friendly against Girvan Amateurs was hastily arranged in order to give the side some much needed game time. Undoubtedly, the star of the show that day was Bertie Auld who scored a double hat-trick, but I feel a special mention of John Divers' brace is necessary, as he was described by a newspaper reporter as "one of the cleverest Celts on view", scoring the seventh and final goals as the Hoops put Girvan to the sword, winning by twelve goals to two.

A few weeks later, Celtic eased past Albion Rovers in the first round of the Scottish Cup, although John did not feature, handing over his starting place to Sammy Wilson for the day on which Charlie Tully made his final Celtic appearance. A replay victory against Clyde in February set up a much anticipated quarter final tie as Celtic drew Rangers, the strongest side in the country and a team they had not beaten in the Scottish Cup at Celtic Park for almost sixty years – 1901 being the last occasion upon which they had enjoyed such a success.

With Charlie Tully now out of the picture for good, there were less forwards at the Club competing for spaces in the starting line-up again, and whilst Divers had unsurprisingly regained a place in the first team for this match, injuries and illness meant Celtic were forced to call-up a few less experienced youngsters also, fielding perhaps one of the youngest forward lines in the history of the Football Club, which read: Matthew McVittie (twenty-one), Mike Jackson (nineteen), Ian Lochhead (nineteen and making only his second appearance for Celtic), Sammy Wilson (twenty-eight) and John Divers (eighteen).

The attacking line, led not by the experienced Sammy Wilson but by its youngest member, John Divers, excelled that day as Celtic treated their supporters to a sight the vast majority of them would never have seen before, a Scottish Cup victory over the Ibrox side at Celtic Park. The following quotes come from three differing news publications, two based in Glasgow and another a broadsheet from further afield – giving us an interesting insight not only into how these colossal matches were viewed in our fair city but in the rest of the country also.

"Weeping grey sky, a mixture of forty thousand spectators and four hundred policemen, and, for backcloth, a graveyard and factory chimneys. This, on Saturday, was what the Glaswegians call "Paradise". If the local name is unfamiliar it was, in fact, Parkhead, the grim looking ground of Celtic Football Club. If the opening act sounds sombre, by the time the curtain came down with a final flourish we had had tension, tumultuous cheering, and a surprising but deserved victory for the home team over Rangers... The pitch was so saturated by heavy rain that the groundsmen were out with forks before kick-off. Soon the pitch had become a trap for any ball artist and yet the game went completely the way of Celtic, who played a much more delicate game than the hard driving but somewhat crude Rangers." [Broadsheet]

"Scott was in his most deadly mood on the right wing, and yet in practically Celtic's first attack, Rangers would surely have been a goal down but for a most superb bit of goalkeeping from Niven. From a clever position, Lochhead pushed a ball through the centre to Divers and the outside-left instantly wheeled and cut the ball along the mud for the back of the Rangers net. In a flash of yellow Niven streaked down on to the sawdust line and smothered the ball while every Celtic fan in the ground was shouting "Goal!" One minute from half-time Telfer, who had looked none too comfortable, made a mistake which cost Rangers a goal. He failed to clear a ball out on the right touch line, and when McVittie's cross came over beyond the far post, Divers came racing in and with his head steered the ball back across the goal and into the net at the far side. Half-time – Celtic 1; Rangers 0." ["The Evening Times"]

The first newspaper which I have quoted later said "...there was Divers flat on his face in the mud having executed a superb header to put the white ball past Nevin." I only mention this quote in particular as it connects rather well with a picture which, personally, I adore. Above the caption, "Divers scores Celtic's first goal against Rangers in the Scottish Cup", it shows John, lying flat on his chest in the mud, looking to his right just as the ball passes the helpless Rangers goalkeeper and bounces an instant before it hits the back of the net – all of this in front of a section of the expectant Celtic support who would proceed to go wild only a second or two after the shutter fell on this snapshot of history.

The article continues: "As goalkeeper and scorer picked themselves up there was a strange sight peculiar to Celtic-Rangers matches. At one end of the ground caps flew in the air, green and white Celtic scarves were brandished, and everyone leaped for joy. At the other end, not a figure stirred. There might have been two different matches in the one arena." [Broadsheet]

"The regular, if hardly rhythmic chant of "Seven, seven, seven" which developed at the covered enclosure end of the ground – the League Cup Final of last season has for some an irresistible and indestructible appeal – was, however, vainly inglorious; much toil and sweat there had yet to be for Celtic before the victory was sure." ["Glasgow Herald"]

"In the fifty-sixth minute, there was a prolonged scramble in the Rangers goalmouth, Caldow dramatically clearing off his line, before McVittie had the Parkhead supporters dancing again. Celtic, unbelievably two goals ahead, were singing now and they had nearly all the best of the remainder of the second half. Nearly all, but not quite, for Murray woke up sufficiently to crack in a header that the promising Haffey only just saved, and, with one minute to go, again used his head and this time won. But the final score of two-one did not really do justice to the winners." [Broadsheet]

Yet, after all of the effort and skill which it took to fell the favourites Rangers, Celtic proceeded to lose heavily by four goals to nil in the following semi-final against St. Mirren, a side whom they were unable to defeat in the league that season, but ultimately finished above when the campaign came to a close. As the biggest of the four sides left in the competition, fresh from their victory over their rivals, I feel it is likely that many Celtic supporters were dreaming of a first Scottish Cup win in five years as the doomed semi-final approached. Hopes would have been high and the crushing defeat which followed must have been hard to accept.

As Celtic began the 1959-60 season, with the previous campaign having fizzled out rather disappointingly, a few notable players made their competitive debuts, including Bobby Carroll, Charlie Gallacher and John Clark. Pat Crerand began to feature alongside Billy McNeill and Bertie Peacock on occasion in the half-back line, preparing for the inevitable departure of Bobby Evans who was, whilst still a fantastically capable footballer, beginning to lose some of the pace and stamina which helped to make him such a special talent. The attacking line remained unpredictable, as players came in and out for most of Celtic's matches that year, as the Hoops rarely fielded the same forward five twice in succession. One of the few players to consistently hold down his starting place throughout the majority of the campaign, save for a few games in the middle of the season, was Divers.

John, alongside other youthful talents such as Bertie Auld and a new kid on the block – who had only made his senior debut a few matches prior to the end of the previous season – Stevie Chalmers, did their best, impressing at points throughout a campaign which was frustrating for the Celts and their supporters. Once again, they had the potential to play some impressive football, and they did so at points, but the regularity with which a section of the team misfired continued to cripple their chances of winning any silverware. For example, it was not uncommon for Celtic to attack well on any given outing, scoring a few goals as they did so, but proceed to draw or lose because the defence played very poorly. Equally, on other days, the defence would stand resolute in the face of an opposition bombardment, but wasteful shooting and substandard passing from the forwards meant the Celts were unable to score at the other end so as to win the game.

As for John, he started the season fairly well, delivering good performances whilst scoring the occasional goal. In mid-November, he netted another hat-trick as the Celts beat Dunfermline Athletic by four goals to two at Celtic Park.

Latterly that season, once he had returned to the starting line-up, John featured in all of Celtic's Scottish Cup ties, as they took three matches to finally vanquish their foes from the previous campaign, St. Mirren. John's contribution proved pivotal in the replay which followed the first tie. This game, which went to extra-time prior to the need for a second replay being confirmed, ended in a four-all draw, and as you would expect the "Evening Times" reported it in typically dramatic style.

"The thirty-eight thousand crowd at Celtic Park last night cheered themselves hoarse as twenty-two heroes, who had reached the heights of physical endeavour, trooped off the field after two hours of non-stop effort in which Celtic and St. Mirren each scored four goals. The Celtic supporters were not only cheering their heroes for having drawn with St. Mirren after all seemed lost, they were cheering the rebirth of Celtic's traditions as cup fighters."

"Last season the same Celtic fans trooped out of Hampden after watching Celtic licked by St. Mirren in the Scottish Cup semi-final. There was little fight in that Celtic side. It was all so different at floodlit Celtic Park last night. The Celtic team started away like champions, galloped to a twenty-five minute lead, missing no end of chances, and then hit real depths in nine horrible Celtic minutes in which St. Mirren built up a three-one interval lead."

"It looked like the end for Celtic, but led by an effervescent Neilly Mochan at centre forward they threw off the shackles of despair and emerged as a team that equalled the greatest Celtic teams in fighting spirit. Before ninety minutes had gone they were level."

At this point, a typically chaotic footballing travesty befell the Celts, putting St. Mirren into the lead again with only minutes to go in the game: "Then came another blow, Kennedy tried to clear a shot eight minutes after the restart of extra time, succeeded only in hitting Bryceland and the ball rebounded against Kennedy's legs before trickling into the Celtic net."

Therefore, the scene was set for John Divers, who had previously scored Celtic's second goal of the evening, to step forward and deny St. Mirren the pleasure of knocking the Celts out of the Scottish Cup for the second year running. The following two quotes from differing Glasgow newspapers describe the Celtic onslaught as they looked for an equaliser, as well as Divers' goal itself.

"But then again the Celts came back. They threw everything but their superb lighting pylons at the St. Mirren defence and just on the one hundred and fifth minute Divers equalised."

"Celtic maintained their will to avoid defeat, and Divers, whose natural strength stood his side in great stead the longer the match lasted, scored the final goal in one hundred and five minutes, having controlled and shot almost in one movement Peacock's lofted free-kick. As the tremendous duel of skill and strength endured to the very end one was glad for both sides' that there was no further goal."

When the second replay of this match finally proceeded on the twenty-ninth of February, Celtic would eventually overcome their opponents via an impressive scoreline of five goals to two. This day will have lived long in the memory of one man in particular, Neil Mochan, who scored all five of Celtic's goals, bagging himself a first half hat-trick before adding to his tally after the break.

Obviously, Divers did not score, but he was still roundly praised by the media men who attended the match and subsequently wrote about it in their respective daily newspapers. The "Glasgow Herald" said: "No doubt they [St. Mirren] now regret the choice of Neilson and McGugan as their wing halves. Colrain and Divers, both strong, thrustful inside-forwards, gave those two a harrowing evening, the pace and strength of Divers in particular overwhelming Neilson."

Despite this victory, Celtic would crash out of the Scottish Cup again, this time losing to Rangers in a comprehensive replay defeat. It could have all been so different for the Celts had John Divers' magnificent header in the first match found the back of the net when Celtic already held a one-nil lead (it was saved stupendously by the Rangers goalkeeper, George Niven), but it was not to be. Although they wouldn't have known it at the time, the Celts – John included – were in the middle of a trophy drought which would last for almost eight years. Yes, the team were to blame at times and yes, those running the Football Club were also, but one contributory factor that must not wholly overlooked was that of bad luck. Nothing seemed to go right for the Hoops, as endless examples of promise and hope inevitably turned to despair. However, this is not to say that there were no good players at Celtic Park, and considering this chapter in particular, this is certainly not to suggest that John Divers was a poor player.

With regards the matter of false promises, the season of 1960-61 was to be equally, if not more harsh on Celtic than the previous campaign. League form improved notably as the Celts increased their points tally and moved up from a ninth place finish to the fourth spot, and they overcame some tricky opponents to reach their first Scottish Cup Final since 1956, but when push came to shove, they would fall again, this time at the final hurdle.

John did not feature in the Scottish Cup Final of 1961 against Dunfermline, the subsequent replay, nor in any match from the middle of February until early May (a little under a fortnight too late to be available for the Final) after he strained his knee ligaments early in the Hoops' second round Scottish Cup tie against Montrose. Whilst his teammates would go on to win that match six-nil, John was simply unable to continue, and it all but spelled an end to his season. However, it is noteworthy that he did manage to return to the first team for the final league fixture against Hearts at home. Celtic lost by three goals to one that day, with neither side playing for anything other than pride, but John did announce his return with a conciliatory goal after "a magnificent run".

Thereafter, as the 1962-63 season began, John solidified his place in the starting line-up once more. The forward line now had a distinctly different look to it, as the departures of figures such as Bertie Auld and Willie Fernie opened up spaces for which others could then compete. It is worth bearing in mind that at this stage John Divers was still only twenty-one years old, and therefore you may be impressed to discover than he played well enough that year to maintain his place in every single starting line-up in the league and both major cup competitions for the entire season.

During this campaign, John scored twenty-five goals in forty-six appearances for Celtic, helping the Hoops to a third place league finish (with an improved points total once again) and another disappointing Scottish Cup semi-final exit. Whilst Celtic opened up their league campaign with a loss, a win, and then a draw, Divers opened his account with a goal on each of the three occasions, the third of which came at Ibrox Park. In mid-December, John would score his second hat-trick for the Celts, as they twice came from behind to beat Hibernian by four goals to three at Celtic Park. This trio was completed with "the most spectacular goal of what was a great day", which arrived with about ten minutes of the tie remaining, to make sure the points would be staying firmly at Celtic Park.

When a potential win in the New Year Derby (which was cancelled due to bad weather) could have sparked Celtic on to bigger and better things that season, riding on a wave of belief and confidence, the reality was that, without the derby, they drew their next two matches, dropping three points in January alone. I should highlight that, even prior to these results, it would have taken an optimistic Celtic fan to think we stood a chance of winning the league. Yes, we had won all eight of our home matches going into the New Year, and our away record appeared to be improving, but like the rest of the pack, we were a large distance behind league leaders Dundee who, although they wouldn't win the league by quite such an extensive margin when the campaign was over, were still well ahead of their competitors at the turn of the year, in seemingly imperious form.

Celtic would eventually fall at the Scottish Cup's semi-final stage once more in 1962, thus dismissing any prospect of ending the continually lengthening trophy drought at Celtic Park. During the following campaign, that of 1962-63, Celtic and John Divers would be introduced to an arena in which they had never before had the chance to take part – European football. They would face tough opponents in the form Spanish side Valencia, and after a four-two loss on the continent in the first leg – in which John Divers did not feature – hopes were high that the Celts could redeem themselves in Glasgow. However, despite John's endeavours as he led the attack having been given the role of centre forward, the Celts were unable to progress. This effort was not helped much when Divers won an early penalty which John Clark proceeded to send high over the crossbar. Despite this, the Hoops did actually take the lead via an own goal, but poor defending, coupled with the talent of the Spaniards, meant Valencia equalised before taking the lead on the night with a little less than ten minutes remaining. Celtic were able to restore some pride by equalising late on, but Valencia, who would eventually go on to win the competition that year, were fairly comfortable winners on an evening when many felt they had been there for the taking.

Only a few days after the aggregate defeat to Valencia, Celtic travelled to Broomfield where they beat Airdrie by six goals to one, with John Divers grabbing his third hat-trick for the Celts. John continued to impress as the season went on, chipping in with the odd goal and often assisting his teammates in setting up their net bound efforts for them. However, unlike the previous season, Divers was not to be an ever-present name on the Celtic team sheet throughout 1962-63. With another influx of youth, one begins to see new names, some of which are instantly recognisable (such as Tommy Gemmell and Jimmy Johnstone), appear in the Celts' line-ups that year, even if it was just on a rare occasion.

One famous story was that as Celtic travelled to Parkhead at the start of the domestic campaign to take on Hearts in the League Cup, John Divers made a critical error which would be almost impossible for a Celtic player nowadays – he forgot his boots. Subsequently, he was informed a few minutes before kick-off that, as punishment, he would not feature that day, and his starting place was given to a sprightly youngster, but more about him in a moment.

The sorry saga which followed was not only played out behind closed doors at Celtic Park, but also amongst the support and, naturally, the Scottish sports media. One article which discussed this affair, which was published prominently in "The Evening Times" (taking up half a page in the sports section), said the following.

"Were Celtic right to leave Johnny Divers out of the team on Saturday because he turned up bootless at Parkhead? Or was it a foolhardy risk to in the very first match of the season in which Celtic are expecting to break through to the real big time in the game? The fans of the "grand old team to play for" have been arguing that one out since the news came out that Divers did not play because he left the tools of his trade at home when he set off for the ground. My verdict – the Celtic decision was bold, brave, and one hundred per cent right."

"I can just hear Mr. Bob Kelly, the Celtic Chairman, when he heard that after all their great preparation for the new season, one of his stars had turned up minus the most important item in his equipment. This is by no means the first time Celtic have left a fit player on the sidelines minutes before a kick-off. A few seasons ago Bertie Auld missed the team bus to Edinburgh when the side were due to play against the same Hearts. Auld, with the help of a taxi and a fast driver, caught up with the other players at lunch time. Sentence for unpunctuality – no game. The Celtic attitude is the right one. They pay good wages and they are entitled to expect nothing less than a one hundred per cent response from their staff. Fortunately for Divers and the club, the boot business did not prove fatal for Celtic."

Returning to the subject of the youngster who replaced John at inside-left, he opened Celtic's goalscoring account for the season after only seven minutes that day: "The strange reading forward line of Lennox, Gallagher, Hughes, Murdoch and Byrne went out and played Hearts off the park. The young Bobby Murdoch does not have his name up in lights and headlines tonight – but he made a most satisfactory debut. For a youngster, pitched in quick, he did a very fair job. Apart from his noticeable natural ability, the thing I liked most about this new first-team man was his astonishing calmness on the field. Not for him the dash all over the field and the quick, excited boot at the ball. He took his time, weighed up the position, and then made his pass or shot."

As is discussed previously, John Divers did force his way back into several starting line-ups after this sorry incident – never forgetting his boots again – but often now he would play alongside Bobby Murdoch, who never really looked back from his impressive debut at Celtic Park. Having been beaten twice by Rangers on league duty, few gave Celtic much of a chance as they met their rivals in the Scottish Cup Final at Hampden in May. Whilst the

Celts had not improved much on their previous season in terms of league performance, Rangers had rediscovered their form, winning the division comfortably.

The Scottish Cup Final of 1963 was a rather dull affair, a poor game played in dreary weather by all accounts. The Celtic goal-keeper, Frank Haffey, was described as having "the game of his life" as Rangers created an almost endless stream of chances, some of which were wastefully sent off target and others heroically saved by the Celtic stopper. Two goals were scored that day though, one for each side, as Rangers took the lead before Murdoch levelled things later on. A draw, of course, meant a replay, which took place eleven days later and the controversy caused by this affair was to rock the Celtic support to its core.

Before we discuss that, I feel it is worthy of mention that Rangers won the replay at a footballing canter, which would have hurt the Celtic support by itself, without the added revelations which would follow. Gair Henderson describes a poor Celtic performance, before questioning the cause of much consternation, their team selection.

"No howl of protest would have gone up at Hampden last night if the referee had stopped this one eleven minutes before the end – stopped it to save the Scottish Cup Final losers Celtic from further punishment. The Celtic supporters who remained on the east terracing, and there were precious few of them – would have regarded an "early closing night" as an act of mercy, for seldom can a Celtic side have been so outplayed from start to finish of any match. Rangers won three-nil, but if they had run up seven goals and removed for all time that seven-one League Cup final stain of 1957, no one would have claimed they were flattered by the score."

"The simple fact of the replay is that Celtic were outclassed in almost every position on the field, and the mass exodus of their supporters just after half-time was not so much criticism of the men on the field but bitter protest against the men who thought up the forward permutation. Before the kick-off Celtic's management had announced their attack as Murdoch and Craig; Hughes; Divers and Chalmers. That looked almost, but not quite, the best line-up inside Parkhead but, incredibly, someone managed to change around every one of the forwards. When they came out onto the field the line read from right to left – Craig and Murdoch; Divers; Chalmers and Hughes; and never has any Celtic forward line put on such a hopeless and futile show for their fans."

Plainly speaking, it was decisions such as this which only reinforced the belief within the Celtic support of that time that it was not always the Club's manager Jimmy McGrory choosing the starting line-up for upcoming matches – especially those of a prominent nature – but Chairman Robert Kelly. To move each forward player from one of his regular positions to those they were less comfortable with was experimental, to say the least. It was certainly not the kind of move any football manager would consider for a replayed Cup Final anyway.

Having said that, it was not just the positioning of the players that infuriated supporters, but also the team line-up itself. Whilst no changes were made to the midfield, the defence, nor the man between the posts, both forward wingers who had featured in the first final (Jimmy Johnstone and Frank Brogan) were dropped without any obvious cause. This was hinted at by Henderson, who questioned why the young Johnstone was left out of proceedings: "The biggest mystery of all was the playing of Bobby Craig at outside-right in preference to the daring and lively Jimmy Johnstone."

For John Divers and his Celtic teammates though, their defeat at Hampden Park would have been difficult to accept. There was undoubtedly talent in the side, with more coming through as the years went by – but they still seemed to lack the consistency, discipline and organisation it would take to win a trophy once again – especially at a time when, on the whole, the quality of the average Scottish football team was perhaps at its zenith. Sadly though, whilst all of those attributes, as well as many more would come to the Football Club in time, bringing with them tremendous success the likes of which the Celtic supporters who stormed out of Hampden Park on that galling May night in 1963 could barely have dreamt of, it would all arrive too late for John.

The following campaign, that of 1963-64, was to see John Divers' last serious involvement in a Celtic shirt, for although he would remain a Celtic player until the end of the 1965-66 season, he would not see any semblance of regular football once Jock Stein arrived to take up the role of Celtic Football Club's fourth manager.

Whilst the Hoops would once again finish the season without a trophy when 1963-64 came to an end – and Rangers had won a second domestic treble – this often forgotten campaign very nearly became one of the most significant in our history, for only a freak away result stopped Celtic from participating in their first European Final. Yes, while Rangers were out of Europe in early October having received a footballing lesson from the mighty Real Madrid, Celtic made it to the last four of the European Cup Winners' Cup, surviving until the end of April.

Considering the Celts' had never made it past the first round of a European competition previously, this was some feat in itself. They began their campaign with a comfortable five-one away win in Switzerland against F.C. Basle which, coincidentally, was the scoreline the last time the two sides had met, away back in 1911. Having opened his goalscoring account for the season only a few days earlier against Third Lanark, John Divers carried on this form by netting Celtic's first goal that day, as the "Glasgow Herald" describes: "Divers, the best forward afield, opened the scoring after twenty-one minutes when he broke through a wall of defenders and deceived Stettler with a twelve yard shot."

A few weeks later, the Swiss side travelled to Glasgow and, once again, they conceded five goals amidst some of the worst weather conditions in which a football match had been played for some time. For this reason, more than five decades on, this tie still holds the record for the lowest home crowd of any of Celtic's European matches. The "Evening Times" of the following day said: "Celtic's heroes in the five-nil European Cup Winners' Cup romp against Basle last night were not the players but the eight thousand fans who deserted home comforts in a night of gale and storm to watch the game at Celtic Park. Surely no-one but the staunchest of football fans would have made such a sacrifice. Consider the facts. Apart from the weather, Celtic had a five-one lead from the first leg in Basle and the Swiss had landed in

Glasgow minus four of their top stars – hardly the situation to attract a big following to Celtic Park. But the gallant eight thousand came."

On that soaking wet night in Glasgow, John Divers scored twice, the first of which is described as follows: "It was three minutes from half-time before Celtic scored again, but it was the best goal of the game. Divers picked up a loose ball, beat two men, and from twenty-five yards hit a low, hard shot." With this, the Celts eased past Basle by ten goals to one on aggregate. It is also worthy of note John Divers became the first Celtic player to score in both legs of a European tie on that miserable night.

Later in the month of October, John scored a hat-trick against Airdrieonians, and he would continue to hold down a place in the Celtic team, both domestically and in European competition, until the spring. During this time, the Celts dispatched Dinamo Zagreb and Slovan Bratislava, soon finding themselves as the only remaining British side in European competition. A couple of weeks later, Celtic drew one-all with St. Johnstone, and John Divers made his final appearance of that season for the Hoops. Presumably, he must have suffered some sort of injury on this occasion, for newspaper reports around ten days later say he is "unfit" to play in the upcoming semi-final against M.T.K. Hungaria in Glasgow. Regardless, John's absence did not hamper his teammates' home performance, for they won by three goals to nil and hence took a healthy lead to Hungary for the second leg. However, the Hoops suffered a disastrous four-nil defeat on the continent, and thus missed out on their chance to appear in a European Final for the first time. To say this loss was due to the absence of John would be a massive exaggeration, for calamitous defending combined with an impressive performance from the home side (as well as a smidgeon of bad luck for good measure) were the main contributory factors to Celtic's demise. This young side had shown tremendous promise, but they had not been able to fulfil it as yet.

Similarly, at the start of the 1964-65 campaign, Rangers travelled to Celtic Park for the Hoops' first home tie of the season. John Divers did feature that day, but it was some of the men who would become Lisbon Lions, like Chalmers and Johnstone, who really shone as Celtic beat their rivals for the first time since August 1960.

As the season progressed, John's first team appearances became increasingly sporadic in nature. Three league outings in October, during which he scored three goals, as well as a brief run of matches just after the New Year were about the total of Divers' contributions that season. He had featured in all three derby matches against Rangers, which included an away league defeat and a League Cup Final loss as well as the early season victory, but that was the sum of it. He did not take part in any of Celtic's four European matches, nor was he to have any impact in Celtic's run to the Scottish Cup Final and subsequent victory therein.

This was a great shame in many senses for John, for he had been with the Club throughout a large portion of the Celts' barren spell and yet he was not given the opportunity to play in a single one of the ties which finally ended the drought, as the Celts finally emerged from the proverbial desert. As I have mentioned previously, this was due not to a lack of individual ability on John's part, but to the increasing prowess of his colleagues. John Divers was a very capable young footballer, but the new crop of talent, featuring the likes of Jimmy Johnstone, Bobby Lennox and Bobby Murdoch limited his chances to make first team appearances. The return of Bertie Auld in January 1965 only worsened matters, as he immediately secured one of the starting places in Celtic's forward line, pushing John Divers further down the pecking order.

A once ever-present Celtic player, with the arrival of Jock Stein and the resurgence of a Football Club most firmly on the rise, was now largely left behind in footballing terms. He was given a handful of outings at the start of the 1965-66 season, but these were to be his last with Celtic Football Club. He made his final appearance for the Hoops in a derby defeat to Rangers at Ibrox in September 1965, but would not officially leave the Club until the end of that campaign.

John Divers scored one hundred and two goals in two hundred and thirty-two league and cup appearances during a stint with the Parkhead Club which lasted a little under a decade. Now,

I'm sure you would all agree this is an admirable record, but in the Celtic ranks of the 1960s and 1970s, such tallies were to become fairly common. However, if I may, I would like to make particular mention of John's final league goal, which came on the twenty-fifth of August 1965, as Celtic eased past Dundee United at Tannadice by virtue of a four-nil scoreline.

The "Glasgow Herald" made a brief mention of this strike: "There was a champagne quality about the play of this latest Celtic blend. Victory was the product of teamwork, and they were an impressive balance of speed, skill and spirit. Their defensive covering allowed United only three potential scoring shots. The Parkhead forwards, backed by a defence that moved swiftly out of retreat, performed with a directness that eventually told, and Divers was their powerful contributor in the first half. By contrast, United proceeded with steadied leisure that in the end never justified itself. Celtic went ahead in thirteen minutes when McBride squared swiftly and Divers shot through a narrow opening into the net from twelve yards."

Of course, there was no mention in any newspaper, nor any other form of media of the true significance of that goal at the time. In fact, this would only become apparent almost a decade later, for it was John Divers' strike which set Celtic on a course which was to lead them to a then unrivalled nine Scottish League Championship titles in a row. In this regard, John's name will live forever, as he finally contributed, albeit in a small manner, to a trophy which Celtic won, after nine valiant years of effort.

Sadly, John Divers would no longer be a Celtic player by the time the league flag returned to Celtic Park, for he was released by the Club only a matter of days before the title was secured. In September 1966, he signed for Partick Thistle and there he would remain until 1969 when he left for Strathclyde University. He studied whilst also playing for their football team, before retiring from the game in 1970. Thereafter, John became Mr. Divers to many, as he enjoyed over three decades in the field of education as a secondary school teacher. The majority of this period was spent at Our Lady and St. Patrick's in Dumbarton, where he was a popular and much loved figure.

Regardless, I feel that John Divers (or "John the Third") should be remembered as perhaps the best of the three Celts to have held the name, and most definitely as a determined, talented Celt. In another era, when Celtic were not quite so good, I have no doubt in saying he would have stayed with the Club for longer than he did, making more appearances and scoring more goals than he was given the chance to do – oh, how the Celtic of the late 1940s would have loved to have a player like him in their ranks, for example.

John Divers passed away on the twenty-third of September 2014, at the age of seventy-four. In the days following his death, the "Glasgow Herald" astutely highlighted that "John Divers [Jr.]... John Divers Sr., and Patsy Gallagher...Three men from the same bloodline, played more than one thousand games and scored more than four hundred goals for Glasgow Celtic [between them]."

However, ignoring family ties and focusing purely on the three men discussed in this book linked by name alone, it is abundantly clear that all three John Divers to have played for Celtic brought unique talents and attributes to Parkhead. They may not be the most famous Celts of all time, but their individual contributions to three wholly different eras in the Club's history make them all very worthy of our admiration and respect.

"The Chronicles of Willie Maley: "The Bould, Bould Celts""

"By Willie Maley, Celtic F.C. Manager"

"The close of the actual season of 1888-89 did not mean the finish of football for the Celtic, and until July of 1889 the team played a lot of unofficial games, chiefly to benefit charities or country clubs. Just to give one item of history, the Celts sent a fairly strong team to Neilston to play a charity game, and got beaten by four to three. [Arthurlie's] defeat of our team in a Scottish Cup tie is still paraded in the Answers to the Correspondents [section of newspapers] every few weeks, had not the honour of being the first Renfrewshire team to defeat the "bould, bould Celts."

"Again teams composed of the celebrities from the leading teams went all around Scotland, playing exhibition games against the locals, and I, like others, often thought these matches were "means to an end." The gate drawings were, as a rule, divided between the teams, making the suggestion quite feasible."

"The Association also took some of their International teams on tour to spread the light, and I remember one special trip to Aberdeen, where the English International team of that year had a great time of it before the record gate for Aberdeen up to that date of £59 11s. One of the funniest items of that tour, showing the "make yourself at home" style of the touring clubs of that day, was a raid through the night on this hotel larder by McLaren and company, resulting in a midnight feed and the consternation of the proprietor in the morning when he found his table supplies had mysteriously vanished."

"We won another Cup that year. We got entered somehow in a second XI competition for the Kilsyth Charity Cup, in which we met Renton, Kilsyth Wanderers, and one or two other teams. We had a fairly strong team, strengthened by Dowds, Jerry Reynolds (from Carfin) and myself, and won by five goals in the final, in which I got nearly finished by the [tough] centre half of the Kilsyth Wanderers, in which I think Patrick (later to join St. Mirren) played goal against us. This cup was a great joke with us for a long time. The cup had never been seen by any of us until the presentation, and quite proudly John Glass came out with us to the ceremony. The joke will be understood when I say Glass carried the cup home in his jacket pocket. I believe it was stolen out of Glass' house not long after that, and I am afraid the thief would get as big a disappointment as we did then. It was another cup, however, Glass used to say."

"An Amateur Sprinter"

"I ran a good deal at amateur sports that season, as did my brother Tom, but as he went in for regular training, whilst I mixed mine with football playing, I did not do much good. Tom, however, had a great season, and won a heap of prizes. He broke the two hundred and twenty yards' record at St. Mirren sports, for which he had been specially trained, but the powers that be would not pass it [accept it as an official record]. Celtic stock was not in favour then. His best performance that year was in the Clydesdale Harriers' sports in June at Ibrox, where he won the open one hundred and two hundred and twenty yards' races from virtual scratch. If Tom had applied himself properly to the game, I am certain he would have won the championship that year, but he never could stick to training. I remember him running once at Hampden in an evening meeting, in which I also competed. I was put out early in the one hundred yards' heats, Tom coming on much later. I was getting dressed, when Arthur Geake rushed into me and said that someone told him Tom had burst a blood vessel and was spitting up blood. I dashed out to see Tom sitting on the grass at the finishing post. When I got to him and asked him what was wrong, he looked up and told me he had been sick, as he had to rush from school to get up in time. He had a feed of cherries on the way, and with a "return to the light" of the red cherries someone had imagined the worst."

"A Celt of Tremendous Character"

Celtic Football Club have competed in all manner of friendly competitions and tournaments over the years, ranging from those which were taken tremendously seriously to others where the results were considered largely meaningless. Equally, our relevant participations therein have culminated in everything from remarkable victories to disappointing defeats. Thankfully, it has been many decades since the Club has been involved in a tournament specifically scheduled to mark the end of national wartime or to raise funds during a conflict. Perhaps I am idealistic, but I for one hope there is never any need for Celtic or any other teams to compete in such post-war fixtures again.

Regardless, such opinions do not mean we should simply ignore the stories of the tournaments such as these which have taken place in the past. After all, Celtic did enjoy some successes in this sense, winning both the "Navy and Army War Fund Shield" (defeating Queen's Park, Clydebank and Morton in the process in 1918) and the "Victory in Europe Cup" (overcoming Queen's Park by a single corner kick after Rangers declined their invite to participate in 1945).

Of course, with a few notable exceptions, such as the Empire Exhibition tournament of 1938 and the Coronation Cup of 1953, thoughts and tales of most one-off competitions tend to retreat with some pace towards the rear of supporters' minds. In this regard, the "Victory Cup" of 1946 is not alone and yet, as happens so often, when you begin to peel back the layers, you discover there is actually far more to the "Victory Cup" than may first meet the eye.

Firstly, to all intents and purposes, Celtic have actually won this "one-off" tournament on fifteen occasions (at the time of writing), with our last triumph arriving in 2015. Ironically, it was only that victory in the Cup Final over Dundee United which brought our success rate in such matches back up to fifty percent.

Prior to that fixture and the goals from Kris Commons and James Forrest, the Celts had actually lost more of these finals than they had won. Yes, the aforementioned "Victory Cup" is essentially the same tournament which we all refer to nowadays as the "Scottish League Cup".

With its origins steeped in one of several regional competitions put in place during the Second World War, it was initially known as the "Southern League Cup", beginning its life in 1940 before – officially – coming to a halt in 1946. During this time, Rangers won the tournament on four occasions, finishing as runners-up in the other two years. Celtic never even reached one of these finals, so you would be forgiven for wondering where I am going with this, but stay with me. Simply because the history of this competition may not appear to be a big issue for Celtic does not mean it is irrelevant, and it most certainly remains a bone of contention for the fans of the only other Scottish football club never to have known life outside of the country's top division, Aberdeen.

To cut a long story short, the "Southern League Cup" was only truly a southern competition from its inception until 1944-45. Of course, World War Two came to an end in Europe on the eighth of May 1945, with the conflict only officially ceasing in the Pacific theatre with the unconditional surrender of Japan a little over three months later. For this reason, coupled with the fact Scotland would take some time to truly recover and find its peacetime feet once more, competitive football did not begin in officialdom here until the 1946-47 season. However, with no more Nazi air raids or missile strikes to worry about, black out and travel restrictions in the United Kingdom were lifted around a year earlier, meaning sides from all over the country could face each other once again.

With this in mind, the number of teams participating in the "Southern League Cup" doubled in 1946 from that which had done so in 1945, and for the first time a very credible argument could be made to say that the tournament was no longer a regional competition in anything other than name, but a national one. As such, the winners of the tournament – Aberdeen, who beat Rangers in the final – are right to feel aggrieved that, to this day, they are officially denied what was in truth their first piece of major silverware.

Adding insult to injury for the thousands who made up the Aberdeen faithful at that time, they would lose the first official Scottish League Cup Final to Rangers a year later in 1947, but it gets worse for those of a red persuasion. Incredibly, having won the Southern League Cup in the May of 1946, the northern side were promptly ordered to hand the trophy back to the Scottish Football Association so that it could become the prize for their one-off "Victory Cup" tournament. The trophy would not see the inside of Aberdeen's boardroom again until October 1955, almost a decade later, when it would finally be allowed to stay long enough to gather a modicum of dust.

Therefore, the "Victory Cup" will always be a contentious issue for many Aberdeen fans – after all some would speculate the tournament was only really staged in order to appease Rangers who had missed the previous such competition (albeit by it choice) – and yet for those of us who support the Celts, the "Victory Cup" will always have more sinister connotations for the personal effect it had on the man who was then one of our finest representatives, the indomitable George Paterson.

Born on the twenty-sixth of September 1914 in the small town of Denny near Falkirk, George Denholm Paterson emerged into a world gripped by its first global conflict. Less than two months previous, the Great War had begun, and fighting would not cease until after his fourth birthday. Relatively little appears to be known of George's early life, save for the fact he was clearly a talented footballer, plying his trade – and impressing – with Denny High School, Denny Y.M.C.A., Carrowbank Juveniles and Dunipace Juveniles before finally signing for Celtic in the spring of 1932.

Standing at around five feet and seven inches in height and weighing a little over eleven stones, it could be said that George was born to be a half-back, coupling mobility with strength. Shortly after the first anniversary of his signing for Celtic, the name "Paterson" would appear on a Celtic team sheet for the first time as George, aged only nineteen, made his competitive debut in a Scottish League match against Airdrieonians.

Coming only days after Celtic's Scottish Cup Final triumph against Motherwell, Paterson replaced the injured Jimmy McGrory, one of the greatest strikers of all time, for what would be the Celts' last home match of their league campaign. However George, still playing as a centre forward at this the earliest stage of his professional career, seemingly took everything in his stride, scoring the first of the home side's goals in a narrow two-one win in the East End of Glasgow. His goal was described in "The Scotsman" newspaper: "Celtic were without Kennaway, McGrory and Napier in this, their last home league engagement, last evening. Playing with the assistance of a strong wind, Airdrie were soon attacking, but the home backs were safe. The visitors were keen, and Connor took a lot of watching, although each time Celtic got near the Airdrie goal they were extremely dangerous. H. O'Donnell was given a great opportunity to open the scoring when he was allowed to travel goalwards without opposition, while the visitors defence stood claiming off-side against Paterson. The winger got close in and shot, but Morrison saved, and O'Donnell shot past from the rebound. A minute later, however, he made amends by sending over a fine cross which Paterson headed through, the ball striking the post and the goalkeeper before entering the net. This was ten minutes before the interval."

Therefore, only thirty-five minutes into his Celtic career, George had opened his goalscoring account at Parkhead. Nobody would have known then that these goals would become collector's items of sorts, with Paterson only adding another seventeen to his tally over the next thirteen years or so. Of course, his positional change would account for that to a large degree but no matter, a fine young man had just taken his first steps with the team he would go on to serve with ability, distinction and faith.

Celtic finished fourth in the league table that year, a little behind third placed Heart of Midlothian and some distance away from runners-up Motherwell and champions Rangers. George featured once more in Celtic's last game of the season away at Dens Park, but neither he nor many of his teammates gained any plaudits for their respective performances, with the visitors suffering a disappointing three-nil defeat. In truth, with the benefit of hindsight, Celtic had done well to win the Scottish Cup in what had been a mediocre season otherwise, and to do so by keeping a clean sheet against Motherwell (the highest scoring league side during that campaign with a remarkable one hundred and fourteen goals scored) was particularly impressive.

The next season, that of 1933-34, saw George make only one senior appearance as Celtic took on Rangers in the replay of the semi-final of the Glasgow Cup. Celtic would go on to lose by two goals to one that day, much to the dismay of everyone associated with the Club. Whilst newspaper reports highlight the scrappy, unkempt nature of large parts of the match, it appears that Rangers edged the tie in terms of performance. The members of their forward line, particularly Robert "Bobby" Main (a winger who spent over a decade at Ibrox) and Alex Stevenson (an inside-left born in Dublin who played for the Irish Free State and later went on to manage the Republic of Ireland), were praised very highly by the football correspondents of the time.

Notably, the latter of these two men was the only individual in almost a century (1916-2013) born in what is now the Republic of Ireland to play for an Ibrox club. It was only the arrival of Jon Daly which stopped this record from growing in magnitude.

Regardless, whilst the half-backs and full-backs of Celtic struggled to contain the in-form Rangers attack on that day in 1933, the Celts forward line were not enjoying much success themselves. A report from "The Scotsman" read: "Celtic are trying to form a new forward line; it is a difficult problem. They have energy in plenty, but more guile is required."

It is of no coincidence then, especially without the presence of a gradually aging yet still very dangerous McGrory, that a transitional forward line would struggle away from home against the side who were, at that point in time, the best team in the country. Despite this, flickers of Paterson's potential (as well as that of the side as a whole) were evident, as the same article later said, "Celtic had punch, however, and it was only a splendid save by Dawson which stopped a shot from Paterson following the free kick..."

Ironically, having survived several waves of Rangers' attacks, Celtic held their opponents to a one apiece scoreline until five minutes from the end of the match, when a scruffy shot beat the Celts' keeper before bobbling over the line only to be cleared as it did so. The away side protested the referee's decision, but the goal stood and thus Rangers progressed to the final. To be fair, it must be said that newspaper reports of the time do back up the opinion that the referee, Mr. H. Watson, made the correct call. However, what is clear is that George Paterson had just endured a somewhat controversial defeat to Rangers, perhaps signifying a key episode en route to the events of the "Victory Cup" well over a decade later.

Throughout the remainder of the season, George would not make any further competitive appearances for the Celts, who eventually finished the campaign third in the league table, with a sizeable margin of nineteen points separating them from first place finishers Rangers. Approximately one month on from the cessation of this season though, George reappeared in the senior side for a friendly against a North of France select side – a game which Celtic lost by four goals to two.

Whilst on their trip to the continent, which totalled a little less than a week in length, the players and officials of Celtic Football Club visited the scenes of some of the most intense fighting of the Great War, touring the battlefields before attending a luncheon in Ypres, a short distance across the border in Belgium. They then returned to France, where the friendly match was played outside Lille. The impact of Paterson's visit to these battlefields remains unclear, but it is likely it had some effect on the young man.

As the summer passed, it was soon time for the new football season to kick-off. George may well have been hopeful of inclusion in the Celts' first league squad of the campaign (a four-one win at home to Kilmarnock) but as previously, his potential slot was filled by William Hughes. However, George wouldn't have to wait long for the sustained first team football which he desired.

Paterson would make his first appearance of the 1934-35 season in what turned out to be a remarkably feisty encounter with Heart of Midlothian at Tynecastle. In a match which saw the debut of a youngster by the name of Jimmy Delaney, over thirty-thousand spectators packed the stands and terracing hoping to see a fine game. Thus, despite the fact the tie finished as a goalless draw, that is what they were treated to, with "The Scotsman" newspaper describing proceedings as "fast and exciting" in their match report which was published on the following Monday.

The article continued, making reference to the nastier events of the day: "A few "incidents" enlivened the second half. After Harkness had made a brilliant clearance Reid and H. O'Donnell almost came to blows and had to be lectured by the referee. Later, Paterson of the Celtic went down heavily and caused the referee to interrupt a promising Hearts' attack. When the player leapt to his feet apparently unhurt, there was a noisy demonstration, and quarrelling at the south-west corner of the field led to some of the crowd leaping the barrier. The police shepherded them back, and play was not interrupted." As for Paterson himself, he received fair praise for his performance alongside his colleagues, with the "Glasgow Herald" saying: "The drastic changes in the composition of Celtic's team were of vital interest. All the newcomers played with great zest, and it was this dash which rattled Hearts. Delaney showed distinct promise on the wing, and Dawson and Paterson merited further trial."

In the coming weeks, George would enjoy "further trial" as the previous report dubbed it, featuring in the two remaining league games of the month of August (away to Motherwell and home to St. Johnstone respectively) as well as playing in Jimmy McGrory's benefit match against Rangers. Subsequently, after Celtic had failed to win any of these fixtures – although the result of the latter was of little serious consequence – Paterson dropped out of the side for a period of eight matches (including two derbies) with William Hughes temporarily clinging on to his starting position. At this point in time, Maley was clearly caught in a dilemma of sorts regarding his team selection. Of the eight matches previously referenced, Celtic only managed to attain three victories therein, and after their fourth defeat of September arrived away against Albion Rovers at Cliftonhill, the longest serving Celtic manager of all time decided to try the young George Paterson at left-half once more.

In the following away league tie against Dundee, the earliest benefits of this decision began to show. Celtic kept only their fourth league clean sheet thus far, two of which had come when Paterson was last present in the side. Sadly though, thanks to Celtic's inability to score themselves, the match ended goalless, but it was clear Paterson's presence had positive effects, with the "Glasgow Herald" saying: "Celtic would extract the greater satisfaction from the game, as there was a suggestion of better team balance than in many recent matches. Particular improvement was evident at half-back, where Geatons had one of his best days and both Paterson and Napier let little past them."

It would take another fortnight for George Paterson to enjoy only his second victory as a senior Celtic player (from nine attempts, the only other being his debut) as the Celts beat Clyde away. This match also saw the return of Jimmy McGrory to the side, who had not featured since the four-two loss to Hamilton almost a month earlier due to injury.

From here on in, Celtic found their form and began to steadily climb the table, going on a run of nine straight victories. Paterson, who scored four penalties during this spell, enjoyed fine personal form and went on to hold his place in the Celtic side for the remainder of the league season. Discussing a four-two away victory against St. Mirren towards the end of this streak, "The Scotsman" said of George's prowess from twelve yards: "Two of the Celtic goals – one each half – resulted from penalty kicks. These came about through St. Mirren defenders downing opposing forwards. Paterson was the man entrusted with the kicks, and he made no mistake." In all, George scored eight goals during the 1934-35 season – all of which came from the penalty spot – and this would represent his best ever goals tally for any given campaign come the eventual end of his career.

During the 1935-36 season, George Paterson would miss only a couple of Celtic's thirty-eight league matches. In the course of time, the Celts would come good that year but matters most certainly began in disappointing fashion as Celtic slumped to a three-one defeat at Pittodrie on the opening day of the season.

Despite a poor showing from Celtic at the edge of the North Sea, the debut of a young half-back signed from Queen's Park, Willie Lyon (a man whom I discussed in more detail in my first book) would prove pivotal. Previously, Paterson and Geatons had essentially established themselves as Maley's first choice left and right halves respectively, but the long serving manager had, up until that point, struggled to find any truly worthy replacement at centre-half since the departure of the legendary Jimmy McStay (who, of course, would eventually succeed Maley as the second Celtic manager) in the summer of 1934. However, personified in the twenty-three year old Lyon, he had found that which he had been seeking. Equally, twenty-eight year old Geatons and his compatriot Paterson, still only twenty-one, had found a fine partner indeed.

Thus, having suffered their opening day defeat at Aberdeen on the fourth of August, Celtic, with their newly formed half-back trio, would not lose again until over four months had passed, eventually succumbing to Dunfermline Athletic in the middle of December by a single goal. In September, after racking up seven consecutive victories, the Celts would travel to Ibrox to face champions Rangers, a side whom they had not beaten on their own turf in the league for fifteen years. Celtic would go into the tie without Jimmy McGrory, who was again injured, and when one considers the fact Rangers had previously scored thirty goals in eight matches until that point (an average of almost four per game), it is clear the visitors would have quite a task at hand.

However, the Celts would take all of this pressure and speculation in their stride, ultimately delivering one of their finest derby performances in many years. In a hotly contested match, the first half came and went without any score. However, the tie ignited less than five minutes after the interval when the home side took the lead. A determined Celtic soon showed their resilience though, equalising from a corner only a few moments later. The visitors would then go on to take the lead approximately fifteen minutes from the end, before Celtic goalkeeper Joe Kennaway saved a penalty just prior to full time to secure a vital win for his team. Heaps of praise were lavished upon the Celtic players in the hours and days which followed, the half-backs being no different from the rest in this regard.

"The Scotsman" described the tackling from each side that day as "intensely keen", before proceeding to make specific reference to George, saying: "Both teams were well served in defence. Paterson was a clever, forcing half-back for Celtic". Equally, the "Glasgow Herald" said his colleagues Lyons and Geatons "played a big part" in Celtic's victory, the end of which was marked by a pitch invasion of jubilant travelling supporters.

It may sound somewhat clichéd, but this win must have given the Celtic players (as well as the fans) a tremendous amount of belief back in the autumn of 1935. It had been a decade since the Club were last Champions of Scotland, with an aging McGrory the only remaining first team player from that time. The Celts had been gradually climbing the table with passing seasons, but to knock a fairly dominant Rangers side – who had won eight of the last nine league titles – off of their perch by actually winning the Championship once again was an entirely different prospect altogether.

Yet, that was exactly what Celtic would go on to do. Not only would they top the table, dropping points on only six occasions throughout the entire season, they did so in an impressive style, scoring more goals and conceding less than any other team. In two years, they had shaved twenty goals off of those which they conceded in a single season, culminating in the league winning campaign where they averaged less than one goal conceded per match. Also, this record becomes all the more impressive when we consider the fact Celtic conceded thirteen of these thirty-three goals in four matches, meaning they only gave away twenty goals to their opponents in the other thirty-four ties. Likewise, matters also improved going forward, with the Hoops scoring thirty-seven more goals in 1935-36 than they had done two years earlier (one hundred and fifteen in all).

Now, credit for this title win must go to all areas – and members – of the Celtic squad of the time. After all, to win a League Championship, you must have the best overall record of all the clubs, and this can only be achieved via a joint effort from all involved. In saying that, the role of Celtic's half-back line cannot be underestimated when we consider the success of the 1935-36 league campaign. Geatons, Lyon and Paterson were integral, embodying the linchpin which held the defensive structure of the side together whilst also providing the launch pad for many of the team's attacking movements. Even back in the 1930s, both winning the ball back from your opponents and effective retention of it thereafter were critical attributes to successful sides, and the Celts' half-back trio most certainly possessed them in abundance.

The following year, Celtic would surrender the league title to their rivals once again, conceding more often and scoring less than they had done by a considerable margin compared to their record of the previous season. Several factors can be attributed to this, with a continued reliance on Jimmy McGrory – now thirty-two – for goals, combined with less being scored by other players and also occasional changes to defensive and goalkeeping selections.

However, Celtic did go on to win the Scottish Cup of 1937, defeating Aberdeen in that famous final before the biggest crowd ever to officially attend a European club match. Whilst Chic Geatons took the majority of the half-back plaudits that day – having had one of the games of his life and being described as "faultless" by one newspaper reporter – George Paterson also received much credit, notably from the "London Times" (who did not tend to cover Scottish Football terribly often or in any great detail), saying "The winners' half-backs broke up Aberdeen's attacks with ease, and fed their forwards admirably. Lyon held Armstrong, who never got going, and Geatons was the perfect half-back. Paterson's sturdy defence constantly broke down the Aberdeen right wing."

The season of 1937-38, the penultimate pre-war campaign, did not begin particularly well for the Scottish Cup holders. Having only managed a two-all draw against Queen of the South on the opening day of the league calendar, they proceeded to record just three victories from their first seven fixtures, which culminated in a three-one defeat by defending champions Rangers at Ibrox Park in September. After this loss, Celtic found themselves in eighth place in the league standings with only eight points to their name. Four points ahead at the top of the table were unlikely leaders Dundee, who enjoyed the luxury of having played one game less thus far and who had just beaten Aberdeen at Pittodrie that very weekend, whilst Motherwell and Rangers sat poised only two points off the leaders. It is fair to say then, that whilst the Celts had not enjoyed the best of starts to their campaign, there was still a long way to go and they certainly still in the running for the Championship at this point.

In the next fixture, George Paterson would fill in at full-back for the absent Jock Morrison as the Celts emerged victorious from a hotly contested tie away against Morton, thanks to a late headed goal from Willie Buchan. Subsequently, the final appearance (characteristically marked by one last goal) of Jimmy McGrory prior to his departure for the managerial role at Kilmarnock signalled an evident change within the Celtic side. Without the presence of McGrory competing for a starting place, Celtic were finally able to play a fairly settled forward line for the remainder of the season, and as such enjoyed great success as the likes of Crum, MacDonald and Divers scored goal after goal. A consecutive run of thirteen league victories, from the end of November to mid-March tightened Celtic's grip on the championship, leaving them three points ahead of second placed Hearts with two matches in hand. As the headline in the "Glasgow Herald" said on the Monday after the Celts' thirteenth consecutive league triumph, "Celtic in Sight of League Championship – Nine Points Needed from Eight Matches".

Therefore, after a temporary slump in form, three wins followed by a three-one victory away to St. Mirren proved enough to guarantee their place as the Champions of Scotland – a title they would not hold again until 1954. Regardless, the Celts would triumph in the Empire Exhibition Trophy before finishing runners-up in the league table the following season.

During this period, George Paterson was rewarded with the first of only two Scottish international caps which he would receive over the course of his career. However, despite the fact the Scots emerged from their British International Championship match against Ireland in Belfast with a victory, George did not enjoy the greatest of personal showings as this excerpt from the "Glasgow Herald" highlights (although it must be said the Scottish defence were never really threatened to any significant extent): "[Bill] Shankly was, all things considered, the best Scottish half-back, alike in defence and distribution. Paterson, always useful, seemed to be affected by the "gluey" pitch, and scarcely reached his best club form."

George would not appear in a Scotland line-up again until 1946. With the fog of war looming heavy on the horizon, the league campaign of 1939-40 ceased after only five matches. The last of these ties for Celtic, played the day before Prime Minister Neville Chamberlain declared the country to be at war, was a one-nil victory over Clyde at Celtic Park. Watched by a crowd of only five thousand people, it is difficult to imagine the feelings of those in the stand and on the terracing that afternoon, all undoubtedly shouldering the collective knowledge their lives were about to change inextricably. Perhaps the match provided them all with one last moment of solace in the face of what lay before them, but I am simply speculating, for I cannot – and hope never to be able to – understand such emotions. Fittingly though, George Paterson – alongside Chic Geatons – was described by the correspondent for "The Scotsman" as the Celts' "master purveyors" in his report of the match, hinting again at what could have been for Paterson (and many others) had his football career been allowed to continue unhindered in the absence of war.

Like countless others during the years of conflict which followed, George did that which he felt obliged to do, joining the Royal Air Force. However, he would return to feature in foot-balling fixtures occasionally, not only with Celtic but the likes of Arsenal, Blackpool and Leicester City as a guest of sorts. Indeed, having seen him appear for the last of the three previously mentioned sides, then Leicester City manager Tom Bromilow (the great Liverpool left-half who made over three hundred appearances for the club, mostly during the 1920s) said Paterson was "one of the best wing-halves I have ever seen".

On New Year's Day 1945, Celtic travelled to Ibrox for the traditional derby match, with the home side sitting quite a way in front of their visitors in the southern league standings. Of course, much of Rangers' success (albeit unofficial) during this period of time can be attributed to the fact that whilst many players largely left their footballing roles to aid the war effort in one manner or another (front line soldiers, miners etc), only returning for the odd game here and there, the majority of the Rangers' squad instead found work in the shipyards for the entirety of the conflict. Regardless, one of the men who had returned to play for Celtic that cold winter's day was George Paterson, and although the result may not have mattered too much in the grand scheme of things, I presume I am safe in saying it will have brought much joy and cheer to those Celtic supporters in attendance. The "Glasgow Herald", a newspaper which had now been reduced to only eight pages in length due to wartime restrictions on materials, said this.

"Celtic's Narrow Victory – Paterson Sole Scorer. The big attraction of the New Year's Day football was the clash of Rangers and Celtic at Ibrox, where Celtic triumphed by the only goal of the game. The attendance was seventy thousand, the biggest league gate of the season. The match, however, did not reach a high standard, and mistakes were frequent. In the first half Paton, in the act of shooting from twelve yards, slipped and lost a fine chance for Celtic, whose defenders kept the rival forwards out of the picture. Paterson scored the vital goal three minutes after the change of ends."

For the record, I feel it is worthy of mention to say that if you had opened an edition of the aforementioned newspaper on the second of January 1945, you would have come to the previous match report before you reached the pages which discussed the events of the ongoing World War. Of course, this is a largely meaningless fact, but it does prove once more that sport, particularly football involving either (or both in this case) of the city's two biggest football clubs, most certainly provided an escape of sorts for the residents of Glasgow at a very difficult point in history.

A year later, towards the end of the January of 1946, George would see himself recalled to the Scotland squad for a challenge match against Belgium at Hampden Park. A last minute equaliser from a James Delaney penalty (James had already scored once midway through the second half) meant the tie finished in a two-all draw, and prevented the Belgians from breaking a barrier which would nowadays seem somewhat unbelievable, for had they held out for their victory, they would have been the first international side from the European continent to win on British soil.

Returning to the initial story discussed at the start of this chapter, it was only after the eventual cessation of fighting that the world gradually began to readapt to peacetime again. Of course, this process would take many years, but as the Scottish Football Association geared up for the restart of competitive, national league football for the 1946-47 season, the "Victory Cup" was held in the April, May and June of 1946. In the early rounds, Celtic scored thirteen goals in two matches against St. Johnstone, before disposing of Queen of the South and Raith Rovers en route to the competition's semi-final stage. Rangers, the side whom they had lost by three goals to one to in the semi-final of the Glasgow Cup only a couple of weeks earlier lay in wait, and it would certainly be a memorable encounter.

The first semi-final ended in a goalless draw, with Celtic largely owing their opportunity to replay the tie to goalkeeper Willie Miller, whose performance the sports correspondents in attendance could not praise highly enough, with one saying "Miller's uncanny anticipation of the flight of the ball, whether on the ground or in the air, had to be seen to be believed."

The replay would be played on the evening of the fifth of June 1946. Unlike its goalless counterpart, this tie and the events which took place therein continue to cry out across the ages, and that alone should make it a very worthy topic of our interest. As a preface to this match and the controversy which still surrounds it, allow me to begin by quoting the line which concluded one major newspaper's match report the following day, "Celtic were left with seven men and a cripple".

As the two sides took to the field, presumably Rangers were considered by many to be favourites. After all, they had dominated the previous match and won the Glasgow Cup fixture also, but according to the "Glasgow Herald", it was actually Celtic who threatened in the early minutes of what was a hard fought contest.

"The greasy ball and blustery wind had not prevented both teams from giving a first-half display that was highly credible. Celtic, with a most unusual assortment of forwards, used the ball to extremely good advantage in the early minutes. Kiernan and Paterson being especially useful in contriving to keep the ball on the ground when they made a pass. But with the wind against them the Celtic defence found many of their clearances ballooning back on them and, as on Saturday, Miller had hardly an idle minute. Once again this goalkeeper played magnificently, as did Hogg and Mallan."

Despite Celtic's reasonable start to proceedings, they found themselves behind come half time, thanks to a fine goal from William Waddell, who went on to manage the Ibrox club in later years. A few minutes after this strike the referee, Matthew Dale, came to the fore for the first time. For the sake of clarity, allow me to highlight that Dale was far from a popular figure within the ranks of the Celtic support, as questions had been widely asked regarding his alleged bias towards one team (and I'm sure you can work out to which side such allegations referred). Anyway, only moments had passed since the opening goal when the Celtic forward Jimmy Sirrell was sent flying by a poor tackle from Rangers full-back Jock Shaw, and despite the fact that the injured Sirrell had been left writhing about on the Hampden turf, no foul was given, much to the dismay of those of a green and white persuasion. This sense of injustice was only inflamed in the minutes which followed when Rangers were awarded a very soft-free kick indeed, all whilst Sirrell continued to limp around the field, doing his best to continue.

It was at this point, as the players prepared for the upcoming free-kick, [that] referee Matthew Dale attempted to place the ball in the desired spot before losing his balance and keeling over. Presuming the official had simply lost his footing, George Paterson held out his hand and helped Dale to his feet once more. However, as he did so, Paterson caught an inexplicable whiff of the referee's breath, which he noticed smelled distinctly of alcohol.

Understandably, Paterson was unhappy about this, but all he received for his protestations was the first caution of his entire Celtic career (which amounted to over fourteen years), and the first half drew to a close without further incident of note.

During the interval, the Celtic players were so upset by the condition of the referee that they insisted their manager Jimmy McGrory take it to a higher level, and as such Robert Kelly was informed. He then presented the concerns of the players to the secretary of the Scottish Football Association, George Graham, and insisted that appropriate action must be taken. Graham assured Kelly that the matter would be suitably addressed, but as the players re-emerged on to the Hampden turf for the second half, those in green and white jerseys were flabbergasted to discover Matthew Dale had been allowed to continue in his role. Now, whether this was a decision based on bias or one made in order to save themselves the embarrassment of having to explain such a change to the Scottish press cannot be known for certain. However, what is not debatable is that not only did this decision harm Celtic's chances of winning the tie, but it would also contribute to one of the most farcical halves of football the Scottish game has ever seen.

At the time though, all was not lost, for despite the fact Dale would continue, it would be Celtic playing with the benefit of the wind in the second half, whilst the defence of Rangers would have to deal with the difficulty of a strong gust blowing towards them.

However, any hopes which Celtic had of a revival would have been dashed as, only one minute into the second half, the pattern of the first forty-five minutes was allowed to continue after another poor tackle went unpunished. This time the victim would be John "Jackie" Gallacher who, like Jimmy Sirrell, had also felt the effects of a foul challenge in the first half. As a result of this second assault, Gallacher was moved to the wing and left hobbling around the park. A short time later, he was downed again, and was simply unable to continue in any capacity, finally having to be stretchered from the field.

Approximately twenty minutes would then pass, with Matthew Dale awarding virtually every decision in favour of the side in blue, before the most infamous incident occurred. Still leading by a single goal to nil, Rangers continued to press for a second to assure their victory against the now ten man Celtic, but so far, despite putting together several threatening periods of attacking play, they had been unsuccessful in this regard. Of course, in all likelihood they could well have closed their ranks and focussed on defence rather than offence in order to ensure their win, for Celtic did not appear to have much chance of scoring now, but there would be no need for either tactic when Rangers centre forward William Thornton went down inside the Celtic box and Matthew Dale duly obliged by awarding the Ibrox side the softest of penalty kicks.

By now, it is safe to assume that the proverbial powder keg was primed to explode, such was the levels of anger and disgust being felt not only by the Celtic fans in attendance, but also the Celtic players on the field. George Paterson, a man who had a well-known reputation for being cool and collected, was now utterly incensed. Upon picking up the ball in the seconds after Dale had made his decision to award the spot kick, he outright refused to give it back to the official or any member of the opposition. Such a show of disdain was bound to provoke a reaction from the referee, who proceeded to send the Celtic man off for being brazen and rebellious enough to attempt to publicly challenge his authority. However, if Dale had thought that would be the end of such a mutiny, he would be wrong, as he discovered very shortly.

As the nine remaining Celtic players watched their comrade depart the field, I doubt the nineteen year old Jimmy Mallan was the only one who felt aggrieved by this decision, but unlike his teammates, the young full-back decided to take matters into his own hands. Whilst everyone else stood still and Paterson trailed off the field, Mallan moved over to the penalty spot and began to vigorously scrape it away with the sole of his boot. Upon Dale eventually moving to place the ball down, it is said the young then offered some line such as "look, there's no penalty spot ref", without making any reference to his immediate intentions. It was then Mallan did something I am certain other Celtic players have dreamt of doing throughout the ages, as once the ball had been placed on the turf and Rangers half-back George Young prepared to take the kick, Jimmy ran forward and hoofed the ball away before he could do so. Unsurprisingly, this enraged Matthew Dale who promptly gave Mallan his marching orders, as sheer and unbridled carnage ensued on the Hampden terracing.

In the immediate aftermath, as those Celtic players still on the field considered abandoning the game in protest, Matt Lynch was the most prominent in his attempts to urge his friends to walk off. However, according to the "Dundee Courier", "captain Bobby Hogg intervened and they remained."

George Young would eventually score his penalty kick, but in the seconds which followed one Celtic supporter emerged from the terracing and attempted to hit referee with a glass bottle. Mercifully, his attempt was dashed as he was halted just before he was able to do any damage, but the mood in the stadium was now bordering on poisonous. The same Dundee newspaper then made a reference to "free fights...taking place on the terracing", whilst the "Aberdeen Journal" stated that "suddenly there appeared from under the South Stand close on one hundred policemen, who, rushing among the spectators, soon succeeded in restoring [some] order." The rest of the match would be played out at walking pace, with Rangers simply keeping the ball against the eight men of Celtic, one of whom could barely walk.

As the final whistle sounded, the remaining Celtic supporters trudged home with a combination of disgruntlement in their guts and injustice in their hearts, whilst one would assume the Rangers supporters were a much cheerier bunch at that time all things considered. As for those at Celtic Football Club, they were certainly not happy with the referee's showing that evening, but nothing could be done to change the result.

However, in a manner not entirely dissimilar to the legacy of the so-called "shame game" (March 2011), the punishments handed out in 1946 by the governing body as a result were utterly perplexing in their nature. For the sake of clarity, allow me to remind you all that the modern fixture in question was a Scottish Cup replay which saw three Rangers players sent off at Celtic Park, some of whom physically laid their hands on referee Callum Murray, whilst a bit of post-match pushing and shoving between Neil Lennon and Ally McCoist ensued after the latter said something in the ear of the Irishman which, to this day, remains unpublicised. Such displays, not only from professional footballers but from grown men were embarrassing, but all of that paled into insignificance upon the announcement of the results of the Scottish Football Association's disciplinary proceedings, which entailed no punishments for any of the offenders dressed in blue (minimal financial fines aside). Now, who was the only individual to face any serious sanction following this sordid affair? Yes, you guessed it, Neil Lennon, simply for having the gall to react to whatever was said by Mr. McCoist (which was presumably provocative in nature).

Returning to 1946 however, the parallels become all too clear to see, and will likely lead many of you reading this to ask the same question I find myself pondering – "How much has really changed over the last seventy years?" I will leave it to these quotations from "The Scotsman" to outline the punishments handed out following the semi-final replay of the "Victory Cup".

"The Referee's Committee of the S.F.A. yesterday announced their decision in connection with the incident in the Victory Cup tie between Celtic and Rangers at Hampden. Paterson and Mallan of Celtic are suspended for three months and Lynch of Celtic for one month, to date from August 10. The Celtic Club were fined fifty pounds."

The previous passage comes from the thirteenth of June 1946, only a little over a week after the tie was played. Now, one could rightly question why it was left to the "Referee's Committee" to decide on punishment in these affairs, since a strong argument could be made to say that, with the accusations being levelled against one of their colleagues in mind, they could not possibly be impartial in this instance. However, if such a case was made by those in control of Celtic, it was ignored, as were their appeals, with these snippets arriving in the press at the start of July and the middle of September respectively.

"At a meeting of the S.F.A. Council yesterday, the Council rejected an appeal by M. Lynch of Celtic, against the sentence of one month suspensions imposed recently by the Referee's Committee. The player denied that on the occasion of the replayed Victory Cup tie at Hampden Park against Rangers, following the ordering off of J. Mallan, he invited and incited members of the Celtic team to leave the field. After hearing a statement by Mr. R. Williamson (Morton), Chairman of the Referee's Committee, the Council agreed unanimously that the appeal be dismissed."

"An application by Celtic F.C. for a reduction of the suspension sentence passed on two of their players George Paterson and J. Mallan was refused yesterday by the S.F.A. Executive Committee at a meeting in Glasgow. The players were ordered off during the Celtic-Rangers Victory Cup tie at Hampden Park on June 5, and at a subsequent meeting of the Referee's Committee, they were each suspended for three months until November 10."

Therefore, it came to pass that each of the three Celtic players handed suspensions would not see them repealed or reduced, whilst one must presume that Matthew Dale was allowed to continue in his normal role, without punishment, as he was back refereeing top flight matches only weeks into the new season. Matthew Lynch would reappear in a Celtic line-up as the Hoops took on Queen of the South on the fourteenth of September 1946 – the first match to be played after he had served his sentence. He would stay with the Club until the end of the 1947-48 season. Similarly, Jimmy Mallan would again turn out as a Celtic player, although he was not selected to play a match until over a month after his suspension had expired, as Clyde visited Celtic Park in mid-December. He too would remain a popular figure at the Football Club, remaining there until the spring of 1953.

However, fate would not be so kind to George Paterson, who was deeply affected by the events of that day at Hampden Park. Upset to such a serious extent not only by his ordering off and subsequent suspension but also by a sense of unfairness and bias, he became disillusioned with the national game which he loved so fiercely and allegedly considered quitting the sport altogether. Thankfully, this threat did not come to pass, but a little over a month prior to the end of his suspension, he left Celtic for Brentford, with inside-forward Gerry McAloon moving in the opposite direction. During his career at Parkhead, George made two hundred and eighty-three appearances, scoring eighteen times, winning two Scottish League Championships, one Scottish Cup and the Empire Exhibition Trophy.

In all, he would make more than sixty outings for Brentford during his three years at Griffin Park. However, he was unable to help them avoid relegation from the English top flight in his first season and as such played out his final two campaigns there as "The Bees" languished around the lower to middle end of the Second Division. Now in the twilight of his playing career, George would return to Celtic Park once more as Brentford travelled north for a friendly match in late September 1949. As one would expect, he was given a rousing reception at Parkhead alongside fellow Celts Malcolm MacDonald and John Paton, who also played with the London club at the time. Of this trio, the "Glasgow Herald" said: "Paterson has slowed down considerably but retains his skill, and MacDonald, now the English club's trainer coach, is as clever a ball player as ever, though he did not unduly exert himself. Paton was disappointing." The match itself was a fairly even affair, culminating in a two-all draw. George scored the second of Brentford's goals with a deflected shot struck from all of thirty yards, but according to one newspaper, his reaction to this told its own story, as he "hung his head", looking "ashamed".

Subsequently, George would go on to become the player manager of Yeovil Town in the October of 1949. Less than a year prior to Paterson's appointment, Yeovil Town would record a victory which is still considered to be one of the greatest F.A. Cup upsets of all-time, knocking out big spending Sunderland thanks to an extra time winner in the fourth round of the tournament. Regardless, the Scot would oversee one hundred competitive matches during a two year stay in Somerset, guiding "The Glovers" to forty-six victories and twenty-two draws, whilst bringing home two Somerset Professional Cups in the process.

On the fifteenth of October 1951, George Paterson left Yeovil Town behind him, taking over the managerial reins for a brief spell with Stirling Albion, who would finish the 1951-52 campaign firmly rooted to the bottom of the Scottish League Division A (the top flight), managing only to attain fifteen points from thirty league fixtures. George then vacated what would be his final managerial role, instead returning to his home at Celtic Park, working with the reserve squad as a trainer and also as a scout for a time.

George Denholm Paterson died on the tenth of December 1985 in New Zealand, not too long after he had emigrated to the opposite side of the globe. He was seventy-one years of age at the time of his passing. A Celt of tremendous character, he undoubtedly deserves to be remembered by the modern day support not only for his service to the Football Club, but for his integrity and ethics. Yes, a combination of bias and shambolic decision making would cut his time at Celtic Park short, very likely costing him the chance to become the club captain, but that should not tarnish his achievements both before and after the events at Hampden Park.

Poignantly, of all of the plaudits which George received for his endeavours as a footballer, perhaps the most impressive of these came over two decades after the end of his involvement in the sport at any level, as his former teammate Jimmy McGrory published his book, "A Lifetime in Paradise: The Jimmy McGrory Story." In the final chapter of this work, McGrory names his greatest ever Celtic eleven, of which George is awarded the left-half position. Now, when one considers that his half-back compatriots in this imaginary team are Billy McNeill and Bobby Murdoch, it clearly indicates the calibre of player which McGrory considered George Paterson to be. Therefore, we should all be proud to call him one of our own.

"The Chronicles of Willie Maley:
"Early Cup Struggles""

"By Willie Maley, Manager, Celtic F.C."

"My notes bring me now to the start of the season 1889-90. I shall however, from now on, deal only with the chief items of each season."

"Our second year of competitive existence, 1889-90, found our team not much changed from the famous lot of 1888-89, but in one or two cases time had, as usual; made a call on some of the older ones. McLaren developing slowness enabled Peter Dowds, to my mind the greatest wing-half I have ever seen, to come into his own. Then we had young Cunningham, coming on well as an extreme left-winger to the exclusion of the older Coleman and T. E. Maley."

"The season itself as far as honours were concerned found us still only able to boast of the North-Eastern Cup as our only honour. We had a bad time of it that year in the Cup-ties at the hands, or feet if you like, of Queen's Park, for they dusted us in both the Scottish and Glasgow Cup-ties in games which were most exciting and strenuous. The Queen's team in these days had a "punch" with them in the shape of big, strong defenders, and they asked and gave no mercy. What a contrast to the present team, or their teams of recent years, as far as physique goes! Tom Robertson, who had forsaken the charms of Gourlay Park with its "heights and hollows" for the "turf" of Hampden, was a great man for the Queen's that year, and his long experience pulled the team through many a time. Arnott and Smellie, too, were in their prime just then, and were a treat to see, the one for his beautiful clean kicking and tackling, and the other for his almost "maniacal" enthusiasm he put into all his work."

"Over the Glasgow Cup Final played at Cathkin between us there was a deal of bad blood. The game itself was played in a very hot mood, and a lot of things occurred on both sides which did not [contribute greatly] to anyone's credit. The referee, Tom Park, of Cambuslang, was, to our mind, very much at fault on this occasion, and so much so that two of our players stupidly made to leave the field during the game rather than suffer any more, as they said, at his hands. Rightly or wrongly we of course could not have that, and our committee present soon sent them back to the fray. Our representative to the Glasgow Association, when the protest we lodged against the refereeing on this occasion came up, withdrew from the Association, stating he was the first and would be the last Celtic representative there. Needless to say the temper of that day soon passed away, and in later years as we came to be what we are today, I am proud to say that we are the best of friends with the Amateurs of Hampden."

"The lack of fixtures became painfully evident that year, and from the big lot of English clubs which we had to bring to keep our weekly engagement list going it soon was seen that something on the lines of the English League was needed, and so the following year saw the results of the committee's labours, when the Scottish League was formally inaugurated with ten clubs."

"I referred above to the qualities of Peter Dowds, now, alas, numbered with our great and growing roll of departed friends. He was a medium built lad as far as height was concerned, but he was of the very sturdy type we see so often. A quick eye and equally good with both feet, Peter could play well in any position, and he played all over the shop for us, but was especially good, I thought, at left-half, where he could deliver a very powerful shot, and when he finally got Doyle behind him he completed an almost perfect defence. A quiet, unassuming lad, and one who could enjoy a joke with as hearty a laugh as one could hear, poor Peter died very young, and in him also was lost to Scottish football one of its brightest exponents."

"That year we had a lot of bother with Groves, who had in the summer signed on for Everton and taken their "fine gold." On our discovering this, Glass's usual persuasive eloquence was at once put into play to thwart the wiles of one who would later adorn our team – Dan Doyle, who was then in Everton, where with Andrew Hannah, late of Renton, they made history, and go down in posterity in the story of English League football as the essence of fearlessness in defence. They were regular stonewallers, and a terror to their opponents."

"Fred Geary's Speed"

"We had Everton down at Celtic Park on twelfth of October 1889, when Dan Doyle got a reception which was very mixed in view of the Groves affair, and the game was remarkable for the wonderful speed displayed by the Everton centre, Fred Geary, who beat us himself, and also for the wicked display of Holt, their International and diminutive centre-half. Madden and he had a regular field day, Madden carrying a black eye for the following week in memory of same. Holt was very clever, but most unscrupulous, and failing to get a man one way he always made certain that there was the other way of stopping him."

"We visited Everton in April, 1890, and got beaten again, but in between times they came to Parkhead on the first of January 1890, when we overcame them by three to two. Holt did not venture back to Celtic Park in this game, which was chiefly remarkable for the left-wing displays on both sides – Millward and Chadwick for Everton, and Coleman and T. E. Maley for Celts, my brother scoring two very fine goals that day."

"The Glasgow Hibs, an opposition body of mushroom growth and similar existence, had now grown to shape, and played for a short time, having the assistance at various times of some of our cast-off's, and even Jerry Reynolds appeared [briefly] in their ranks. As I have already said, the club really grew out of personal jealousies, and in no branch of life have I seen such seed bearing decent fruit. The club had amongst its members several persons who had seceded from our club in the hopes of promotion, and on their not paying their annual subscriptions when due, so their names were erased from the roll of our membership."

"When the League Was Formed"

"The season 1889-90 was a famous one in many ways, and several incidents in that season come back to me as I think over the past. The Glasgow Association in that year numbered twenty-eight clubs. To the present day follower of that game that will sound extraordinary, but it is a fact nevertheless, and the only club outside the city boundaries was Cambuslang, now, of course, with twenty-one of the other clubs of that year's membership, extinct. For this professionalism was the chief reason, but junior football now takes the place of senior football in districts where Thistle, Cowlairs, Northern, and many other such well-known names then existed."

"We had, at the close of that season, a regular invasion by English clubs, whose travels were not always for holiday purposes alone, and many good men were thereby inveigled [persuaded] to travel South to the "gold mines" supposed to exist in Lancashire and the Midlands, not to speak of the North-Eastern districts, where Tom Watson was making a name for himself and his team. Neilly McCallum, our greatest right winger of all time, was coaxed away by Blackburn Rovers to join Harry Campbell, his old mate in the famous Renton team, but Neilly soon returned to us after a short stay in smoky Lancashire. Then McKeown was always on the go, and threatening every day to travel afield, but we eventually got sick of his threats, and he was at last told to go, but, like the wayward chap he was, he wouldn't leave then. Poor Mick, the wander lust finished him later on – tragically."

"Friends of the Celts"

"My good friend and old-time clubmate, Jerry Reynolds, was a bit sore about me reminding him last week of his days with Glasgow Hibs, but as these were very short I am pleased to be able to say that Jerry, wherever he played, was always a Celt first. His coming to us that year was a bit of a joke. We found ourselves short of a back to face Queen's Park, and with Jerry always in our eye in Carfin Shamrock, where he was then playing, a deputation awaited Jerry at the little village of Carfin at 2 a.m. one morning. Secrecy was very necessary then, as the Shamrock were also in the Scottish ties, and needed all the men they could hold [once players had featured in a Scottish Cup fixture with one team they could not do so with any other until the following season]. Like Red Indians on the trail, Glass and Co. got to Jerry's door in the miners' row where he lived, and arousing the house as quietly as possible, Jerry was coaxed, cajoled and finally commandeered as he stood in shirt, trousers and socks, and driven to Glasgow to a hotel, to be togged up next day and taken away to the country preparatory to his appearing in the green and white. That year again we gave five hundred pounds to charities."

"The scarcity of fixtures which I referred to before as the cause of so many English teams coming North, brought on the League, and it was finally formed at the end of that season, ten clubs [contesting] it the first year, two of them, Cambuslang and Cowlairs, now being extinct. The movement brought forth all sorts of gloomy prophecies, and the leading athletic papers argued strongly against the League principle as being a selfish one, calculated to drive out the country club and limit competition. The League has proved its worth, and to it, and it alone, Scottish football owes its strong position today...Queen's Park declined to join the body, but later years brought them that wisdom which enabled them to apply for membership...they are as keen members today as Celtic or any other professional club."

"What Would You Do Without Celtic?"

Occasionally in life, as I presume you will all appreciate, matters do not transpire in the manner which you may necessarily expect. Of course, the writing process is not exempt from such twists and turns, and I was reminded of this as I picked up the phone to call an elderly gentleman by the name of William Maxwell, whom I was set to interview with the purpose of penning a chapter similar to this one. A few moments later, William answered the phone.

Thereafter, I went through my usual spiel, explaining who I was and what I was aiming to do (which turned out to be a slightly pointless exercise as Mr. Maxwell had read my first work), before asking the gentleman in question whether or not he'd like to speak to me for what would eventually become my second book. Promptly, he answered "Yes, but I'm not going to." For a few seconds, this left me somewhat puzzled until he continued, "I'd love to speak to you son, but I want you to have the best chapter possible, and I don't think you'll get that by talking to me. You should speak to my pal instead, he's seen a lot more than I have and his memory, with regards Celtic at least, is probably a bit better than my own. I've actually got him sitting here next to me now, I'll just pass you over to him…his name is Pat."

Quickly, I found myself – not for the first time I may add – on the proverbial hop. Whilst I had been given a little bit of information about William from one of his family members whom I had spoken to previously, I knew nothing of Pat other than his name, so I must confess I was slightly unprepared as the phone was passed between the two men. Subsequently, I said hello and again ran through my introductory piece. Pat was very pleasant as it turned out, and after a short discussion, he gave me his address and we arranged a day and time for me to visit him – and so ended one of the more surreal, but ultimately important, phone calls of my life thus far.

In later months, midway through the series of interviews which followed, Pat would explain that he was initially slightly wary about the prospect of recounting much of his life story to a stranger, but once we had met he was happy to proceed. "I really enjoy it when you come over", he told me, "It gets my brain going and gives me something to look forward to, but more than that, it's just great to speak to someone who has such an interest in the history of the Football Club, particularly the periods I lived through." For the record, I relished these conversations also. After all, it's not every day you have the chance to sit down with someone who attended some of the biggest and most important matches which Celtic have been involved in. As you will come to realise in this chapter, Pat is a very likable gentleman with an infectious love of Celtic Football Club, and I can sincerely say it was a great pleasure to spend some time in his company.

Upon our initial meeting, my immediate impressions of Pat as a man were two-fold. Firstly, he was clearly a friendly individual, but secondly, and perhaps more notably for a man eighty years of age, his mobility appeared to be remarkably good. His living room was a simple and tidy affair, with couches surrounding a television and pictures adorning the walls. Of these, family photographs took pride of place, but I could not help but notice the presence of a large black and white autographed print of Billy McNeill lifting the European Cup. A wry smile spread across my face when I spotted this, as I knew Pat had been in Lisbon that day in 1967, but we shall to come to that later. Naively, I did wonder if this was the only such Celtic memorabilia on display in the house, but I would be proven wrong momentarily, as Pat – who was busying himself making a couple of cups of coffee – told me to take a wander upstairs and go to the room at the end of the hall, before our discussions began in earnest.

En route, it quickly became apparent that the previously referenced picture of the captain of the Lisbon Lions was not the only such Celtic related piece on show as everyone from Jock Stein to Lubomir Moravcik stared down from the walls around me. It was then that I opened the door to a small box room, probably only big enough to be classed as a bedroom by an estate agent, as in reality it would be a tight fit. Now, it is safe to say that this room was unlike any which I have had the pleasure of seeing previously, for it was covered from the floor to the ceiling – and that is genuinely no exaggeration – in Celtic memorabilia. Prints, posters, programmes and newspaper cut-outs covered every available area of wall space. Other items such as scarves, hats, books and DVD's made the carpet all but invisible, and even the roof had pieces stuck to it, tickets and the like. There was so much adoration for one subject matter crammed into such a small space that I would liken it not a spare bedroom but to a shrine.

Naturally, as I returned to the living room downstairs, where a large cup of hot coffee was now waiting for me – as was Pat – I was rather enthusiastic about the prospect of learning more about the room. After all, it didn't strike me as the sort of project someone would start and finish in a day or two, but it was then I discovered there was a notable tinge of sadness attached to it, as Pat explained he was a widower. Carrying on, he informed me that he had lost his wife of over thirty years, Betty, in the mid-1990s. Obviously, such a loss had an enormous impact on him, and as they have done for so many other people at one point or another when tragedy strikes, Celtic somehow found a way to help take Pat's mind off things, even if only for a few brief minutes here and there. As such, he began to work on transforming the spare room into what it is today.

"I had never planned for it to turn out as it did, it just started when I was moving a few things around here and there. For the first time ever, I found myself living alone and I thought it'd be good for me to personalise the house a little bit to my own liking. I found not only the Celtic paraphernalia itself, but the memories and thoughts which the items brought forth in my mind helped me immensely, so I'm really rather proud of the collection I've assembled", he said.

Turning our attention now to the early days of his life, Patrick McManus (who prefers to be known simply as "Pat" as you have likely established by now) was born in Turner Street, Garngad, on the twenty-fourth of October 1934. A few days later, Celtic beat Dunfermline Athletic by three goals to nil, thanks to a brace from

Frank O'Donnell in the first ten minutes of play and a second half goal from Willie Buchan, which secured the points for the Celts. Reflecting on this, I enquired as to whether or not Pat thought his father would have attended that match, and he responded positively, telling me his dad rarely missed a game prior to his days in the army. Of course, it will come as no surprise to you when I say that Pat came from a long line of proud Celtic supporters, including his grandfather Robert, who was one of the thousands who walked the whole distance from Glasgow to Cardenden in Fife for the funeral of John Thomson in 1931.

Although he wouldn't have known it at the time Pat, along with millions of other children of all nationalities and backgrounds, had been born into a world on the verge of war. Even before he had attended his first Celtic match, he recalls being marched out to the bomb shelters located in the middle of the street at eleven o'clock nightly, during the height of the Nazi air raids over Glasgow in the early 1940s.

"I wasn't really old enough to be able to truly comprehend what was happening in those days", he told me, "I know that to be the case because if I had, I would have been terrified, and that sort of anxiety never leaves the people unfortunate enough to experience it. My friends and I knew nothing different, we had no grasp of what peacetime was like, so we just made the best of it and got on with our lives. The women of Garngad deserve immense credit for that though. Keep in mind, there weren't many men around because they'd all been called up for the war effort – my father included – but the women were so good to all the kids. Every night, in the shelters, they'd start singing or telling us stories to take our minds off of the air raids. Looking back on it as an adult, they must have been petrified with fear themselves, but they didn't show it and they really kept our spirits up, trying to turn it into a family adventure rather than anything to be frightened of. I just wish I could thank them for all that they did for me and the other children."

Before continuing, it is perhaps worthy of note that many of the people who grew up in Garngad –with one James Edward McGrory perhaps being the most famous resident – seem to attest to the fact that the area breeds people with a particular amount of resilience. It is not alone in this regard, but it is this toughness, coupled with the strong family and community spirit present there, which Pat attributes to himself and many others. According to Pat, "You can take the boy out of Garngad, but you can't take Garngad out of the boy."

Sadly though, regardless of any individual fortitude they may have possessed in the past, many of those who fought during the Second World War were unable to dispense with the memories and effects of the almost unspeakable horrors they had witnessed therein. Pat's father – also called Pat – was one of these men, who largely retreated into himself in the years following the conflict.

"I rarely ever got to have much of a conversation with him after the war", Pat recalled, "Clearly, he was badly affected psychologically by it. A member of the Highland Light Infantry, based in Maryhill, he was part of the group chased out of Dunkirk by the advancing Nazis, before being involved in some of the fierce fighting which went on in the North of Africa later in the war. He lost his brother Sandy during those years also – he was killed in Burma – and in truth, my dad never really got over the whole thing. Nobody had much of a clue about mental illness back then, so he didn't receive any of the help which would be offered nowadays. He was never the same man, and even from a sporting perspective I found that difficult to deal with, as we were never able to go to the football together nor could I really talk to him about the good old days when he watched Celtic. It was a real shame, and I dread to think how many men and their families had to deal with similar problems when they returned home. It was very hard."

In the summer of 1943, at the age of eight, Pat would make his first trip to see Celtic with his Uncle Tommy (who was exempt from military service owing to the fact he worked in the shipyards) as they took on Rangers in a tournament known as the Summer Cup. This competition, one of the regional trophies up for grabs during the Second World War, was competed for annually by representatives of the Southern League. Celtic, a poor side by their standards during this time period, never even reached the final during any season in which the cup was contested. As a point of interest, the trophy itself sits proudly at Easter Road nowadays.

Anyway, I shall leave it to the words of Pat himself to describe the build-up to the match: "I can still remember my first game, walking up and over Garngad Hill with my uncle, past the cigarette factory and down towards the East End of the city. When I look back on it now, it must have been some walk to the ground and back, but everyone did stuff like that in those days, so I thought nothing of it. As we approached Celtic Park, the crowds began to get thicker and thicker, and I can distinctly remember thinking to myself, "How can all these people fit into a football ground and still see the match?" Anyway, once we had made our way through the turnstiles I was passed down to the front of the Celtic end, behind the goal. I remember being impressed by the scale of the event itself, but regrettably Celtic Park wasn't up to much in those days."

Unsurprisingly, neither were Celtic, who would go on to lose by four goals to nil. Around a week later, Pat recalled that he was playing football in the street and encountered his uncle walking home from work with a friend. Tommy proceeded to tell him to come up to his house shortly as he had a surprise for him, and Pat duly obliged. Arriving there, Tommy's wife opened the door, before Pat wandered in to find his uncle and the man he had been walking with inside. Here, Pat says he remembers thinking that he did not know the man standing in front of him, despite his uncle asking "Don't you recognise him, Pat?"

There may well have been a slight familiarity about him, but Pat was stumped, before his uncle formally introduced him to Alex Venters of Rangers, one of the finest inside-forwards ever to pull on the blue jersey of the Ibrox club. To give him his due, Alex told the young Pat not to be too disappointed about the defeat which Celtic had endured in the days previous. Of this encounter, Pat said simply: "He was a lovely man – a really nice guy – but I'd be lying if I said I didn't hate him when he was on the park, because more often than not he helped to make our lives a misery. He seemed to score against Celtic more often than he did against most teams, but maybe he was just that sort of big game player."

Notably, Alex Venters was not the only famous footballing face whom Pat had the pleasure of meeting as a child, as he explained: "Being a Garngad boy it wasn't an uncommon sight to see Jimmy McGrory, or Mr. McGrory as I referred to him back then, wandering about with a newspaper under his arm and a pipe in his mouth. He seemed like a cut above to me, refined if you will. He spoke fluently and appeared to be well educated – or at least better educated than I was. Whether it was me or any of the other kids, he'd always go out of his way to say a few words to you, even if you were one of the more shy children. He had time for everyone. Mr. McGrory was such a pleasant man."

Yet, whilst his relatively common encounters with Celtic's greatest striker seemed normal to Pat, another meeting with an equally large presence in the history of the Football Club seemed much more extraordinary to the young boy, partly because it was a one-off and also as it did not occur in his home streets of Garngad, but in the bustling city centre.

"It was my birthday", Pat began, "and my mother Lizzy and I were in the town. I think I must have just turned seven or eight because I was still a young lad at this point and most of my memories any earlier than this are fairly cloudy at best. Anyway, my mum had bought me a copy of "The Story of the Celtic" as a birthday present, and I'd assume some of your readers will know before I say it who wrote that particular book, as it was none other than Willie Maley himself. Now, he had a restaurant in Queen Street called "The Bank" [which is now a Vodka Bar at the time of writing] and while we were walking past that day, my mum decided to chance her arm and see if Mr. Maley was there. We approached the front door where there was a man in a suit and a hat, clearly a concierge of some sort, and after my mum had conversed with him for a short time, he told us to wait and disappeared off into the building."

"A few minutes passed and I began to fidget, before the same man appeared and told us to come inside. As we entered the restaurant, I felt immediately uneasy because it was a nice place, and all of the people there were well dressed, apart from me and my mother since we didn't have a lot of money. Anyway, as we began to walk across the restaurant, down a central aisle, a huge figure of a man emerged from a backroom and started to walk towards us – it was Mr. Maley. Quickly, I straightened up and after my mother spoke to him briefly, he leant down and said something along the lines of "Hello Pat, it's nice to meet you. I hope you have a very happy birthday and keep behaving well for your mother". He then signed my book, smiled and said his goodbyes, and within a few seconds me and my mum found ourselves back out on Queen Street. It was a small gesture in the grand scheme of things, but even now it means a great deal to me that Mr. Maley was willing to show us an act of kindness like that. I've still got the book too."

Certainly, witnessing a defeat against Rangers was not the happiest of starts to a life following Celtic for the young Pat, but things would improve. Little would he have known then that one day, a little more than two decades later, he would be there to see a Football Club formed for the maintenance of dinner tables for the children and the unemployed reach its sporting pinnacle by playing a style of football which became the envy of the world.

However, as we all know, the journey to future successes was not to be an easy one, and as such I feel I must make special mention of a match Pat attended which may not be the most glamourous or well-remembered fixture of all time, but one which was a critically important one for the Football Club nonetheless. Although I shall not tell the story of this tie in immense detail here as I have done so elsewhere at some length and do not wish to repeat myself, it is sufficient to say that going into our final match of the 1947-48 league season, away at Dundee, Celtic and their supporters knew it was a must win. Had they failed to do so and other results gone against them, the Hoops risked unprecedented relegation to the second tier of Scottish Football, but thankfully it wasn't to be.

Of the match itself, which ultimately ended in a three-two win for Celtic thanks to a hat-trick from new signing Jock Weir (the third goal of which arrived with only seconds of the tie remaining), Pat said: "It's intriguing when I think back over all I've seen in my life as a Celtic supporter, of all the joyous successes, to recall that the first really pivotal match I attended was the day when we avoided relegation. Over the course of that season, the support were aware of the fact the team weren't up to much, but nobody really thought we would have ended up coming so close to the edge. People were confident we would stay up, but that doesn't mean the prospect of relegation didn't make us all very nervous."

"When we went one up early on, everyone breathed a sigh of relief, but around the hour mark we suddenly found ourselves trailing two-one, and I can't say I wasn't worried. I think we all were, whether or not we like to admit it. An equaliser with about twenty minutes left just made the tension even worse, as everybody, including the players, knew one bit of magic or a single mistake could decide our fate. Emotions were running very high, so I think that's why when Jock Weir put us three-two up just before full time the travelling support went completely crazy. In all honesty, I've never seen more exuberant, passionate celebrations as a Celtic supporter than I did that day in Dundee. As that ball hit the net, you could feel the weight of the nerves being lifted off everybody's shoulders, and the away support just exploded. I don't remember much about the game itself, but that goal, the immediate reaction to it and the celebrations which followed will live with me forever."

Around that time too, it was not just Celtic who found the going difficult. Pat, who attended St. Roch's Junior Secondary School, was set to leave formal education and emerge into the working world – not something which was always an easy task for Catholic people in Glasgow. "I was the dux at school, but I lost out on being top in the final exam we ever sat by one point to a girl in my class. She's probably forgotten all about that by now, but I still remember it purely because I came second", Pat told me jokingly. "In all seriousness though, in the days following that I found myself, at the age of sixteen, out and about in search of work as no further forms of education were available to me at that time. My mother had tried to smarten me up a bit, making sure I'd had a bath and that I wore some of my better clothes, but initially it was all in vain. I visited many potential workplaces, only to be told there were no vacancies available, which was fair enough. However, it did annoy me when people would ask me what my name was and where I went to school before giving me that answer. Eventually though, I did get a lucky break and found work as a saw doctor. Ironically, I was the first Catholic the firm had ever employed – to such an extent that on my first day everyone knew who I was purely because of that fact – but I must say that the gentleman who chose to give me the job was Sammy Marshall, one of the groundsmen at Ibrox at the time, so not everyone was discriminatory in nature. It wasn't the most glamourous job in the world, but I was very grateful to have it, and equally so to Mr. Marshall for giving me the opportunity."

It was during this period in his life that Pat would flirt briefly with the possibility of making a career not as a saw doctor, but as a footballer, having played with the Scottish schoolboy side and drawing some relatively minor attention from a few clubs, including Celtic. At sixteen years old, he would sign for Huddersfield Town, proceeding to leave home for a year against his parents' wishes to play for the West Yorkshire club. However, despite the efforts which he made playing as an inside-left forward, Pat was never able to break into the senior side, eventually deciding to return home to Glasgow as he found the lack of first team football to be frustrating. This was to be the end of his short footballing career. Nowadays, he does not so much regret his decision to give up the game as acknowledge the fact things could have been different had he chosen to follow another path in his life, as he explained to me.

"I always felt I was a decent player as a lad," he told me, "perhaps nothing special but decent enough. I always wanted to play for St. Roch's or Celtic, but the former thought I was too small to be effective and the latter, although they did look at me fleetingly – as they did with countless players – clearly didn't think I was quite up to their standards, which is not something I hold against them. I was optimistic when the move down south to Huddersfield came together, but it wasn't easy being away from home, particularly when I couldn't seem to force my way out of the reserve side. This may sound silly, but my football career was hampered by myself and my adoration for Celtic more than anything else. When I played with teams in and around Glasgow, I regularly missed training sessions and games to go to whatever match Celtic were scheduled to play, and this quickly worked against me. I think it was clear to people that I was more interested in watching one team than I was in playing for almost any other, and that attitude probably killed off any chance I had of making it in the sport myself. However, I must reiterate the point that I don't regret the choices which I made. I honestly don't believe I could have played against the Celts for any other side anyway, so it maybe wasn't a bad thing that I never had the opportunity to do so."

Whilst the trials and tribulations during the post war years prior to the arrival of Jock Stein in 1965 are well documented, there were still some high points for the Celtic supporters to enjoy. One of the most notable examples of these arrived in 1953, when the Celts, along with seven other sides, readied themselves to take part in a one-off knockout tournament, the Coronation Cup. Pat gleefully recalled his memories of the time leading up to this competition: "Nobody really gave us much of a chance of winning the Coronation Cup", he said, "and to be fair, you wouldn't have found too many people within our own support who seriously thought we would do it either, although to save face with our work colleagues and the like we may well have said otherwise in public. However, putting that aside, everyone was really excited by the prospect of the tournament being held in Glasgow. There was a buzz about the place. Don't forget, there was no such thing as competitive European football at this point in time, so the prospect of us being able to face the likes of Arsenal, Manchester United, Newcastle United or Tottenham Hotspur – the English teams – was mouth-watering. Of course, as it turned out, we played the first two from that list and beat them both, and it was magnificent. To win any competition is worth celebrating, but to win that tournament was an enormous finger in the eye of the establishment, and that meant a lot to us all. The only downside is that we believed then that it would be a major turning point for the Club and that great things would quickly follow, but sadly that wasn't to be the case. It was a bit of a false dawn, in truth."

Subsequently, Celtic would win a famous league and cup double in 1954, but these were to be the last successes they would see in either competition until Stein's Celtic won the Scottish Cup again in 1965. However, there was to be one last triumph for the Celtic support of the 1950s to savour, as they attempted to retain the Scottish League Cup (which they had won the previous year for the first time against Partick Thistle), taking on Rangers in the next final on the nineteenth of October 1957. As ever Pat, now only a few days shy of his twenty-third birthday, was one of the eighty-two thousand strong crowd in attendance, and I doubt he could have wished for his Football Club to deliver a better birthday present than they did that day.

"I was standing more or less on the eighteen yard line at the Celtic end", Pat told me – again with that distinctive smile growing wider as memories of a special victory returned to him – "Our team then always had promise, and on occasion could play fantastic football, but they also had the potential to let you down badly, something they did relatively often in one way or another. Despite that, I did believe we could win that match, but I could never have envisaged doing so by such a convincing scoreline. It was a lovely autumn day, which regardless of when they were born any Glaswegian will know is a rarity at that time of the year, and as we found ourselves leading two-nil at half time, the Celtic support was in a buoyant mood as you'd expect. We scored again soon after the break, but then Rangers did so a few moments later to make it three-one."

"At this point, a few slight nerves crept in. After all, we were all expecting a resurgent showing from Rangers as the second half progressed, as they didn't often play whole games so poorly, but their goal turned out to be just a blip for us. There was no mass exodus from the blue terracing, as I genuinely think they believed they could pull it back from three-one, but we soon extinguished any hope of such a comeback with three quick goals after that. Willie Fernie, who was absolutely sensational, made it seven with a late penalty, and as the final whistle went, we were delirious. In all honesty, I think most Celtic supporters in attendance were stunned by the severity of the defeat which we inflicted on

Rangers, but it would prove to be another success which the Club failed to capitalise on in the long term."

Almost a decade later, Jock Stein would return to Celtic Park and begin to return the Club to its former glory and beyond. Firstly, a Scottish Cup Final against his old side Dunfermline Athletic loomed, which Celtic won by three goals to two. Briefly, Pat said the following of that match, and of the return of Big Jock: "I never had any doubt we would win that day against Dunfermline, even when we were twice behind. We had a good side, and you could tell how determined the players were to get the victory, not only for themselves or the fans, but for Mr. Stein also, and to their credit they did just that. Stein quickly became a massively popular figure, because he had a way of making the support – both as a collective and on an individual basis – feel important."

Equally, whilst these days brought significant changes at Celtic Park, they also saw similarly big events occurring in Pat's life. A move to an engineering works in Southampton followed a brief spell spent as a football coach in London for the Garngad man, who settled on the south coast of England with his new wife, Betty. Here, they would start a family, becoming parents to two daughters, Elizabeth and Sharon. However, despite the fact he was so far away from Glasgow, Pat's relationship with Celtic continued to flourish, with him making the eight hundred and fifty mile round trip in the car to watch the Hoops on a relatively regular basis.

"I only really came up the road in those days for the big games, although I would have liked to have been at every match. Quite often, I'd actually make a trip up and Betty wouldn't even know about it – I'd tell her I was on a night shift or there was a really big project on at work – whilst in reality I was on my way to Hampden or wherever. Looking back on it, I've no idea how I managed to do it so often. I know I was a younger man, but those sorts of journeys really took it out of me, and I wasn't even the one driving, that was usually one of my friends. It was worth it though, particularly if the team put on a good show and managed to attain a positive result."

As our discussions continued, Pat admitted there was a distinct possibility that his wife did indeed know about several of his secret trips up to Scotland, but simply allowed it as she knew how much it meant to him. Of course, as the years passed, Pat's journeys began not only to include Celtic's domestic matches, but their fledgling steps into the European arena also, beginning with a three-one away win against Nantes at the end of November 1966. Approximately five hundred supporters made this journey, and it would be worth all of their efforts as the Celts would rally after going a goal behind to secure a crucial win by the previously referenced scoreline. Now is perhaps an apt moment to discuss a few of Pat's favourite Celtic players, three of whom played that night in the west of France, with one subsequently given the nickname of "Pou de Ciel" ("The Flying Flea") by the local press pack.

Pat remains adamant after watching Celtic for over seventy years that Jimmy Johnstone was the most talented player whom he has ever had the pleasure of watching play in the green and white Hoops. "Jinky was the best", he told me, "That doesn't mean he was my favourite, but in terms of raw, natural talent, he was the best I've ever seen." Clearly, that evening, some of the locals agreed Johnstone was a special player, as the "Glasgow Herald" reported: "…the French crowd delighted in the speed and trickery of Johnstone." Bobby Murdoch, another player whom Pat continues to rank above many others, was also widely praised for his performance, helping to set up Celtic's second goal as he "chipped a perfect ball through a gap in the defence" which Bobby Lennox ran on to and scored.

Yet, even amongst such a plethora of talent in that team, Pat holds one man not on a level all his own, but in the highest regard nonetheless. "If I'd to pick a favourite from that team", he said, "I'd struggle to look past Bertie Auld. He was incredible. He embodied, in my mind at least, what it meant to be a Celtic player. He wasn't just skilful, he was as hard as nails when the situation required it. However, what I respect him for most is that, even now, he has time for every single Celtic fan he meets. He's a lovely man – a true gentlemen – and in an age when some modern players seem to consider interacting with the public to be a chore, he thrives on it, because he understands if he hadn't made it as a player he would be one of the cheering crowd. We may never find another talent like Johnstone, but we'll definitely never find another character like wee Bertie." Again, the "Glasgow Herald" agreed with such assumptions when discussing the Nantes tie, saying: "Celtic's best player tonight was Auld, whose industry and use of the ball was not matched by any man on either side."

Thereafter, having followed Celtic to France in the second round of the competition earlier that season, Pat would again journey to the continent in May, but on this occasion, it was for the biggest club fixture of them all, the European Cup Final. Celtic's opponents, the Italian champions Inter Milan, had won both the 1964 and 1965 tournaments, and were therefore – rightly – considered to be formidable adversaries. Despite this, amongst Pat and his friends, confidence levels were high. "Lisbon was a beautiful city", Pat told me, "bathed in gorgeous sunshine, it was a glorious place to visit, although I must say that it wasn't just the weather which made it so nice, but the people who lived there. They were so friendly, treating us all as if we were guests in their homes rather than simply visitors to their city. The language barrier proved slightly tricky, but sitting in the sun with a cold beer in front of us, it would have been a very relaxing experience had there not been any football to worry about. However, in saying that, we really weren't concerned. To me, it just seemed as if it was meant to be for Celtic that day, even before we'd made our way to the stadium. I couldn't stop my mind from repeating the same phrase over and over: "This is our time, this is our time.""

Of course, so it would prove to be, as Pat McManus and his friends took their places inside the Estádio Nacional, adjacent to the penalty box at the end of the ground in which Stevie Chalmers' European Cup winning goal would nestle in the corner of the net. Pat continued his recollections as follows: "The victory meant so much to us that day, and although we went behind early on thanks to the penalty which the Italians scored, the Celtic supporters in attendance never lost faith. As the team continued to surge forward over and over again, they were roared on by the travelling Celts, and once the first goal arrived, we knew things were in the process of going our way. With the benefit of hindsight, I really am amazed we didn't manage to win the match more convincingly, such were the levels of domination of display. To win the European Cup at all was a magnificent achievement, one which I feel was appreciated that little bit more by the older members of the support who could remember the poor days which followed the end of the Second World War, but above all else the manner in which we won that final, showing the skill, flare and attacking prowess which we did, is something that I'll always be proud of. It was a quintessential Celtic performance, to win the biggest club match there is by playing the Celtic way, particularly with eleven men from in and around Glasgow, was simply stunning. It was a privilege to be there."

As the decades passed, Pat would continue to follow Celtic to triumphs and disappointments alike, and whilst managers, players, owners and indeed stadia would all change, he remained a regular attendee, a footballing stalwart whose presence in the stands and terracing would continue for many years yet. A permanent return to Scotland would also occur, with the McManus family settling just outside the city of Glasgow.

Progressing to much more recent times, Pat's life would change forever following the St. Patrick's Day weekend match at home to Kilmarnock a few years ago. Celtic lost the League Cup tie by a single goal to nil, but that would pale into insignificance later in the day, as he stepped off the pavement near a local petrol station. There, he was struck by a taxi which pulled in at the last second after the passenger on board had asked the driver to stop so she could use the cash machine. Subsequently, Pat was hospitalised with, amongst other injuries, a broken hip. Now, an event such as this may have finished off a lesser man, but not Mr. McManus, whose thoughts inevitably turned to football again in the coming weeks. One night, between two and three weeks on from his accident, a doctor who had become friendly with Pat during his time in hospital said to him, "I see you've got a big game at the weekend", referring to Celtic's trip to Rugby Park whereby a victory would guarantee them the league title. Unsurprisingly, the man was taken aback by the answer this question received, as Pat said "Aye, I know, I'm going". The conversation then continued as follows:

"What do you mean you're "going"? I've not signed you out", replied the Doctor.

"Aye, but you'll need to sign me out just for the game", said Pat.

Eventually, after some discussion, a compromise was reached, with the agreement being that Pat – who was still unable to walk – could go to the game providing he promised to return to the hospital straight after it, without any trip to the pub or wherever for any sort of celebration. Subsequently, without access to a wheelchair, the men from Pat's supporters' club bus took turns to carry him from the vehicle to Rugby Park, where they would watch Celtic win by six goals to nil, as green and white clad supporters filled three sides of the stadium. All joking aside, this action, albeit perhaps somewhat ill-advised from a health standpoint, embodied the determination Pat had to recover from his injuries. By his own admission, his memory is not what it once was, something he often lamented when we spoke. "In days gone by", he told me, "I could have rhymed off exact dates and scorelines for matches, but you'll have to forgive me now for sometimes only being able to give you a rough idea. It can be quite frustrating at times, because occasionally I won't be able to remember something and I can't help but wonder whether the fact I am temporarily unable to is just a result of my age or an effect of the accident. It sowed a seed of doubt in my mind, and it has taken me a while to learn to cope with that."

Nowadays, the pace of Pat's life may be slightly slower than it was in days gone by, but not by as large a margin as you may expect, as he was one of the thousands who travelled to Italy for last season's tie with Inter Milan. Initially just a loving father, he is now a proud grandfather and great grandfather, and it is clear he's happily content in his patriarchal role – and rightly so. Every morning, he attends Mass and occasionally treats himself to a trip in to Celtic Park thereafter, not to watch a game but simply to wander around and enjoy the spectacle of the place, appreciating how much it has changed during his lifetime and allowing his mind to drift back to great days gone by.

At one point towards the end of our discussions, I posed the following question to Pat, "What would you do without Celtic?" The reply was almost instantaneous, "I'd probably just die!" This answer was, of course, intended to be largely comical in nature, but the undertones attached to it hint somewhat at the impact our Football Club can have on individuals in their day to day lives, and this is something which must never be underestimated.

In closing, I feel it is sufficient to say that from a personal point of view I consider Pat McManus to be a revelation of sorts. Although people say age is only a number, I am of the opinion that to still be attending nigh on every domestic home and away match, as well as the odd European away game at the age of almost eighty-one is a spectacular achievement in itself. Of course, Pat doesn't think so. As I've said he just considers it to be his passion in life, one which he will follow to the utmost of his abilities until he is no longer able to do so, but as a young man – and I have no doubt there will be many other young men and women who would agree with me when I say this – if I had the opportunity to still be doing what Pat does when I myself am that age, I would be one of the happiest people alive. It may sound clichéd to say – that his loving family aside, of course – Celtic Football Club and all those associated with it are Pat McManus' life.

"Celtic by Numbers:
"The Main Attraction""

At the end of the 2013-14 season, Celtic Park hosted the Scottish Cup Final for the eighth time in the history of the competition (excluding replays). Notably, Celtic have never won the Scottish Cup at Celtic Park and, in fact, they have only ever managed to reach the final there on one occasion, all the way back in 1901-02, when they lost to Hibernian by a single goal to nil. Of course, we shouldn't complain too much in one sense, as since that day, we have won the Scottish Cup thirty-three times, whereas the Edinburgh side have yet to register another success in the competition.

Anyway, with this in mind, I decided to examine the Scottish Cup Final in more detail than I ever have before. For some unknown reason, I have always held a love for the competition, and although it has undoubtedly lost some of its prestige and prowess with the introduction of European Football and debatably the Scottish League Cup, I still feel it represents one of the pinnacles of the Scottish game.

In all, there have been one hundred and thirty Scottish Cup Finals held to date, excluding replays and, in a few cases, second replays also. Whilst the competition first took place one hundred and forty-one years ago, it has only seen Scottish Cup Finals take place in one hundred and twenty-nine of those years, thanks a break for two World Wars and a walkover for Queen's Park in the 1884 Final. As you will all be aware, Celtic have been the most successful side in the history of the Scottish Cup, having reached the Final fifty-four times and won the trophy on thirty-six occasions – a rather neat ratio of two successes for every failure at the final hurdle.

Now, if we take a moment to consider Celtic's impact on the tournament, and particularly the Scottish Cup Final itself, an interesting pattern appears to develop. Ignoring Scottish Cup tournaments prior to Celtic's formation as, of course, they could not have taken part in them, we quickly find that the participation of Celtic Football Club in Scottish Cup Finals generally correlates notably with the highest recorded attendances at these matches to date.

In Celtic's first season in existence, the Club reached the Scottish Cup Final and, despite a disappointing loss to Third Lanark at Hampden, did something no other club has done in their inaugural year by getting there. Approximately seventeen thousand people attended the first of the two matches, and although the result was declared void (Third Lanark won by three goals to one), this represented the highest Scottish Cup Final crowd ever at that point in time. A few years later in 1892, when Celtic reached their second such Final, this record was broken as forty thousand people flocked to Ibrox Park to see Celtic defeat Queen's Park and win their first Scottish Cup (Celtic won both matches, although the first was declared void).

Sometime later, in 1904, Celtic and Rangers met in the Final for the third time, and over sixty-four thousand people saw Jimmy Quinn's hat-trick at Hampden – the first in any Scottish Cup Final – haul Celtic back from two goals behind to an unlikely victory. Again, in 1909, the two teams met at Hampden Park and despite the riot which ensued after the first replay meaning the Scottish Cup was withheld by the Scottish Football Association, it is noteworthy that this once again represented a record crowd at such a match with seventy thousand spectators in attendance.

Continuing in this record breaking vein, we come to the Scottish Cup Final of 1920, the case which provides the exception to the green and white involvement, as approximately ninety-five thousand people packed themselves together to witness Kilmarnock win their first Scottish Cup, defeating Albion Rovers by three goals to two at Celtic Park. The crowd smashed the previous record and whilst in later years Scottish Cup Finals which were played between two provincial clubs were not as highly attended as those in the years around them, the lack of such a match for six years thanks to the First World War meant that a vast number of neutral spectators paid to take in the affair for themselves.

Anyway, moving onwards to 1926, Celtic, the holders of the Scottish Cup, faced St. Mirren at Hampden Park, and as the attendance was totted up, it became clear that the record had been surpassed once more. Regrettably, the majority of the ninety-eight thousand spectators left Hampden heartbroken, as Celtic slumped to a two-nil defeat, destroying their hopes of a domestic double. Of course, as with any Cup Final, some supporters did leave the ground happy though, as St. Mirren secured the Cup for the first time.

Finally, in 1937, the record attendance for the Scottish Cup Final was broken for the last time, as one hundred and forty-seven thousand, three hundred and sixty-five people squeezed inside Hampden Park to see Celtic defeat Aberdeen by two goals to one. As is discussed in my first book, the true number of spectators at this tie (and many like it), was likely to have been far, far higher than the official attendance would suggest. In fact, the Scottish Football Museum at Hampden Park contest that a truer figure may have been somewhere in the region of one hundred and eighty thousand – or three full modern day Celtic Parks at once. To contextualise that somewhat, with the population of Scotland in 1937 believed to have been just under the five million mark, one can say that approximately one in every twenty-seven people in Scotland attended the match at Hampden Park that day. Presently, about one in every ninety people in the country make their way to Celtic Park whenever it is at full capacity. Of course, for the record, these calculations do not take into account those supporters travelling from outside of Scotland.

For the sake of this statistical analysis, I shall stick to the official figures, but already one thing has become abundantly clear, Celtic Football Club have been and continue to be the biggest crowd-pullers in Scotland. Of the seven occasions upon which the record attendance for the Scottish Cup Final has been broken since the formation of the Football Club, Celtic, and therefore their legions of supporters, have been directly involved in six of them – more than any other club – and this is no coincidence.

Even when one considers the Scottish Cup Finals held after the Second World War (since the record set by the 1937 Scottish

Cup Final will likely never be broken), similar trends can be seen, although the contests between Celtic and Rangers, which had then become world famous, would often draw some of the biggest crowds in later days.

Only on seven occasions in all of history has the official attendance figure for the Scottish Cup Final passed the one hundred and thirty thousand mark. Six of these occurred post World War Two, with the other being the aforementioned 1937 Final. Of these seven matches, five have involved Celtic, more than any other Football Club once again. Interestingly though, the highest post war attendance for such a tie is actually held by the clash between Motherwell and Dundee in 1952, when "The Steelmen" won the first of their two Scottish Cups.

Still, before I conclude, I would like to indulge you all in a few numbers which I think should make us all proud of Scottish Football – granted, it's not perfect – but I'm sure you'll enjoy the next couple of paragraphs nonetheless.

Over the years, if we ignore replays and matches declared null and void for the moment, just shy of eight million, two hundred thousand people have attended Scottish Cup Finals alone, with an average of sixty-three thousand people present on each occasion. When one considers the fact that many of the crowds numbered less than ten thousand in the earliest days of the competition (prior to Celtic's inception), this becomes even more impressive.

After all, more people have attended Scottish Cup Finals over the years than every European Cup Final, World Cup Final, and SuperBowl combined. This gap is steadily closing, but with more than a couple of hundred thousand spectators currently the difference, this statistic will hold true for a little while yet.

"Our First Captain:
"On to the Boardroom""

A few months later, Celtic would carry on as they had finished off previously, opening the new season of 1893-94 with another five-nil victory, this time over Third Lanark. A comfortable away win at Dundee followed, before a disappointing goalless draw with Dumbarton at Celtic Park preceded the Celts' trip to Ibrox, which fell early in the calendar that year. There, Rangers would competitively defeat Celtic in the Scottish League for the first time in their history and it would not be the last occasion upon which the Ibrox side gave us what could only be described as a battering, reversing the scoreline of the previously referenced Glasgow Merchant's Charity Cup Final and winning by five goals to nil themselves.

Undoubtedly, such a hefty defeat stung the Celts, who responded by winning their next twelve matches, nine of which were competitive, overcoming the likes of Heart of Midlothian along the way, as well as English sides Sunderland (champions) and Preston North End (runner's-up). However, when they faced Rangers again, this time in the Glasgow Cup semi-finals, Celtic again fell by the wayside, losing by a solitary goal to nil.

Following on from this, Celtic once more responded positively by winning their next nine competitive fixtures, securing their hold on the top place in the Scottish League and making their way to their fourth Scottish Cup Final in the process. Having scored twenty-five goals in the four matches which led to the final, the Celts would almost always have been the clear favourites to win the trophy against any Scottish side, but once again they were faced with their bogey team that season – the only side to beat them so far, in fact – Rangers. In horrendous weather, the Ibrox side marched out into the lead, and despite a late point from Willie Maley, it was the light blues who won the Scottish Cup for the first time, winning by three goals to one and leaving Celtic with one Scottish Cup Final victory from four attempts – hardly the sort of record befitting of the Club considering how well they had done in their early years. Regardless, the Celts would have something to celebrate soon after, as they retained their Scottish League title, becoming the first side to do so alone (you may recall that Dumbarton were joint winners of the first championship, before winning the second by themselves). Kelly would then captain Scotland once again to a convincing five-two victory over Wales before the spring was at an end.

The following league season, 1894-95, did not start well for the Celts, who first drew with Dundee before losing at Third Lanark, these two away results being interspersed with a victory over St. Bernard's at Celtic Park. They then endured a gruelling two-all draw in the first round of the Glasgow Cup with Battlefield (minus James Kelly, it has to be said), before winning a pulsating derby match with Rangers by a score of five goals to three in the league the following weekend. James Kelly returned for that match and on the page which the "Celtic Wiki" website has devoted to this fixture, they cite a quote from the "Glasgow Observer Catholic Newspaper":

"The game produced more fouls on the part of one team than I have ever witnessed, and I am informed by Celtic players that the language some of the Rangers' players used was most disgraceful – "Fenian", "Papist", "Irish" – all being hurled with, of course, the most vulgar accompaniments."

Now, whilst it is generally accepted that the sectarian policies of Rangers Football Club only truly became entrenched upon the arrival of Bill Struth at Ibrox Park around the end of World War One, such evidence suggests that there was certainly a feeling of anti-Irishness and anti-Catholicism being harboured by some of the players and, one would presume, some of the fans around this time, although it must be said that this was likely not to have been only applicable to the Ibrox club. I can only despair when I imagine the reaction of those Celtic players who played that day if they had known that such terms would still be in fairly common public use more than a century later.

Following on from that victory, the Celts made their way past Battlefield at the second attempt, thanks in part to two goals from centre forward Walter Lees. Having played briefly with the Celts in 1892 he had since been with Lincoln City south of the border. However, having returned to Parkhead, the Celts were accused of using illegal monetary incentives to tempt Walter back to the Club, and thus until the matter was resolved, no English side would be allowed to face Celtic for a friendly match on order of the Football Association. Therefore, only a couple of weeks later, after scoring three goals in his four appearances for the Celts (including those in his previous spell), Walter would be sent back to Lincoln City.

Regardless, his goals against Battlefield would prove to have been worth something for less than two months later, having since surpassed Clyde and Cowlairs, Celtic defeated Rangers by a two goal margin for the second time that season to win the Glasgow Cup, their third such triumph in what was, in the past, a popular competition indeed. Thereafter, the Celts comfortably dispatched Queen's Park in the first round of the Scottish Cup before losing to Hibernian in the same tournament, subsequently being reinstated, and then eventually being knocked out in rather disappointing fashion by Dundee in the next round.

Celtic would then travel to Tynecastle knowing that a victory was crucial if they were to have even a chance of clawing back Hearts' lead at the top of the league table. In the modern day, the situation going into such a vital match would have seemed somewhat out of the ordinary, for although Celtic trailed the Edinburgh side by eleven points, the visitors had five games in hand on their opponents – thanks, in large part, to Celtic's progression through cup competitions, with a few replays and a spot of bad weather along the way too. This meant that as the teams ran out, Hearts had only two matches other than this one to play before their league season was at an end, whilst the Celts had seven.

The home side stormed to a four-nil victory, declaring themselves the Champions of Scotland in all but officialdom in the process, as it would have required a truly fantastical run of results for their lead to be overturned. Notably though, one cannot blame this defeat on the number of matches in which Celtic had played that season, as they had not contested a single tie for almost a month prior to their trip to Edinburgh. In all likelihood, the defeat can be put to the fact that Heart of Midlothian were, at that time, a superior side to Celtic, having also won the previous league tie that season at Celtic Park. They adapted better to difficult conditions underfoot at Tynecastle (described by one newspaper as being the result of "melting snow") and, once they scored their first goal and had their tails up, it is unlikely any Scottish team would have able to stop them.

However, having then went on to draw one-all at Ibrox in one of their remaining league fixtures, the season would end with some minor celebrations for the Celts, as they beat Rangers fournil in the final of the Glasgow Charity's Merchants Cup Final at Cathkin Park. This meant that despite disappointing results in both the Scottish League and the Scottish Cup during the season of 1894-95, the Celts did still have two pieces of silverware to show for their efforts.

The season of 1895-96 was to be a better one for Celtic and, in many senses for James Kelly, who would enjoy some real high points domestically, interspersed with the odd low. The early running saw the Celts start their league campaign fairly positively – despite losses to both Edinburgh sides in the autumn – winning at Ibrox, Carolina Port (Dundee's home at that stage) and Boghead Park. There was also the famous eleven-nil home victory over Dundee which remains Celtic's largest competitive victory, whilst the Celts quietly progressed through the various rounds of the Glasgow Cup until, once again, they found themselves in the final.

Here, they would face an old foe in the form of Queen's Park and this would be one of James Kelly's finest hours, coming less than a month after his thirtieth birthday. When one considers the Celtic line-up that day, we are allowed a glimpse into the quality of the players at Parkhead at that point in time, which included not only the great James Kelly, but the maverick Dan Doyle, a clever but tough half-back line with Willie Maley and Barney Battles Sr. on either side of their captain, and an attacking array which boasted the likes of James Blessington, John Madden and

Sandy McMahon. Despite the fact that Queen's Park were undoubtedly still a good side, it is interesting to think how differently they would have treated such a match against Celtic had it taken place five years earlier. By 1895, the complacency associated with playing this new club had worn off, as the Celts had firmly established themselves as one of the finest teams in Scottish football.

The following is from the "Notes on Sports" section of the "Glasgow Herald": "A grand display of football was witnessed on Ibrox Park on Saturday afternoon when the Queen's Park and the Celtic played off the final tie for the Glasgow Cup. Finals are not usually associated with good football, but Saturday's was an exception to the rule, as play throughout was of the most brilliant description. There never was a dull moment and the spectators from start to finish were kept at a high pitch of excitement. The Celtic led off in good style and they quickly opened the scoring. Shortly after this a remarkable change came over the game, the Queen's playing with determination and vigour, and not only did they equalise, but at half-time they actually led by three goals to one."

"With such a pull the Queen's supporters were confident that their favourites would win, and the manner they commenced the second half in gave them additional hope. For fully ten minutes they rushed everything before them, rendering the Celtic backs almost helpless, and they almost added to their score. From this time on to the finish, however, the game underwent another remarkable transformation. The Celtic, chiefly owing to the spirited efforts of Kelly, romped away at great pace, fairly overwhelming the Queen's defence, and, scoring goal after goal, they ran out the winners of one of the greatest matches ever witnessed."

A few of the individual incidents from the match are described within the match report which featured in the same newspaper, as it discusses the second half in some detail. From this, it is clear to see that Celtic were most certainly struggling (to such a degree Queen's Park were guilty of some level of showboating), until their determination and ability won through, led by their captain, James Kelly.

"There were twenty-five thousand spectators present. There was a break in, but the crowd remained quite orderly. The Queen's started with ten men, but despite that fact they had the best of the opening passages, and Cameron very nearly scored, the ball just hitting the post. Allison came on the field after a few minutes play, completing the Queen's team."

"The Celtic pulled themselves together, but they never looked like a winning team, the amateurs fairly taking it out of them and playing them at every turn. What was considered to be the weak spot in the Queen's armour proved itself to be the strongest, Gillespie and Smith playing splendidly at the back, and repelling all the attacks of the Celtic. The Queen's never played in pluckier or more determined fashion, and it was these factors which took the Celts by surprise, and fairly pulverised them, at all events during the first ten minutes. The Queen's were cheered to the echo, and well did they deserve it, for never did a team respond more nobly to the calls made upon them. There was no weak division in the whole lot. The Celtic forwards were blocked, baffled and beaten back in all directions, while the Queen's forward fairly played Meechan and Doyle, meeting them in fearless style and playing them to perfection."

"After twenty minutes play [of the second half] the Celtic scored their second goal, Anderson rushing out of his goal and missing the ball, which was shot in by Ferguson. The game looked a bit more open, and the Celts chances improved. Kelly was in the thick of the fray, and to his efforts especially were due the Celts revival. After thirty minutes the Celts equalised, and were now playing in their true form. McMahon scored the third and equalising point. It was a death and life struggle full of excitement as each team tried its hardest to get the leading goal."

"The Queen's broke away, and Crookston just missed heading the ball through. There could be no doubt the Celts improved vastly towards the close, and they fairly redeemed their reputation. The transformation came as a surprise, just as everyone thought they were completely "bottled up", and only a save from Anderson prevented them from getting the leading goal."

"Just twelve minutes from the close the Celtic scored the fourth and leading goal. The Queen's protested on the ground of offside, but the point was allowed. The Queen's seemed upset at the decision, and the Celtic, putting on the pressure at a tremendous rate, scored the fifth goal. The Queen's tried hard to stem the tide, but it was no use. It was disheartening and disappointing to be beaten after such a display for over an hour. The Celts added another goal just on the call of time, and the game ended as follows: – Celts, 6 goals. Queen's, 3 goals."

Queen's Park would have their revenge of sorts in January, when they knocked Celtic out of the Scottish Cup at Parkhead by a margin of four goals to two, but with a second successive Glasgow Cup triumph to their names, the Celts pushed on to win their third Scottish League title, eventually finishing the campaign four points clear of their closest competitors, Rangers, whom they had defeated both home and away, scoring ten goals in the process. Also, the twenty-eighth of March 1896 would see James Kelly pull on a Scotland jersey for the final time, captaining his country for the fourth match in succession (considering only games in which he appeared) and finishing his international career with a three-all away draw against Ireland.

Now, we turn our attention to the season of 1896-97, the last which saw any involvement from Celtic's first captain as a player. Whilst the Celts would ultimately finish the campaign without any silverware to their name (thanks partly to the infamous player strike discussed in another chapter), they did come close, only failing to make it three Glasgow Cup victories on the bounce after a two-one replay defeat in the final against Rangers, who would also go on to lift the Scottish Cup. Considering this was the season when Celtic suffered the first giant-killing in their history, losing to lowly Arthurlie in the first round of the national knockout tournament, I suppose I should take the stance of the less said about that the better, particularly for Kelly's sake, who would have been most disappointed to lose such a match, especially with his Scottish Cup pedigree in mind. The league itself was one of the most hotly contested championships for years, with all five teams who featured in the top half of the standings finishing within six points of eventual winners, Hearts. Celtic's relative lack of goals cost them dearly as they ended the campaign four points off the top spot, for they had conceded fewer than any other side in the two league divisions, a lasting testament to the influence Kelly had upon the defensive line.

In truth, it is regrettable to think that James Kelly's playing career came to an end with four consecutive losses, which began with a two-nil defeat at Ibrox on the nineteenth of December 1896 and culminated with a two-nil away loss to St. Mirren in Paisley in mid-March 1897. Had Celtic won their remaining three league matches (the fourth loss I mentioned previously was the Scottish Cup tie against Arthurlie), they would have been crowned as the Champions of Scotland, and what a fitting end to a great playing career that would have been for Kelly, but it wasn't to be. Again, this must have troubled the captain, who was always known to be a fierce competitor who detested losing, and this would continue to be the case long after he stopped taking part in matches himself. Therefore James Kelly, one of the first Celtic stars, enjoyed his last competitive victory in a Celtic shirt on the twelfth of December 1896, as the Celts eased past Clyde by a margin of four goals to one at Parkhead. At that point, Celtic topped the Scottish League table, but by the time their captain officially retired on the thirteenth of April 1897, they lay fourth in the league standings as I have said.

Before considering James' later life, allow me to quote a correspondent writing for the "Dundee Evening Telegraph" who recounts his overall thoughts on Kelly as a player, almost a decade on from his retirement.

"Possessed of great speed, a keen eye and untiring energy, Kelly was an almost ideal half-back. To see him dash across, say thirty yards, when a wing half was beaten, and nimbly rob the forwards was something not to be readily forgotten. Of rather short stature, he was nevertheless of good substance…and never had to shirk his work for physical reasons. If he had a weakness it was in placing, and probably the swiftness of his work accounted for this. The forward who could beat Kelly required a head start. His honours were numerous…Kelly was absolutely the best centre half-back in Scotland in his day."

Taking up a role as a director following on from the decision to turn the Club into a limited liability company in June 1897,

James Kelly was a member of the first ever Celtic Board (previously a committee had run the Club). A little over a decade later in 1909, following on from the sad death of John H. McLaughlin, who had held the role of Chairman during the intervening period, Kelly was elected to this role. Clearly, this was indicative of the high standing in which his peers regarded him, and he served in this sense dutifully until 1914, when he resigned owing to other work commitments, returning to a directorship at the club. Now may be an apt moment upon which to make a broader point as we consider that James' successor as Chairman, Tom White – along with the man who followed him, Robert Kelly – held the reins of power at the Football Club for the majority of the next six decades. I believe it is critical to point out that whilst the influences of the Kellys and the Whites will always be contentious (justifiably so), James Kelly had largely a very positive impact on the Football Club over the years, so nobody should tar him with the same brush as his descendants nor punish him for their shortcomings.

Considering more personal matters, the Census of the United Kingdom carried out in 1911 gives us some insight into the home life of James Kelly, then Chairman of Celtic Football Club. As a resident of Blantyre, he lived alongside fifteen other people in a house – albeit a spacious one – as it is listed as having thirteen rooms with one or more windows. He and his wife Margaret have five sons (Francis, Charles, Robert, David and Joseph) and four daughters (Agnes, Bride, Margaret and Jane Elizabeth). At this point the youngest, Joseph, is listed as being only a month old. They were accompanied in the house by three female servants ranging from nineteen to fifty in terms of age, with another woman (perhaps an extended family member) listed as a visitor, and a nurse present also.

Whilst James' profession is listed as a "sports merchant", he also spent much time working with the local council and school board. Clearly, a few of his male relatives inherited some of his footballing prowess, with his son Francis signing for Motherwell from Blantyre Victoria in 1915; son Charles joining Queen's Park in 1920 after a spell with Blantyre Celtic; and nephew John

Broadley being acquired by Hibernian having impressed as a junior with St. Roch's in 1926. Also, his daughter Bride would marry Celtic player William Hughes in 1934 whilst another of his sons, Robert, would go on to become Chairman of the Football Club himself in 1947, to which I have previously made reference.

James Kelly died on the twentieth of February 1932, at the age of sixty-six, as a life devoted to sport and particularly Celtic Football Club finally came to an end. Having died late on Saturday night – the day upon which the "Edinburgh Evening News" reported he was "lying seriously ill at his home" – his passing was reported by the "Glasgow Herald" on the following Monday.

"Death of Mr. James Kelly – Original Member of Celtic F.C. – Mr. James Kelly, J.P., a director and ex-Chairman of the Glasgow Celtic Football Club, died at his residence, Thornhill, Blantyre, on Saturday night. Mr. Kelly's fatal illness was a direct result of an injury which he sustained when playing for the Celtic football team many years ago – a severe injury to his head. He accompanied the Celtic team on their American tour last year, and shortly after his return home he complained of a recurrence of the pains in his head. The funeral will take place to St. Patrick's Cemetery, New Stevenston, tomorrow, following Requiem Mass at St. Joseph's R.C. Church, Blantyre. Mr. Kelly is survived by his wife and a grown-up family of four sons and four daughters. His eldest son, Frank, was killed whilst serving with the Glasgow Highlanders in France."

"Mr. Kelly…was one of the best known sporting personalities in Scotland. In addition to his football and many business interests, he took a very active part in public affairs. He served for many years on the old School Board in Blantyre, and later represented the Stonefield Division of Blantyre on the Lanark County Council. He resigned from this position some years ago, and was appointed a Justice of the Peace for Lanarkshire. Prior to becoming one of the original Celtic football team Mr. Kelly was a member of the famous Renton team and played for them against West Bromwich Albion for "the championship of the world." In 1888, he played centre half-back in the first game between Celtic and Rangers."

In all, James Kelly made one hundred and thirty-nine competitive League and Scottish Cup appearances for Celtic Football Club, scoring eleven goals in the process. He will forever hold the honour of having been the first man to captain the Celts, and his services, both on and off of the field of play, remain just as important and worthy of remembrance now as they did over a century ago. James Kelly led us to our first three Scottish League Championships, our inaugural Scottish Cup win, four Glasgow Cups, four Glasgow Merchant's Charity Cups and, of course, to our first trophy of all, the Glasgow North Eastern Cup, which the Club won in both 1889 and 1890. He also made eight senior appearances for Scotland, captaining his country on four occasions and scoring one goal also. Undoubtedly, he led by example and provided a beacon for both his teammates and the Celtic support to follow, especially as he played in the time before the Football Club's first manager, Willie Maley, had taken up his role. He was one of the figureheads which helped a new Football Club, formed in the East End of Glasgow with the aim of raising money to improve the standards of living of the sick, hungry and needy, rise to become the biggest footballing side in the country – a Club which would one day conquer Europe with an attacking style of play which was the envy of the world. The legacy of James Kelly has not, and must never be forgotten. He remains a Celt of the highest calibre.

In his book, "The Story of the Celtic, 1888-1938", Willie Maley paid the following tribute to his departed comrade, and it is upon this note which I wish to bring this series of chapters to an end.

"His fame as a player needs no recounting as his name is known wherever the game is played. As a centre-half he had few equals and no superior. Of a kindly disposition, his work on the Club's Board of Management was great, and his memory will live long with those privileged to know him...May the turf he loved to tread in life rest kindly on him in his last sleep."

"Tales of Their Time:
"Our Very First Game""

In the summer of 1972, the "Celtic View" published the previous headline above a sublime article which discussed the exploits of one Dan Drake, a ninety-four year old man who had followed the Football Club from its debut match in 1888. However, before proceeding to the piece itself, allow me to expand a little upon Dan's background.

Born in 1878, Daniel Drake was the second son of Samuel and Cecilia Drake, an iron turner and home keeper by trade. Married on the nineteenth of July 1874 at St. Patrick's Chapel in Glasgow, Samuel and Cecilia (née McEwan) had six children, although it appears only four of them survived infancy to be named in subsequent census records; Philip (two years Dan's senior), Daniel, Sarah (two years Dan's junior) and Cecilia (five years Dan's junior). Whilst all of his siblings are listed as having been born in Glasgow, Dan appears unique, as his place of birth is said to have been England, although no more specific details are given than this. Regardless, whilst the census of 1891 has him listed as a twelve year old school pupil living with his family in an area of Anderston long since replaced by Glasgow's network of motorways and dual carriageways, Dan had moved up to Maryhill at some point in the next two decades.

In the 1911 census – with Celtic not having long since finished their famous streak of six Scottish League Championships in a row – Dan was a thirty-two year old tailor, living with his mother and sister (both Cecilia's). The former was now a widow, with Dan's dad Samuel having died around a year earlier, whilst the latter worked as a sewing machinist, possibly with her brother. Dan would have been in his sixties when World War Two broke out, contextualising the age of the man somewhat. Whilst he would retell some of his footballing experiences to the Celtic View as follows, I felt his wider life story – sparse though the detail may be – was worthy of inclusion. Daniel Drake died in 1976 at the age of ninety-seven, having seen everything from Celtic's birth to their European Cup glory and nine Scottish League Championships in a row – a life well lived.

"The Celtic View" – Summer 1972

"Dan Drake is an alert and fit-looking man of ninety-four who can remember the first Celtic games of 1888 and enjoys talking about them. Mr. Drake was a boy of ten when his father took him and his brother to see Celtic play their first game as a club. "My father didn't know the first thing about football," Mr. Drake said, "but my brother and I were keen and my father took us to see the Celts to encourage our interest in the sport. Sitting in a room of the Home run by the Little Sisters of the Poor at Roystonhill in Glasgow, Mr. Drake, who must be one of Celtic's oldest supporters, warmed to his favourite subject. He said: "You used to go down Dalmarnock Street to the old Celtic ground (Barrs Lemonade occupy the site now behind Janefield Cemetery) and although it wasn't very big it held several thousand spectators quite comfortably."

"Uphill – "As a matter of fact, although the park had a small stand, many of the more able fans climbed on to the cemetery boundary wall for a better view of the matches. At that time the site of the present Celtic Park was a large piece of waste ground with a huge crater in the middle which was about thirty or forty feet deep. In those days there was no Scottish League competition. The programme, apart from cup-ties, was filled up with games against famous English sides like the Corinthians, Mitchell's St. George's, Bolton Wanderers and Burnley. Celtic were founded to provide charity, but no one can really appreciate just how successful they were in those very hard times. They also gave an interest to the down-trodden Irish community in Glasgow who were able to identify themselves with the uphill fight of the club.""

"Speaking of the players in that first game, Mr. Drake said they came from all over the country but they combined as though they had played football together for years. In the first game Celtic beat Rangers five-two before a crowd of about two thousand spectators. But it was as he spoke of great individuals that Mr. Drake really got into his stride. He said: "Peter Dowds was about the best half-back I ever saw play, but my outstanding memory of a Celtic half-back line was that of Willie Maley, James Kelly and Paddy Gallagher (not to be confused with Patsy Gallagher). That was the half-back line in the Celtic team of 1892 that won the Scottish Cup, Glasgow Cup, Charity Cup and finished runners-up in the Scottish League Championship which had just started the previous year. Other outstanding players I remember included Willie Groves, who was a great ball player, and James McLaren, a left-half from Hibernian known as "The General". Mickey McKeown, Neilly McCallum and Johnny Madden were other great players I remember.""

""Talking of Johnny Madden, he went to Prague at the beginning of the century, and became a national figure as a result of his wonderful coaching of footballers. The great thing about the Celtic teams was their ability to play football on the ground. They combined so well in their passing that people who disliked them used to say they needed a carpet to play football. One problem Celtic had in the beginning was finding a really good goalkeeper but that was solved with the arrival of Dan McArthur. He was on the small side but his timing and agility more than made up for his lack of height. Although most people consider John Thomson to have been the greatest Celtic goalkeeper of all time, I think Thomson and McArthur were so outstanding you couldn't say one was better than the other.""

""The best full-back partnership was that of Jerry Reynolds and Dan Doyle, though strangely enough they were very different types of players. Reynolds could head the ball as far as most players could kick it, and Doyle could kick a long ball with deadly accuracy. Doyle used to be a torment to opposition players when taking free-kicks. He could hit the ball right into the opponents' penalty area from his own half of the field, but if anyone moved as he ran to hit it he just stopped dead and started his run all over again. This seemed to have an unsettling effect on defences. I also remember with joy the great left-wing partnership of Sandy McMahon and Johnny Campbell who each seemed instinctively to know what the other was going to do. Celtic had, in fact, signed the Benburb left-wing of Barney Crossan and Campbell but Crossan couldn't oust McMahon from the inside-left spot. In the middle of the 1890s, however, Crossan won a Scottish Cup medal with the now defunct St. Bernard's whom he had joined from Celtic.""

"According to Mr. Drake, Celtic's other outstanding quality was their tremendous fighting spirit, a quality which has remained with the club since their early difficult days. One great example of this he remembers, was in a Glasgow Cup final against Rangers at old Cathkin Park. Celtic lost Willie Maley and Sandy McMahon early in the game through injury, but the nine remaining players rolled up their sleeves and won by two goals to nil. Mr. Drake hasn't seen Celtic now for about two years, but he thinks the club's success is attributable to three main qualities: Good football, the will to win, and discipline on and off the park."

"Smile – "What Willie Maley did for half a century," he said, "has been carried on by Jimmy McGrory and Jock Stein and, judging by the players they've got at present, Mr. Stein can go on adding successes to those which he has already won. Considering all the things that have happened in Celtic's history I think the greatest triumph of all has just been completed – winning seven League Championships in succession. I don't think I'll see that feat equalled in my lifetime," concluded Mr. Drake with a suspicion of a smile."

"This Was a Lisbon Lion"

Throughout the decades and centuries, it is entirely possible that the achievements of one Celtic side will continue to shine brighter than any other, unless some unknown triumphs of a future team await the Club's supporters in the coming years. Whether people refer to this group of men as the Lisbon Lions, the Kings of Europe or indeed simply the greatest Celtic team of all, the names of Ronnie Simpson; Jim Craig and Tommy Gemmell; Bobby Murdoch, Billy McNeill and John Clark; Jimmy Johnstone, Willie Wallace, Stevie Chalmers, Bertie Auld and Bobby Lennox will live as long as the Football Club itself and perhaps beyond, such were the scale of their successes during the 1966-67 season. Equally, the names of the manager Jock Stein and his coaching staff, with Sean Fallon being the most prominent, will also be held sacred by the fan base. Yet, these are not the only men whose names should be revered, as other Celts within the wider playing squad made vital contributions en route to victories in each competition in which the Football Club entered that season.

John Hughes, Joe McBride and Charlie Gallacher all featured in Celtic's run to the European Cup Final in Lisbon, whilst David Cattanach, John Cushley, John Fallon (the substitute goalkeeper throughout the European campaign) and Ian Young all appeared in at least one domestic tie over the course of the season. Trainer Neil Mochan, physio Bob Rooney and masseur Jimmy Steele are also due much credit, but having given all of these men their due, allow me to introduce the only man not previously mentioned who pulled on a Celtic jersey that season, William O'Neill.

Born on the thirtieth of December 1940, he was one of those lucky men whose childhood dreams of growing up to play for the Football Club he adored would come true. Willie's earliest involvement in football – other than out on the streets presumably – came at school, as he represented both Sacred Heart and Our Lady of Fatima, before enjoying a spell with junior side St. Anthony's.

It would be here that the young man, standing at five feet and ten inches in height, would catch the attention of those at Celtic Park. A lifelong supporter of the Football Club, one can only imagine the emotions involved as Willie put pen to paper and signed for the Celts in the middle of October 1959.

From a historical point of view, I have only been able to find one other Celtic player who made their senior debut for the Football Club in a comparable manner to that which Willie O'Neill did, as he was called up to feature in his first senior game against Dunfermline Athletic – in the replay of the 1961 Scottish Cup Final. For the record, this man was William McCafferty, who played for Celtic against Hibernian in the Scottish Cup Final defeat of 1902. McCafferty would only appear once more for the Celts thereafter, before his departure for Stenhousemuir in 1903. Returning to 1961 though, Celtic had not won the old trophy since 1954, having suffered numerous semi-final and final defeats during the intervening period, and thus the pressure was on the Celts to perform. The first fixture had finished goalless, meaning a crowd of almost eighty-eight thousand spectators would arrive at Hampden on the following Wednesday for the replay which was set to kick-off at quarter past six in the evening.

Twenty-four hours prior to the match, Willie would likely not have given himself any chance of being selected to play, but on the Tuesday night, the Celts' then left-back of choice Jim Kennedy was rushed into hospital with a bout of acute appendicitis. As such, the Hoops would require a late replacement, and the twenty year old was called upon. On the day of the game, the "Evening Times" devoted an entire article to Willie, not only discussing the pressure which he would inevitably find himself under but also the faith which one man above all others, Sean Fallon, had in him and voiced loudly, as follows.

"Sean Fallon's Verdict on the New Celt – O'Neill is a Real Good One! One hundred thousand pairs of eyes will stare hard at Hampden tonight! They will be watching every move made by a 20 year old boy in a Celtic jersey. The boy is Willie O'Neill, and he will be facing this three-fold ordeal – (1) He will be playing in Celtic's top team for the first time in his life. (2) He will be playing in Celtic's most important game of the season. (3) He will have to beat both the Dunfermline right wing, and the famous Hampden roar."

"O'Neill has been called up to the green and white colours because the seasoned Jim Kennedy was rushed to a Paisley hospital last night for an appendicitis operation. Now the big talking point in Scotland today is this – "Are Celtic taking an outrageous gamble in throwing O'Neill into the Hampden arena to face a one hundred thousand strong crowd when he is used to playing before supporters numbered only in their hundreds?" One man who supports the O'Neill promotion one hundred per cent is Celtic coach Sean Fallon. He says – "This boy is good. He came to us from St. Anthony's with a first class reputation. He has both the temperament and the physique needed for the big time. He stands 5ft 10 inches, in his boots, and he weighs 11½ stones. He has been playing extremely well in the reserves all season. He will not let us down! And I believe we will win."

"O'Neill has won his chance of a coveted and unexpected gold Cup medal because of the admirable Celtic policy of giving every youngster his opportunity no matter when it comes along. The Sean Fallon view on this point is – "The policy is right. If a player is an understudy to a first team man it is only fair to give him his chance. It is the best possible encouragement to the young-sters who are knocking at the first team door". The bright new-comer is a plater in a Clyde shipyard…He turned up for Celtic's training session today looking both cool and calm. Yes, Celtic trained a matter of hours before the 6.15 kick-off at Hampden. All top team players were called to Celtic Park at lunchtime, they did some loosening up exercises and they stayed together for a light meal and then moved out to Hampden one hour before the start of the replay."

Of course, as has been well documented, the match would not transpire to be one of those glorious evenings forever written into Celtic folklore, as Jock Stein's Dunfermline won by two goals to nil. By all accounts, the majority of the Celts' forward line was toothless in its attempts to beat the Pars' goalkeeper Eddie Connachan, who had one of the games of his life. Trailing one-nil and pushing forward desperately in search of an unlikely equaliser, Celtic were caught out in the final minutes of the match and their opponents capitalised on their error, putting the result beyond doubt and causing a barrage of bottles and other objects to rain down from the green and white terracing. For the third time since the famous double of 1954, Celtic had fallen at the last of the Scottish Cup hurdles, and understandably everyone associated with the Club, players and supporters alike, would have felt dejected.

Interestingly, Willie was one of the few Celtic players to receive some praise for their individual showing in the days which would follow, with the "Glasgow Herald" saying "O'Neill gave a most creditable, cool display in his first big match; he certainly deserved a winner's medal much more than his forward colleagues." Perhaps the most ironic point of note regarding this whole affair was that had Jim Kennedy not been struck down by health concerns, Willie O'Neill would very likely have been one of the few Celts celebrating that night in late April 1961, as the Celtic reserves went to Tynecastle and came away with a victory by six goals to three to secure the Reserve League Championship. Bertie Auld, whose departure to Birmingham City was now imminent, netted two of the goals. However, despite the inevitable disappointment which came with the result at Hampden, I cannot imagine any young player would have given up their place in such a prestigious match in order to play in a reserve tie. Critically, Willie now had his foot in the door, and with Jim Kennedy out of action for the small amount of the season which remained, he would have at least four more opportunities to show everyone what he could do.

The first of the two league fixtures involved would come away at Fir Park, the ground upon which Celtic suffered their worst ever defeat just days after their Scottish Cup Final exertions of 1937. However, despite not enjoying the same calibre of result in the Cup Final as they had done over two decades previously, the Celts of 1961 did achieve a better scoreline in Motherwell this time, but only just, with a late Willie Fernie goal meaning the match was drawn two-all. However, early on in the tie, Willie O'Neill would intervene in a manner which he would emulate most famously a little over five years later. The "Evening Times" briefly makes mention of this, saying "Immediately after the start there was a very near thing at the Celtic end when a Roberts' effort could have brought a goal if O'Neill had not been on the goal line to clear with Haffey well out of reach."

Willie's other performances before the close of play that season, a three-one home loss in the final remaining league tie against Hearts and two successive draws which led to Celtic jointly holding the Glasgow Charities Cup were not worthy of much note, but due to the return of Jim Kennedy to full fitness for the start of the 1961-62 season, Willie would not appear in a senior Celtic line-up again until the following March. As such, he would wait almost a year between pulling on a Celtic jersey as a senior player for the first time and enjoying his inaugural victory.

Willie's chance would only come again owing to the fact that Jim Kennedy was suffering from an injury once more. Willie deputised for two matches in succession as Celtic won by two goals to nil at home against Aberdeen and five goals to nil away at St. Mirren. On the eve of the second fixture, the "Evening Times" said the following whilst confirming Kennedy would again be absent at Love Street: "There will be no return for Celtic left-back Jim Kennedy against St. Mirren at Love Street tonight… Kennedy, who missed Saturday's game against Aberdeen with a leg strain, was at Parkhead today for a fitness test. During the check-up he still felt pain from the injury and manager Jimmy McGrory decided not to risk Jim in tonight's game. However, the good news for Celtic fans is that Jim should be off the unfit list in ample time for Saturday's cup semi-final against St. Mirren at Ibrox. Willie O'Neill, who did so well as Kennedy's deputy against Aberdeen, will play again tonight…"

Less than a week after Willie featured in the trouncing of St. Mirren, a similar Celtic side would lose by three goals to one to them in the semi-finals of the Scottish Cup. The Celts' defence was very poor that day, but it would not be fair of me to pin such a disastrous result on the returning Jim Kennedy. The following season, that of 1962-63, Willie O'Neill clocked up more than ten appearances over the course of a campaign for the first time, as well as playing in Celtic Football Club's debut pair of European matches.

Having played in just two senior league and cup competitive matches in the last year and only three in total as September 1962 neared an end, Willie would be thrown in at the deep end once more as the Celts prepared to take on Valencia in Spain. There is no mention prior to match day itself of McGrory's intention to pick O'Neill, although it was known that he was part of the twenty-one man squad which travelled. The "Evening Times" said the following of his selection in an article adjoined by a picture of O'Neill, with the caption "Surprise choice for left-half".

"The Celtic Party have been astonished to find so much rain. A fortnight ago they were told by a friend just back from Spain that there had been no rain for three months. Indeed, he advised the players to take white Panama hats with them! But Celtic are delighted not only with their reception and hospitality in Valencia, but with the playing conditions for their Fairs Cities Cup tie. They have been working hard at training and the latest news from their hotel headquarters, miles outside of the city, is that Price will not play and that young Willie O'Neill will take over at left-half. The forward line has not yet been named."

Celtic went on to lose their first leg clash by four goals to two, but praise for Willie O'Neill came from an unlikely source, as a correspondent writing for the Spanish newspaper "Marca" said: "We liked the Celtic side. They played steadily, with smooth movement. Crerand and O'Neill were very good. The defence with the giant McNeill is made up of players who are tough, but who play a clean and noble game."

During the intervening period between the two legs, which totalled nearly an entire month, Willie O'Neill held on to his place in the Celtic side as they racked up victories against Raith Rovers, Motherwell and Dundee United, although he would return to his more accomplished left-back role for the last of these three victories. Draws against Kilmarnock in the league and Rangers in the Glasgow Cup (purportedly the first floodlit night match played between the two Glasgow giants) meant the Celts did not suffer another defeat before they were set to play the return leg against Valencia.

Therefore, whilst it would not be easy, Celtic retained a hope of progression to the next round of European competition as the Spanish side came to Glasgow with a two goal lead. However, despite the fact the Celts would not lose, things most certainly did not go to plan as the home side could only manage a two-all draw. Yet, minutes into the second half, with the score still goalless, Celtic were given a lifeline as the "Evening Times" described.

"Huge tears rolled down the cheeks of Senor Manuel Verdu at Parkhead last night when he sliced a clearance past his own goalkeeper [into the net] and gave Celtic a wonderful chance of catching up on Valencia in the Fair Cities Cup Tie. The right-back was desolated by his blunder. He beat his head with his fists, he threw himself to the ground and tried to bury his head in the turf, and his anguish was such that the Spanish trainer had to rush on to the field and croon words to the effect – "There, there, son – not to worry.""

Sadly though, as the article continues, it goes on to discuss how it would not be Senor Verdu crying in despair at the end of the night. "The Celtic supporter is made of much sterner stuff, but I imagine a number of them felt like joining Mr. Verdu in a good cry. Most Celtic teams I have seen in the past ten years would have sent this Valencia team packing in short order and without further interest in the tournament. Valencia on this showing did not rate even the classification "moderate", and they could and should have been hammered…The blame for the 2-2 draw and the 6-4 overall defeat can be laid right at the feet of the forward line, and not on McNamee and O'Neill, who had to deputise for Billy McNeill and Jim Kennedy."

In the weeks which followed, Celtic would fail to register a win in three league matches against Queen of the South, Dundee and Partick Thistle. Thereafter, William Price would return to the side and William O'Neill would disappear into the background again until April 1963. However, for the sake of clarity, I feel it is worthy of mention that Celtic edged out Rangers by three goals to two in the replay of the previously drawn Glasgow Cup match. The Hoops would make their way to the final of the competition that year, before falling to Third Lanark, but O'Neill did not see action in either of the two Glasgow Cup fixtures which Celtic contested after the win over Rangers. Regardless, Willie O'Neill would only play a handful more matches for Celtic that year whilst Jim Kennedy was out of action once again in the spring. These included a five-two victory over Raith Rovers in the semi-final of the Scottish Cup, which set up a final tie with Rangers. The Ibrox side won the trophy via a replay, but Willie was not chosen to feature in either of the two final matches.

However, Willie's next senior appearance for Celtic would come against Rangers as it happened, as the Celts travelled to Ibrox for their second league match of the 1963-64 season. Once again though, those wearing green and white would find themselves on the losing side, and having subsequently appeared in a four-all draw with Third Lanark, Willie would vanish into the ether once more.

Although Willie did not feature in any of the fixtures involved, Celtic built on their European experiences of the previous year by making it all the way to the European Cup Winners' Cup semi-finals. Here, they would enjoy a commanding three-nil first leg lead against M.T.K. Hungaria, but would infamously collapse as they suffered a terrible four-nil loss on the continent, denying them a place in the final which was due to be held at Hampden Park in Glasgow. Several of the team who would feature in Lisbon in 1967 were holding down starting positions during the 1963-64 season, and with Jim Kennedy moving forward to left-half, Willie O'Neill may well have fancied his chances of securing the left-back slot for himself. However, this wasn't to be the case, as a young man by the name of Tommy Gemmell proved talented enough to make the position his own. O'Neill did play in the three domestic matches running up to the first leg of the European Cup Winners' Cup semi-final owing to a minor injury sustained by Gemmell, but he would again be dropped upon Gemmell's return to fitness.

Willie was used sparingly the following season once more, playing in just a handful of matches, at left-half more often than not. Again, the most notable of these ties came in the European cauldron, as Celtic welcomed F.C. Barcelona to the East End of

Glasgow for the first time. The Hoops had lost the first leg by three goals to one, and in an article very much reminiscent of previous such pieces, the "Evening Times" broke the surprising news of O'Neill's potential involvement on the day of the game, before reflecting on Barcelona's movements that morning.

"Jim Kennedy today failed to pass a fitness test and is out of tonight's return Fairs Cities' Cup tie with Barcelona...Kennedy was at Celtic Park early this morning and trainer Bob Rooney worked hard on the badly bruised foot for more than an hour. At the end Jim still felt pain and rather than let the team down he immediately called off. Willie O'Neill, who has not played in the top team this season, is almost certain to be called in to fill the gap."

"Barcelona's players, reasonably happy with their three-one lead from the first leg, had the quietest possible day, although they did not sleep late. They were out for fresh but damp Glasgow air just after breakfast, and in the afternoon they rested in bed before the conference to decide the tactics for tonight. All the signs point to a defensive plan, despite hints that the Spaniards will go out early for more goals."

Clearly, the newspaper had done their homework, as the home leg finished goalless and the Catalans secured their place in the next round of the competition. Celtic were incapable of breaking down a determined and well organised defensive unit, who proved themselves to be deserving winners over the course of two legs. Notably, media reports do suggest a certain affinity did develop between the two clubs in 1964, although they would not see each other in competitive action for four decades thereafter. However, though the men wearing the red and blue shirts may have changed during those years, their abilities of close control and passing did not, something of which to be proud.

"Barcelona...turned out to be the most sporting Continental side yet to visit Glasgow, and the one good thing to emerge from last night's proceedings was that in defeat Celtic have struck up a valuable friendship for the future. Of the match itself, all that need be said is that the Spaniards were infinitely superior at passing the ball. They had no need to waste a second bringing it under control. They could flick it and pass it to a team mate in a quarter of the time it took Celtic players to stop the ball and think out their next move."

That aside, Willie featured very little that season as I have said. However, with the arrival of a new manager in the form of Jock Stein in the spring of 1965, he may well have hoped such a situation would improve on an individual basis. The following campaign of 1965-66 suggested this was not to be the case – at least not initially – as Willie O'Neill failed to make a single senior appearance for the Celts for the first time in any full season since he signed for the Club. It is likely that many players would have seen this as their proverbial death knell at any given Football Club, quickly deciding that a move elsewhere would promptly be in order, but not Willie, who continued to dig in and work hard, believing his chance – however big or small it would eventually turn out to be – would come at some point, and he would be proven correct in glorious fashion.

Bizarrely, he would not only have his own efforts nor Jock Stein to thank for this, but the University of Glasgow's School of Dentistry, as I shall explain. Jim Craig, the excellent full-back and the man who continues to be a wonderful ambassador for all things related to Celtic Football Club in the modern day was, as many people know, a dental student. As such, whilst Celtic departed on their summer tour of North America in the middle of May 1966 – which started just days after the end of the previous league calendar – Craig had no choice but to forget the sights and sounds of Bermuda, Los Angeles, New York and the like, but instead focus on sitting his final university exams. As such, Willie was given the opportunity to feature in nine of the eleven matches which Celtic played on the tour, establishing his place as a first team regular seriously for the first and only time during his Celtic career.

Speaking in 2011, Jim Craig himself said of this time: "I had been the man in charge [of the shirt] at the end of the previous season, but then I missed the tour because I was sitting my finals during that summer and it took me until November to get back in again. Willie was a really intelligent full-back but he was probably a throwback to an earlier generation, when full-backs were a bit more static and did not come over the halfway line so much. Possibly, he was playing his career about ten years too late in terms of football evolution, but he was an excellent player."

And so it would be that for the first half of Celtic's greatest ever season Willie O'Neill, the man who had grown up supporting the Football Club and patiently awaited his opportunities as a player, would feature in nigh on every game, with Jim Craig only truly taking over his role in the side again in January 1967. Jim Craig is correct in his assertion that he did not return to the side on league duty until November 1966, but he did also play in one Scottish League Cup match on the third of September that year, which is a match remembered not for its scoreline nor indeed for the home appearance of St. Mirren "in a strip of all scarlet for the day", but for the fact that around the sixty-five minute mark, Willie O'Neill became the first player in the history of Celtic Football Club to come on, officially, as a substitute. For the record, he replaced Jimmy Johnstone, who had to be taken to the pavilion "with what appeared to be concussion from an earlier collision".

A fortnight later, Celtic welcomed Rangers to Parkhead for just the second match of the 1966-67 league calendar. On this day, the Celts stormed to a two goal lead even quicker than they did in the famous six-two match of August 2000, but unlike that occasion there would be no more scoring recorded. This was in part due to the intervention of one man, Willie O'Neill, as the "Evening Times" describes: "Nearest approach to a Rangers goal came when Johnston hit a cross low into the goalmouth. As always, there were plenty of Celts around to cope with this little emergency – but suddenly Alex Smith spread his feet apart and allowed the ball to run through his legs. Celtic did not expect this one, and the slowly moving ball was almost over the line before O'Neill sprang to life and cleared."

Again, this hinted at perhaps the most famous personal moment Willie would have, which arrived roughly six weeks later as Celtic again faced Rangers in the Scottish League Cup Final at Hampden Park, before a crowd of almost ninety-five thousand spectators. The Hoops were considered to be the pre-match favourites for the tie, but as the following newspaper report describes, matters did not prove to be so easy and conclusive as some had predicted.

"Celtic won the League Cup at Hampden for the second year in succession with a goal as golden as the sun, a goal of the kind that they have been gathering by the dozen this season... streamlined, swift and devastating in its power and efficiency. It was a goal...worthy of this tremendously exciting, lightning fast, and physically tough Final. But it was also a goal which made a complete mockery of the run of play, which did a shocking injustice to Rangers' best performance of the season and which left the Stein Stunners fortunate victors. We watched, unbelieving, as odds on favourites Celtic were pushed back on their heels by this revitalised Ibrox side. Long before the end the cocksure cantrips had given place to desperate, neck or nothing clearances, and the cool method which has been the Parkhead hallmark had vanished in a frantic scramble for safety. And yet...Rangers, for all their heroics must accept that they beat themselves by their own appalling inefficiency in their opponents' penalty box."

Late on in the match, such inefficiency was laid bare as, to all intents and purposes at least, a Rangers player managed to miss an open goal and in doing so allow Willie O'Neill just enough time to scramble back and prevent an equaliser with a remarkable goal line clearance. The following quote, taken from the same article as is previously referenced, described this, as well as offering thoughts on Celtic's triumph as a whole.

"Three minutes later there was an even more incredible miss when a Johnston pass left Alex Smith in the clear with Simpson beaten. But, somehow, the inside man managed to stumble over the ball. At that, it was still trickling goalwards when O'Neill came up to scramble it clear...It is of course the mark of champions that they can win in such circumstances. But, for once, the Celtic victory heroes were their defenders...the splendid Clark, the stout-hearted Gemmell and O'Neill, the methodical Murdoch and McNeill. And that great veteran, Ronnie Simpson."

In the days and hours of celebration which followed this victory, Willie O'Neill was praised to almost the same extent as the scorer of the winning goal, Bobby Lennox. Clearly, with the manner in which the majority of the game had been going in mind, many Celtic supporters were unsure that they would have been able to recover had their opponents equalised, such was the number of chances they managed to create as the match progressed. O'Neill's efforts were held in high regard by his fellow players likewise, as the famous dressing room photograph which shows the buoyant Celtic team posing with the Scottish League Cup sat atop Willie's head in the middle of the shot encapsulates. The joy and the centre of attention caught therein are clear to see, and one cannot underestimate the psychological impact this victory likely had – at least domestically – on the Celts going forward that season. Willie O'Neill may not be remembered as the scorer of a famous goal, but he should most certainly be remembered, at least partly, as the man who made sure the first of the six trophies amassed in the 1966-67 season did indeed return to Celtic Park.

Willie would also play an important role in helping to secure the Glasgow Cup a little over a week later, setting up the third of the four goals which Celtic scored without reply in the final against Partick Thistle on a Monday night at Parkhead. The "Glasgow Herald", describing the second and third goals from that evening said: "Such was Celtic's dominance that Murdoch and Clark were more often than not up to lend added weight to the forwards, and it was because of a foul on the left-half that Celtic scored their second in twenty-four minutes. Gallagher pitched a thirty yard free kick into the Thistle goalmouth and Lennox, that prince of marksmen, hooked the ball powerfully into the net. Only two minutes later the same player scored Celtic's third, this time with a glancing header from a cross by O'Neill, and it seemed nothing could prevent them from going on to reach double figures, so obviously outclassed were Thistle in all facets of the game."

Willie O'Neill also featured in Celtic's first four European encounters that season, both home and away against F.C. Zurich in the first round of the European Cup and F.C. Nantes thereafter. All four of these matches finished in victories for the Parkhead side, each with a winning margin of two goals or better. As a defender, Willie would likely have been particularly happy with the fact the Celts only conceded two goals during these fixtures, whilst scoring eleven themselves, boding well for what was to come after the turn of the year. However, Willie would only turn out once for the Celts after New Year in the 1966-67 season, as Dunfermline visited Celtic Park on the eighteenth of March.

Celtic's calendar was busy at this stage, with recent victories over Vojvodina Novi Sad and Queen's Park securing their places in the semi-finals of both the European and Scottish Cups respectively, all whilst they obliged their league calendar, attempting to maintain the pressure on Rangers who led the table at that time (albeit thanks in part to having played more league matches than the Hoops thus far). Jim Craig had taken an ankle knock ten days earlier against then Yugoslavian champions Vojvodina, and as such was still out of contention when the Dunfermline match came around. Davie Cattanach had been called upon to replace Craig against Queen's Park – which was, by chance, the day upon which Sean Connery (still a Celtic supporter at this point in time, bizarre as that statement may appear nowadays) had several photographs taken with the Celtic team – and as such neither Craig nor O'Neill featured in the famous shots. Regardless, Stein saw fit to alter his full-back pairing again for the league match against the Pars, swapping O'Neill for Cattanach and shifting Tommy Gemmell to the right-back slot. Celtic won the match by three goals to two and kept the pressure up on the Ibrox side in the fight for the League Championship.

Willie O'Neill would not make another competitive appearance for the Celts until the following season though, watching from the sidelines and the stands as his colleagues continued to forge onwards to glory. However, nobody can ever make the claim that his contributions en route to such triumphs for the Football Club were not of critical importance. Willie played in the first seventeen consecutive fixtures of the 1966-67 league calendar (with his league total taken to eighteen by the March appearance against Dunfermline Athletic); started in nine of the ten games involved in Celtic's retention of the Scottish League Cup (whilst appearing as a substitute in the other); participated in four of the nine matches during the triumphant European Cup run and also featured in the Glasgow Cup. Such efforts were vital, and it is my belief they should continue to be considered as such to this day.

Speaking to the "Sunday Mail" in 1997, Willie recounted his experiences of that sunny evening in Lisbon. He said, "There was no room for some of the squad in the dugout [a bench in this case] so Joe McBride, Jim Brogan and I were given tickets to sit in with the fans on the other side of the ground. That was great because we could really let ourselves go even though we had blazers and ties on. The fans loved us being there and we ended up going just as daft as them during the game. I remember when we were a goal down and the boys were pounding the Inter goal but Sarti was pulling off save after save. The fans were saying "We're never gonnae score" but we were calming them down and telling them not to worry because we knew it was meant to be our day. The goals did come and the scenes were just incredible."

"We tried to make our way straight to the dressing room but it took us about an hour to get there because it was just mental with everyone cuddling and just in another world. We thought we'd be missing out on the celebrations but when we got back to the dressing room the lads still had their strips on and it was party time."

"Jock made a meal of the boys who didn't play in the final. He took me aside in the dressing room and told me I had played my part in the run just as much as anybody else. I appreciated the gesture and it was just typical of the man. I'd have preferred if he hadn't made a fuss because it was only then that it really hit me that I hadn't played. It hurt me but I genuinely felt part of it. The other boys made sure of that because we had a team spirit second to none."

Finally, making reference to the European Cup itself and how he looked back on the team's achievements with the benefit of hindsight, Willie continued: "It was six hours before I got to hold it [the trophy] and my God it was heavy. But it wasn't until we paraded around the Parkhead track on top of a lorry that it hit home what we'd achieved. It was so special and it made me a very proud man. You know, when I look at some of today's players and the huge amounts they earn it doesn't make me envious because money could never buy my memories."

Also, it must be highlighted that Willie did play in one of the highest profile friendly matches of all time in the weeks which followed Celtic's glorious day in Lisbon, as Real Madrid welcomed Celtic to the Santiago Bernabeu for the testimonial match of the legendary Alfredo di Stefano. The fixture was attended by a crowd of approximately one hundred and twenty thousand people who watched the Hoops emerge victorious by a single goal to nil. As has been widely publicised, it was little Jimmy Johnstone who stole the show that night, becoming the darling of the Madrid crowd, but much praise was also due to the other Celtic players who featured, including Willie.

The Spanish newspaper "Marca" said "Celtic, great European champions, score a deserved victory over worthy opponents Madrid. It was a beautiful night of football. We thank Celtic, and are grateful to Real Madrid for being worthy of the occasion. The Scots played stronger and better football, and deserved their victory...May the football which Celtic play stay amongst us in Spanish style. Amen."

The following season of 1967-68 would see Willie O'Neill used more sporadically than he had been during the previous campaign. He enjoyed a few appearances in the League Cup before being dropped for the semi-final tie against Morton, but would be called upon on Cup Final day itself at half-time, as Bertie Auld had sustained a deep cut to his ankle and was deemed to be unable to continue. Celtic would defeat Dundee and win the Scottish League Cup by five goals to three in the end. Immediately thereafter, the squad travelled thousands of miles around the globe to face Racing Club of Argentina in the return leg of the Intercontinental Club Cup. The Celts had edged the first leg in Glasgow by a single goal to nil, somewhat making up for the unexpected first round European Cup exit inflicted by Dynamo Kiev in the weeks previous.

Willie O'Neill did not feature in any of these three matches, but would start the second leg against Racing Club in the unusual role of an inside-left forward, continuing his time as cover for Bertie Auld. Occasionally overshadowed by the so-called "Battle of Montevideo" (the play-off tie), the second leg in Buenos Aires was undoubtedly the opening salvo in what transpired to be a bloody South American campaign – literally. Before the match had even begun, Celtic were forced to substitute their goalkeeper, as Ronnie Simpson had his head split open by a missile apparently thrown from the crowd. The tie itself was hard fought to say the least, and after a two-one defeat, with no away goals rule in effect in this tournament, the Hoops faced a trip to Uruguay for the deciding match.

Whilst I am being speculative here, I cannot help but wonder whether this would be one of – if indeed not the only – occasion upon which Willie O'Neill would not have been overly disappointed to find his name did not appear on a Celtic team sheet. The play-off match which ensued cannot truly be described as a game of football, but as a sporting war. Six players were given red cards, and this whole shambolic affair ended with Racing Club winning by a single goal to nil. In truth, it is likely Celtic will never contest a match of such physicality and aggression again, and thankfully so.

Willie would play in the four league games which directly followed the Celtic squad's return home, as the Hoops racked up four straight victories without conceding a single goal. However, only a couple of appearances against Kilmarnock and Aberdeen in March would follow, both of which were again Celtic wins by a healthy margin. The following campaign, that of 1968-69, would ultimately prove to be Willie O'Neill's last as a Celtic player, but happily he would feature in the first team here and there, picking up Scottish League, Scottish Cup and Scottish League Cup winners' medals along the way. After all, bowing out at the end of a treble winning season isn't a bad way to go, certainly from a supporter's perspective.

The footballing year began with a trip to Ibrox for the first of Celtic's Scottish League Cup ties. Fighting both on the terracing and in several locations around the city took up significantly more newspaper column inches than the game itself, highlighting that the fixture was not the greatest ever played between the two sides, with a couple of goals from Willie Wallace giving the Celts the victory. Ironically, on the day of the match the "Evening Times" seemed genuinely impressed that "before the kick-off the number of arrests was one – and that from the Rangers' end", but then later the same newspaper carried a front page story about the "sickening" behaviour of supporters at the match.

Amidst this article, one of the stories perhaps showed, in some respects at least, how little has changed during the passing of the last half century: "Among those fined at Govan were two Belfast men…Each was fined ten pounds for breach of the peace in Paisley Road West. They were seen by police wearing Celtic scarves, standing in the roadway gesticulating, waving their scarves, and challenging other supporters in buses to come out and fight. [One man] told the court Rangers supporters in buses were spitting at them. [The other] told Bailie Trainer [the judge] they would not return to an "Old Firm" game."

Willie O'Neill played that day and in each of the next five Scottish League Cup ties in which Celtic were involved, but would be dropped for the partnership of Jim Craig and Tommy Gemmell for the Hoops' ten-nil annihilation of Hamilton Academicals on the eleventh of September 1968. Willie would not manage to regain a place in the starting line-up for any of the remaining League Cup fixtures, as the Celts won the trophy for the fourth consecutive season, with his last match in this competition for Celtic coming in a six-one away win at Firhill.

League duty would be a rare treat for Willie that year with a five-two win over Falkirk being his last outing at Celtic Park, although he did feature in Celtic's first European Cup tie of the campaign away at St. Etienne also. This disappointing two-nil defeat, which the Hoops would dramatically overturn in the return leg at Celtic Park, would be the final European appearance for O'Neill. Willie's only Scottish Cup involvement would come as Celtic beat Clyde by three goals to nil en route to a quarter final meeting with St. Johnstone.

Therefore, within a month of Celtic beating Hibernian to win the Scottish League Cup and in the days which followed the

Hoops' Scottish Cup Final triumph over Rangers, Willie, who had been at the Football Club just shy of a decade, made his last appearance in a Celtic shirt as the Celts defeated Dundee by two goals to one at Dens Park. Although the result was largely of no great significance thanks to the fact Celtic had already secured the League Championship, it is nice to know that the last time Willie O'Neill left the field as a Celtic player he did so as a winner.

Less than a fortnight later, Willie signed for Carlisle United, where he would feature to some extent before an ankle injury forced him to announce his retirement after about two years, at the age of just thirty-one. Subsequently, he managed St. Roch's for a time and became a much loved member of staff at the famous Gallowgate "Baird's Bar", where he would never shirk from talking to adoring fans and showing off his much beloved medals. Willie O'Neill died at the age of seventy on the twenty-eighth of April 2011, having achieved a great deal in his life.

In all, he made eighty-six league and cup appearances for Celtic without ever scoring a goal. If nothing else, this statistic highlights the difference in his approach to playing as a full-back compared to say, Tommy Gemmell. During his time at Celtic Park, he amassed a collection of three Scottish League Championship winners' medals, three Scottish Cup winners' medals, four Scottish League Cup winners' medals, five Glasgow Cup winners' medals, one Glasgow Charity Cup winners' medal and, most importantly, one European Cup winners' medal.

Not simply from a historian's point of view, but also from that of a fan, it is clear to me that every single Celtic player's contributions – regardless of their respective size – were truly vital during the Football Club's finest season of all. It is a rare occasion indeed when a footballing eleven achieve great things over the course of any given campaign, as to do so, one almost always requires a great squad, with individuals capable of slotting into the team seamlessly and upholding the standards of play expected of them. Eleven men alone do not win European Cups. Willie O'Neill was an almost perfect example of this type of player, and it is very apt that he was the man to become Celtic's first ever substitute. His name may not be shouted from the proverbial rooftops like that of a Billy McNeill, Jimmy Johnstone or Bobby Murdoch, but it should be treasured within the annals of a proud footballing history regardless. Willie's individual attitude and efforts, embodying loyalty and perseverance, all of which he focused not on himself but on helping the Football Club which he supported from his first until his dying days in any way he could are a testament to that fact. Make no mistake about it, this was a Lisbon Lion and his roar will reverberate through time as loudly as all the rest.

"A Different Ball Game Altogether"

Across the eras contained within the history of Celtic Football Club, there have been many figures whom the Celtic support have considered to be tough (or "hard" to use a Glaswegian term). However, some of the modern day players who exhibit this attribute may not have appeared to be so physically dominating had they played one hundred years ago when it was a different ball game altogether. Some of these bruisers have been famous simply for their physicality, whilst others who often tended to be real favourites on the green and white terracing were capable of the rare feat of combining strength with skill. Of these, one of the greatest was Daniel "Dan" McArthur.

Born in Old Monkland, Lanarkshire, on the ninth of August 1867, almost a century before the Club he would go on to star for would eventually reach its pinnacle, Dan began his footballing journey with Parkhead Star and Parkhead Juniors, before going on trial with Cowlairs in the November of 1891. However, Celtic would swoop for the young man in April 1892, and over the course of the next decade, he would become as firm a fixture at the new Celtic Park as Dan Doyle or Sandy McMahon. Why then, to some extent at least, is his story not more familiar to us today? Well, I suppose one theory may simply be that in the early days of the game, when goals aplenty tended to be scored in many matches, few people remember those sworn to guard the posts.

Before continuing, I feel it is necessary to remind you that goalkeeping in the late nineteenth century was a very different job to that which it is nowadays. There were very little in the way of rules for the protection of goalkeepers, and being in possession of the ball as a custodian was essentially just an excuse for any nearby opposition players to attack you in an attempt to obtain it for themselves. As such, relatively few goalkeepers during the period in which Dan McArthur played did so at a high level for any great length of time, such was the deterioration their bodies underwent as a result of such physical tactics being employed against them.

McArthur would make his Celtic debut on the tenth of September 1892, replacing the injured Joseph Cullen for a league match at home to Abercorn. In the end, Celtic would win a thrilling game by three goals to two, but for the sake of brevity I shall simply quote what the match report in the "Glasgow Herald" had to say with regards goalkeeping: "It was quite unfortunate that the home custodian, Cullen, was unable to take his place between the uprights owing to an injury...the Abercorn again forced their opponents back, and Munro shot right into McArthur's hands. The clever young custodian was quite equal to the occasion."

However, despite putting in a solid display on his debut, Dan would lose his place to the regular stopper when the Celts played their next match a fortnight later, a two-all draw with Rangers. In fact, almost two years would pass until the name of McArthur featured again on a Celtic team sheet for a league or cup game. Dan would make his second appearance as the Celts suffered a two-one defeat at the first Cathkin Park (situated a few hundred yards north of the later site) against Third Lanark. Despite this disappointment, McArthur's first clean sheet would arrive in the next fixture as his side notched up a three-nil victory over St. Mirren, before a five-three home win against Rangers followed. Poor losses both home and away to Hearts essentially nullified any chance of Celtic retaining their status as the champions of the Scottish League, but seventeen appearances in Celtic's twenty-two Scottish League and Scottish Cup matches during the 1894-95 season proved Dan McArthur to be the new Celtic goalkeeper of choice.

This quickly gained him international recognition, as he made his debut for Scotland in a three-one home win over Ireland at the end of March 1895, before being selected to play against England at Goodison Park just a week later. The home side would win the day by a three goal margin in Liverpool, but the "Glasgow Herald" did not pin the blame for this on Dan, saying of his performance: "In goal, McArthur acquitted himself fairly well."

The following domestic campaign would be a happy one (although McArthur would not be recalled to the Scotland squad for several years), as after recovering from a fairly poor start to the league season, the Celts won eleven fixtures on the trot. As well as racking up what remains their largest ever victory (an eleven-nil win against Dundee), they became the champions for the second time. Also, it is worthy of note that Celtic only conceded twenty-five goals in the league that season, eleven fewer than any other side. Only twice in their league history had the Celts conceded fewer, and those came in the inaugural league campaign of 1890-91 and its successor.

The next season saw Celtic finish a disappointing fourth in the league standings, but they did set a new club record in terms of goals conceded, allowing their opponents to score only eighteen times in eighteen games, fewer than they had done in any previous year. Of these, half were conceded by Cullen, although Dan played more league games than he did. Critically, Dan McArthur cannot take any blame for the infamous first round Scottish Cup exit to lowly Arthurlie that season as he did not play that fateful day.

As 1897 became 1898, Dan McArthur enjoyed what was undoubtedly his finest league season as a goalkeeper, helping the Celts to another League Championship title by appearing in seventeen of the eighteen league matches contested, and again setting a new Celtic Park record by conceding only twelve goals (Celtic conceded thirteen league goals that season, with the other being conceded by John Docherty, whom the Celts had loaned from Dumbarton after McArthur had been injured midway through the league campaign). However, another defeat – this time by three goals to two – against Third Lanark would see Celtic once more knocked out of the Scottish Cup fairly early on in proceedings. Gladly though, Dan McArthur wouldn't have long to wait to pick up his first Scottish Cup winners' medal.

In the 1898-99 season, Celtic would enjoy a year of somewhat mixed fortunes. In the league, Rangers were deserved champions, winning every single one of their eighteen fixtures, including two ties against Celtic in which they scored four times each. Celtic and

McArthur kept only three clean sheets, finally finishing the league in third place, having conceded almost twice the number of goals as the Ibrox side. Yet, as the league season ceased only a week into January, the Scottish Cup began. Thirteen goals scored and only two against saw Celtic progress past the Sixth Galloway Rifle Volunteers, St. Bernard's and Queen's Park en route to the semi-final stage. Here, a four-two win over Port Glasgow saw the Celts reach the final for the first time since 1894, when they were beaten by the same side they would face in the 1899 contest, Rangers. However, the outcome would be different on this occasion, as the Celts won by two goals to nil and, after featuring in all five ties along the way, Dan McArthur was a Scottish Cup winner at last. When one considers the fact that Rangers averaged more than four goals per game played in the league that season, McArthur's feat – undoubtedly aided by the performance of his defenders – of keeping a clean sheet in the biggest match of the domestic calendar becomes an even more admirable achievement. Also, 1899 would see Dan make his third and final international appearance as the Scots hammered the Welsh by six goals to nil in Wrexham.

Over the course of the next league season, Dan McArthur would miss almost half of the matches played, predominantly through injury, such was his habit of being hurt or knocked out by opposition players in his attempts to protect his charge. However, he would once again feature in every Scottish Cup tie which Celtic played – including a semi-final replay against Rangers in which he kept another clean sheet to see his side through to the final – as the Celts went on to lift the Scottish Cup for the second season in succession.

Another mediocre league campaign followed in 1900-01, but again Celtic reached the Scottish Cup Final, losing on this occasion to Heart of Midlothian by four goals to three. Sadly, this match would signal that the end was nigh for McArthur, who was criticised (perhaps not entirely unjustifiably so) as his mistakes and errors contributed to the Edinburgh side managing to score four times. The goal which proved to be the winner came late on. After "McArthur, who saved feebly" spilled a shot, an attacker pounced on the loose ball and neatly dispatched it to settle the tie once and for all. Undoubtedly, such a loss would have hurt Dan personally, but it must be said that the defeat cannot be blamed on him alone.

Dan McArthur would make his final Celtic appearance on the sixteenth of September 1901, as Celtic beat Hibernian in Edinburgh. In all, he played for Celtic one hundred and twenty times in the league and Scottish Cup, keeping thirty-six clean sheets in an era when these were often few and far between. An integral part of a Football Club which was only just reaching its teenage years, his contributions, whilst not perfect, were invaluable as Celtic found the first goalkeeper to truly settle and represent the Club on more than one hundred occasions. Awarded three international caps by Scotland, he also made a solitary appearance for Queen's Park before retiring with broken ribs. He died approximately four decades later, at the age of seventy-six, on the eleventh of November 1943. As one would expect, his funeral was attended by Willie Maley amongst several other representatives of Celtic Football Club. He is fondly remembered to this day. After many knocks, bruises and injuries, he can finally rest in peace, safe in the knowledge other men valiantly protect the Celtic goalmouth now and will continue to do so in the future.

"From Pathé to Podcasts"

Memories are tricky things to quantify. In fact, you could say that not even science fully understands them yet, and in this sense, you would be correct. When we consider the subject of memory, several questions spring to mind (no pun intended), such as "Why do we remember certain things and not others?" and "Is there a limit as to how much we can physically remember?" The answers to both of these questions remain somewhat unclear, but despite this, there are particular trends we can note and make deductions from.

For example, it is abundantly clear that people are far more likely to recall incidents which were particularly out of the ordinary and/or large in scale. These recollections are often personified by people who can readily recall exactly where they were or what they were doing when they heard about a particularly large piece of breaking news, whether it was the assassination of President John Fitzgerald Kennedy in 1963, the Lockerbie Bombing in 1988 or the events of the eleventh of September 2001. Now, each of these incidents were tragedies in their own right, and one would deduce that pain and astonishment were emotions linked to the brain's natural storage of an individual's experiences on those given days.

However, humans do not simply remember horrific and agonising experiences, but happy and joyous ones also. Whilst family occasions such as weddings and births are likely to be the most prominent examples of these, the majority of such events only tend to be remembered by a relatively small number of people because they were the only ones who were directly involved. Therefore, if we are to consider why large numbers of people recall certain happy days, there are few more appropriate theatres to examine than those of sport – and in our case, football matches involving the only Scottish side to lift the European Cup – Celtic.

Now, I think it's safe to say that one could easily compile a large enough collection of Celtic related memories to write a book on those alone. After all, the Football Club has an enormous fan base, and each of those supporters will have their own stories of their time following Celtic. Importantly though, it's not just our individual memories which can provide an interesting topic of discussion, but our collective ones also. Football lends itself to these recollections because, generally speaking, whilst we all make our way to and from games alone or with a few friends or family members, and whilst we all do our own unique things on match days, when the game itself is in progress, it tends to be the main focus of all of our attentions – hence creating shared memories in the process.

Before I continue, another noteworthy aspect of this topic is that the game of football, and critically the manner in which people view the sport, has changed dramatically over the course of time. Whilst taking in a match between Hearts and Celtic in Edinburgh in the nineteenth century would have necessitated a rail or road journey to the nation's capital for a Glaswegian Celt, supporters in the modern day can generally tune in from virtually anywhere on the planet, providing they have access to a television or an internet connection.

This progression of sports broadcasting (which first began with radio before television and eventually online streaming took over), brought another phenomenon along with it which, although it is bemoaned by many at times, has come to form an integral part of many people's collective footballing memories – commentary.

In a similar sense to that of the previously discussed "I remember where I was when…" phenomenon, commentary has become something millions of people around the world directly correlate with memorable sporting moments. Referring to Celtic in particular, the fact that most supporters now take in matches regularly via television means that they are exposed to the sound of a commentator's voice whether they like it or not – unless they mute their television, of course.

For example, as Celtic romped to a historic six-two victory over Rangers on the twenty-seventh of August 2000, many supporters, including my ten year old self, were not fortunate enough to be able to drink in this spectacle in person. Now, whilst I do not recall too much about my life as a ten year old, I do remember this game clearly. After all, as a child who grew up in the 1990s, scoring six goals against Rangers was, for me anyway, totally unheard of.

As Henrik Larsson ran through on goal and perfectly chipped the ball high over the head of the oncoming Stefan Klos, I watched it dip just under the bar and nestle in the back of the net. Yet, if I think of that goal now, I simply cannot see it in my mind's eye without hearing the words and voices of the Sky Sports commentators which accompanied it. Therefore, I'll leave Ian Crocker and Davie Provan to kick things off in this chapter, with one of my personal favourites, embedded in their coverage of the game as a whole.

Ian Crocker (I.C.): "Bobby Petta with an early surge...and he'll get a free kick."

Davie Provan (D.P.): "Well, that's what Martin O'Neill will be looking for plenty of this afternoon. Bobby Petta, full tilt here down the left hand side, clearly tripped there, and it gives Celtic a free kick. Well, in fact, Stuart Dougal has given the corner."

I.C.: "Moravcik sends it in, and Stubbs and Larsson are there! And it's turned in, by Chris Sutton! Unbelievable, Chris Sutton makes an immediate impact! And Celtic are in front!"

D.P.: "Well, I bet he can hardly believe his luck Ian, a gift from God for Chris Sutton! Lorenzo Amoruso is screaming at the stand-side linesman for offside here. It sits up nicely for Sutton at the back post, I think he's on, two Rangers players on the goal line, it breaks perfectly for him. Stefan Klos with no chance whatsoever, and as you see there he's well onside, and Celtic, Chris Sutton and Martin O'Neill have the start of their dreams." [Celtic 1, Rangers 0]

I.C.: "Celtic, seeking their second. Moravcik, sends it in, and they have a second! And it's Petrov, who wasn't picked up, and it gets better and better for Martin O'Neill and for Celtic. A quite incredible start!"

D.P.: "Well, this is...deplorable marking here at the back post from Rangers, Stiliyan Petrov just runs off Fernando Ricksen.

Good ball in by Moravcik, but the marking is woeful there. Plenty of pace on the ball, into a great area for Petrov to come and attack it." [Celtic 2, Rangers 0]

I.C.: "Moravcik, could be in, and they're queueing up here! It's another one! For Paul Lambert! Three for Celtic, and in Paradise, this is the stuff that Celtic dreams are made of."

D.P.: "That all came from a very good advantage by Stuart Dougal, Bobby Petta was fouled wide right. He let the play go on, claims for offside, Moravcik clearly on though, checks back, has the presence [of mind] to pick out the supporting Lambert. Amoruso can't get close enough to him to close the shot down. Moravcik has time to look up, he sees Lambert, and Lambert could not have struck it any sweeter. Well, it's "Mission Impossible" for Rangers now." [Celtic 3, Rangers 0]

I.C.: "Sutton, sets up Larsson here. Larsson, oh he's in! Henrik Larsson! That is sensational! He missed all four Old Firm games last season, but he rather enjoys making up for lost time! World class."

D.P: "Well, that is world class Ian, a special goal from a very special player. Chris Sutton does magnificently well in the first place to win it over Amoruso. Larsson, on his way, look at that skill, and he has the confidence, the composure, and the technique to chip it over Stefan Klos. Look at the arrogance in that finish. That, as you say, is the mark of a world class player. Absolutely magnificent." [Celtic 4, Rangers 1]

I.C.: "Petta delivers, Larsson's header! He's done it again! It's a double for Henrik Larsson, it's number five for Celtic!"

D.P.: "Well, once again it's a wonderful goal Ian but once again you have to question the marking at the back for Rangers. Good delivery, whipped in by Petta, but look at the room that Henrik Larsson had, Barry Ferguson the nearest to him, and he's three yards off him! And it doesn't get any easier for strikers than this, a lot of work still to be done though and Larsson applies the deftest of headers to find the corner." [Celtic 5, Rangers 2]

I.C.: "Petta now has released Stephane Mahe, have Celtic got another one left in them? Sutton is there! Yes they have! Sutton scores, it's six of the best – of the very best, today – for Celtic."

D.P.: "It's a great striker's goal Ian, because he can't have much left, gas in his tank, but he still makes sure he's at the back post when the ball comes in here. And he has to make up a lot of ground, you see him on the far side there, times the run to perfection, drifts off Amoruso, one touch is enough and what an Old Firm debut for Chris Sutton. Martin O'Neill said all he lacked is confidence. Well, he certainly won't lack it now. He's a hero in the East End of Glasgow today." [Celtic 6, Rangers 2].

Now, with progression of technology which I referenced previously in mind, you must forgive me for largely ignoring the first few decades of Celtic's existence, because prior to the Scottish Cup Final of 1927, in which Celtic defeated East Fife by three goals to one, no Scottish Cup Final had ever been covered live on the radio in Scotland. Celtic's victory over their lower league opposition provided a unique opportunity, and laid the foundation for everything from "Super Scoreboard" to "Celtic TV".

However, prior to the end of World War Two, it appears that nigh on all video highlights of football matches were silent films, with perhaps a piano or something similar accompanying them in the cinema venues in which they were designed to be shown. As such, some of the first Celtic fixtures whose highlights include audio commentary were the 1951 and 1954 Scottish Cup Finals, against Motherwell and Aberdeen respectively, and even then this audio was added to the films after the fact. Whilst we shall focus predominantly on the latter match in this chapter, I feel that one brief snippet of commentary from the 1951 tie is worthy of note for no reason other than the fact it proves commentators were not always as slick in their delivery as many of their modern day equivalents. With Celtic leading by one goal to nil, play becomes increasingly scrappy in the middle of the field, resulting in a Motherwell player losing his feet repeatedly whilst trying to maintain some semblance of possession. However, our commentator described the scene as follows: "Resuming, Motherwell attack but Paton is brought down. He gets up, but he's down again. He's a stickler all right. He gets up again and he's down again! This could go on forever but this time referee Mowat intervenes, four times down in as many seconds is plenty."

Whilst some of these early examples of commentary are delivered in an amusing style, it must be said that there was undoubtedly a certain amount of charm attached to the whole process also. Perhaps the natural passing of the decades has contributed to this romanticism somewhat, but I find it heart-warming when grainy footage accompanied by grandiose introductory music appear on a screen before me. The commentators too were wonderfully different to that which we listen to nowadays, with posh English accents and a vocabulary which would seem out of place on a modern sports channel. Indeed, such broadcast characteristics are irrevocably linked to a bygone era, but one of which surviving remnants will be enjoyed for years to come. Therefore, to indulge in this momentarily, let us turn our focus to the Scottish Cup Final of 1954.

"Once again Hampden Park is the setting for the most important date in Scotland's soccer calendar, the Cup Final. Celtic, in hooped jerseys, kick off against Aberdeen. One hundred and thirty-four thousand ticket holders watch…there were plenty of thrills in the first half, but still no score at the halfway mark. Play resumes with Leggat taking a corner for Aberdeen. Still quite unruffled, the Celtic defence works the ball away and off they go again. Mochan centres the ball but Young puts it into his own net! A gift goal for Celtic!" [Celtic 1, Aberdeen 0]

"Aberdeen open up now and fight back grimly. Hamilton passes to Buckley who beats Bonnar and there is the equaliser! Both goals scored within a minute." [Celtic 1, Aberdeen 1]

"About thirty minutes after half time, Celtic go away on another raid. Fernie forces the ball through to Fallon, who left foots it into the net! Two-one to Celtic is how it ends, and Jock Stein [whose surname was pronounced completely wrongly] receives the winners' cup. Celtic, as well as topping the league, take the cup home for the seventeenth time in their history." [Celtic 2, Aberdeen 1]

Moving on into the 1960s, the dulcet tones of one commentator's voice in particular, Kenneth Wolstenholme (the man who uttered the legendary phrase – "They think it's all over, it is now!" – at the 1966 World Cup Final), were to become

synonymous with some of Celtic's greatest victories. The return of
the previously mentioned Celtic captain Jock Stein as manager
sparked a revival at the Club, the first solid evidence of which
came in the Scottish Cup Final of 1965. This is the earliest fixture
discussed in this chapter which has the benefit of live commentary,
rather than that which was recorded later. Equally, the days of
added commentary were numbered by this point, and as such
I have included both Wolstenholme's audio and that which
accompanied the British Pathé News report of the game, allowing
you to compare the two. Please note, Dunfermline took the lead
twice in the following tie, and we pick up proceedings with the
Hoops one-nil down at a packed Hampden Park.

Kenneth Wolstenholme (K.W.): "Clark, Gallacher, could be
something here, Gallacher! Auld running in, Auld scores! A great
try that slapped against the cross bar and then Bertie Auld
equalises for Celtic on the half hour mark. And in the terracing,
look at that sea of joy! Well, let's see what happens now. One-all!"
[Celtic 1, Dunfermline Athletic 1]

British Pathé News (B.P.N.): "Celtic began to wonder if they'd
have their fifth cup final failure, and the game was half an hour
old before they equalised. Inside-right Charlie Gallacher hit the
bar, Bertie Auld scored from the rebound. So, Celtic were back in
the game to the delight of their supporters in the one hundred and
eight thousand crowd." [Celtic 1, Dunfermline Athletic 1]

K.W: "Gemmell, tackling Edwards, Auld, Lennox, Hughes,
and Auld! Auld equalises for the second time. Auld scores Celtic's
second goal and also his second of the match. Seven minutes in the
second half, two-all. What excitement!" [Celtic 2, Dunfermline
Athletic 2]

B.P.N.: "Celtic kicked off in the second half one goal down,
nothing to worry about, just enough to spur them to redoubled
effort. And now we saw flashes of the great Celtic. Jim Heriot got
Dunfermline out of danger, only to find that Celtic had tasted
blood. A pass found Bobby Lennox, Lennox centred, Bertie Auld
fired in a great shot!" [Celtic 2, Dunfermline Athletic 2]

K.W.: "Hughes, Lennox, Thomson moving in to tackle him,
very happy to give away a corner. The man who takes all the

Celtic corner kicks, Gallacher. And it's gone off a head into the net, by McNeill! The Celtic captain and centre-half, Billy McNeill, races up there to head in what could very well be the goal which will win the Scottish Cup for Celtic for the first time in eleven years!" [Celtic 3, Dunfermline Athletic 2]

B.P.N.: "When a draw seemed likely, Lennox won a corner for Celtic. Charlie Gallacher's kick went to the head of Billy McNeill, the winning goal, and what a scene it was! So, for the eighteenth time in the history of this amazing club, Celtic won the Scottish Cup. A final they'll talk about for years!" [Celtic 3, Dunfermline Athletic 2]

A couple of seasons later, it was Kenneth Wolstenholme who again provided the commentary for an enormous tie, with the European Cup up for grabs on this occasion. Although a large Celtic support travelled to Lisbon for the final, the majority of fans, mostly due to a lack of finance as opposed to a lack of desire, were still stuck at home in front of a television. Now, if I may, allow me to take you back to late May 1967, as we enjoy the commentary from both of Celtic's goals, as well as the trophy presentation itself. Again, we join proceedings with the Celts trailing their opponents by a single goal.

Kenneth Wolstenholme (K.W.): "Gemmell, across to Craig, Murdoch. Ah, you get the quickest of split second chances against a defence like Inter's. Now Clark, to Murdoch, in comes Craig. Gemmell! He's scored a great goal! He's done it! Gemmell! A great goal! Seventeen minutes of the second half gone, and that could be the goal that wins it for Celtic because Inter now have to come out. Well, Tommy Gemmell has done this time and time again for Celtic, but it looks as if they've been right up against it, a packed defence, a concrete wall, and he's come through…and scored an outstanding goal. He's been itching to do that, I was talking to him last night. I asked him if he'd do it again and he said he would – and he has done now! Now then, the interesting thing is we've seen Inter Milan be magnificent in defence, but they've got to come out and do a spot of attacking. At one goal each, Celtic have done the impossible, they've broken the rock of Inter's defence." [Celtic 1, Inter Milan 1]

K.W.: "Somebody has suggested that the only way Inter Milan will score is if one of the Celtic players were to put through his own goal. Five minutes left now, one goal each. Gemmell, Murdoch, it's there! Celtic have scored! I think Chalmers put it in but it doesn't matter! Murdoch shot, there's a kilted gentleman on the pitch! It's only five minutes to go, and without a doubt, the European Cup is on its way to Glasgow! Stevie Chalmers put it in, and Celtic are cock-a-hoop now! With five minutes to go, they've taken the lead, and Inter Milan, who couldn't come back when they had an equalising goal against them, will never surely be able to come back now Celtic have taken the lead. And glory is hovering over Parkhead!" [Celtic 2, Inter Milan 1]

The close and a final line which I personally adore now follows, K.W.: "A minute left, and Celtic are in the lead, two-one [at this stage, the "Celtic Song" is clearly audible as it rolls down off of the surrounding terracing into the television microphone]. A Celtic throw, but everyone has decided now it's all over, and I think the people who know more than anyone that it's all over are the players of Inter Milan. There is a moat around this ground, but I reckon that's not going to stop the Celtic fans. Thirty seconds, between Celtic and the European Cup. Only seconds left, the referee looks at his two linesmen, the whistle will go any moment now. The referee, just looking at his watch, he's brought his watch into play, and the whistle is going! And Celtic, have won the European Cup! A fantastic victory by a great team. Celtic have won, the goalscorers, Gemmell and Chalmers. And on to the field come thousands of Celtic fans! This is a great moment, a fantastic moment for Scottish Football, a deserved victory and a great performance by Celtic, the spirits of Inter Milan completely crushed. Glasgow, Scotland, Great Britain, Europe, now belongs to Celtic!"

K.W.: "A magnificent performance, and quite frankly it's been a privilege to be here! I've supported Celtic because they are an attacking team, and everybody who's been here, all the commentators from all the lands all over Europe have been talking to me at half-time and saying how amazingly well this Celtic team has been playing and how they might succeed if they kept it up in the second half. Well, they did just that! I care not a jot for the reputation of Inter, it's now lying in threads. It is, in fact, the end of an era, it is the end of the Catenaccio, of this era of the tremendously tight defensive play by Inter."

Later, in the aftermath of the match itself, Wolstenholme continues: "A fantastic performance by Celtic, the first non-Latin team to win the European Cup. Their supporters have come from everywhere. We're waiting now, for the presentation of this cup, but goodness knows where, and how, or when, they're going to present it. But I think far more important is the fact that Celtic have won...football has triumphed over this dreary, dull defensive play and perhaps now, teams will begin to copy the attacking style of Celtic."

K.W.: "And there's the Cup that Celtic have won, there's the Cup that Celtic have won. We're now, we're now trying to find out where the Celtic team have gone. We think they've gone to the dressing room. We're looking around, I don't think we've ever had such scenes at the end of a European Cup Final, we can't see any players in there, in that mob. We think that Tommy Gemmell is there. We are, we are looking around to try and find a team to give this cup to, because no team has more worthily won it than Celtic."

K.W.: "And now, the moment we all awaited, the moment we all prayed for. Billy McNeill, coming through this packed crowd, to receive the European Cup. And there's Archie MacPherson trying to, trying to get the crowd to disperse – that's his voice on the public address."

Before the commentator utters his next word, McNeill lifts the European Cup high above his head into the Portuguese air.

K.W.: "Well done Billy McNeill, a fantastic moment, for Celtic! And how well they deserve it, everything they've entered this season, they have won! And so, there's the great scene, Billy McNeill lifts the European Cup for Celtic. Remember, BBC One tomorrow night will show you the scene at 9.30 when Celtic get back. Go to Parkhead or watch on television, not to the airport. And so, it's "well done Celtic", and its goodbye to you from Lisbon."

However, it is not always the role of the commentator simply to add a vocal accompaniment to sporting events themselves, but to those which can occur in and around the stadia which host them also. Turning our attention to the 1980 Scottish Cup Final between Celtic and Rangers for a moment, we find Alex Cameron and Archie MacPherson each carrying out their respective duties. Firstly, we shall consider Cameron's thoughts on the solitary goal which won the Scottish Cup for Celtic, before crossing over to Archie MacPherson, who highlights his shock regarding the unfolding events post-match which have since become synonymous with that day.

Alex Cameron: "Corner. Provan going to take it, probably saying to himself "I'd love to make this one really count." Headed away by Dawson, kicked back by Sneddon and headed by Forsyth. McGrain! An astonishing goal by McGrain! Danny McGrain has scored! McGrain hit the ball there, finely deflected off McCluskey. McCluskey getting the final credit, there he is right in the middle of your picture, watch it again. Out it comes to McGrain, he volleys it forward, a flick there by McCluskey away, well away, from McCloy, and McCluskey has scored the goal which could very well be the winner in this Scottish Cup Final."

Archie MacPherson (A.M.): "They've come right across, they're spilling right on to the pitch, and indeed Rangers supporters are coming on now. And where are the police? For heaven's sake, where are the police? ... I'm not going to hide my feelings about this – this is – this is ridiculous that this should have happened at the Scottish Cup Final. So much for fences round the ground, and here's another charge! Here's another charge! The place is now absolute pandemonium and turmoil, these are sad and disgraceful scenes... These supporters [referring to the Celtic fans] didn't come on belligerently, they came on to congratulate their team, but that was enough to signal a counter-charge from the other end.

A.M.: "There are casualties in the left-hand goal mouth, the ambulance men are on there, and this is...like a scene out of "Apocalypse Now"... At the end of the day, let's not kid ourselves, these supporters hate each other, and they itch to get at each other... It's all a game of football isn't it? Why, oh why? ...People are limping away bloodied from Hampden Park... I feel sorry, particularly, for young boys who have come unaccompanied to this. I'll tell you, I wouldn't let children come unaccompanied again to this sort of match, it is far too dangerous."

Happily, a much more peaceable pitch invasion would be sparked six years later, as the Celtic supporters once again spilled out of the terracing – this time at Love Street – to celebrate a historic League Championship win. Undoubtedly one of the most dramatic finishes to any season, the words "Love Street 1986" and "Albert Kidd" will always warm the hearts of those supporters who remember it. For the sake of record keeping, I should highlight that on the final day of the league calendar, Celtic sat in second place, trailing Heart of Midlothian. To all but the most optimistic of people, the Edinburgh side appeared to be likely champions, as the only way they could be stopped would be if they lost their match against Dundee and Celtic were victorious against St. Mirren by a margin of three goals or better. Dundee had lost more matches than they had won that season, so on the face of it, the Celts' hopes hung by a thread and yet, the fates would align. Therefore, I shall leave you largely to the words of Jock Brown, the television commentator that day, to describe each of Celtic's goals and some of the lengthy celebrations which understandably followed.

Jock Brown (J.B.): "Johnston, challenged in the end by Hamilton, but once again Celtic now have a corner kick – and a great header by Brian McClair! Six minutes gone and McClair does it again for Celtic. Well, it couldn't have been simpler or more effective. An in-swinger from Archdeacon, McClair with a run towards the near post, a powerful header and Stewart was left stranded." [St. Mirren 0, Celtic 1]

J.B: "McClair doing well, wrinkling the ball free to McStay. Here's Mo Johnston, it's there! Mo Johnston, the Celtic fan's hero [not a description which would be used in the modern day], thirty-two minutes of the first half gone, and it's two-nil to Celtic."

I shall interject here briefly to say that no written or spoken description of Celtic's third goal that day will ever do the beautiful interplay which preceded it justice. The passing and the movement by those both on and off of the ball was sublime, and it is my belief it remains one of the finest team goals ever scored by a Celtic eleven. I would urge any of you who have not seen this goal – or simply those who wish to enjoy it again – to seek it out on the internet. It is attacking football at its finest.

J.B.: "McGrain with a delicate ball to Murdo MacLeod, here's Paul McStay finding Aitken. Now McGrain, Celtic, in full fly now as McClair gets free on the right, there's Johnston! Absolutely magnificent! One of the goals of the season! Set up inside the Celtic half, the...ball from McGrain releasing Brian McClair – his pace – the final pass to Johnston was perfect." [St. Mirren 0, Celtic 3]

J.B.: "McGrain, Murdo MacLeod, Burns. No question about it, Celtic are certainly playing like champions. Archdeacon, testing Paul Wilson, makes his way to the byline – here's Murdo MacLeod now [who steps over the ball and lets it run beyond him] – McStay! Four-nil for Celtic! Paul McStay thundering in goal number four, it was down to the creative play of Archdeacon on the left. Look at the way he gets away from Wilson and holds off the challenge, then the dummy from Murdo MacLeod and how about this for a thunderous finish."

J.B.: "Whyte to McStay, St. Mirren trying to play Celtic offside. They've failed, here's Johnston, now Murdo MacLeod, McClair! Nine minutes into the second half, five-nil to Celtic, and that was certainly with a tinge of good fortune. McStay beat the offside trap, Johnston hanging back, going forward, playing it back to McLeod who tried a shot at goal – miscued completely – and McClair took advantage, the ball landing at his right knee."

Again, it is difficult to adequately describe the scale of the following snippet. Paul McStay proceeds down the right wing before crossing the ball, which is gathered at the second attempt by the St. Mirren goalkeeper, Stewart. As he does so, a number of Celtic supporters situated on the terracing behind the goal (presumably those with transistor radios) begin to celebrate, and within a matter of seconds thousands are leaping up and down taking full part in the joyous commotion which inevitably ensued following Dundee's opening goal.

J.B.: "Paul McStay, well Stewart needed two bites…now that must be a goal for Dundee! Sheer bedlam around the stadium! Well, you don't need to hear any more news than that, Dundee clearly have scored at Dens and its lift off here at Love Street. Well, what incredible scenes."

J.B.: "Speirs with the lay-off, and there's the final whistle! Celtic have won by five goals to nil. Danny McGrain goes on to convey the news of the position at Dens Park, the Celtic supporters invade the field. There's still no news at all from Dens to confirm the final whistle has gone but surely now it's only a formality to hear that Celtic have won the League Championship in the most dramatic fashion."

J.B.: "And the celebrations continue despite the steady downpour of rain. None of these Celtic supporters have noticed the difference and I'm sure the players feel exactly the same. Well, these are the happy scenes which looked impossible just about a week ago, but with a tremendous finish to the season, Celtic going fourteen games undefeated, they've come through to win on the last possible day of the season. With just minutes left, when they got the news from Dens Park about Dundee beating Hearts, the celebrations began and they've been going on ever since. The rain teeming down and the Celtic players now going right round the stadium on their lap of honour and on the performance this afternoon, they're certainly worthy champions!"

Therefore it would come to pass that Celtic Football Club, who had done all they could do to ensure they had the possibility of winning the league that day in early May 1986 would be helped by an unlikely source in the form of Albert Kidd. Brought on as a late substitute for Tosh McKinlay (who himself would later go on to play for Celtic), Kidd had not scored all season until that point, but two goals in the final ten minutes of proceedings that day would deprive Hearts of their first title since 1960 and cause the Celtic (and indeed Hibernian) supporters to forever hail him as a cult hero. Comically, it is said that when news initially reached Ibrox of Kidd's goal at Dens Park, many within the home crowd celebrated, presuming it had been the Hearts' player Walter Kidd who had scored. However, happiness soon turned to gloom at

Ibrox, as the Celts secured another League Championship title and Rangers finished fifth from ten teams, level on points with Dundee.

Moving forward by a little over a decade, another monumental campaign for Celtic in 1997-98 also brought with it some magnificent commentary. The first example, when Martin Tyler and Andy Gray describe and react to Paul Lambert's first goal in the Hoops (against Rangers in the New Year derby), is sure to bring cheer to any Celtic fan.

Martin Tyler (M.T.): "Now Larsson, a second one will surely settle it for Celtic. That's Lambert! Oh! What a way to settle it! Paul Lambert! No chance for Goram, no chance now for Rangers today."

At this point, Andy Gray intercedes, and in typically dramatic fashion, analyses a phenomenal strike.

Andy Gray (A.G.): "For twenty minutes, his job has been defensive, to get Gascoigne, to shackle him, but he gets forward, and he hits the most stunning of strikes that he's ever likely to hit in his career. It's unstoppable, it's unsaveable. It's an absolutely magnificent way for Celtic to finish their afternoon. Take that! You just do not save them. Take a bow son, that's a great goal... in a game like this."

M.T.: "His first goal for Celtic, he'll never hit a better one. Paul Lambert."

As we all know too well, that wasn't to be the last of the dramatic days for Celtic that season. Although, it has to be said, such a derby victory proved crucial not only in terms of points, but also in terms of believe and spirit. Thereafter, it all came down to the final round of matches, as Celtic faced St. Johnstone at home and Rangers travelled to Dundee United. Rob MacLean described the action at Parkhead for "Sportscene".

Before I begin to quote Mr. MacLean, I feel I should mention that "The Fields of Athenry" is clearly audible ringing around the ground prior to the beginning of this first quotation, hinting somewhat at the electric atmosphere inside the new Celtic Park that day.

Rob MacLean (R.M.): "Time for Main, not the best of clearances, picked up by Paul Lambert. Now with Henrik Larsson,

Donnelly is alongside him, Larsson, lining up for the shot! What a start for Celtic! Two minutes gone, and Larsson makes the breakthrough. Henrik Larsson's nineteenth goal of the season, but it's only his second in the last twelve games. And that will settle the Celtic nerves. Powerfully struck, it was curving and dipping as well. Alan Main could only watch as the shot exploded in the net behind him, and there's a jubilant reaction down on the trackside from Wim Jansen. It must be difficult for the players to hear themselves talking to each other, such is the din around Celtic Park. What a start for these Celtic supporters." [Celtic 1, St. Johnstone 0]

Whilst Henrik's early strike may have been the best possible opening for Celtic, the rest of the first half came and went without any further scoring. This was not to be a nice, easy five-nil win where victory is assured from the first quarter of an hour or so. With Rangers leading at Tannadice, everybody inside Celtic Park and across the Celtic supporting world was all too aware that an equaliser from St. Johnstone, be it a forty yard screamer or a paltry defensive error, would take their collective dreams and crush them into the most painful of sporting agonies. Celtic had to look to extend their lead, but to do so cautiously – this was not a time for all-out attack. Eventually, it fell to one of the more improbable men to become an idol, in a style perhaps somewhat fitting with regards the Club's past liking for unlikely heroes.

R.M.: "Celtic make a significant change, on comes nine goal Harald Brattbakk in place of Simon Donnelly who has put a power of work into this, he must be exhausted, and Celtic will hope that Harald Brattbakk can make it double figures for his tally and give them a more comfortable lead."

"...Came off the top of Marc Rieper's head, now Lee Jenkinson, got the ball through the legs of Tom Boyd but slipped as he did so. Boyd's looking for a possible pass, waiting for the McNamara run. It's a good pass. In for Harald Brattbakk!"

As the ball leaves the Norwegian's foot, MacLean pauses – seemingly as did time – and as the supporters realise the ball has indeed beaten the goalkeeper and found its target, a collective cry of "yes" the likes of which Celtic Park has only seen on a rare occasion is heard to go up before the commentator continues.

R.M.: "He's done it! Harald Brattbakk scores the goal which may well give Celtic the title. He's been much maligned since he came here, he's had an awful lot to prove, maybe that's the perfect answer! Twenty-eight minutes of the second half gone, a sweeping move downfield, the Boyd pass, first time in from McNamara, and there's a top class finish from Brattbakk. His tenth goal of the season, and that one surely has a gilt edge to it, and what did that mean on the touchline? There's your answer. Celtic Park is almost literally bouncing at the moment, as these Celtic supporters sing and dance." [Celtic 2, St. Johnstone 0]

Now, as the full time whistle grows imminent, the commentator reflects on the anticipation of the squad members not directly involved that day, before heralding in the new champions of Scotland.

R.M.: "And some of the Celtic players not involved today [at the mouth of the tunnel leaping up and down], ready to join the celebrations – Malky Mackay, Darren Jackson, Stewart Kerr, Tosh McKinlay, David Hannah, Stephane Mahe, Tommy Johnson – all there, all ready for a party. And down on the touchline, the gaffer Fergus McCann making sure that everything goes as it should go for the final whistle...The long wait is over! Celtic have won the Championship!"

Whilst Rangers secured the two titles which immediately followed Celtic's first league win in a decade, the pendulum swung firmly back across Glasgow as the first full season of the new century began and Celtic won their first treble since 1969. A fine indication of this supremacy came on the twenty-ninth of April 2001, as the Hoops travelled to Ibrox having already confirmed themselves as the champions of Scotland once again. Ian Crocker and Davie Provan (who is particularly fond of the word "composure") describe the action, with the tie goalless approaching the midpoint of the second half.

Ian Crocker (I.C.): "Lennon's free kick. Larsson, into the path of Lubomir Moravcik! He's through and he's scored! It's one-nil to the Champions, and it's little Lubo!"

Davie Provan (D.P.): "Well Henrik Larsson does magnificently Ian, to hold it up, under pressure from Bert Konterman. Needed a bit of support, it came from Moravcik, who was prepared to get forward and help him, and from there on in he had the composure to pick his spot." [Rangers 0, Celtic 1]

I.C.: "Maloney's flick, oh Moravcik is going to be in again here! Where are Rangers? Lubomir Moravcik, is he going to get a second? [At this point, having eluded Fernando Ricksen with a deft touch and change of direction, Lubo calmly slots the ball into the goalmouth at the Celtic end, beating Stefan Klos at his near post]. You better believe he is! It's a double for Moravcik, and Celtic are heading for their first win over Rangers at Ibrox for six and a half years!"

D.P.: "Well, he couldn't have shown any more composure Ian. Wonderful finish by a wonderful footballer!" [Rangers 0, Celtic 2]

I.C.: "Away by Ferguson, here's Tugay. Oh, Tugay stumbled, McNamara, slips it through! Henrik Larsson, round the keeper, the angle is a bit acute but that doesn't matter! He's done it! It's a fabulous fifty goals in a season, for Henrik Larsson, and that is the perfect end, to a perfect day, in a perfect season."

D.P.: "Tugay caught in possession, Jackie McNamara looking for a runner. Larsson shows enough composure to get round the keeper, tucks it away and, well, I think we've used all the adjectives for this man, Ian. Once again, it's a special finish from a very special striker." [Rangers 0, Celtic 3]

I.C.: "It's all over. The Celtic fans must be wondering if it can get better than this, but they will know that it can, because they have the Scottish Cup Final coming up in a month's time." [Full time]

Of course, it would get better for Celtic, who defeated Hibernian by three goals to nil in the Scottish Cup Final and completed a domestic treble as I have mentioned. However, a couple of years later during the 2002-03 campaign, Celtic would win nothing, and yet many regard it to be our finest season for many decades. Therefore, I'd like to pick up the commentary action in the second round of the UEFA Cup, away against Blackburn Rovers, with the microphone in the hands of Alan Green.

Alan Green (A.G.): "He scored enough goals at the Darwin End in his Blackburn days, Chris Sutton... Petrov will go across to take the corner, in front of the Celtic supporters who are having quite a night... Sutton! Oh yes! On the ground where he scored so many for Blackburn Rovers, Chris Sutton probably settles this UEFA Cup tie for Celtic. It was the near post header, Blackburn had been warned. Look at these scenes of jubilation among the Scottish supporters, and this means now that Celtic have a three-nil aggregate lead. Sutton's header, Friedel could only get a hand to it, and Trevor, Blackburn now need four. It's impossible, isn't it?!"

Anyway, Celtic progressed to the quarter finals for their second "Battle of Britain" of that season, and if the English press had set themselves up for a fall after being overly confident Blackburn Rovers would beat the Hoops, many presumed the mighty Liverpool would steamroller over their Scottish opponents, but alas, it wasn't to be for the Anfield club. Both goals described below are from an English commentator on Eurosport (which is not the coverage the majority of people see of the match nowadays), and whilst I cannot convey the clear tone of shock in his voice for you in writing – particularly as the Celts scored their second goal – I can, at least, quote exactly what he said for you all to enjoy.

"Larsson, leaves it for Thompson, goal for Celtic! Alan Thompson, right at the end of this first half! Oh, that makes things very interesting [the camera then pans over the celebrating away supporters] – they certainly think so. Look at the Liverpool wall here, that's terrible. Steven Gerrard, if only he'd stayed on terra firma, that wouldn't have got through. Full credit to Thompson." [Liverpool 0, Celtic 1]

"This is John Hartson. One-two with Larsson – it's opened up here for John Hartson. What a goal! And curtains for Liverpool surely. It's the sort of thing you're used to seeing in comics. Hartson, delightful one-two with Henrik Larsson... [At this point, a Celtic supporter can be heard shouting "What a goal!" near one of the television microphones]... And well, Anfield just opened up for him there and he's buried it... [Again, our microphone man becomes audible over the English commentator – "What a goal Celtic! What a goal!"]… Well, with nine minutes to go, there's no way Liverpool are coming back from this. Great stuff, it bent away from Dudek. Great stuff!" [Liverpool 0, Celtic 2]

And so, after all of that, as well as a one-all draw at Celtic Park in the first leg of the semi-final against Boavista, Celtic's chances of reaching their first European final in thirty-three years lay ultimately in their success or failure in one match, away in the north of Portugal. Typically, it was Henrik Larsson who scored the crucial goal and, in the days and weeks which followed, one commentator's name was irrevocably linked with the great Swede, and one of his finest moments. Ladies and gentlemen, I give you Peter Martin.

Peter Martin (P.M.): "Sutton, flicking it into Larsson. Larsson, edge of the box, tries to play it into Hartson. Larsson's got a chance here! Oh it's in the net! Goal! Goal! Goal! Henrik Larsson scores! It's the goal Celtic wanted! They are one-nil up, they've got the goal! His name is Henrik Larsson!"

P.M.: "Douglas, kicks the ball. It's all over! Celtic are in the UEFA Cup Final! What a result in Portugal! The Celtic players are in the air, they're cuddling each other, Bobo Balde is flat out on the grass! What a performance here by Celtic!"

Perhaps what makes Peter Martin's commentary so memorable is the fact that he clearly enjoyed the moments he described above. Peter himself remains tight-lipped as to who his loyalties lie with in the world of Scottish football – after all, it is part of his job to maintain as high a degree of neutrality as possible – but outbursts like those above may well have hinted, not so subtly, to the answer to this question. Regardless, the fact Mr. Martin was utterly ecstatic when he commentated on Larsson's strike in Portugal is the reason his voice will go down in history alongside Henrik's goal. Had a more dreary, or less passionate commentator covered the game, I have no doubt in my mind that whilst the goal would, of course, be remembered in glorious detail by the majority of Celtic supporters, the commentary which accompanied it would not. It was a perfect way to sum up the mass outburst of joy felt across the Celtic supporting world that night in 2003, and whilst I'm sure Mr. Martin would play down this accolade, it just wouldn't be the same without it. His screaming words were the cherry, placed on the icing, atop the proverbial cake.

In 2007, a very different looking Celtic side would write their own names into the history books by securing only our third League Championship and Scottish Cup double since the centenary season (including the treble of 2000/01). Whilst the Scottish Cup Final would be won by a goal from Jean-Joel Perrier Doumbe a little more than a month later, the league title was secured in the most dramatic fashion, with a ninety-third minute Shunsuke Nakamura free kick giving Celtic not only the three points, but the Championship, against Kilmarnock at Rugby Park. With the score level at one goal apiece, Ian Crocker describes a moment which will live forevermore.

I.C.: "Celtic fans, inside Rugby Park; watching at home; watching at pubs and clubs; watching around the world, holding their breath. If anyone can do it, he can. Nakamura! He has done it! Isn't that just typical? What a way to win the title, and how fitting that the goal should be scored so late, and should be scored by Shunsuke Nakamura! They've had to wait for the title, but good things come, to those, who wait. Celtic, Champions!"

Now, we shall move on to another one of my personal favourites. It is a well-known fact that some of Celtic's greatest derby results have come when they have been considered to be large underdogs – whether one refers to ten men winning the league or the following example. To beat your rivals when you were favourites was one thing, but to do so, seemingly against all the odds, was something quite different.

When Celtic walked out on to the pitch at Ibrox Park on the second of January 2011, they were without club captain Scott Brown, as well as striker Gary Hooper; Korean pairing Ki Sung-Yeung and Cha Du Ri; and veteran playmaker Shaun Maloney, amongst others. I doubt I was the only one who thought that afternoon could be a painful one, with so many key players unavailable for selection and our only striker, Georgios Samaras, without a goal to his name all season. However, my fears were unfounded. Celtic won two-nil thanks to a brace from the Greek

Gazelle, coupled with some remarkably skilful and determined defending. Once again, the words of Ian Crocker and his co-commentator Davie Provan will live long in the memory.

I.C.: "Foster, gave it away to Ledley. Samaras is chasing this! And McGregor's come way out! Georgios Samaras scores for Celtic! Happy New Year to the men in Hoops! They have the lead at Ibrox!"

D.P.: "Well, if anyone in green and white today deserves a goal, it's Georgios Samaras. I think he's been terrific. Very often the whipping boy, he's been terrific this afternoon. Allan McGregor, I'm afraid, has to hold his hands up. Why he commits there, I've no idea. Samaras, always favourite to get there first. Davie Weir trying to make up the ground to get goal side, but can't close the angle on Samaras. The first touch is exquisite, pretty small target from that angle, but it's a terrific finish from Celtic's best player this afternoon..."

Continuing on this theme of green and white clad underdogs, I would like to conclude this chapter with one of Celtic's greatest – and possibly most unexpected – moments of late. As Jordi Alba scored a last gasp winner in the Camp Nou in the autumn of 2012, my heart sank and I plunged my head into my hands whilst the Barcelona support, whom I was sat amongst, celebrated exuberantly. At that stage, I could never have believed I would watch Celtic defeat the Catalan giants only a couple of weeks later.

It took several beers to drown my sorrows that night, but the pain would only eventually be washed away by my subsequent attendance at Celtic's one hundred and twenty-fifth anniversary celebrations – an event I remain honoured to have been privy to. That night, in the cramped, hot surroundings of St Mary's Church in the Calton, I was reminded of why Celtic Football Club is so very special indeed. A unique atmosphere was created by those who filled the building, as well as those prominent figures who spoke – an atmosphere not of a birthday party or a football match, but of something more; something unique; something special. On a balcony high above the church floor, I watched the Barcelona directors in attendance, as well as many famous faces associated with Celtic whom you will all be familiar with, and

I found that many of these individuals were visibly moved by the celebration going on around them.

Yet, even after all of that – the hope, the memories, the romanticism and the grandeur – I could not bring myself to believe we would beat that Barcelona side. When we did, I was utterly amazed, and I doubt any Celtic supporter could have asked for a better birthday gift for the Football Club. Whilst most people will recall Sky Sports' commentary, which ended with the popular "Wow! Wow! Wow!" line, I would like to draw your attention to a less widely known piece that accompanied the match – no, not Krys Kujawa's infamous "Tony f*****g Watt!" magnificent though it was – but that of Alan Green and Craig Brown on BBC Radio 5 Live. Both Celtic goals, as well as the nervy finish which followed Lionel Messi's consolation goal, are described below.

Please note that on the original recording, both commentators are initially shouting and bawling over each other as the second goal approaches and is subsequently scored, such is the excitement being felt by the two men. However, for the sake of being able to follow what each man is saying, I have spilt each individual's dialogue apart in order to gleam some clarity from the situation.

Alan Green (A.G.): "It's going to be played in, left footed by Lustig. Oh, is that? Actually, it's Mulgrew to cross. Mulgrew, left footed corner, in towards the far post, header and in! It's a goal for Celtic! Wanyama has put them in front. Free on the far post, his header was true, precisely what Celtic needed. Celtic one, Barcelona nil!"

Craig Brown (C.B.): "Yeah, it's a wonderful start for Celtic, great delivery by Mulgrew, left footed in-swinging corner, right over the top, and there was Wanyama. He outjumped his marker... Song. Quite clearly, much more powerful than Alex Song, and he headed it into the back of the net. A wonderful start for Celtic, and a thoroughly deserved header for that corner kick."

A.G.: "Oh and the ball breaks forward, here's an opportunity! Watt! For history! Watt makes it two-nil! Sensational! The eighteen year old has only been on the pitch a few minutes. It's a long clearance upfield by Celtic, Watt was after it, through into the penalty area, a right foot shot, low past Valdés. What a night at Celtic Park. Celtic two, Barcelona nil!"

C.B.: "Oh! Oh! Tony, Tony Watt's through, wonderful goal Tony Watt! Wonderful goal! What a wonderful goal from the young lad. He could easily have bottled that one, right through in the inside-right position and he rifled it into the net. Good long ball forward to him, he outsprint the Barcelona defence and stroked it across the keeper. Tony Watt, the hero for Celtic."

A.G.: "Villa and Piqué, Piqué's now up as an additional striker. Throw in to Barcelona on the far side. It's the final whistle at Parkhead! What a night for Celtic! A day after they celebrate one hundred and twenty-five years of existence, and this is as great a victory in European Football, even equal to that great night in Lisbon."

C.B.: "Yes, I think so, and everyone on their feet, everyone applauding the Celtic team, thoroughly deserved victory, and I just think it's one of the most famous victories in the history of Celtic."

I feel that is a rather apt note upon which to end this chapter, for whilst the constant reference to this victory – sometimes as a defence in the face of subsequent disappointments – became somewhat maligned, especially online, it does not take anything away from the fact that Celtic defeated the best team the world had seen in quite some time that evening, matching them over two games also (in terms of scoreline at least). Personally, I would not rank this victory alongside Lisbon as the English commentators suggested, but it was certainly one of the finest nights we have enjoyed in the modern era.

Ironically, the progress of technology which spawned the invention of radio and eventually television allowed the art of commentary to become eternally interwoven with the sport we all love. It is regrettable that the growth of this media and its financial clout has directly impacted upon Celtic's ability to compete at the highest echelons of the game. This is a great shame, and one which I hope will be suitably rectified in the future.

All I would ask is that the next time you criticise a commentator for saying something you disagree with (something

I do also), remember that their words will be recorded and replayed for generations to come. It is not as easy a job as it may seem. Indeed, the rise in fan commentary over the last decade or so has proven this to be the case, with some individuals being much more adept at the pursuit than others. To commentate fluently, clearly, and describe developing matters as they occur can be quite a task, all whilst not speaking too much or too little. Some of these men and women are far from perfect, but they have provided an audible legacy which will forever be linked the exploits of Celtic Football Club, and for this, we owe many of them our thanks.

"The Chronicles of Willie Maley: "I'll Take Root and Flourish""

"By W. Maley, Manager, Celtic F.C."

"Season 1890-91 was a most interesting year in our history, and one still fresh with stirring memories. We held that season, in August, our first athletic sports, and we had as our guests Dan Bulger, the greatest hurdler Ireland ever had, and big, cheery, Tom Donovan, the champion long jumper. Our players were, of course, all amateurs in those days, and we had a regular field day amongst the prizes. Tom won the open one hundred yards, Kelly won the open two hundred and twenty yards, and I won the players' two hundred and twenty and ran second in the one hundred yards. I was also one of the winning five-a-side, which beat Cambuslang in the final. I had the pleasure that day, for the first time since the club's inception, of having my parents present to see the show, and I sent them home in a cab with a load of silver plate, the happiest couple in the country."

"Our football season started with a bad knock, as Renton – soon to be suspended – wiped out our lot in the opening game at Parkhead by four to one, chiefly caused, however, by an inglorious display between the posts of the "Auld General" [James McLaren], as we had no goalkeeper at the time. We at once secured one, however, in Bell of Mauchline, who played previously for Dumbarton, and redeemed ourselves at Tynecastle the following Saturday, when we wiped out the Hearts in the opening League game by five to nil, with the following team, which will show our forces starting that year: – Bell; Reynolds and McKeown; Maley, Kelly and McLaren; Madden, Dowds, Groves, Dunbar and Crossan."

"A Memorable Match"

"A fortnight later we met the Rangers for the first time in a Scottish tie. James Kelly had been suspended just then, and so McCallum came into the team. His namesake Neilly had by this time gone over to Nottingham Forest, to be followed very soon by W. Groves to West Bromwich Albion. The game was a very hard one, but we conquered (not for the last time in these ties) by one to nil over our great rivals to be, and divided a gate of over four hundred pounds."

"We got our walking ticket that year at the feet of Dumbarton, by three to nil. On a wretched day, with the ground all slush through a heavy snowstorm, both clubs protested going out on the ground conditions, but Dumbarton, when in a winning position, withdrew their protest, and when the case came before the S.F.A., we lost our appeal for a replay by the casting vote of the Chairman."

"That season our second eleven also made history by winning the Scottish Second Eleven Cup, beating St. Mirren in the final by thirteen to one, St. Mirren scoring first. Our reserves' record that year is worth reproducing: – Played thirty-six games, won thirty, lost nil, drawn six, scored one hundred and eighty-seven goals and lost thirty-two. We won our first big honour that year in the Glasgow Cup, on the fourteenth of February 1891, beating Third Lanark on Hampden by four to nil."

"We secured some new men that year, chief of whom were the famous left wing of later years, Sandy McMahon and Johnnie Campbell. Sandy came to us from the Hibs, and Campbell from Benburb. In our Scottish ties with Royal Albert, Campbell was partnered with Barney Crossan, [with Sandy] not eligible for the Glasgow or Scottish ties. Crossan eventually was dropped with the coming of Sandy McMahon, and went to Preston North End."

"Tour in England"

"We toured in England, March twenty-seventh to thirty-first, and played Bolton, Ardwick (now Manchester City), Blackburn Rovers, and Sheffield Wednesday, scoring in turn two-all, seven-two, two-nil and three-one, in all fourteen goals to five, and earning for ourselves great praise in the English Press, and at the same time too much prominence for our left wing, whose play was marvellous throughout the trip. At Bolton, Campbell and McMahon were coaxed into a little bar parlour, and a huge bag of gold laid before them to affix their names for Bolton Wanderers, but the lads would not have it, and came home to do great work for their home team. We had great jinks on this tour, McKeown [at a circus], feeding the hippopotamus with copies of newspapers, pocket handkerchiefs, post cards etc. Just before we left for home Gallagher had a letter delivered to him containing a pawn ticket for his top-coat which some wag had obligingly "popped" in case Pat might lose it. With the pawn shop closed for the night, of course, the erstwhile "calm and quiet" Pat was a sight to see, but needless to say the coat arrived home safely a day or two afterwards, and Pat had not to pay carriage."

"Our affairs at Celtic Park, whilst financially good, were not so harmonious at that time as they had been. We actually had a strike amongst some of our "amateurs" of that day for a rise in the allowances made them, but thanks to some common sense talk by two of our Board today, Messrs. Kelly and Dunbar, the matter soon righted itself and a month or two saw us rid of the malcontents. To show the depth of the feeling, I might cite the case of my brother Tom and the late J. H. McLaughlin, both standing for one seat on the S.F.A., and, of course, neither getting in. When matters ultimately did come right the foundations were all the stronger, and prepared the way for the united and happy combination of recent years, although even after the year I refer to we experienced the string of the place-seeker and factionist."

"The great point of difference was the question of a paid official, and with the club growing as it was it is hardly to be conceived now that such a necessary step should have been opposed by some of the sound business men who fought so hard against it then."

"Scottish Cup Won For the First Time"

"Season 1891-92 was our first great year as cup winners, and we started the game that season with a very much improved lot from that which won the Glasgow Cup for the first time in 1890-91.

We had secured Tom Duff as goalkeeper, from Cowlairs, thus making a position where we had never really had complete satisfaction – one free from anxiety. With the coming of the famous amnesty law of the S.F.A., which permitted Scottish players who had been playing in England to return to "home and whitewash," we were able to secure the return of Neilly McCallum, and to enlist the services of Doyle and A. Brady from Everton. McKeown had deserted us for Blackburn Rovers, after many threats of departure. Doyle and Brady made their debut for us against Cowlairs on the tenth of August 1891. Tommy Dunbar, a brother of our present director, was at that time first reserve, but feeling that opportunity was not to come his way; owing to the strength of our other reserves, he went over to Rangers later on that season. English agents still worried our lot, McMahon being offered one hundred and thirty pounds down, three pounds per week."

"My First Cap"

"I secured my first International cap that year, playing for Scotland against Canada at Ibrox, and I was also picked to play against Sheffield and London in the same season, but against the latter had to call off through injuries which afflicted me a lot [then]."

"Our team soon showed its real worth, and we started off by retaining the Glasgow Cup, defeating Clyde in the final on a cruel wintery day by seven to one, the weather being so bad that several of the Clyde collapsed near the finish of the game."

"In the League we took a good position, and it looked as if we were to win our first League flag, but two bad performances near the end of the race robbed us of the honour. Our lot were big, strong and fast, and in the front line we had five of the cleverest forwards who ever played, and individually fit to play in any team. McMahon and Campbell at this time were at their very best, and it was a treat to watch them, their understanding and feinting being marvellous, while McMahon's head work has never been equalled. McCallum and Brady, though playing a game quite different, were a very dangerous pair, and as shots were outstanding. In Madden we had a very elusive centre. Behind we had a solid defence, which feared nothing, and could take on any heavyweights going. Duff, too, until he fell victim to rheumatics that season, was unbeatable at times."

"New Year's Day found us get a terrific shock and a rude awakening that [eventually] did us good. Dumbarton, our closest rivals for the League flag, and ultimately winners that year, beat us eight to nil at Celtic Park [in a friendly]. We had our full team bar Kelly, injured, for whom John Cherrie, the Clyde captain, played. Dumbarton played a great game, but the season of the year was the real cause of our set back, which was, however, only very temporary, as next day we whacked Third Lanark at Cathkin by three to one, and next day beat the Rangers by two to nil. Dumbarton went to Tynecastle the day after they played us, and got beaten seven to one."

"A New Goalkeeper"

"Duff's rheumatism put him out of football after this game, and we secured from Benburb, the Scottish Junior Champions...the services of their clever goalie, Joe Cullen. Poor Joe, he was one of the cheeriest pals I ever had...He was always smiling. He played many good games for us in his day. He played his first game in a Scottish tie with Cowlairs on the sixteenth of January 1892, which we won by four to one. Our Scottish Cup progress that year, up to the final, saw us beating in turn, St. Mirren, Kilmarnock Athletic (of which my good friend Charlie Smith, now a director of Kilmarnock, was then a shining light), Cowlairs, Rangers, and finally meeting Queen's Park in the final, played on the twelfth of March at Ibrox. The excitement started, the crowd broke onto the field, and this led to a mutual protest by both clubs against the game being counted a tie. We won by one to nil, but (contrary to what certain other clubs of whom we had experience did), the Queen's and ourselves stood to the protest lodged, and the game was ordered to be replayed, which it was on the ninth of April, the delay being caused by trial games, and the English, Irish and Welsh Internationals. The second game was an eye-opener for the Queen's supporters, as our lot walked away with the "goods," winning by five to one. Both sides showed changes, Dowds playing centre for us [instead of] Madden, injured, and Sellars playing back for Queen's, [replacing] the redoubtable Walter Arnott. Our lot stamped themselves that day as the champions of Scotland without a doubt, and their football was delightful to watch."

"We won the Charity Cup that year, beating Rangers in the final, and thus having our name engraved for the first time on two of the biggest honours in Scottish football."

"Our ground at [the old] Celtic Park saw us for the last time at the end of that season, as the rent was raised from fifty pounds to four hundred and fifty pounds. As we could not have that we secured the present ground, and had the first sod laid by Michael Davitt, M.P., who received on our behalf the Glasgow Cup from the Association at the same time. The "poet" of the period wrote a poem on the sod, which was put down to this strain:-

> *"On an alien sod like yourselves I am here,*
> *I'll take root and flourish, of that never fear;*
> *And though I'll be crossed sore and oft by your foes;*
> *You'll find me as hardy as the Thistle or Rose;*
> *If model you need, on your own pitch you have it;*
> *Let your play honour me and my friend Michael Davitt."*

"In these days of lack of sentiment, the touch of bringing a sod across from Ireland for our new field may not be in keeping with present ideas, but it was the touch which made us all throw ourselves, heart and soul, into the work at hand."

"Our three-leaved-shamrock success of that year had not been touched by any other club since the inception of the competitions, and so we started our record-making career of cup-winning."

"The Soul and the Spirit"

On the second of November 1983, a determined Celtic side strode out of the tunnel at their home stadium in their away kits, ready to face their hooped visitors – Sporting Clube de Portugal – before a raucous crowd. The official attendance would be given in the days which followed as thirty-nine thousand, one hundred and eighty-three, but as I draw this book to a close, I would like only to focus on three of them; my grandfather (also Francis), his brother (Charlie), and my father (another Francis – we're an imaginative bunch when it comes to names as you can likely tell). The reasons behind my decision to do so will become clear in a few moments, but first allow me to take you all back to that night in Glasgow's East End and set the scene appropriately.

At the beginning of the 1983-84 season, Celtic joined St. Mirren and sixty-two other sides in the UEFA Cup, a two-leg knock-out tournament. The first round saw some closely fought encounters with giants Real Madrid falling to the unlikely sword of Sparta Praha, whilst other teams such as eventual winners Tottenham Hotspur cruised on to the second stage via double-figure victories over smaller outfits (Spurs beat Drogheda United fourteen-nil over two legs). As for Celtic, they initially knocked out Danish side A.G.F. Aarhus by a fairly comprehensive margin, thanks to wins both home and away, whilst St. Mirren were eliminated by Feyenoord.

The draw for the second round of proceedings saw the Celts paired with Sporting (better known as Sporting Lisbon by many), one of the clubs from a city which will forever be linked with the proud history of Celtic Football Club. To emphasise this point further, the travelling team stayed in the same hotel during this visit as the Lisbon Lions had done a little over sixteen years earlier, and were permitted by the home side to wear their famous hooped jerseys rather than a changed strip in the first leg. Almost seventy thousand people packed the Estádio Alvalade that night, and despite Celtic threatening to grab an away goal early on through Murdo MacLeod, the visitors would eventually fall to a two-nil defeat after a brace from Rui Jordao.

Therefore, having failed to win two of their three domestic ties in the interim period between the pair of European games, Celtic knew they would have to overturn this two goal deficit in Glasgow if they were to progress to the next round of the UEFA Cup. At this point, the Celts had only ever achieved such a feat once previously, against French side Saint Etienne in 1968. Ironically, there are some similarities to be found between both matches, for in 1968 and 1983 Celtic lost each first leg two-nil away against sides who also wore green and white as their main colours, and in each case, the Celts were ultimately fortunate to return home still in contention in the tie.

It was clear the home side would face an uphill struggle in Glasgow, as Sporting and their manager – a certain Dr. Jozef Venglos – came to town. It then came to pass that for what may have been the first time since the introduction of the Hoops in 1903, the home supporters at Celtic Park found themselves cheering not for the players wearing those jerseys, but rather those in the lime green kits. Of course, even to an outsider, it wouldn't have taken long that night to ascertain which team was which, for many of those in Hoops had tanned skin, dark hair and moustaches, whilst those in the green were much paler, some of whom had ginger hair also.

However, if one had to judge the sides purely on the football which they played that night, many may well have presumed Celtic were indeed the Latin team, for some of their short, sharp passing, incisive running and exquisite finishing was truly spectacular. Tommy Burns headed Celtic into the lead early on, and sporadic Sporting attacks aside, it soon became clear who the team in the ascendancy were. The Portuguese side's goalkeeper, Béla Katzirz, was called into action more than once by Paul McStay amongst others, and only a couple of minutes before the end of the first half, a Davie Provan corner was chested down by Tom McAdam, who promptly proceeded to smash the ball home, sending those in the stand and terracing wild.

Subsequently, before many of those in attendance had likely taken a breath, Celtic scored again through Brian McClair and the home fans who had been going wild previously now found themselves in a state of positive rapture upon the sounding of the half-time whistle. In the second period, the Celts kept up the pressure, scoring two late goals thanks to Murdo MacLeod and Frank McGarvey, eventually finishing the match as five-nil winners and progressing via a five-two aggregate scoreline to the third round of the UEFA Cup, where they would be knocked out by eventual semi-finalists, Nottingham Forest.

Now, those of you who are not still wallowing in thoughts of that sensational night against Sporting may be wondering what this all has to do with my family members whom I referred to earlier. Indeed, according to my father, they would probably just be amazed to have been directly mentioned in a Celtic book at all, but that is not my sole intention. In fact, I presume some of you reading this were likely at the five-nil match I have discussed, alongside them. However, the critical point is that whilst my father is still with us and my great uncle Charlie died when I was very young, the victory over Sporting Lisbon was to be the last Celtic match my grandfather – a man whom I never had the pleasure of meeting – was ever to attend.

Having been born on the twenty-ninth of October 1921, a day upon which Celtic recorded a league victory over Ayr United at Celtic Park, he would not live beyond the September of 1984, having been taken from us by a condition which presently remains incurable, Motor Neurone Disease. A Celtic fan all of his life, he grew up at a time when the likes of Jimmy McGrory were strutting their stuff, providing a temporary escape for all of those poor, hardworking families who followed the Celts. Shot in both legs in the Second World War, he returned home to Glasgow on medical leave for a few months, before returning to Europe as the Allies battled the fascist forces of Nazi-controlled Germany. In later life, he leapt and danced about atop my grandmother's new couch – something which she was as protective of as she was proud – as Stevie Chalmers scored the winning goal in the European Cup Final of 1967, and he wholeheartedly enjoyed many of the Celts' triumphs thereafter. Yet, less than a year after making his way through the turnstile of a football stadium for the last time, he was gone from this world.

In my previous book, I devoted a chapter to the first match which I had the pleasure of attending with my father, as Celtic beat Aberdeen by three goals to nil on the twentieth of April 1997, whilst now I feel I must make mention of a grimmer subject. Put simply, any of us who have ever seen Celtic in the flesh will, one day, do so for the final time. That may appear to be a somewhat morbid thought, but I believe it is one we must all accept and address if we are to do the best by those supporters who will follow the Club in future. Fundamentally, if the research and time involved in writing these books has taught me anything, it is this – we as Celtic supporters, as a fan base, have three roles in life – to support the team and the charitable deeds of the Football Club, to do our utmost to continue the good name of the Celtic support, and to ensure we leave the Football Club in as strong a position as possible for those younger members of the support to enjoy in years we will never see ourselves.

Of course, this is not something to dwell on, but it is most certainly something of which we should all be aware. To follow Celtic is to enjoy the trials and tribulations of a sporting roller-coaster ride, with the ecstatic highs tempered at times by the gut-wrenching lows, but just as players come and go, so do supporters, albeit mercifully on much longer timelines. Whether we like it or not, the fact is that one day, our rollercoaster car will pull into the station and we will depart, but we must all be buoyed by the fact that when our time comes, another Celtic fan somewhere will undoubtedly be just beginning their ride, ready to see what the next decades have to come; the results to savour; the performances to enjoy; the songs to sing and the stars to behold. This, ladies and gentleman, is what Celtic is all about. It is not simply a Football Club, it is – as I have said before – a living, breathing entity which we all contribute to in our own individual way – and providing the Club is in a better state than that in which I found it when I leave Celtic Park behind me for the final time, hopefully many years from now, I will be content in the knowledge I have done my part.

As the song says, "We are Celtic supporters; Faithful through and through; Over and over we will follow you…" It does not say "I", but "We", and although I doubt the larger point I am referring to was in the mind of whoever penned that song, it is poignantly accurate, because neither you nor I will be around forever, but we – as a collective support – will be for as long as the Football Club is in existence. In future years, this young upstart may well be considered a veteran of sorts, but such a thought presently seems surreal. People will be impressed that someone of my age saw Henrik Larsson and Lubomir Moravcik in person just as I am by those few who remain who watched Jimmy McGrory and Willie Fernie, and the Earth shall continue to spin. The greatest legacy which we all leave as Celtic supporters is the Club itself, passed down from generation to generation, and it warms my heart to think that my grandfather would likely be enormously proud of how his Club has developed into that which I follow today.

He was an individual supporter; my great uncle Charlie was an individual supporter; myself, my father and our family are individual supporters; and you reading this are an individual supporter. Yet, as a group, we are the soul and the spirit of Celtic Football Club.

CPSIA information can be obtained at www.ICGtesting.com
Printed in the USA
LVOW11s2310101115

461894LV00001B/377/P